DREAM CITY

DREAM CITY

Race, Power, and the Decline of Washington, D.C.

HARRY JAFFE
TOM SHERWOOD

CONTENTS

For information, address Harry S. Jaffe and Tom Sherwood c/o David Black Agency, 335 Adams Street, Brooklyn, NY 11201.

Print ISBN: 978-0-7867-5593-6
eBook ISBN: 978-0-7867-5594-3

Cover design by Antonella Iannarino

Distributed by Argo Navis Author Services

ACKNOWLEDGEMENTS

My friend and colleague Chuck Conconi once told me that writing a book is like walking through a room full of mashed potatoes. He's right. And most days one of my three daughters would wade in and ask: "Is the book done yet?"

David Black, our literary agent, did everything but write the book. He coaxed and cajoled us through the early stages. He became my coach, my therapist, my punching bag, and through it all, my friend, who said long before I believed him that I could write a book. If not for his patience and deft negotiations, the book would have stayed in manuscript form.

I needed many editors. Brian Kelly, my editor at large, helped at the conceptual stage and kept me on course during long diner lunches and squash matches. Jane Leavy was our most careful reader. She made me reach deeper into myself and the material, and like the best editors, made it better. Gerri Hirshey read and said what I needed to hear, when I needed to hear it. Marc Jaffe gave "strength to my elbow" and provided a crucial mid-course correction. Barbara Marcus cut the fat with a scalpel. We're also indebted to Paul Aron at Prentice-Hall Press for recognizing the value of our book and taking it through the early stages; and to Dominick Aufuso and Cassie Jones at Simon & Schuster for their patience and commitment in seeing it through to the end.

The reporting for this book began years ago while I was writing for *Regardie's,* the gutsy monthly magazine that flourished in the eighties. Bill Regardie was the best publisher imaginable. He gave me the time and the space to develop an understanding of the "money, power, and greed" that make Washington tick. At *Washingtonian,* I want to thank Jack Limpert, my editor, and publishers Philip and Eleanor Merrill for their forbearance during the actual writing. Mark Plotkin introduced me to city politics, as he reminds me all the time.

Tom and I owe a great debt to all our sources. Hundreds of people were willing to share their recollections, insights, and emotions, even though many of the events were painful and unpleasant to recall. My special thanks to Al Arrington, Carol Thompson Cole, and Carroll Harvey for their generosity in time and spirit.

Finally, I want to acknowledge my friend John Wilson, who was perhaps my deepest and most constant source. He was there during many of the events that we describe. He knew the characters and gave us the unvarnished truth about them. I only wish that he were here to read it and tell us everything that we missed.

—Harry S. Jaffe

First, I want to acknowledge someone I don't know. A few years ago, a burly man sat next to my son and me in Florida during a spring-training baseball game between the Boston Red Sox and the Baltimore Orioles. The man turned to me and said derisively, "Oh, you're from Washington. You must either work for the government or be on welfare."

Such bigotry stung, and inspired me to tell the country more about the nation's capital.

For this project, I thank Harry Jaffe for proposing a book on Washington and seeing the value of my work as a journalist with ties to the city's diverse black communities. And my appreciation to Harry's wife, Cindy Morgan Jaffe, whose empathetic support was matched by her counsel on substance.

Thanks to my son, Peyton. Even as I am having my first book published, he's getting his first driver's license. Both make me very nervous, but my son unfailingly makes me proud. And to Deborah Jones

Sherwood, his mother, for being such a good one and for encouraging me early on to reach further than I could see.

I'm grateful to sustaining friends Nancy Lewis and Gene Bachinski, superior journalists both, who, while they taught me the value of fine food and wine (they feed me a lot), offer me the warmth of unyielding loyalty. To Bob Galano and Terry Dale, for true friendship and frequent refuge from a weary land. And to Phyllis Jones, passionate and committed, with unusual understanding of local Washington and its racial complexity.

A posthumous debt of gratitude to Herbert Denton, *Washington Post* city editor, who encouraged my initial interest in hometown Washington, and to *Post* editor Milton Coleman, whose support and enthusiasm allowed me the opportunity to write so much about it.

My thanks to the many good District government workers who each day try to do a difficult job made even more difficult by decades of poor management. And, finally, an acknowledgment of debt and appreciation to the tens of thousands of black middle-class Washingtonians who are not featured in this book—the individuals and families who do not make the news but each ordinary day make their homes, businesses, and communities places of pride and decency. They deserve so much more recognition, appreciation, and help than their government—or the media—is likely ever to give them.

—Tom Sherwood

*In memory of my father, Josef, who taught me to love books.
And for my mother, Zelda, who believes in me*

Harry S. Jaffe

*For my son, Peyton, who once innocently illuminated all the time
spent on this project by telling a caller, "He's not here; he's working
on that damn book."*

Tom Sherwood

PREFACE

to the 20th Anniversary Edition

When Kaya Henderson, the District's school chancellor, moved into her home in the Brookland neighborhood in 2001, her street of tidy row homes was solidly African American. The Northeast section of the nation's capital off South Dakota Avenue near Providence Hospital had been home to DC's black middle class for decades.

"That's not the case any longer," Henderson told us one fall afternoon in 2013. She stood on her porch and looked across the street. "White families have moved into those houses. Some have children, and the kids are starting to play together. It's a good thing, but I can't say there isn't some tension."

Henderson's neighborhood was hardly unique. It was the new normal across Washington, D.C. Reflecting demographic changes taking place nationwide, younger people were moving into the city, most were white and quite a few hoped to raise families in neighborhoods that had been largely African American.

Since Dream City was published in 1994, the city behind the monuments had transformed itself. From politics to society, demographics to development, sports to culinary culture, the District of

Columbia barely resembled the town we described twenty years ago. Except for one constant: Marion Barry was still in office, representing Ward 8 on the D.C. council.

When we put the last period on the print edition, Sharon Pratt Kelly was finishing her term as mayor, which most saw as a failure. Marion Barry had served six months in jail for a cocaine conviction and had won a seat representing Ward 8 on the council. He was contemplating a run for mayor.

"You can't talk him out of it," said Courtland Cox, who had helped orchestrate Barry's rise to power in the 1960s.

In late 1994, after we sent our book to the printer, Barry won an unprecedented fourth term.

By many measures, the District under Kelly had sunk to its nadir that year. The city budget was running a deficit projected to reach $1 billion. Police reported 399 homicides. Crack wars still bloodied the streets. Residents were fleeing the city; the population had dipped below 590,000, headed for a low of 569,230 five years later. The development boom that had rebuilt parts of downtown had nearly ground to a halt. Public schools ranked lowest in the country, infant mortality the highest.

Dismayed at Barry's return to office and fearing the capital city would go bankrupt, Congress installed a financial control board to oversee the city's budget and manage the government. The federal panel reduced Barry to a second class mayor. It was his last term as chief executive.

Cut to 2014.

New residents streaming into the city at 1,100 a month have increased the population beyond 646,000; that's nearly 100,000 above the 1998 low point. Neighborhoods like Shaw, once home to Black Broadway, teemed with white residents, new bars and a residential building boom chronicled in the *New York Times* and *Wall Street Journal.* Still more new residents -- mostly young, white professionals -- were moving east into LaDroit Park and crossing North Capital

Street into Kaya Henderson's Brookland and further east across the Anacostia River.

In 1960, the District became the first major American city to have a majority black population. African Americans peaked at 71 percent of the city in 1970. By 2014 that number was hovering at 50 percent and slipping.

Chocolate City had turned mocha.

In Dream City, we chronicled the birth of the District's limited self-government under the 1973 Home Rule Act. The city's first elected council in 1974 had 11 black members and two whites. In 2014 the council had seven white members and six black. The chairman, elected at large, was Phil Mendelson, one of the seven white majority.

Cranes once again defined the city's skyline, from downtown to Georgetown and up 14th Street to Columbia Heights. They hovered over long-neglected Southwest and Southeast waterfronts along the Anacostia River. Major league baseball returned to the District in 2005, and the new National's stadium by the Anacostia helped jump start development.

Remember that Stokely Carmichael helped start the 1968 riots by chucking a brick through the window of People's Drug Store at the corner of 14th and U Streets in Shaw? And Marion Barry had made a symbolic point of locating the Franklin Reeves Municipal Center at that same corner in the late 1980s? In early 2014 the city was negotiating to trade the Reeves building as part of a land swap to build a new soccer stadium. So much for symbolism.

The city's homicide rate dropped to 88 in 2012, its lowest since the 1960s and 400 fewer than its height in 1991.

The city's public schools, though still struggling, were no longer the worst in the nation. Test scores were beginning to rise, and the student population was starting to increase for the first time in decades.

We will take you from 1994 to 2014 in a new section after the original Epilogue.

How and why did Washington, D.C., resurrect itself? From the control board to surprise Mayor Anthony Williams and upstart Mayor Adrian Fenty, how did the streets become safer, the schools less dismal, the complexion more Caucasian? Why did scandal and corruption take down three promising black politicians, each the son of a prominent leader in D.C. and the Civil Rights Movement? How did U.S. Attorney Ronald Machen, an African American lawyer from Detroit, investigate and unravel dirty political contributions that corrupted council and mayoral elections, including Mayor Vince Gray's 2010 victory over Fenty? Machen's investigation raised questions about Gray's ethics and hovered over the 2014 mayoral campaign.

Meanwhile, Marion Barry remained on the political stage. African American voters in Ward 8 — the District's poorest neighborhoods east of the Anacostia River — had again elected him to the council. As his health deteriorated, he reached his late-70s, and his influence waned, he tried to play the political Godfather. Even as we put the finishing touches on our new account, Barry confounded critics. He emerged from hospital stays and recuperation to campaign for Vince Gray's reelection.

As Courtland Cox once said: "You can't talk him out of it."

INTRODUCTION

The president-elect came to Washington on November 17, 1992—not the capital that serves as the backdrop for the evening news, but the Washington that provides the setting for our book, the city beyond the monuments.

Bill Clinton picked a block on Georgia Avenue in the heart of what once was a thriving black business community. After twelve years of Marion Barry as mayor and the Republicans in the White House, that strip of Georgia Avenue is receding into the urban wasteland. Storefronts are boarded up, winos stagger around by day, storeowners consider deadly robberies a cost of doing business, and crack dealers hunt one another down after dark. The incoming leader of the world's most powerful nation spoke with the shop owners and the local politicians, promised Georgia Avenue and the city more jobs, more credit, safe streets, better housing. Then he departed in a sea of secret service agents.

"Haven't we heard all that before?" a middle-aged black man in the crowd asked. We had to agree. LBJ promised self-rule in 1967, Nixon promised to rebuild the riot zones in 1969, and George Bush in 1989 orchestrated a cocaine bust across from the White House and declared war on drugs, beginning on the streets of D.C. Charles Dickens called the capital "a city of magnificent intentions" in 1842, and 150 years later the phrase still applies.

Millions of students and tourists come every year to see the capital's broad downtown streets, lined with the symbols of federal power and history: the White House, the Capitol, the FBI Building, the National Archives, the Smithsonian Institution. This is the majestic city of monuments to presidential icons Jefferson, Washington, and Lincoln, of Cherry Blossom Festivals and inaugural celebrations. Americans feel that this federal city belongs to them, but if they lay claim to the national treasures, they can't deny their collective responsibility for the other Washington where drugs, murder, and poverty are testaments to the nation's failure. Washington is America's city, in glorious myth and tragic reality.

Our story is about local Washington, a town where bad things happen in good neighborhoods and terrifying things can happen in poor neighborhoods. Here is the sixty-nine-square-mile city that—despite its well-established black and white upper classes, its six major universities, and the rich tradition of the activist black church—jails more black men than it graduates from high school every year. It's a city where white men and foreign investors own virtually all the commercial real estate, though 70 percent of the population is African-American; where black babies die at rates higher than in any other American city, higher than in many third-world nations; where the rate of AIDS cases among children is rising faster than in any other place in the nation; where a small deer herd thrives in Rock Creek National Park while a half-mile east of the forest young black gangs prey on one another and where the murder rate from 1989 to 1991 made the city the country's killing capital.

No other city in America is as tormented or polarized by race, class, and power as the District of Columbia. It is the stage for sweeping national events and international summits, and it is the setting for modern urban atrocities: A teenager shoots a black woman in a car because he "felt like killing someone"; two Washington men throw a mother out of her car in the suburbs and drag her to a gory death when she tries to save her two-year-old daughter; a shotgun slayer terrorizes a neighborhood for two months, randomly shooting twelve people and killing three before he's caught. The fact that this city lies in the shadow of the fortresses of American power only sharpens the pain and the paradox.

How did these two cities develop side by side? How can they co-exist? What went wrong? What can be done?

It's questions such as these that have motivated us to write this book. As journalists who cover the city, live in the city, and raise our families in the city, we confront them every day. Our work takes us from the White House to city hall; from gleaming downtown office buildings to public housing projects; from a congressional hearing to the scene of a gangland murder. It's a difficult city to grasp and understand. But we can't escape the conclusion that a single undercurrent binds its disparate parts: Racism and racial insecurities made Washington what it is today.

The capital is like most big cities in that regard, but the racial and class divisions loom larger and become more stark on the national stage, in the garish light of the international media. Washington officially became the country's first majority black city in the 1960 census, yet it's still rightly called "the last colony," ultimately controlled by white lawmakers in Congress and the local white business elite. It's commonly held that the city is united only by its hometown football team, the Washington Redskins, but the team has a painful racist past. It was the last pro team to hire blacks. Former owner George Preston Marshall agreed to integrate the team only under pressure from John F. Kennedy 's interior secretary, Stuart Udall. When Marshall finally hired black running back Bobby Mitchell in 1961, the Ku Klux Klan demonstrated at RFK Stadium. *Post* sportswriter Shirley Povich said the team's colors should have been burgundy, gold, and Caucasian.

On the other hand, the city's African-American political establishment has controlled the District government since 1974 and certainly bears much responsibility for the city's shame. America's sickness in the last quarter of the twentieth century rises from the chasm between the races, and nowhere is the gulf wider, deeper, and more evident than in the capital, a small city where fear and racism rule the streets.

Which brings us to Marion Barry, Jr., the man who bridged the chasm to get elected mayor in 1978, exploited it to stay in power, and now more than anyone in American politics personifies the distance between blacks and whites.

It is impossible to separate the man from the city or from the African-American odyssey. Barr y takes us from black serfdom in the Mississippi Delta to black power, to black politics, to the defiant summer of 1990 when black teenagers rediscovered Malcolm X and wore T-shirts saying "It's a black thing, you wouldn't understand. " Barry burst on the capital city in 1965 when the entire nation still believed in the altruistic ethos of the Kennedy White House, the War on Poverty, and Lyndon Baines Johnson's Great Society. Barry was the personification and distillation of that idealistic moment in American history. The whole idea of Marion Barry appealed directly to the liberal soul: He was the son of a sharecropper who became a leading civil rights activist and rose through the political establishment to executive power in the capital city.

The young Barry was a natural leader and a skilled politician. He could remember a name, stir a crowd, charm white businessmen, and connect heart-to-heart with the poorest blacks. Liberalsbelieved that he could relate to underclass blacks and help lift them into the system. But Barry, like many other dark-skinned African-Americans from the rural South, never was accepted by Washington's "high yellow," native aristocrats. They—not the whites—called him "a cotton pickin' nigger." The class differences are central to his story and to the city's current crisis.

Much was riding on the success of Barry's administration.African-Americans look to Washington as a beacon of pride because of its thriving black middle class and its black aristocracy. Barry came into power with a coterie of stars from the civil rights movement who wanted to prove that a black government could manage the nation's capital after a century of white control. From the city streets to the back rooms of the Barry regime, we explore what became of that dream.

During his fall, Barry's descent into drug addiction, abuse of-women, demagoguery, and eventual arrest eerily mirrored the city's own decline into murder and crack. It became a destructive pas de deux, the man and the city, in a vortex of despair, to that moment during his trial in the summer of 1990 when the entire world saw the FBI videotape of Mayor Barry drawing so deeply from a pipe filled with crack cocaine. Here, for the first time, is the inside story of the investigation, or as Barry saw it, the vendetta.

Mattie Taylor, a black woman whom Barry crushed in the 1986 mayor's race, said, "I can't understand why the people love him so." Seven years later, after he'd been humiliated, defeated, and jailed, many still love him. In 1992 the city's poorest ward elected him to the city council, and in 1994, he's rebuilding his citywide political base. When some Washingtonians refer to "the mayor," they're still talking about Marion, and Mattie Taylor's words still hang in the air. We hear them mostly from white people, who ridicule Barry as a venal charlatan who betrayed his people, confirmed every racist stereotype of black men, and wrecked the city. They simply can't see why anyone of any color or any class would hold him up as a leader. Yet for many African-Americans, especially from the lower economic classes, Barry will always be a hero. Though he shifted with every po-litical wind, Barry maintained a facade of defiance. Blacks saw him as a man who refused to "bow down to Mr. Charlie," even as Mr. Char-lie helped create him and kept him in power. At some emotional level that defiance touches every African-American, regardless of class or color. Their reaction is an indication of just how insecure and alien-ated black Americans still feel, and the white response shows how lit-tle they understand the African-American predicament.

Marion Barry, like the problem of race in America, won't go away.

Our story covers the period from 1964 to 1994 because it spans the time of great change for America, for its capital city, and for Mar-ion Barry. Congress established the home rule government twenty years ago; now, even as that government is close to bankruptcy, Jesse Jackson and others are calling for Congress to grant full statehood. The opposite—federal receivership—is just as likely. This could have been the tale of the dream city that so many have sought to make it. Instead, it has become a nightmare for the city and the nation.

CHAPTER 1

ANTECEDENTS: PARLIAMENT OF RACISTS

Tell all the colored folks to listen to me,
Don't try to buy no home in Washington, D.C.
'Cause it's a bourgeois town!
—*Leadbelly, circa 1940*

Acker Street, a short lane about six blocks east of the U.S. Capitol, is a place where small-town Washington brushes up against the federal city, once with deadly results.

It is a quaint street, almost toy like, as if its two-story, brick row houses were made in miniature. They front right on the sidewalk, giving the street an intimate feel, and many are gussied up with a bay window or wrought iron security bars. A few decades ago Acker Street was home to both black and white clerks who worked for Congress or at the Navy Yard, but in the 1990s it has an urban mix, Washington style. A sprinkling of congressmen and senators live nearby. A crack house set up shop in the neighborhood. On Acker Street there are a few black families that bought years ago and stayed. There are some single mothers and one excongresswoman. There are a few gay couples. But for the most part the cozy street is home to young Capitol Hill aides who come to Washington to seek their fortunes, to change the world, or to work for a year between college and graduate school. In one sense, it is the integrated urban landscape

1

that Martin Luther King, Jr., dreamed of in his "beloved community." In another sense it's a neighborhood in transition, where aspiring white college graduates share turf with many desperate black high school dropouts.

Tom Barnes moved to a two-bedroom townhouse on Acker Street in the late fall of 1991. He'd come to the capital over a year before, immediately after graduating from the University of Alabama in Tuscaloosa, his hometown. He was twenty-five, of average build, with fair skin and. blond hair that he cut short and brushed to the side in a neat, fraternity style. In high school he sang in the choir, in college he was president of his fraternity, and in his Capitol Hill office he was a rising star. He'd taken an internship with Alabama senator Richard Shelby, a friend of the Barnes family, and quickly landed a full-time job on Shelby's staff. He worked hard, laughed easily, and wore wild ties. His coworkers called him "the all-American."

On Saturday evening, January 11, 1992, Tom Barnes looked in the cupboard and discovered that he was out of coffee for Sunday brunch. He told his roommate, Toof Brown, that he was going to the corner store on Maryland Avenue for a can of grounds. "Be right back," he said. It was a chilly winter evening, and the streets were glistening from an afternoon rain. Barnes put on duck boots and a light parka over his corduroy shirt and jeans. He walked out the front door at 7:30 and headed toward Seventh Street.

You can search from one end of Washington to the other and not come across another place quite like Acker Street. It reminds one of certain sections of downtown Philadelphia or of North Boston. The rest of Washington doesn't compare easily with other American cities, whether the comparison is of downtown business districts, the wealthiest enclaves, the middle-class communities, or the poorest parts. The capital city is unique, by design.

Pierre L'Enfant laid out the city in four quadrants with a midpoint at the U.S. Capitol, but his greatest imprint is the city's scale in height. Under his design-backed up by congressional law—no private building can be higher than 160 feet, so the skyline is dominated by the 555-foot Washington Monument and the pearly white Capitol dome. The American capital has the feel of a low-slung European city, rarely overpowering and quite manageable.

Every state in the Union has a street named after it in Washington, and each one conjures up particular images. Wisconsin Avenue is the most ritzy. It begins at the foot of Georgetown by the Potomac River, runs north through the spine of the upper-class community where Katharine Graham and Pamela Harriman live. It rises up a hill where the new Russian Embassy bristles with microwave dishes and listening devices, skirts the U.S. Naval Observatory grounds where the vice-president lives. It passes the giant Gothic Washington National Cathedral and nearby Sidwell Friends, Chelsea Clinton's school, and continues through the pure white neighborhood of Friendship Heights where it aspires to be the capital's version of Rodeo Drive (Neiman Marcus, Gucci, Saks) as it crosses into Maryland.

Massachusetts Avenue is a more egalitarian street. It begins at the Maryland line northwest of Wisconsin, angles sharply through the embassy district toward the city center, cuts through the hip, gay, polyglot brownstone community of Dupont Circle. Then it heads toward Capitol Hill where it pauses in a rough neighborhood that has its share of shootings by the Anacostia River. Rhode Island Avenue slashes east from the downtown through middle-class neighborhoods before it crosses into Maryland on the city's eastern border amid a trashy neon mix of used car lots, check-cashing joints, and more liquor stores than any other spot in the city.

The capital has major streets that most white Washingtonians barely know and rarely travel. South Dakota Avenue is so far east that it doesn't even exist on most tourist maps, but it's home to some of the city's most stable, black middle-class communities with fine schools, good hospitals, stately brick homes, and hundred -year-old churches. Minnesota Avenue begins and ends east of the Anacostia

River, and that makes all the difference. Where Wisconsin is white and rich, Minnesota is black and largely poor.

Pennsylvania Avenue also traverses both the Anacostia River and Rock Creek Park, the two physical features that define Washington's economic and racial patterns as surely as the Potomac River separates the District from Virginia. Whites for the most part live "west of the park," where the public elementary schools are the best in the city and Volvo sells more station wagons than in virtually any other place in the nation. East of the park is where 95 percent of the city's African-American population, primarily middle class, calls home. That leaves the poor folks. They live "east of the river," meaning the Anacostia River, the nation's most endangered urban waterway, according to the American River's Council. It's a slow-moving, wide, and muddy waterway that empties into the Potomac at Hains Point. Five bridges cross the Anacostia, but the people who live there are disconnected and easy to abandon. Not all are poor, but nearly 100 percent are African-American, and too many are dispossessed.

Poverty is not that easy to see in the capital. It has few bombed out, trashed neighborhoods like Manhattan's South Bronx or Philadelphia's barren streets bordering North Broad Street. Washington hides its poor in public housing complexes that don't look rotten until you take a good look. They are hellholes to the people who live there and to the police who try to keep order. Valley Green, Langston Terrace, Barry Farms are killing fields with stairwells. But the most deceptive and disturbing aspect of the capital city may be that nice-looking neighborhoods can be deadly. Some neat streets of brick row homes with flowers in their yards and fresh coats of paint on their porches turn into open-air drug markets after dark. And there are the neighborhoods on Capitol Hill that are, as the real estate agents say, in transition—quaint places where bad things can happen, like Acker Street.

A small group of black teenagers approached Tom Barnes from behind as he reached the corner. Precisely what happened next isn't clear. According to police reports and subsequent court testimony, there were two, perhaps three assailants. One was named Edward, another Stanley, the third went by the nickname Toy. They had a handgun.

"Give me all your money or I'm going to bust a cap in you, " Toy told Barnes, according to police testimony.

"Leave me alone," Barnes responded and turned up the street. One of the teenagers then passed a handgun to another, who put it behind Tom Barnes 's left ear and fired one shot. Barnes's face hit the pavement with such force that it seemed as if he'd been severely beaten. The assailants rifted his pockets and ran.

Police arrived in minutes and assumed that he'd been hit by a car. It wasn't until he was X-rayed at the hospital an hour later that doctors discovered the bullet. It had entered just over his ear, ripped through the base of his brain, and lodged in his jaw, leaving a blood clot and swelling in its wake. Word spread quickly through Shelby's staff to Barnes's parents, Don and Susan, in Tuscaloosa. They arrived in Washington early Sunday and joined Shelby's entire staff in a vigil at Washington Hospital Center's trauma unit. Tom was in a coma.

The *Tuscaloosa News* editorial the next morning ran under the headline "A Capitol Outrage" and said: "The nation 's capital seemingly has self-destructed over the past decade. Beset by drug-related violence, Washington has become a national disgrace, an American embarrassment."

Tom Barnes never regained consciousness. He died on Wednesday at 8:30 p.m., four days after he was shot. The new year was only fifteen days old, but he .was already the twenty-second person slain in Washington. The city was keeping pace with its record 489 murders the previous year, ensuring that the capital of the free world would retain its title as the nation' s murder capital, more deadly than Detroit, more bloody than Manhattan, as random as L.A.

Tom Barnes's hometown paper called him "a good young man in a town that has gone bad.

"His shooting should outrage Washington as much as it outrages Tuscaloosa."

Senator Richard Shelby was outraged.

He'd known Tom Barnes since he was a toddler, he said, and he didn't intend to let his killing pass quietly. Shelby asked the Senate to make the death penalty legal in the District.

Meanwhile the police had launched a manhunt with twenty cops and a few homicide detectives. Shelby put a ten-thousanddollar bounty on the killer. "We don't experience that kind of outpouring when it's John Doe lingering because we have that all the time," a police spokesman said. The dragnet pulled in Lloyd Hardy, seventeen, who was jailed without bond on a first-degree murder charge. A bond hearing on February 28 drew a tense crowd of Shelby staffers on one side and Lloyd Hardy' s friends and relatives on the other. Three days later prosecutors were forced to release Hardy because a key witness admitted that he had lied. Hardy was mobbed by well-wishers, including his grand mother, Willie Hardy, a former D.C. council member.

"They threw out the net and they said, 'Find somebody' and they found somebody—another black youth," she told *The Washington Post.* "This black youth had never committed a crime. This was the wrong one. As long as they fish out and get a black child, that satisfies them."

Shelby said in a statement that he was "disappointed."

Ascending to the Senate floor on March 8, 1992, Shelby said he would be "hard pressed to describe the criminal behavior in Washington as 'civilized society.' In just five years the homicide rate has more than doubled. People are using guns to settle arguments about clothes and girlfriends. They are 'smoking' others because they feel like it. They will even 'bust a cap in you' if they don't like the way you look at them."

This played well among voters in Tuscaloosa, but in the District, which didn't elect Shelby or any other senator, it was seen as a racially motivated attack on home rule. Shelby's legislation failed, but he did succeed in forcing the District to hold a referendum on the issue.

On November 3, 1992, District voters went to the polls and soundly defeated Shelby's initiative. It's not that they didn't favor the death penalty. Many black Washingtonians are quite conservative, law-and-order advocates. And it's not that they didn't think that Tom Barnes's murderer should pay with his life. They just resented a white senator from Alabama telling them that they needed a death penalty to make their streets safe.

"I'm in favor of the death penalty," said city council chairman John Wilson, a civil rights movement veteran who'd been clubbed by Alabama sheriffs, "but I don't want someone who we didn't elect ordering us to take the vote."

In other words, it wasn't a question of right and wrong, it was a question of race and power—white lawmakers in Congress telling black people in the city how to run their lives. This is the dynamic that underscores every debate, every decision, every relationship. No one can understand Washington without appreciating the debilitating impact of federal control that has been at various times patronizing, neglectful, and racist. It is a political reality that has a bearing on Tom Barnes's death, Richard Shelby's reaction, and the city's backlash.

Racism is used to rationalize so much that often the term becomes meaningless, but it's impossible to dismiss the fact that raw discrimination against blacks was for years at the root of Congress's relationship with the District of Columbia.

The year was 1890 when another Alabama senator, John Tyler Morgan, set the tone. Alexander "Boss" Shepherd 's massive public works projects had bankrupted Washington's short-lived territorial government that was elected by black and white voters. Senator Morgan, a tall plantation owner and former officer in the Confederate army, took to the Senate floor to explain why Congress had taken the right to vote from Washington. It was necessary, he said, to "burn down the barn to get rid of the rats...the rats being the negro population and the barn being the government of the District of Columbia.

"Now, the historical fact is simply this," he said, "that the negroes came into this District from Virginia and Maryland and from other places; I know dozens of them here now who flocked in from Alabama...they came in here and they took possession of a certain part of the political power of this District...and there was but one way to get out—so Congress thought, so this able committee thought—and that was to deny the right of suffrage entirely to every human being in the District and have every office here controlled by appointment instead of by election...in order to get rid of this load of negro suffrage that was flooded in upon them.

"That is the true statement," he affirmed. "History cannot be reversed. No man can misunderstand it."

The horrible beauty of Senator Morgan's soliloquy is that it sets out so clearly how and why Congress eviscerated the city's ability to control its destiny, provide for its citizens, and develop a political identity. True, Article 1, Section 8 of the Constitution gives Congress jurisdiction over the seat of government, but the framers didn't have racist intentions. In one sense, Congress, following Morgan's unvarnished racism, perverted its constitutional authority. On the other hand, the racism was a natural outgrowth of the city's birth in the summer of 1783, when the infant Congress was on the run, literally.

A mob of soldiers demanding back pay had surrounded the building in Philadelphia where the first Congress was meeting. The congressmen talked the armed men out of violence long enough to make their escape to temporary shelter in Princeton, New Jersey, and the legislators spent the next few years sampling cities in search of a permanent home. The vagabond Congress tried Philadelphia and New York, Trenton and Annapolis. For a time it seemed the acrimonious search might split the union. President George Washington wanted the government to be within a horse-and -buggy rid e of his farm at Mount Vernon. Bowing to Washington's wishes and cutting a deal to pay war debts at the same time, Congress designated a ten-mile-square area above the confluence of the Potomac and the Anacostia rivers, midway between the Appalachian Mountains and the Chesapeake Bay, as the seat of government.

Other world capitals—London, Rome, or Tokyo for example—were ancient, thriving cities before they became modern political centers. When the new government moved from Philadelphia to Washington in 1800, the 131 officials and their families found themselves in a village with muddy lanes, cattle in the streets, and no room at the inns. The setting was gorgeous, however. Wooded hills and plateaus overlooked bluffs by the two rivers. The Mall was pastureland, and there was a good bit of swamp, as *The New York Times* sniffed.

But it was the proximity to the South, not the deal or the setting, that sealed the fate of the city that would grow around the federal government. Placing the capital between Maryland and Virginia saddled it with slavery and put it in the thrall of southern senators and congressmen.

Senator Morgan was among the first in a long line of southern segregationists who ruled Washington with devastating results for African-Americans, particularly the forty thousand former slaves who sought refuge in the capital after the Civil War.

What they found was not unlike what greeted the European immigrants who arrived in Manhattan. The northern city had tenements; Washington had alleys. When L'Enfant designed the capital, he drew in broad alleys behind the rows of houses that fronted directly on the sidewalks. The city's housing stock couldn't accommodate the black newcomers, so many alleys sprouted shacks. For a time Irish immigrants competed with the blacks, but eventually the Irish left. Washington 's alleys would be slums for the next eighty years.

Still, Washington was the promised land for black sharecroppers fleeing the harshness of the Deep South. In the decades before, during and after World War II, trains called the Chicken Bone Express brought a steady stream of black refugees into the capital. Many African-Americans were poorly educated and unprepared for city life. They crammed into shantytowns and ghettos in the city's Southeast and Southwest neighborhoods, shunned by the established black communities and ignored by the whites. In 1934 the city's infant mortality rate reached 66.1 per 1,000 births, second among major cities only to New Orleans. Crime in the slums soared, and the city's murder rate was more than twice New York's. *Newsweek* wrote a story in 1941 that tagged Washington the "Murder Capital of the U.S."

Malcolm X, then known as Malcolm Little, visited the capital in 1941. He'd just moved from Boston to New York, where he'd taken a job as a dishwasher on The Colonial, the New York to Washington train. On his first layover he did some sightseeing.

"I was astounded," he observed in his autobiography, "to find in the nation 's capital, just a few blocks from Capitol Hill, thousands of Negroes living worse than any I'd ever seen in the poorest sections of Roxbury; in dirt-floor shacks along unspeakably filthy lanes with names like Pig Alley and Goat Alley. I had seen a lot, but never such a dense concentration of stumblebums, pushers, hookers, public crapshooters, even little kids running around at midnight begging for pennies, half-naked and bare footed. Some of the railroad cooks and waiters had told me to be very careful because muggings, knifings and robberies went on every night among these Negroes…just a few blocks from the White House.

"But I saw other Negroes better off; they lived in blocks of run-down red brick houses. The old 'Colonial' railroaders had told me about Washington having a lot of 'middle class' Negroes with Howard University degrees, who were working as laborers, janitors, porters, guards, taxi-drivers, and the like. For the Negro in Washington, mail carrying was a prestige job."

Which was exactly the way Congress liked it.

The city was under the direct control of committees that were the least prestigious in Congress. They were a proving ground for junior members or a dumping ground for embarrassing ones. Blacks in Washington had endured slavery, the restrictive Black Codes of the 1830s, and the riots of 1919, but Congress made the racism institutional.

In 1938 the Community Chest published *First City-Worst City,* a devastating exposé of Washington's slums. Backed by the report, the city asked Congress for $3.2 million for health care, housing, and education. The chairman of the House Subcommittee on District Appropriations, a Mississippi farmer named Ross Collins, cut it to $900,000. Elwood Street, a city welfare official, asked Collins to appropriate funds for the National Training School for Girls, which was overflowing with teenage black girls who'd come to Washington alone and destitute.

"If I went along with your ideas, Mr. Street," Collins said, "I'd never keep my seat in Congress. My constituents wouldn't stand for spending money on niggers."

Collins was enlightened compared to Senator Theodore Bilbo, a short, troll-like white supremacist from Poplarville, Mississippi. Bilbo survived bribery scandals in Mississippi before he was elected to the Senate in 1934, when he described his opponent as "begotten in a nigger graveyard at night." In tirades on the Senate floor, he opposed an antilynching law and proposed an amendment to the 1938 work-relief bill that would have deported 12 million blacks to Liberia. He was proud of his membership in the Ku Klux Klan and wrote a book entitled *Take Your Choice—Segregation or Mongrelization.*

In 1944 Bilbo became chairman of the District Committee and let loose his racism on the city. He was nicknamed "the Mayor of Washington," but he was no joke for African-Americans. He proposed that twenty-two thousand blacks be driven out of the alleys and sent back to farms, shipped back to Africa, or put in a "self-liquidating" stadium. "If you go through the government departments," he once said, "there are so many niggers it's like a black cloud all around you." Until he died in the summer of 1947, Bilbo did his best to deny funds to any cause that might help the city's poor blacks.

In the 1950s the segregationist running Washington from Capitol Hill was Congressman John L. McMillan of South Carolina. As chairman of the House District Committee, "Johnny Mack" treated the city as if it were his plantation and turned the District Building into a fiefdom for his own patronage jobs. He kept the city's social service budget low, held down local taxes, and applied taxes to construction projects at the behest of the white business community. When bills or proposals on self-government came up, McMillan refused to hold hearings. In 1950 the Senate actually passed a bill granting home rule, but McMillan let it die in his committee.

The white business community, represented by the Board of Trade, held more political power than the three commissioners appointed by the president. The businessmen simply leapfrogged the commissioners and went straight to McMillan's committee. Board of Trade executive director William Press would drop.by to sip cocktails and negotiate the business community 's legislation poolside at the home of James Clark, McMillan's committee clerk.

What Congress denied in the form of political power, the federal bureaucracy gave back in the form of jobs. A government job was a ticket to the American Dream, and Washington developed the largest and most stable black middle class in the nation. It lived in relative harmony for two decades after the war along with strong Greek, Italian, Jewish, and Irish Catholic communities. The black middle class was sandwiched between a small class of black aristocrats and the poor blacks who couldn't make it out of the alleys. The result was a rigid caste system reflected by skin color.

"It was a segregated city among blacks, " says Calvin Rolark, Jr., who came to Washington from the South in 1952 and started a weekly newspaper. "The lighter-skinned blacks didn't associate with the darker blacks, and the Howard University blacks didn't associate with anyone."

The city's poor blacks, crammed into the Southwest slums, suffered the most. The slums occupied a 113-block area south of the Mall and northeast of the Washington Channel, about a quarter mile from the Capitol. An estimated 22,539 people lived there in 1950, and nearly 80 percent were black. Hundreds of houses didn't have indoor toilets. The city fathers decided that the entire neighborhood would have to be obliterated. Led by *Washington Post* publisher Philip Graham and an elite group of white businessmen in the Federal City Council, the redevelopment forces promised to improve the lives of the people in the slums. The *Post* carried a series describing a new neighborhood of apartments and homes "for all income bracket s though predominantly within reach of middle and lower income families."

The project began in 1952 as a $500 million package to create a city within a city. Phil Graham brought in New York builder William Zeckendorf and a fledgling architect named I. M. Pei. Bulldozers razed the slums in a year, but it took twenty-five years to complete the construction of apartments, office buildings, and homes. An entire community was demolished and dispersed in the process. It became known as "Negro removal. " In 1959 Eleanor Roosevelt toured the neighborhood and asked a simple question: "What has happened to the people who once lived here?"

The answer is one reason why middle-class black and white communities across the city went into decline. The city relocated twenty-five thousand people to public housing projects in the Northeast and Southeast parts of the city in the midst of stable, middle-class black neighborhoods, but the juxtaposition didn't help the poor. The housing projects were allowed to deteriorate, and the surrounding neighborhoods took a turn for the worse. Poor families that didn't find their way into public housing were scattered across the city into other poor neighborhoods.

An editorial in the *Post* later admitted that "in all candor it must be conceded that the motivation has been more economic than social, and that a total assault on poor housing here, as elsewhere, remains to be mounted."

Desegregation came early to the capital, but there was no homegrown mass movement, so black Washingtonians didn't feel a part of the process.

By 1954, President Dwight Eisenhower had ordered the desegregation of all schools and public accommodations, thanks in part to a genteel crusade by liberal whites and professional blacks. But still, there was no home rule, no politics, no local control. Black Washingtonians still had no responsibility for the way their city was governed. Congress still ran the city as if it were a department of the federal government. In a perverse way, desegregation did irreparable harm. Under segregation Washington entered the 1950s as a city of neighborhoods where blacks and whites actually lived together in many communities, and black middle-class families held their own communities together with roots in the schools and churches. By the end of the decade the capital was quickly becoming two separate cities polarized by color and class. But above all, nearly a century of congressional control had created a leaderless, passive city full of politically docile people.

This became abundantly clear to Adam Clayton Powell, Jr., who called a voter registration rally on January 24, 1964, at All Souls Church, a landmark perched high on Sixteenth Street in Adams Morgan with a commanding view of the city, the Washington Monument, and the Capitol dome some three miles away.

The flamboyant congressman from Harlem was the most influential black politician of the day. Voters in his hometown ·adored his defiance of white power and sent him back to Congress term after term despite his publicized escapades with wine and women. He could draw a crowd on any street corner in Harlem, and he expected a decent turnout in Washington that chilly day. The civil rights movement was reaching a crescendo, but much depended on who would occupy the White House for the next four years—Lynd on Baines Johnson or Barry Goldwater. The coming election was the first time that District residents could cast a ballot for president, thanks to the Twenty-third Amendment, which Congress had passed in 1960.

Powell arrived fifteen minutes late, but there were only a few people in the church. He paced in the Reverend David Eaton's small study as a few more straggled in. He waited an hour. Finally, he walked onto the pulpit to address the small gathering.

"I have never seen a city in the United States as apathetic as this one," he railed. "This is our first chance to be political men and women. We are colonials here in this District. The District of Columbia is the Canal Zone of the United States."

For an ambitious young man named Marion S. Barry, Jr., and the very political young activists who wanted to take their southern civil rights movement to the northern cities, Washington's apathy and lack of leadership would provide the perfect opportunity to take control.

CHAPTER 2

ROOTS OF ANGER

We weren't poor....We always had plenty to eat, clothes, a decent place to live.
—Mattie Cummings, Marion Barry's mother

The two police officers weren't looking for trouble, but the spring night was raw and jumpy.

It was about midnight as police officer Thomas J. Tague and his partner, Albert Catalano, were patrolling northern Shaw, Washington's little Harlem, the infamous Thirteenth Precinct. The streets were jammed with people leaving the movie houses. Crowds were gathered on street corners, and heroin deals were going down in the alleys. The two cops were the only white faces for blocks.

Upper Shaw had been Washington's hippest neighborhood into the 1940s and early 1950s, when black culture had flowered in the segregated capital city. Back then U Street between Sixteenth and Ninth streets had thumped with the beat of a thriving community, especially at night. Duke Ellington, Count Basie, and Pearl Bailey played the Howard Theater on Florida Avenue. Louis Armstrong blew his horn at the Lincoln Theater. Jazz and be-bop tunes spilled out of glittering nightclubs like the Caverns or Cecelia's or the Casbah, a hot spot for Latin dancing. Handsome young black men turned out in double-breasted suits. A few hip white couples came for an earful of jazz. Flashing neon signs lit up the night.

But by the late 1960s the neighborhood had gone sour. Integration had killed off the black theaters and nightclubs. Many black middle-class families had fled to the suburbs. Liquor stores on every corner did a brisk business in pints in paper bags. Teenagers in doorags ran the streets. Upper Shaw, once the mecca of black culture, was part of "Shameful Shaw," the heart of the uptown ghetto, heroin central.

Tommy Tague pulled his paddy wagon to a stop at the light at the corner of Thirteenth and U streets. A tall, lean black man and two women started to cross against the light. The women pointed at the police and turned back, but the man grinned and kept walking in a slow strut. Two cars screeched to a stop to avoid hitting him.

Tague leaned over to Catalano. "Isn't this some shit?" he said. The jaywalker was Marion Barry, Jr., out for a midnight stroll, not looking for trouble but not afraid of a confrontation, either. He glared at Tague and continued to the corner. Barry had been in town less than two years, but already he was a minor legend among many poor blacks and young civil rights activists. His angry face, with its pencil-thin Fu Manchu mustache and goatee, and his trademark white suit and Panama hat set the pace for the activists' new style of defiance.

Tague rolled down his window.

"Hey, you," he said. "Can't you tell the color of a streetlight? "

"Fuck you and fuck the light, too," Barry said.

"Oh, for crissakes," Tague mumbled to Catalano.

Tague was a wiry man with big ears and a face so young that it made him look like a kid playing cop under his oversize blue patrolman 's hat. He and his young partner were used to the role of young white officers enforcing the law over African-Americans. Washington's police force was more than' 80 percent white in a town that was 65 percent black. To most blacks, the police were an occupation army, and a deadly one at that. In 1967 and part of 1968 city police killed thirteen African-Americans, including one whose offense was as petty as stealing a bag of cookies. It was called "justifiable homicide." The black community had complained about police brutality for years, but little had changed except for the mounting age. Tague didn't see it that way. He was · born in Washington and raised six blocks from the White House near Mount Vernon Square when it was a working-class, integrated neighborhood. It was his city, too. His father, a ScotchIrishman, was a special policeman for the railroads, and his uncles were city cops. Tague had been on the force for ten years by the time he ran into Barry. He already had a reputation as a tough character who made lots of arrests. The city's police force was full of Tommy Tagues. He leaned out his window and looked Barry up and down.

"Say, boy, " he said. "You must have a lot of money. It's illegal to cross against the light—gonna cost you five dollars."

"Bullshit, motherfucker," Barry shot back.

Tague was used to black men who obeyed his commands. This was a new development.

"Just let me see something with your name on it," Tague said.

"I don't need to show you nothing, you white dogs," Barry said. "I ain't going to show you any fucking identification."

Tague jumped out, told Barry he was under arrest, and ordered him into the paddy wagon. Barry's two friends had run to the nearby local headquarters of SNCC, the Student Nonviolent Coordinating Committee, and returned with reinforcements. A large crowd encircled the wagon. The two white cops stood amid a sea of angry black faces.

"Hey, man, cut him loose," someone shouted from the crowd. "Honkey pigs. Let the brother go."

A man jumped Tague and freed Barry. Tague and Barry squared off. Barry kicked Tague in the shins, grabbed his thumb, and bent it back. For an instant Tague thought about pulling his service revolver, but he checked the odds and decided to get help instead. Catalano radioed for backup, and squad cars converged on the scene from every direction. More than a dozen uniformed and plainclothes police rushed in to force Barry toward the wagon, but he broke out and decked officer Robert Sharkey with a blow to the side of the head before the police succeeded in cuffing Barry and locking him in the wagon. On the way to the precinct house, he tried to kick out the window because, he said, the cuffs were too tight.

At the Thirteenth Precinct Barry was guarded by patrolman Leonard Gray, a mountainous black officer. Some of the city's black police officers had reputations for being as brutal as the whites. Gray sat Barry down.

"Keep your hands off of me, you big Uncle Tom," Barry said.

"You say that one more time and I'll punch you so hard in the stomach you'll wish you were never born," Gray said.

The officers placed Barry alone in a holding cell. His clothes were disheveled, but he was otherwise unharmed by the scuffle. He was booked on charges of resisting arrest and damaging government property for smashing the police wagon door. Two lawyers arrived to get him out: Frank Reeves, a prominent and politically active black attorney, and Landon "Jack" Dowdy, Jr., an ardent liberal Irishman. Barry emerged from the cell with his pants torn and his face bruised. The police said Barry faked the injuries and ripped his own clothes; Barry claimed they had beat him.

"I've seen people really beaten up," Dowdy would say later. "It was not all that bad. We may have dramatized it."

At 3:00 a.m., after paying $1,015 in bail, Marion Barry was back on the street, a martyr in the making.

Tommy Tague saw Barry as just a nuisance on the street. He wasn't alone in the view.

"The majority of black Washingtonians thought that Marion was a thug," says radio and television veteran Jerry Phillips, a fifth-generation member of the city's black elite, whose members were acutely aware of intraracial castes by upbringing, skin color, and language. "They saw him as one of the 'cotton-pickin' niggers' who came to our city from down South."

Barry may have been poor, by choice, but he wasn't a street dude or a thug. In the lexicon of the streets he was a 'Bama, a hayseed from the South, but even that description was too simplistic. Marion Barry was actually a well-educated man, a few hours shy of a doctoral degree in chemistry, which qualified him to be a member in good standing in the black bourgeoisie. His street affectation in 1967 was more political than personal.

The prevailing myth holds that Marion Barry grew up in the Mississippi Delta. The truth is, he lived in Memphis, Tennessee, and from the time he was four in 1940 until he finished college in 1958. In those years before and after World War II, the rough-and-tumble Mississippi river town was the first stop for waves of sharecroppers escaping the poverty and virtual serfdom of the Mississippi Delta. Memphis could be mean, but it offered hope. Marion Barry was four years old when he and his family arrived from Itta Bena, Mississippi, a speck of a town in the heart of the Delta. He was born there on March 6, 1936. In the landscape of the civil rights movement, Itta Bena is located down the road from a town called Money. It was there in 1955 that Emmett Till, a fourteen-year-old black boy visiting from Chicago, was lynched for the indiscretion of saying "Bye, Baby" to a white woman on a dare. News of the lynching shocked the nation, but by that time, young Marion was out of the Delta, and he never returned.

Barry left Mississippi without his father, and that may be the most indelible aspect of his early life. What happened to him remains a mystery. Beyond the fact that he was a farmer, Barry says he has no recollection. "My father is dead," he told Thomas Rose, a graduate student writing a thesis on black activists in 1962. Barry's mother, Mattie, told interviewers that his father was a handyman, that she had two daughters with him, and that he died when Barry was five or six. The only clear fact is that Barry, like many children of sharecroppers, came from a broken home and lacked a father figure.

In Memphis, Mattie Barry worked as a domestic, took her children to Arkansas in season to chop cotton, and worked on the line at a meat-packing plant where she met and later married David Cummings, a butcher. Cummings had three daughters by a previous marriage; he and Mattie had two more girls. So Barry lived with his mother, his stepfather, and seven sisters: two whole sisters, two half sisters, and three stepsisters. The family of ten lived in a four-room "shotgun" shack shaped like a boxcar on Kentucky Avenue in the Foot Hill public housing projects of South Memphis, a maze of un-paved streets in the 1940s. Marion slept on the couch and stoked the wood stove every morning. David Cummings worked seven days a week and had little time for his stepson. "Marion didn't have much of a father figure to the best of my knowledge, " says Calvin Rolark, Jr., the Washington businessman who lived in Memphis at the time. But Cummings brought home the bacon, literally, along with slabs of beef for big Sunday suppers.

"We weren't poor," Mattie Cummings once said. "It was just so many mouths. We always had plenty to eat, clothes, a decent place to live."

From the age of eleven Barry was aggressively working his way out of poverty. It was a familiar sight at the Kentucky Avenue bus stop: Marion Barry, dressed in his Sunday suit, urging on his two younger sisters to sing for loose change. In fifth grade he sold sandwiches at school with the extra bologna from the slaughterhouse. He delivered the *Memphis Press Scimitar,* bagged groceries, and later waited ta-bles. He saved his small wages and bought a suit when he got to high school. He did well enough at Booker T. Washington High School to get into the National Honor Society. He joined the Boy Scouts and became one of the first black Eagle Scouts in Memphis.

Barry graduated from high school in 1954, the year that the U.S. Supreme Court ordered the desegregation of public schools, and following the advice of a shop teacher, he prepared to become a plasterer. His friend William Hawkins encouraged him to apply to LeMoyne College, a small school in South Memphis founded in 1870 with a bequest of twenty thousand dollars from Dr. Francis LeMoyne, a white abolitionist from Washington, Pennsylvania. Most of the professors were white, and two radicals set Marion Barry on a course of protest.

He'd been short as a child, but by the time Barry entered college he was tall, thin, clean-cut, and handsome. His mustache was neatly trimmed, his eyes were large and sincere. He wore ties and jackets or cardigan sweaters with his school emblem on the breast pocket. He pledged the Alpha Phi Alpha fraternity, joined the Naval Reserve, played on the basketball team, and became active in student government.

"I got involved just almost like I had come out of the dark into the light," he said in the 1962 interview with Tom Rose.

Two liberal, white professors—Richard Stoverman, a mathematics teacher, and James Lowrey—focused the light on revolution. At mandatory church sermons, Stoverman or Lowrey delivered lectures about the Korean War, oppression in all corners of the globe, and the need to join the drive of Dr. Martin Luther King, Jr., against the evils of segregation.

"They preached nonviolent disobedience," said Ulysses Campbell, Jr., a fraternity brother who attended LeMoyne with Barry. "They had a tremendous effect on many of us, but especially on Marion." Barry got so fired up that his fraternity brothers dubbed him Marion "Shepilov" Barry after a Soviet propagandist. His buddies called him "Shep."

In March 1958, midway through his senior year, Barry jumped into the Memphis bus desegregation case and got his first taste of notoriety for publicly rebuking a white city lawyer and member of LeMoyne's board. In the midst of the controversy, NAACP executive director Roy Wilkins took the stage of the Masonic Temple in South Memphis and called Barry to the podium, saying he had "the courage of a lion." Barry delivered a two-minute speech about "the Negroes' fight against the forces of bigotry and reaction." He basked in the glow of his first moment as a leader in the movement. "Marion started to believe that he was sort of a messiah, " LeMoyne president Hollis Price later said.

And local segregationists burned a cross on Mattie Cummings's lawn.

The nation was on the verge of great changes as 1959 gave way to 1960. John F. Kennedy was organizing his run for the presidency. Martin Luther King, Jr., was struggling to keep the Southern Christian Leadership Conference (SCLC) in the forefront of the movement. FBI director J. Edgar Hoover was trying to link King with communists. White teenagers were rocking and rolling with Elvis Presley and beginning to receive the radical message from Jack Kerouac and Allen Ginsburg. A new ethic was shaping a whole generation of college activists, inspired in many ways by the nonviolent philosophy of Mahatma Gandhi.

Barry applied to graduate schools in chemistry to avoid being drafted into the U.S. Army. He chose Fisk University in Nashville, Tennessee. It was a fateful move. Barry started an NAACP chapter and was perfectly positioned when Dr. King asked James Lawson to organize the Nashville students in the summer of 1959. Born and educated in the North, Lawson was a light-skinned African-American with sharp features, thick-rimmed glasses, and a passionate dedication to Gandhi's theories of nonviolence. Lawson quickly tested his tactics on the streets of Nashville with small protests, lunch counter sit-ins, and picket lines. Marion Barry was one of his first student volunteers, along with John Lewis, a theology student at Nashville's American Baptist Theo logical Seminary, and Diane Nash, a student from Chicago who would become one of the first women leaders in the movement. Together they formed the Nashville Central Committee, one of the strongest and most cohesive student civil rights organizations in the South.

"We were the pacesetters," says Nash, "and Marion was certainly one of the staunchest and most consistent members. We thought it was our task to get the movement started."

On February 1, 1960, four black freshmen from North Carolina Agricultural and Technical College put on their ties and jackets and took the sit-in movement to the Woolworth lunch counter in downtown Greensboro. News of their protest spread, and the Greensboro sit-ins brought the disparate student protests together. Lawson and his Nashville group marched on the downtown lunch counters for two days during the week after the Greensboro demonstrations. On Friday, the police threatened arrests. That night the students gathered at the First Baptist Church. They were middle-class kids: The coeds wore stockings and skirts; the young men dressed in coats and ties. Marion Barry, by then a twenty-four-year-old graduate student, was one of the leaders who coached and inspired the crowd.

On March 19, 1960, Barry returned to Memphis to lead a drive to desegregate the public library. The protest led to another arrest, according to FBI records, for disorderly conduct and loitering. Student protests spread to other cities in Tennessee, North Carolina, South Carolina, and Virginia. The stage was set for the birth of SNCC.

When the sit-in movement caught fire, Ella Baker was Martin Luther King, Jr.'s executive secretary at the SCLC in Atlanta. Miss Baker, the granddaughter of a slave, was a tough, veteran organizer who had worked with the NAACP, helped establish the Congress of Racial Equality, and wanted to bring the students together. She put out the word that students were to meet at Shaw University in Raleigh, North Carolina, on April 15, 1960. Students descended on Raleigh from Howard University in Washington, D.C., all the way to Tougaloo College in the Mississippi Delta. Shaw's parking lots were packed with battered Volkswagen bugs and beat-up Fords. Gathered that day were the young men and women who would be fire-hosed in Mississippi, beaten in Birmingham, attacked by police dogs in Atlanta. The images of their blood running in the streets would be beamed by television into American living rooms and change the course of history. "We really believed in the creation of an interracial democracy," John Lewis says. "We bought into the dream, the vision that we could build on our successes in the lunch counter sit-ins to transform society at large."

Martin Luther King, Jr., came to Raleigh in hopes of bringing the southern, black students under his wing. But Jim Lawson and Ella Baker encouraged them to create an independent organization free from CORE, NAACP, or SCLC. When her chance to speak arrived, she told them that their movement was "more than about Cokes and hamburgers," they were capable of moving the nation. In response, the students formed an independent organization and called it the Student Nonviolent Coordinating Committee (SNCC), known from that day on as "snick."

On the last day of the Shaw conference, the students met to elect a chairman. Jim Lawson could have had the job, but he stepped aside to allow a student to take charge. A political brawl erupted between factions from Atlanta and Nashville. After hours of debate in the Shaw gymnasium, the students made a deal: SNCC would be headquartered in Atlanta; Nashville would get the chair. Their first choice was Diane Nash, but at the time of the morning vote, Nash was taking a shower at the YWCA. John Lewis believes that the vote was deliberately taken while she was absent.

"The student movement was the essence of male chauvinism," he says. "Diane was a devoted, beautiful leader, but she was the wrong sex. There was a desire to emphasize and showcase black manhood."

With Nash out of the running, the Nashville group promoted Marion Barry, who worked the gymnasium seeking votes. Barry was older than most of the students, and many looked up to him. He had Ella Baker's support, too, and the combination helped him become SNCC's first chairman. Immediately after the meeting, Barry returned to Nashville to complete his studies. He left the work of moving SNCC into a dingy, windowless room in Atlanta to Ella Baker and a white theology student named Jane Stembridge.

Barry had yet to take on the personality of a street tough, says Stembridge. "I remember Marion as a teddy bear and a ladies' man, but not in a sexist way," she says. "He would sit back in his short-sleeve shirts at the interminable meetings and wonder when they'd finish so he could get some chicken and beer."

Two months after his election, Barry took SNCC's demands, drafted by Stembridge and Baker, to the 1960 Democratic convention in Los Angeles. The nation had yet to focus on civil rights. The news of the day revolved around foreign affairs—Sputnik, the missile gap, the downing of Gary Powers's U-2 spy plane over Russia—and John Kennedy, the Democrats' rising star. Barry and Bernard "Jelly" Lee, who would become Martin Luther King's closest aide, testified before the Democratic platform committee. Kennedy's people controlled the platform committee under the command of Chester Bowles, a Connecticut liberal who held down the left wing of JFK's group. Bowles and Harris Wofford, Kennedy's liaison to the movement, had put together a strong civil rights plank that they thought would satisfy mainstream blacks without alienating Kennedy's southern white supporters. In the ten minutes that they had to present their testimony, Barry and Lee nearly ruined the compromise.

"For 350 years, the American Negro has been sent to the back door in education, housing, employment, and the rights of citizenship at the polls," Barry testified. "We have come to urge that this convention not only speak to those issues but pledge itself to see that the full weight of the federal government is used to eradicate our national shame, Jim Crow, and second-class citizen ship." Barry, who had little contact with local Washington, D.C., at the time, even asked the Democrats to "provide self-government to the voteless residents of our nation 's capital."

The Democrats adopted some of SNCC's proposals, and Barry got his first serious mention in the national media.

"The Southerners had decided they would risk no open fight unless goaded beyond resistance," the *New York Post* correspondent wrote. "Roy Wilkins didn't goad them. Walter Reuther didn't goad them. But a college boy did—Marion Barry. "

Jane Stembridge sent the clipping to Barry with a note that read: "Don't let it go to your head." After five months as chairman of SNCC, Barry resigned and went north to the University of Kansas for a year and then returned to the University of Tennessee to work toward his doctorate in chemistry It was in this period between 1961 and 1964 that black students took their assault on segregation and bigotry into the teeth of the most violent and hostile communities: places like Albany, Georgia, and Ruleville, Mississippi, the home of Senator John O. Eastland.

"Barry would show up at meetings, dash in and dash out," recalls John Lewis. "He had a way of being in but not in." Barry helped to plan the Freedom Rides that led to the beating of students and the firebombing of buses, but he was not one of the riders. "As I recall," says Diane Nash, who led the riders, "Marion did not get on the bus."

In late 1961, within a few months of his return to school, Marion Barry was at an Alpha Phi Alpha party at Tennessee State University in Nashville when he met a beautiful young woman. He asked for her name and her phone number and suggested that she drive him home after the party. She was coy, but eventually gave Barry her number and her name: Blantie Charlesetta Evans. Barry pursued her, coming down often from Knoxville. They were married in a Nashville church on March 3, 1962, three days before Barry's twenty-sixth birthday and in the company of family and friends, including John Lewis.

Barry returned to Knoxville to finish his degree, while Blantie remained in Nashville, working and living with her parents. They saw each other on weekends. Academia was no haven from racism. When he took a teaching assistantship at the University of Tennessee, where he was the only black chemistry graduate student, he was barred from teaching white students. It was easy for the wives of white students to get jobs with the university, but Barry couldn't get work for Blantie. In 1964, frustrated by the racial barriers, he abandoned his degree and joined SNCC as a full-time organizer and fundraiser. A court found that he abandoned his marriage, too. According to divorce papers filed in 1969, Blantie Evans alleged that Barry "disappeared in June, 1964," and left her "impoverished."

As white students rode south for the Mississippi Summer Project, Barry was raising money in Chicago. He was there when three northern activists—James Chaney, Michael Schwerner, and An drew Goodman—were abducted and killed by white gunmen after attending a meeting on the night of June 20, 1964, in Meridian, Mississippi.

"I believe that that experience changed Marion in a fundamental way," says Mary Treadwell, who would become his second wife nearly a decade later. "It gave him and the other movement folk a tremendous sense of abandon, a sense that life must be lived one day at a time because tomorrow they might die on a dirt road in a town like Oxford, Mississippi."

Barry and his male comrades lived on a constant rush of confrontation and rebellion, of late-night meetings and clashes with cops, of weekends in jail and rallies on roiling campuses. They expected the women to prove their commitment in other ways. In the words of Stokely Carmichael: "A woman's place in the movement is prone."

"You had to prove your commitment by putting your body in the movement," John Lewis says. "It was a come-on to women. This was male chauvinism at its best, or its worst. " But Marion Barry pushed the sexual liberation of the movement over the line. "He was abusive," says Lewis. "He knocked women around."

In 1964 a white woman on the SNCC staff shocked the executive committee with complaints that Barry had sexually assaulted her. The charges were serious enough that Lewis called a special executive committee meeting to air the matter. The incident didn't surprise some SNCC activists. "Marion was legendary in the South in terms of pursuing women," said one. It was rumored, for example, that Barry had had an affair with the girlfriend of one of the lawmen in McComb, Mississippi, a small town where SNCC waged a bloody voter registration drive in 1961. Lewis thought that Barry 's leadership position in the southern movement might be in jeopardy, but Barry already had one foot out of the South. A split was developing between those who wanted to keep SNCC focused on organizing voter drives in the South and those who wanted to take the movement into the northern cities. Barry went north.

In June of 1965, after working the Manhattan cocktail circuit with Harry Belafonte and other entertainers as chief fundraiser for Friends of SNCC, Marion Barry moved to Washington, D.C., to become head of the local SNCC office.

The city was in the midst of wrenching changes brought on by integration. Ten years earlier Washington had been evenly populated by blacks and whites, and the two races lived side by side in many neighborhoods. Anacostia, Georgetown and Capitol Hill were biracial communities. First and Rhode Island, where Barry set up shop, was once an Irish Catholic enclave; now it was part of the ghetto spreading twenty blocks north from the Capitol. Working-class whites had abandoned the inner city for the suburbs, and wealthy whites who stayed within the District settled almost exclusively in the far northwest neighborhoods across Rock Creek Park, which provided a green Maginot Line between the races and made the whites feel secure in a city where they represented just over 30 percent of the population.

Barry moved into an apartment above the SNCC office at 107 Rhode Island Avenue NW, a row house that sat between two boarded-up buildings in a tough neighborhood ten blocks north of the U.S. Capitol. On July 13, after surveying the scene for a month, he wrote a brief memo to SNCC headquarters in Atlanta. "Washington is a strange city and it is very political. SNCC here by and large is either unliked or unknown."

In the South, Barry and the students of SNCC had faced an array of villains and worked toward crystal-clear goals. Taking the moral high ground, they had been the forces of good battling the evils of racism. Reporters from big-city dailies and networks covered their confrontations and wrote sympathetic dispatches. Even in Manhattan, Barry was a minor celebrity. In Washington, he was a trouble-maker.

Barry would walk down Fourteenth Street on the edge of the Shaw neighborhood and greet the shopkeepers, who were members in good standing of the local black bourgeoisie.

"Hey, brother," he would say. ·"What's happening?"

"Don't give me that brother bullshit," some would respond. "I'm not your damn brother. Take that shit back down South."

They didn't go for black power, either.

To make matters worse, the field of social action and organizing was already crowded. The United Planning Organization, an offshoot of the federal War on Poverty, had a budget of $7 million in Washington and used it to hire former SNCC activists to aid individuals and neighborhood groups. The NAACP was active in Washington along with CORE and the Urban League. SNCC's Washington office had been largely a fundraising arm, similar to the one in New York. It was run by a series of white activists. One of them, Liz Levy, tied SNCC to Temple Sinai, the city's most progressive synagogue. Charles E. Smith, on his way to becoming one of the city top real estate moguls, helped SNCC hold fundraisers at the Jewish Community Center. SNCC also did a good job of cultivating liberals in Congress, among them Republican senator Jacob Javits of New York and Democratic congressman Don Edwards of San Francisco.

But Barry wasn't satisfied just with raising money. He sensed that SNCC was losing its clout and that the civil rights movement itself was moving into a new phase that could find its form in the nation's capital. He also believed that he could exploit the city's volatile ingredients: a white economic power structure; a political system controlled by racists on Capitol Hill; a black community that was spoiled and docile at the top, and sick and frustrated at the bottom. The traditional civil rights groups with middle-class emphasis couldn't or wouldn't reach the poorest blacks, but Barry was uniquely prepared: SNCC had given him an education in community confrontation. All he needed was a cause.

In December, D. C. Transit, the company that operated Washington's public transportation system, announced that it would increase the bus fare from twenty cents to twenty-five cents a rid e. Barry was in the SNCC office one day shortly after the announcement when L. D. Pratt walked through the door. A middle-aged, balding white man who wore pork-pie hats and smoked cigars, Pratt didn't exactly fit in with the twenty-something SNCC radicals. He had been a corn farmer until he left Kansas in 1961 and moved east with his wifc, Polly. Pratt fancied himself a radical economist along populist lines; he believed that society could be transformed only if the people took control of the economic structure and broke large corporations down into local cooperatives. His favorite tactic was the boycott. Pratt had tried his theories out on other civil rights activists, including the Reverend Walter Fauntroy of the SCLC, but everyone had turned him away.

Pratt told Barry that protesting the fare hike with a citywide boycott could spark a mass movement. D.C. Tran sit's riders were primarily poor and black, so the increase would hurt them. No one had been brash enough to attempt anything like it before. And the man, who owned D.C. Transit, O. Roy Chalk, was the caricature of a capitalist villain. Chalk was an eccentric New Yorker who, in his heyday in the 1950s, owned real estate in Manhattan, airlines in South America, and railroads in the Amazon. He bought the Capital Transit Company in 1956 for five hundred thousand dollars and squeezed it for cash. He drove Rolls-Royces and Cadillacs, owned yachts, and sported an evil looking, pencil-thin mustache and dark glasses. Here then, Pratt explained, was "the Buslord," Marion Barry's first bogeyman.

Barry latched on to the idea, and they spent the next month organizing. They decided to focus on the Benning Road line, a main artery that ran through ·black communities in the city's Northeast quadrant. With a staff of ten full-time workers and a few dozen volunteers, Pratt and Barry analyzed the bus system's weak points, lined up volunteers to chauffeur some riders, set up phone banks to advise others, posted notices in key parts of the city, and set a date: January 24, 1966.

The day dawned bright and cold with temperatures in the twenties and chilly winds whipping the streets. Bus stops were deserted. The buses were empty. SNCC's chauffeur system worked, and thousands of commuters hitchhiked, walked, or stayed home. By the day's end, an estimated seventy-five thousand riders had stayed off the buses and cost O. Roy Chalk more than twenty-seven thousand dollars.

Declaring victory that afternoon, Barry called a press conference at SNCC headquarters and said the boycott was "an outpouring of spontaneous anger" that might be "the beginning of a mass movement. "

President Lyndon Baines Johnson loved the capital city and called it home for most of his life. He arrived in the 1930s as a congressional aide, made friends, sent his children to the local private schools, and put down roots. He always considered the passage of a home-rule charter, giving the District an independent political system, to be part of his civil rights agenda. He believed that the whole nation saw the injustice of a majority black city that was run by white congressmen.

In the summer of 1965 a home-rule bill, generated by the city's Democratic party, was moving through Congress. The president had plenty on his mind that season: Americans were beginning to die in great numbers in Vietnam's Mekong Delta, and his civil rights agenda—the Voting Rights Act—was still in the making. Nevertheless, Johnson placed his political capital behind home rule. The remnants of the segregationists girded for a floor fight in the fall and looked for allies. They found some in the Metropolitan Washington Board of Trade. The white business organization had fought home rule for decades. With three innocuous, appointed commissioners running the city, it had immense power and control, perhaps more than any other local business group in the nation. When Congressman John McMillan held hearings on District affairs, the Board of

Trade testified on an equal footing with the city's three appointed commissioners.

In November, as the home-rule bill neared a vote, the Board of Trade gave its version of the debate in a mass mailing to newspapers across the country. "The fact is that a great many Washingtonians—including an overwhelming majority of local professional and business leaders—are opposed to pending home rule legislation," the letter said.

The letter was misleading at best, but it worked. Newspapers published it and negative mail rained on Congress as the crucial December vote approached. That helped California Congressman

B. F. Sisk pass a weaker bill that died in the Senate, effectively killing the home-rule campaign.

President Johnson ran into Charles Horsky, his aide in charge of the legislation, at the White House. "You really screwed up, " LBJ said. "This was one of the most bitter defeats for me."

But in the Board of Trade's success, Marion Barry and L. D. Pratt saw another opportunity. They persuaded the NAACP, Walter Fauntroy, and others to join Free D.C, unveiled at a news conference on February 21, 1966. "We want to free D.C. from our enemies: the people who make it impossible for us to do anything about lousy schools, brutal cops, slumlords, welfare investigators who go on midnight raids, employers who discriminate in hiring, and a host of other ills that run rampant through our city," Barry declared. "The people in this city are tired of Gestapo cops who break into their homes illegally and arrest them on flimsy charges."

Barry was the activist in his prime, dressed straight for the occasion in white shirt, thin tie, dark sport coat, no dark sunglasses, close-cropped hair. He looked exactly like the ministers lined up behind him at Fauntroy's church. In town for just eight months, Barry was already at the helm of the biggest mass movement local Washington had ever seen, speaking for the people and wrapped in the arms of the clergy.

"The people in this city," he said, "are tired of a school system that causes 18,000 students to drop out of school in five years while during that same period only 15,000 students graduated. The people in this city are tired of Senator Robert Byrd taking bread away from hungry children by making it all but impossible for families to receive welfare aid in D.C.

"Who is it that keeps D.C. in political slavery?" Barry asked. "The Southern white segregationists led by John McMillan have gotten together with the moneylord merchants of this city to op pose our right to vote…. We can't hurt McMillan or Byrd, but we can hurt the moneylord merchants of this city."

The Free D.C. campaign was largely L. D. Pratt's brainstorm. Merchants were asked to post bright orange stickers that read "FREE D.C." and to ante up a donation of five dollars. If they didn't comply, pickets would be set up at their stores. The city was soon deluged with handbills depicting a black man in a neck manacle held down by caricatures of Byrd, McMillan, and the "D.C. Power Structure," a fat, balding white man.

Barry personally put the squeeze on storeowners. With Pratt and John W. Diggs, a black barber enlisted as a leader of the movement, he walked into McBride's, a variety store owned by Milton Blechman, who said he'd be happy to sign a petition, display the Free D.C. sign, and donate one hundred dollars.

"We've examined your firm's financial standing," L. D. Pratt said. Blechman owned two variety stores and four small clothing shops. "We've decided that your fair share is more."

"How does one thousand dollars sound?" Barry asked.

It didn't sound too good. Blechman said one hundred dollars was plenty.

"Well," Barry said. "This makes it difficult. We'll be back tomorrow afternoon."

The trio walked down the street to Morton 's, a clothing store owned by Mortimer Lebowitz, a liberal Jew who'd worked in the civil rights movement in Alabama and also contributed to SNCC. Lebowitz gave Barry and his comrades a warm reception and offered a donation, but Pratt and Barry wanted more.

"We think that you can afford $650," Pratt said. Lebowitz told them to leave. Diggs quit Free D.C. over the incidents.

The tactics and the demand for donations hit a raw nerve in Congress. Senator Alan Bible, a Nevada Democrat and home-rule advocate who chaired the District oversight committee, called the campaign "blackmail." McMillan held a closed-door hearing with the U .S. attorney to see if Barry' s new organization was violating any laws. He emerged and said, "Trying to extort money cannot be tolerated in the nation's capital."

Blechman called David Abramson, his advertising agent, for advice. Abramson was relatively new in Washington. He came from Boston via New York. He had worked radio in Miami and for Pepsi in Manhattan. Blechman was sure his hotshot ad man would know what to do.

"What are you asking me for?" Abramson said. "I'm an ad guy ."

"Yeah, but you 're from New York," Blechman said. "You know about these things."

Abramson contacted Assist ant U.S. Attorney Tim Murphy, who was considering pressing racketeering charges against Barry, but neither Blechman nor Lebowitz would make a formal complaint. The prospect of legal trouble and adverse publicity about strong-arm tactics prompted moderates, including the NAACP, to drop out of Free D.C., but hundreds of stores put up the Free D.C. signs, especially along the Fourteenth Street and H Street corridors where most of the customers were black. Volunteers started showing up at SNCC headquarters and helped fill the picket lines that were thrown up in front of Hecht's and Kann's, two large downtown department stores that refused Barry's demands.

The net effect of the Free D.C. Movement on Capitol Hill was negligible, but in the city, the balance of power began to shift. The newspapers wrote column after column about the protests and the boycotts, and Barry, the "civil rights chieftain," started to become a household word. *The Washington Post 's* young reporters of the day—Bob Kaiser, Carl Bernstein, Stuart Auerbach, and Dan Morgan—eagerly covered Barry. Officially, the Board of Trade didn't budge from its opposition to home rule, but some companies and larger corporations came out in favor of political independence for the city.

"This is a movement," Barry told *The Washington Post* at the end of April. "And as in a war, strategy and tactics change from day to day. What was true yesterday might not be true today.... Our friends and enemies should understand this."

Even at that early moment in his political development, Barry worked to make friends of his enemies, a trait that would become a trademark.

On June 20, 1966, with interest in the Free D.C. Movement waning, he called for a demonstration in front of the Fleming Building at 800 Seventeenth Street NW, where Board of Trade president F. Elwood Davis's law firm was located. Protesters and the cameramen showed up, but not Barry. Davis, a native Washingtonian who had grown up in a middle-class, integrated neighborhood near downtown, stopped at the microphones on his way into the office and accused Barry of extortion.

"This is typical of Barry's flamboyant, publicity-seeking ways," Davis said before ducking out of the midday sun.

Most of the picketers were gone when Barry joined the line. He was dressed in a seersucker suit and Panama hat, the essence of cool, style, and hip militancy. His mustache had grown and now curled around his mouth to meet his goatee and give him a menacing look. The reporters and TV cameras stayed to hear Barry call Davis "Public Enemy Number One."

A few days later Barry met Davis on the street.

"I just had to do that," Barry said. "You know, I need the atten-tion." "I recognize that," Davis said. "Call me any time. We'll have lunch."

They laughed and had a friendly parting. Davis had to admit that he liked the younger man, and he wasn't alone. David Levy was an-other Washingtonian who was drawn to Barry. He'd walked unan-nounced into the SNCC office on Rhode Island Avenue one day to help Free D.C. The son of a real estate investor who owned a big chunk of Georgetown and a graduate of Harvard Law School, Levy was bored with his job in the Department of the Interior. Free D.C. needed lawyers, and he began to spend more and more time in the movement. He and Barry were arrested in May on a "move on" charge, and they fought it together in court. After a day of protest, Barry and Levy often would hit the local bars or go to Barry's apart-ment to smoke a joint.

"I'm going all the way to the top," Barry used to say, according to Levy. "I'm going to control this city."

As Levy got closer to Barry, he began to see the outlines of his emerging political swagger.

"He was chronically late," Levy says. "He used it as a ploy to make the grand entrance, to keep the spotlight on himself. It was part of his repertoire."

Levy would sit in on negotiating sessions with other civil rights leaders, then walk out and listen to Barry denigrate the deal and run down the others as middle-of-the road, bourgeois Negroes. "This was especially true with Sterling Tucker, at that time head of the Urban League, and Walter Fauntroy, " Levy says. "Basically, Barry's word was worth nothing, and he was contemptuous of the people he was dealing with."

Barry 's relationships with women were characterized by infidelities and betrayal, too.

On his way from New York to Washington in the spring of 1965 he stopped in Wilmington, Delaware, at 3:00 a.m. to see a woman named Kaylynn, who had been infatuated with him. In a letter that found its way into the SNCC archives, she said she regretted allowing "you to put your filthy hands on me," and added: "You use people, take advantage of them and never give one thought that you might be destroying them in the process.... you have betrayed my trust and dishonored me." In Washington Barry's relationship with Betty Garman, a longtime white activist, dissolved in less than six months because monogamy wasn't Barry's way. His role model in matters of morality and style was Adam Clayton Powell.

"Regardless of whether Adam Clayton Powell is good or bad," Barry said at a forum on black power in the Anthony Bowen YMCA, "regardless of whether he is flamboyant or not, regardless of whether he goes to Bermuda or not, we should all support him in this issue because he is being attacked by racists."

A new woman walked into Barry 's life in the summer of 1966. Her name was Mary Treadwell, and their accidental meeting was providential.

Treadwell was the product of an upper-middle-class family from Kentucky; her father was one of the most successful black builders in the lower Midwest. While Barry was struggling to grow up on the poor side of Memphis, Treadwell was going to an integrated high school with the children of doctors and lawyers in the suburbs of Columbus, Ohio. She was recruited by Smith College but chose Fisk University. In 1966, she arrived in Washington expecting to get a law degree while her husband, a white naval officer, was on duty aboard ship.

One day Treadwell was walking out of the phone company building where she was working as a clerk. Free D. C. protesters were picketing and Treadwell recognized Barry, whom she had met briefly at Fisk. Her first reaction was to avoid him. She quickly ducked behind two white executives.

"Look at those monkeys," one man said to the other. "Why don't they go back to the jungle?"

With that, Treadwell turned around, broke into the picket line, grabbed a sign, and started to march. She joined SNCC and eventually became the latest of the strong women that Marion Barry always seemed to need by his side, and in his bed.

The Free D .C. Movement faded away in the fall and winter of 1966, but it had served Barry well.

A *Washington Post* poll placed him fifth among black leaders who had "done the most for Negro people in the area." Faun troy was first and Tucker, an Ohio native, was second. There were other activists contending for the political power that was inexorably shifting away from Congress, the commissioners, and the white businessmen. Julius Hobson, Sr., head of the local CORE chapter, was the least popular but most effective. The straight-talking, pipe-smoking, gnarled militant in pork-pie hat desegregated rental housing, forced downtown stores to hire black clerks, and heaped abuse on the black clergy for creating passive congregations. Rats were overrunning black sections of the city, but the government spent all its rat eradication funds in white sections, until Hobson announced his "rat relocation program" to transfer rodents to Georgetown—and the White House. He also sued the schools to abolish the practice of putting students on different "tracks," according to their abilities, a system that discriminated against blacks, in Robson's view. The Reverend David Eaton was a philosopher-activist, educated at Howard University, Boston University, and Oxford. A tall man who wore cowboy boots to increase his lofty perch, Eaton turned All Souls Church into a radical meeting ground and ran a successful job-training program. Calvin Rolark, Jr., worked behind the scenes and started a community newspaper and eventually the United Black Fund. The Reverend Channing Phillips organized a moderate "Coalition of Conscience" to bargain with the white power structure.

But all the activists and pretenders to power seemed to be standing still as Marion Barry blew past. In the aftermath of Free D.C., he penned long memos to SNCC and sharpened his aim at confrontations that would galvanize the black community's rage. The police were clearly the most obvious villains, and Barry found the perfect bad guy in Private Tommy Tague, who had the temerity to arrest him for jaywalking on that night of March 30, 1967.

The next day at SNCC headquarters Barry's friends wanted to march and riot, but Barry argued for a measured response. He called a press conference, showcased his wounds, and announced the formation of a Citizen Committee for Equal Justice. At one of its first meetings, Julius Hobson suggested that people follow Tague with a bullhorn and harass him for arresting Barry. News of the arrest and Robson 's reaction provoked Congress.

"I would hope the police department, if this scandalous behavior persists, will fill up the jails and find out who is running law enforcement in the city," said North Carolina congressman Basil Whitener.

"It's outright blackmail," proclaimed Congressman B. F. Sisk, the California Democrat who helped kill LBJ's home-rule bill.

Barry stood trial in the court of general sessions in June on the charge of destruction of government property. The courtroom was packed with young blacks, and SNCC organized picketers in front of the courthouse. Barry's attorneys, Landon Dowdy and Frank Reeves, turned the trial into a morality play about police brutality. Dowdy's strategy was simple: Portray Marion Barry as a nonviolent young man who wouldn't think of resisting arrest. Mary Treadwell made sure that Barry came to court in a conservative suit, and Dowdy lined up character witnesses.

"I have known Mr. Barry for more than two years," Bishop Paul Moore, Jr., a white cleric who was head of the city's Episcopal diocese, testified. "He is known as a man of peace, a man of nonviolence.
"

The parade of witnesses continued for nearly an entire day. Howard University Law School dean Clyde Ferguson, the Urban League's Sterling Tucker, more clergymen, a retired police officer, and Free D.C. comrade David Levy all supported Marion Barry and many said they doubted he had done what he was accused of.

A half-dozen officers described a different Marion Barry through detailed accounts of how he tried to fight them off. Barry expected to lose. "I guess I'm going to spend some time in jail," he told Dowdy and Reeves. After deliberating for two hours, the jury of ten blacks and two whites voted to acquit.

"The character witnesses won it for us," says Dowd y. "It was the ministers. " The judge helped, too. Chief Judge Harold Greene, a liberal Jew whose family had been decimated in the Holocaust, identified with the civil rights struggle.

"He asked me more questions than he asked Barry," Tague said. "He put me on trial."

Word of the acquittal touched off a minor celebration around the courthouse, with car horns honking and a crowd of supporters waiting for Barry to speak. He didn't disappoint and declared his case "a great victory for Negroes and poor people."

Ironically, Tommy Tague took the real beating. Black activists picketed his house in Prince Georges County, Maryland, and threw rocks through his window. His dog was poisoned, he suspects by protesters. The picketers used a bullhorn outside his home. A month later, Tague's wife moved out with the children. She later filed for divorce.

"It was a crucial event," says Mary Treadwell, "the test case that everyone was reaching for. Julius Hobson would have loved to have been the one, but it was Marion—a stroke of luck in a way."

"I made Marion Barry," says Tommy Tague.

The man who really made Marion Barry was Willard Wirtz.

CHAPTER 3

PRIDE

*We weren't taking beginning failures. We
were taking end failures.*
*—Marion Barry on the employees of Pride,
Inc.*

Labor Secretary Willard Wirtz paced his office for days during the hot summer of 1967. He had an overwhelming fear that the nation's inner cities were about to blow. He worried even more when he walked out of his air-conditioned office on Constitution Avenue and waded into the wall of humid air that hung over the capital like a wet veil. As miserable as it was on the avenue, he knew it was even worse a few blocks away in the poor neighborhoods.

"There were an astonishing number of minority kids that didn't have work," he says. "Things were getting pretty hot."

The temperature was rising in Detroit, New York, L.A., and other big cities, but one city in particular was giving him heartburn: Washington, D.C. It wouldn't look good if the capital city went up in flames. Wirtz's principal job was to see that it stayed cool.

"This is a helluva situation," Wirtz kept telling his aides. "We can't let this place blow up."

Wirtz, a bushy-browed, bigheaded, bearish man, was one of Lyndon Johnson's point men in the War on Poverty. A protégé of Adlai Stevenson, he'd come to Washington from Illinois in 1962 to become undersecretary of labor to Arthur Goldberg. When John Kennedy made Goldberg his ambassador to the United Nations, Wirtz had taken over at labor. He served in the Kennedy and Johnson administrations during the precise moments when the liberal response to poverty and racial discrimination was conceived and put into place. His friends and colleagues included the core of the liberal Democratic movement: Ted Sorensen, Sargent Shriver, Bill Moyers, Bobby Kennedy, Orville Freeman, John Gardner, and Abe Ribicoff. Together they embodied the spirit that government programs could solve the nation's problems of poverty and hopelessness among black Americans in the big cities.

The philosophy was simple: Federal funds would be applied to cure the root problems and symptoms of the inner-city poor. Through such programs as the Office of Economic Opportunity, the Job Corps, VISTA, Head Start, and Upward Bound, the administration expected to improve education, produce housing, and reduce unemployment.

But Bill Wirtz took a particular slant. He believed that the cycle of poverty could best be broken by creating jobs. He vigorously attacked a 1964 Council of Economic Advisers report that minimized the problems of unemployment. "The Poverty Program must start out with immediate, priority emphasis on employment," he wrote, adding that "the single immediate change which the poverty program could bring about in the lives of most of the poor would be to provide the family head with a regular, decently paid job."

In practice, Wirtz fought hard for programs that would train inner-city youth, and he made sure that Washington was well endowed with job-training funds. But as the summer of 1967 came to a searing climax, Wirtz knew that federal job programs in the capital would end at the beginning of August, which would leave five weeks before school—a very long month of potential hell. He had already funded an array of programs to keep the youths occupied, but nothing seemed to reach the "hard-core unemployed," the tough teenagers in the doo-rags who gathered on street corners.

"We didn't know how much trouble those dudes in Anacostia would get into in those five weeks," he says.

His concern was justified.

On the night of May 1, Clarence T. Brooker went to the corner store to buy some cookies. The store was right around the corner from his home in the projects on Kenilworth Avenue in the city's Northeast quadrant, a neighborhood on the east bank of the Anacostia River that was virtually all black, except for the storeowners. The nineteen-year-old black man—Fat Nasty to his friends—never finished eating the cookies.

Brooker paid for the cookies and walked out of the store, but not before he had hassled the clerk. The clerk called the police. William Rull, a short, white patrolman, responded. He approached Brooker and some friends across the street from the store. When Brooker threw his bag of cookies on the ground, Rull tried to arrest him. The charge? "Throwing trash," according to the police, report. Rull grabbed Brooker, but the youth was too big, and overpowered him and slipped away. Rull chased him down an alley, grabbed him, and they fought. Rull lost his night stick and his tie in the struggle, but he was able to pull out his service revolver. According to the police report, Brooker and Rull had their hands on the pistol when it discharged. According to black teenagers who witnessed the scene, Brooker took off toward some railroad tracks when Rull drew his service revolver and fired two shots—one at Brooker's feet and one into his back. The youth fell to the ground.

"I'm shot," he said.

Other officers arrived, and Brooker told them he was wounded. They didn't see any blood, so they cuffed him, waited for a squad car, and eventually took him to the precinct house for booking.

Brooker kept complaining. Finally, they took off his shirt and saw the hole where the bullet had entered his back. They rushed him to the hospital. Clarence Brooker died a few hours later of massive internal bleeding.

His buddy, Rufus "Catfish" Mayfield, saw the whole street incident. He and Brooker and a few friends hung out together. They were "dudes," the guys Willard Wirtz wanted to help and keep from burning down the city. Mayfield, a wiry young man with a quick wit, was the son of a numbers runner. Though he grew up in the Parkside projects, his father's line of work kept him in new bicycles and fancy clothes. Catfish had been caught stealing cars and wound up in Lorton Youth Center, which gave him the cachet of being an ex-con. He became the comic of the crew. There was nothing funny in his friend's death. He testified at the inquest that Rull shot Brooker in cold blood, and then Rull's fellow officers allowed Brooker to die. The coroner called it a "justifiable homicide."

Mayfield was furious. He wanted to avenge Brooker 's death, to march and protest, but he didn't know how to focus his anger or his energy.

Across town Marion Barry was holding melancholy brainstorming sessions with his friends and fellow activists.

Barry's popularity in the capital wasn't impressing anyone at the national SNCC headquarters. Cleveland Sellers, SNCC's program secretary, questioned Barry's "discipline" in a letter that pointed out his divided loyalties between SNCC and purely local activism. Barry answered the questions in January 1967, when he officially resigned from the Student Nonviolent Coordinating Committee in order to devote all of his energies to creating a political movement in the capital.

"The civil rights direction of protest is dead," he said. "Now we must concentrate on control-economic and political power."

"It's very difficult to talk to a man about his right to vote when the plaster is falling off his wall, or he doesn't have any food, or his kids are hungry," Barry wrote to SNCC before he quit. "It's a hard issue to mobilize people around."

Police brutality was perfect.

On the day that Brooker 's death—and Mayfield's account of it—made the news, Barry walked into his apartment waving the newspaper. Mary Treadwell, L. D. Pratt, and a few friends were there.

"Here's what we've been looking for," Barry said.

Barry needed a way to make common cause with the capital's poor blacks. Barry's dilemma was not unlike Willard Wirtz's: Neither truly understood the culture of these urban black men. Most had dropped out of school, many had police records, and more than a few were gang members and carried guns. Marion Barry was a former small town Eagle Scout who'd made it through nineteen years of schooling.

"On the streets," says Landon Dowdy, Barry's lawyer at the time, "Marion was a 'Bama from the South, and Mary Treadwell was a boojie lady with light skin and a fast mouth."

Barry needed the young blacks as much as Wirtz did, but for different reasons: He wanted to organize them into a political force. In Catfish Mayfield and the shooting of Clarence Brooker, Barry saw an opportunity to protest and to learn the ways of the street. Pratt encouraged Barry to make contact with Mayfield and a week after Brooker was shot, Barry showed up at Mayfield's sister's house.

"I want to help you raise hell about the shooting," Barry told him.

Mayfield had heard about Barry from the bus boycott, the Free D.C. movement, and his work organizing block parties for teenagers in the summer. With a little encouragement, Mayfield agreed to be Barry's guide. He taught him the dialect of the street, the walk, the jive, the mannerisms, the culture. In return, Barry showed Mayfield how to hold a press conference and organize a demonstration. Mayfield quickly organized a protest in front of the Fourteenth Precinct, where Brooker was taken. The demonstration made the news, and Mayfield got a taste of fame.

In late May a grand jury heard evidence on the Brooker shooting. The police testified that Brooker had been shot during a struggle over Rull's revolver. Mayfield testified that Brooker simply was shot in the back. Barry testified for three hours about police brutality in general. The jury went with the police and there was no indictment. But it was a great opportunity for Barry. He hung out all summer long with the Northeast crew, and Catfish Mayfield turned Marion Barry into a street dude.

Barry's ability to connect with the black teenagers distinguished him once again from the city's other civil rights leaders and also drew the attention of Carroll Harvey, the director of the city government's office of community renewal. "Here," thought Harvey, "was our bridge to the young toughs, the kids whom no one else had been able to reach."

Harvey was a tall African-American with a commanding presence and a passion to make Washington work for all of its citizens. He'd been born and raised in the city, but his light skin tone, his intellect, and his social standing had placed him in a different caste than most of the ghetto teenagers. Aiming to be an engineer, he'd gone to Armstrong High School and Howard University. While there, he took a sociology course under E. Franklin Frazier, whose ideas changed Harvey's life.

Frazier was a brilliant, radical thinker who examined the black American experience from a class perspective. In a series of books, including *The Negro in the United States,* Frazier dispassionately described the effects of slavery on the African family, the further destruction of the black family's morals under sharecropping, and the alienation of African-Americans in a dominant white culture. But it was in his last book, *Black Bourgeoisie,* written on a park bench in Paris in the late 1950s, that Frazier set out the theories that intrigued Carroll Harvey.

"As the result of the break with its cultural past, the black bourgeoisie is without cultural roots in either the Negro world—with which it refuses to identify, or the white world which refuses to permit the black bourgeoisie to share its life," Frazier wrote. "Lacking a cultural tradition and rejecting identification with the Negro masses on one hand, and suffering from the contempt of the white world on the other, the black bourgeoisie has developed a deep-seated inferiority complex."

Harvey saw Washington's upper and middle classes—and himself—in Frazier's thesis. He was working as a city planner and engineer, but found himself drawn into the city's social problems. How could he reconcile the races? How could he break down the racism among blacks? And like Wirtz, he wondered how he could keep the city from going up in cinders. In Marion Barry, he saw hope on all levels.

"I thought that he was the only person who could do it," says Harvey. "I know that he was hustling me—God knows I needed him. It was a conscious decision to break the caste system."

Harvey gave Barry space in his District Building office and together they catalogued the city's troubled teenagers by school and the gangs and other associations by neighborhood. Then they tried to bring the leaders in to talk. In July, Harvey helped Barry become a paid consultant for the United Planning Organization, working with "hard-core delinquents" for fifty dollars a day. Harvey became known as the "Godfather," Barry as the "Cooler." One night in late July, street fighting turned into arson in a hot neighborhood, and according to Harvey, Barry went into the alleys to talk to the teenagers and defuse a potential riot.

"It was working," Harvey says.

Willard Wirtz studied the Brooker case and fretted even more. He told his aides to come up with two hundred thousand dollars for a jobs program to get the capital through the last days of summer. To unveil the new project, Wirtz called a meeting at a church not far from where Brooker was shot.

The labor secretary and a lone aide pulled up in front of the darkened church in a dark blue government car. They stepped inside and found their way to the auditorium. It was packed with street toughs. It was hot and absolutely silent.

"I am Willard Wirtz, the secretary of labor, " Wirtz said. "I came here tonight to talk to you about a new, short-term program to train unemployed youths. "

Wirtz explained the project for ten minutes. When he finished, there was dead silence. He looked at his aide and considered leaving. Just then a tall man dressed in a dashiki stood up.

"You may be wondering what's happening," said Marion Barry.

"That's right," Wirtz responded.

"You might be expecting some reaction," Barry said, "but you have three problems. First, you have no idea what's going on here in the ghetto. Two, you wouldn't understand if we told you. And three, you wouldn't know what to do if you did understand. So you can take your program and you know what to do with it."

No one moved or made a sound. Wirtz wasn't angry or frightened, just miffed. He and the aide walked out.

Barry caught up with Wirtz at their car and introduced himself. He was no longer affecting the thug in dashiki. Now Barry was the guy with the degree in chemistry. Wirtz was amazed at the metamorphosis.

"I suppose I should apologize, but I'm not about to," Barry said. "But if you want to talk, I'm willing."

Wirtz looked him over. He'd never heard of Marion Barry before that moment. All he knew was the man who had just humiliated him was offering him half an olive branch. Wirtz was still angry, but so worried about the potential for riots in the capital that he was ready to do just about anything.

"Let's talk, " Wirtz responded. "Come to my office tomorrow morning."

"I'll be there," Barry said.

The next day, Barry showed up at the Labor Department with Carroll Harvey, Mary Treadwell, and David Rusk, the son of Dean Rusk, the secretary of state. Rusk was working as a financial analyst for the Urban League. Barry now was dressed in a tie and jacket.

"What's on your mind? " Barry asked him.

"I told you what I had in mind last night and you didn't seem to like it very much," Wirtz said. "What do you have in mind?"

Barry said that poverty programs weren't reaching the black men whom the policymakers referred to as the hard-core unemployed. Barry wanted to design a program aimed specifically at them.

"Do it," Wirtz said. "But do it fast. I want something in a few days."

Barry, Harvey, and Treadwell called Catfish Mayfield to Barry's apartment where they spent a day figuring out how to use Wirtz's money. There were various plans floating around the city. Harvey himself had developed one; the Reverend Douglas Moore, a local activist, had written another. Harvey polished his version, and two days later the group returned to Wirtz's office. Their plan was simple yet daring. They wanted to set up an independent company that would hire teenagers hanging out on the corners to clean the ghetto streets. The daring aspect was that few believed that street toughs would work for a wage. Barry's proposition challenged the conventional wisdom. He told Wirtz it would cost $250,000 for a one-month pilot program.

"I like it," Wirtz said. "Give it to me in writing, and we can go forward."

"There we go again," Barry said. "Paperwork. Red tape."

They worked all weekend and returned on Monday with a written proposal and incorporation papers for a company called Pride, Incorporated. It would employ five hundred people for five weeks at a cost of $250,000. Cheap, thought Wirtz, if the result was peace in the streets.

"Okay, let's start right away," he said.

The first deal—between Marion Barry and the white liberal establishment —was struck. He would maintain peace in the streets, and the liberals would foot the bill, whether it paid for a job-training project or a political campaign to come. This fundamental transaction was the cornerstone of Barry's political machine. In an ideal sense, the money went to "lift all boats," as the liberals hoped; in a more cynical sense, it went to Barry in return for keeping poor blacks under control.

Barry, Treadwell, and Harvey were stunned at their quick success.

They planned a press conference at noon the following Wednesday to announce the program. Wirtz was in Texas giving a speech that morning when someone slipped him an urgent message to call his assistant, Fred Irwin. Wirtz left the podium and reached Irwin at 11:55, Washington time.

"They're here," Irwin said.

"Great," Wirtz responded. "What's the problem?"

"Catfish Mayfield is supposed to be the chairman of Pride, Inc., and he's been arrested twice for car theft," Irwin said. "Broyhill is fuming."

Republican congressman Joel Broyhill from northern Virginia saw the whole deal as a federal dole for hoodlums. He'd characterized Barry as a bad actor back in 1966, and now he carried his cause to the House floor after the United Planning Organization hired Barry and Mayfield. "Both of these men have long records of civil disobedience and leadership in agitating others to disobey the law," he said. Taxpayers had a right to know if UPO was "running a school for street rioters or just a graduate course for experts in civil disorder."

Wirtz didn't want to embarrass the president and said, "Maybe we should wait."

"Not an option," Irwin said. "These guys are here, and they won't be put off. It's either go or no go."

"Let's wing it," Wirtz said.

At the press conference, Catfish Mayfield took the microphone. He had a fresh, open face and dancing eyes, especially when he took off his menacing dark sunglasses.

"We're after rats," he said. A grin came over his face. "And Broyhill's one of 'em."

Reporters peppered him with questions about his police record.

"Why's everyone so interested in my past? " he asked them. "Is anyone interested in my future?"

After Pride's first week in operation, Mayfield held a celebratory march. Dressed in their matching green coveralls, holding brooms as if they were rifles, and banging on the tops of metal trashcans, the street recruits marched to Pride headquarters to collect their first paychecks. Problem was, they didn't have a parade permit. The police arrested Mayfield, but he was out in a flash, back leading his troops for the moment.

It turns out that Willard Wirtz was acting on more than just his liberal soul and fear of riots. LBJ was still smarting from his loss on the home-rule bill in 1965. He had another proposal working its way through Congress in the summer of 1967 and he wanted nothing to jeopardize it.

Johnson's new plan was a half step toward an independent city government. His legislation would establish an appointed city council with an appointed commissioner/mayor. Congress would still oversee the city's budget and have the opportunity to veto its laws, but Johnson figured that it would put the city on the road to real home rule. The battle lines were quickly drawn, with the usual suspects against change. Although Broyhill and John McMillan testified against the bill, and the Board of Trade still was against it, the plan passed on August 11.

Johnson sought to appease the southerners by appointing a white person to head the new city government. *Washington Post* publisher Katharine Graham and managing editor Ben Bradlee also wanted a white mayor. They met at the White House with presidential aides Joseph Califano and Harry McPherson and suggested for the job criminal lawyer Edward Bennett Williams, former New York governor and future vice-president Nelson Rockefeller, former New York governor Averell Harriman, former secretary of state Dean Acheson, or Sargent Shriver. Attorney General Ramsey Clark passed the plan along to aide Roger Wilkins, the nephew of longtime NAACP chief Roy Wilkins. Clark said Johnson wanted to appoint Wilkins as deputy mayor to serve under the mayor, who would be white. Wilkins insisted it would be foolish to go to the trouble of passing a bill through Congress and then wind up appointing a white mayor. Clark later called Wilkins into his office.

"The president agrees with you," Clark told Wilkins. "He wants to appoint you to be mayor. "

"I don't want to be mayor of Washington, " he said. "I am a New Yorker. I'm planning to go back to New York. The new mayor must be a Washingtonian."

"We've got a problem then," Clark said. "The president is announcing your appointment today at his news conference."

"I'll disavow it," Wilkins said.

"Who should we appoint?" Clark asked.

"Walter Washington," Wilkins said. "He's a solid character. He knows the city government. He's respected by the white community and the black community. He's the one."

Walter Washington was certainly a solid and safe choice. He was a member in good standing of the city's black elite, which he joined by marriage. He was born in Georgia and raised in upstate New York. He scrimped and saved to go to Howard University in the 1930s, where he met Benetta Bullock, daughter of the Reverend George O. Bullock, pastor of the Third Baptist Church, and the scion of one of the city's upper crust black dynasties based in Le Droit Park. Washington graduated from Howard Law School and went into public service with the Alley Dwelling Authority, which later became the National Capital Housing Authority with control over public housing. Washington eventually became director, and when the tenants protested, he would serve tea. Lady Bird Johnson, who 'd worked with Washington on her beautification projects, seconded Wilkins's recommendation.

Washington was working for New York Mayor John Lindsay at the time, and he and Lindsay flew to Washington to meet with Johnson. There was a bit of confusion when Washington got separated from Johnson aide Joseph Califano and the president. "I was lost in the White House," he says. They argued over who would run the police department. Johnson and Katharine Graham wanted the federal government to control the police. Washington refused to take the job unless he had full power over the police. Johnson relented.

But when Califano floated Walter Washington's name on Capitol Hill, he ran into Senator Robert Byrd, Democrat of West Virginia. In his younger days, Byrd had been a kleagle, or organizer, in the Ku Klux Klan, but he renounced his membership when he ran for the Senate in 1952. Nine years later, as chairman of the Senate Appropriations Committee on the District of Columbia, Byrd made headlines and hay back home by cracking down on "welfare cheaters." When Califano told Byrd that Walter Washington would have control over the police, Byrd protested and promised to oppose the appointment.

Johnson ignored Byrd's bluster and moved to appoint Washington, but to appease Congress he gave Washington the official title of mayor/commissioner, not simply mayor. House District Committee chair John McMillan wasn't pleased. When Walter Washington sent his first budget to Congress, McMillan thanked him by delivering a truckload of watermelons to the District Building.

The president needed someone to chair the new city council, but he had problems there as well. His first choice was Max Kampelman, but his appointment ran into trouble in the Senate. Johnson hated to be embarrassed on appointments. He told his aides to find a replacement so that the White House could withdraw Kampelman and simultaneously announce his replacement.

John Hechinger was at a National Symphony Orchestra concert when the White House called. It was Joe Califano on the line. "The president needs to speak with you," Califano said, "tomorrow."

Hechinger was a bookish, unassuming young man who fit well into his square, black-framed eyeglasses. His father, Sidney, started peddling nails in 1911 and built the family hardware company into a do-it-yourself cartel that went on the stock market and made the

Hechingers fabulously wealthy. Sidney was a liberal Jew who empathized with the barriers erected against blacks. He hired black men, promoted them through the ranks, and made the best managers of his stores. John Hechinger was raised with the same sense of fairness, though he grew up in lily-white Northwest neighborhoods. When he took over the family business after graduating from Yale and serving in the Air Force, he was constantly at odds with the Board of Trade. In the 1950s, he made waves by taking two prominent blacks, Charles Duncan and Sterling Tucker, to lunch at Harvey's, then one of the city's most exclusive restaurants. He integrated the Boys ' Clubs. When Carroll Harvey called him in a panic to provide tools for Pride workers on the first day of operation, Hechinger sent over a free truckload.

Hechinger wasn't completely surprised when Johnson tapped him for the city council chairmanship. He knew the Johnsons because their children attended National Cathedral School, an elite Northwest private school. Hechinger's kids had played at Johnson's house back when the president was majority leader and vice-president. Still, Hechinger wasn't sure that he wanted the job. Joe Califano lobbied him to take the post, but the outgoing city commissioners told him it was a thankless job. Hechinger was ready to decline.

It was mid-August when Johnson summoned him to the White House. Hechinger was inside the living quarters when the president burst through the bedroom doorway with a folder under his arm. He was ruddy-faced from the shower. His hair was perfectly slicked back.

"I've made a decision," Johnson told Hechinger. "The papers are here in this folder. I've decided to step up the bombing of Haiphong Harbor. "

That said, the two men exchanged pleasantries, and Johnson began his pitch. He promised Hechinger that he would have the White House behind him, that he would have direct access to cabinet secretaries, that Johnson would treat him as if he were an elected official. Hechinger said that his company needed him. His father had recently named him president, and he couldn't afford the sacrifice. It was, he said, a tough decision.

"I understand, " Johnson said. The president was nose to nose with Hechinger. He had his long arm draped across the smaller man's shoulders. "I wish I could get out from under this decision to bomb North Vietnam, too."

That did it. Hechinger accepted the job. Hechinger was ushered almost immediately into the pressroom, where Johnson announced his appointment. From that day on LBJ treated Walter Washington and Hechinger as if they were powerful, elected officials. "He paid attention to us, invited us to the White House to greet heads of state, ordered his cabinet members to return our calls," says Hechinger. "He'd see me on TV and call to say what a good job we were doing."

It wasn't good enough for Barry and Mayfield, even though Johnson had appointed prominent members of the city's black community to the new city council.

"Either President Johnson can't read or is stupid," Barry told a press conference in September. "Johnson 's setting himself up a dictator role with this list. They should be people who could get elected if there were an election. These men couldn't make it for dog catcher."

The reigning liberal Democrats of the day fell hard for Pride.

Barry gave Senators Edward Kennedy and Edward Brooke of Massachusetts a tour of a rat-infested alley on North Capitol Street with a view of the Capitol dome. He took them for a trip through the nearby ghettos where the houses were falling in and idle men draped themselves on light posts. "These are the folks we're giving jobs to," Barry said.

Hubert Humphrey, with his eyes on the White House, was so enthralled with Pride that in his tour he hopped on a trash wagon and ran it up and down the street.

With that kind of attention and reams of positive press, Barry and Mayfield returned to Wirtz at the end of Pride's five-week pilot program. They wanted to make Pride permanent, and they arrived at the

Department of Labor with a new plan. It called for a whole array of businesses to be staffed by the men from the streets, from gas stations to landscaping services. The cost: $2 million. Wirtz gave them $1.5 million.

Suddenly the idea conceived on the fly over a weekend in July was worth real money and power. Carroll Harvey saw it as a way to "change the lives of people who had dropped out of society—to take them out of bed in the morning, give them a positive, rewarding experience, and put them back to bed at night." Barry also saw it as a perfect opportunity to continue organizing the city's poor people along the lines of the SNCC model and create his political base.

"Barry the pol began to emerge," says Leon Dash, one of *The Washington Post's* first black reporters. "He'd been hostile, almost sullen to reporters when he first came to town, but he became open and accessible—I'd say adroit. He knew he needed good press to keep getting Pride funded."

But he also wanted to be alone at the top. Mary Treadwell was no threat. She was the brains behind the operation and made Barry look good. He shed L. D. Pratt and made Landon Dowdy feel unwelcome because of his skin color. Pride became "a black thing." But there was the matter of Catfish Mayfield, who had a true following among the street toughs. Barry wanted him out, and it wouldn't be easy.

There was always an undercurrent of violence at Pride because many of its employees were gang members and ex-cons. At Pride's early meetings, Treadwell and Barry stationed a bouncer by the door who made sure pistols were dropped in a box before anyone entered. At various times, both Barry and Treadwell carried handguns. Police had discovered robbery rings working out of Pride, and there were reports of some killings by Pride workers. Violence, or the threat of it, was part of the package.

Mayfield started to get the message that Barry wanted him out shortly after the big federal grant came through. Pride held a reception for the newly appointed mayor, Walter Washington, but when

Mayfield tried to take his place on the podium, one of Barry's enforcers blocked his path.

"Marion and Mary said that you aren't supposed to be on the stage no time," the man told Mayfield.

"Bullshit," Mayfield said. "I'm the chairman of this goddamn outfit."

"I don't take my orders from you," Barry 's man said, and Mayfield backed down.

Catfish's strength was among the men in the streets, and he maintained it by cruising the neighborhoods, often in cars rented at Pride's expense. Barry and Treadwell said Mayfield was wasting money and forced him to stay in the office, isolating him from his natural turf. Meanwhile, they worked the streets without him. They stayed up late into the night with Mayfield, learning his contacts. But there was still the matter of Mayfield 's title as chairman and his power to sign checks. Treadwell and Harvey would bring the checks to Mayfield's apartment and have him sign hundreds at a time. By the time Mayfield realized he was being shoved aside, it was too late. He threatened to resign, take his followers with him, and split the organization. Barry came to see him one night just before Thanksgiving.

"Catfish, don't resign," he said. "The people are going to go with me."

"We'll see about that, "Mayfield said. He resigned the next day and called a press conference at Pride headquarters. Mayfield arrived to a room packed with Barry supporters, many of them packing guns and knives. Barry already was on stage when Mayfield walked inside. Surrounded by a handful of friends, Mayfield pushed and shoved his way to the front. The room was on the verge of a brawl.

"I'm coming up," Mayfield told Barry.

"Don't do it, Catfish. It's gonna get ugly if you do."

"I got some things to say."

"You lost your chance. You already resigned. Why don't you keep cool and get out?"

"Okay," Mayfield said, "but I'm not finished." He was, in fact, vanquished.

Ten years later, when Barry was about to take office as mayor, a reporter asked Mayfield what he thought of the city's newly elected leader. "Marion Barry was a carpetbagger in 1966, and I helped this nigger along," he said. "Everything that he has touched in this city he has left in disarray, moving from one position to another. A leopard cannot change his spots."

A week after Barry maneuvered Catfish out of Pride, Stokely Carmichael returned to Washington from a tour of Cuba and North Vietnam. He showed up at Howard University, where West Coast black nationalist Ron Karenga was speaking.

"I'm coming back to Washington to stay, baby," Carmichael told a group outside Cramton Auditorium. "This is our town. Our town."

Inside the auditorium, Carmichael was mobbed by students who wanted him to autograph his new book, *Black Power: The Politics of Liberation in America.* When the meeting broke up, he scanned the crowd and shouted: "Where's Marion? "

Barry emerged and embraced his friend from the SNCC days. "Marion," Carmichael said. "What 's this Pride mess I hear you've been jiving with? "

In the mild-mannered world of Washington politics, Marion Barry was a militant. But to Carmichael and other radical black nationalists, Barry was a collaborator with the white ruling class. They saw Pride as the federal government's way of buying peace in the ghetto. Barry, in that analysis, was a tool of the oppressor.

Barry let Carmichael's question float. As the two men walked off, Carmichael placed his arm around Barry and rattled off a few lines in Spanish.

"You don't know what I'm saying, do you, man?" Carmichael asked. "That's a quote from Che Guevara. It means the duty of the revolutionaries is to lead the revolution."

Barry looked at him and walked off.

A few months later, Carmichael would see how hard it is to control a real revolution

CHAPTER 4

THE UPRISING

Everyone thought Washington was riotproof.
—*John Hechinger, chairman of the appointed city*
council

Martin Luther King, Jr., was despondent when he arrived in Washington on March 31, 1968, to plan the Poor People's Campaign scheduled to take place that summer.

King was watching his nonviolent movement disintegrate around him. His dream of leading America to the promised land of peaceful integration had wilted in the heat of three consecutive summers of violence. The authorities in Washington worried that the Poor People's Campaign would turn ugly. Even NAACP executive director Roy Wilkins said the campaign should be called off because King couldn't control the crowds. King set out to reassure people before an overflow crowd of four thousand at the National Cathedral on Wisconsin Avenue that Sunday night.

"We are not coming to Washington to engage in any histrionic action," he said, "nor are we coming to tear up Washington. I don't like to predict violence, but if nothing is done between now and June to raise ghetto hope, I feel this summer will not only be as bad, but worse than last year."

Most Washingtonians weren't worried. According to the prevailing myth, Washington was riotproof.

Four days and four hours later this bulletin flashed across news wires:

MEMPHIS, TENN. (UPI)—DR. MARTIN LUTHER
KING JR. WAS SHOT AND KILLED LATE THURS-
DAY AS HE STOOD ALONE ON THE BALCONY
OF HIS HOTEL.

Within minutes, everyone at the intersection of Fourteenth and U
streets had heard the word. The main crossroads in the black community already was crowded with late evening commuters , but the tragic
news brought more small crowds into the street. At first the knots of
people stood around stunned and silent, too silent.

Up the street at SCLC headquarters, Stokely Carmichael was sitting between two desks, one foot up on each, on the phone to Memphis.

"Well," he said into the receiver at one point, "if we must die, we
better die fighting back." He hung up the phone. His smooth, handsome face showed little emotion. "Now that they've taken Dr. King
off," he said, "it's time to end this nonviolence bullshit. "

Stokely Carmichael was in Washington by design in the spring of
1968. Fresh from a tour of Hanoi, Havana, Moscow, and Africa, the
SNCC chairman and father of "black power" had decided to make
Washington, D.C., his base for the same reasons that attracted Marion Barry. When he first came to town in January, African-American
activists came together and put him in charge of the Black United
Front. It was a black city, it was a high-profile city, and it could
be his for the taking. Tall, lanky, and dashing in green fatigues and
dark glasses, he hit the street and made his way quickly through the
mounting crowds. Two blocks up Fourteenth Street at the storefront
headquarters of the local SNCC office, he picked up a few lieutenants and burst onto the street waving his hands.

"They took our leader off," he shouted, "so out of respect, we're
gonna ask these stores to close down until Martin Luther King is
laid to rest. If Kennedy had been killed, they'd have done it; so why
not for Dr. King?" He broke onto Fourteenth Street trailing a group
of SNCC workers. His movements during the next few days were

traced by *Post* reporters, whose collaborative book, *Ten Blocks from the White House,* provided the best account of the riots.

In the rear of the Peoples Drug at the northwest corner of Fourteenth and U, a small group was gathered around a transistor radio. President Johnson's gravelly, muted voice came over the box in a statement read from the Oval Office shortly before 9:00 p.m.:

"I know every American of good will joins me in mourning the death of this outstanding leader and in praying for peace and understanding throughout this land," he said. "We can achieve nothing by lawlessness and divisiveness among the American people. Only by joining together and only by working together can we continue to move toward equality and fulfillment for all of our people."

The small audience at the camera counter wasn't buying it, according to *Post* reporter Hollie West, who was at the scene.

"Honky," was the first verdict. Others agreed.

"He's a murderer himself."

"This will mean one thousand Detroits."

Spring is a glorious season that shows off Washington as a city of parks. Flowers bloom in succession, beginning with the daffodils along Rock Creek Park below the P Street Bridge, the tulips on the Capitol grounds, and then the azaleas in rich magentas in front of virtually every home. Until Dr. King was assassinated, the city was preoccupied with the annual Cherry Blossom Festival. Tourists were filling the city's hotels to see the parade and the crowning of the Cherry Blossom Queen , scheduled for Saturday, April 6. The pink buds on the trees surrounding the tidal basin by the Jefferson Memorial were about to burst on cue.

The federal city also was abuzz with the political bombshell that President Johnson had dropped the evening that King spoke at the Washington Cathedral. Numbed by the body counts from the war in Vietnam and tired of facing down segregationists in Congress, Johnson declared over national television: "I shall not seek and I will not accept the nomination of my party for another term." Who would run for the nomination? Could the Democrats hold the White House? Would the cherry blossoms bloom in time for the parade on Saturday? King's prediction of imminent violence didn't register.

What had happened in Watts and Detroit and Newark simply couldn't take place in the capital. The belief rested squarely on two misconceptions. The first was that Washington's black population was prosperous or certainly too middle class to burn its own communities. The second was that the military muscle ringing Washington would deter or instantly quell any serious disturbance to the city's civil calm. The Third Infantry was stationed at Fort Myer just across the Potomac; the Marines were down at Quantico, Virginia; and the Sixth Cavalry was garrisoned minutes away at Fort Meade, Maryland. The troops had been called out in 1967 to protect the Pentagon from antiwar protesters. Surely they could deter a riot.

Police Chief John Layton had been called to the White House inthe fall of 1967 and had tried to reassure Attorney General Ramsey Clark.

"Don't worry," he said. "The police department is fully prepared. But you shouldn't be concerned, because we won't have riots here."

"Why?" asked Patrick Murphy, whom Clark had brought in as a special assistant to advise him on urban unrest.

"Because we have such good relations with the black community," Layton responded.

In fact, Murphy looked into the matter and discovered that Layton hadn't appointed any black officers higher than the rank of captain, and there had been some nasty incidents in street fights, pitting blacks against cops.

The city's collective myopia was also a product of demographics. It was easy to ignore the problems festering within the slums because they were islands in a city of relative wealth. Most of the whites lived west of Rock Creek Park in some of the most sumptuous areas in any American city—Georgetown, Foxhall, and Spring Valley, for example. Of the city's eight hundred thousand residents in 1968, nearly 70 percent were of African-American descent, the highest proportion of any major city, but most were well off. An estimated seventy-five thousand blacks worked for the federal government; many worked two jobs and succeeded in sending their children to college. The vast black middle class lived throughout the city's eastern quadrants. Wealthy blacks lived in the northern reaches of Shepherd Park, a stately community of brick colonials along tree-lined streets named Jonquil, Holly, Kalmia.

There were other reasons to believe that Washington 's blacks wouldn't rebel. Landmark civil rights laws were starting to take effect. Local antipoverty programs such as Head Start and United Planning Organizations hired black s to help the poor. Blacks were moving into leadership positions. Thurgood Marshall had been appointed to the Supreme Court. Washington had an appointed black mayor, a majority black city council, and more black professionals per capita than any other city in the nation. With that kind of stake in the community, why would people take to the streets? Even at Pride, Inc., arguably the organization that was closest to the pulse of the poor, Marion Barry, Mary Treadwell, and Carroll Harvey believed that if the black teenagers hadn't turned the city into cinders in the summer of 1967, it would never burn.

That thought was running through City Council Chairman John Hechinger 's mind as he sat in the District Building and looked north to see the smoke from burning stores wafting over downtown.

"Pearl Harbor wasn't supposed to happen here," he thought. "But my God, it has."

After shutting down the Peoples Drug, Carmichael and the small but growing crowd turned south along Fourteenth Street. They zigzagged from one side to the other and closed stores along the way.

Walter Fauntroy, the local minister whom Johnson had appointed vice-chairman of the city council, confronted him in the middle of the street.

"This is not the way to do it, Stokely," Fauntroy implored. He grabbed Carmichael by the arms, but the wiry younger man broke free. "Let's not get anyone hurt. Let's cool it."

Carmichael kept moving ahead of the crowd.

"All we're asking them to do is close the stores," Carmichael said. "They killed Dr. King."

Fauntroy was somewhat mollified. He returned to SCLC headquarters and arrived on the second floor in time to hear the sound of the plate-glass windows of the Peoples Drug breaking from the impact of a flying brick. It was 9:25. He turned around and spent the next hour pleading for calm on the three local TV stations with other black leaders.

Carmichael doubled back and led the crowd down U Street. In his wake, the crowd had turned into a mob that filled the wide avenue for a block. The majority were teenagers and young men in Afros, goatees, and dark glasses. They weren't revolutionaries, and they were itching to do more than talk, march, and close stores. At the rear of the crowd, people started smashing store windows and heading for the merchandise. SNCC workers tried in vain to stop them.

One of Carmichael's lieutenants saw Mary Treadwell off to the side and sought help. The operations director of Pride had cut a few of her workers out of the mob; the last thing she wanted was to see Pride people busted for rioting. Carmichael knew that Treadwell could handle crowds of rough teenagers and sent someone to enlist her help.

"Mary," he pleaded. "Can you talk to this crowd?"

"Kiss my ass," she responded. "This isn't our style." She went around the corner to the Pride office and fielded a phone call from Carroll Harvey.

"Starmichael is out there with people he can't control," she said. "I'm afraid it's going to go up in flames."

Police Chief John Layton heard about King's assassination but decided to attend the Cherry Blossom Week military program at Fort

Myer in Arlington, Virginia. He wasn't even alerted to the potential for trouble until 10:00 p.m.

The man in control that first night was Patrick Murphy, the public safety director whom President Johnson had installed over Layton to mellow the MPD's penchant for brutality. He represented the restrained approach to urban riot control: Protect people over property; shoot only in self-defense or to protect innocent civilians; and use curfews and tear gas to control crowds. On that first night of rioting, he was at the Washington Hilton, where Vice-President Hubert Humphrey was giving a speech.

"We're giving it the light touch," Murphy told a reporter as the brick went through the window of the Peoples Drug. "There are no great numbers of men visible."

On Fourteenth Street Stokely Carmichael was losing control of the crowd. People dashed past him with booty: toasters, shoes, liquor bottles, all still in their boxes. The sound of a dozen burglar alarm s rang in the night. Looters cleaned out Sam's Pawnbrokers and Rhodes Five & Ten in a flash. Carmichael couldn't finish what he'd started. At 10:30 the architect of the black power movement ducked into a Mustang waiting across the street from SNCC headquarters and escaped.

"This is it, baby, " someone shouted from deep in the crowd, according to reporters on the scene. "This shit's going to hit the fan now. We ought to burn this place down right now. Let's get some white motherfuckers. Let's kill them all now."

By eleven o'clock word of the looting had spread, and people from neighborhoods on both sides of Fourteenth Street joined the free-for-all. Minutes later, a dozen policemen waded into the crowd swinging their white clubs, but they fell back under a volley of stones, bricks, and bottles. Arsonists torched a few small buildings after midnight, but the biggest blaze of the night gutted the Empire Supermarket at 2600 Fourteenth Street. Firemen arrived quickly but the crowd rained bottles and rocks on them. Police responded with tear gas, and headquarters crackled with radio reports of officers surrounded by mobs and helpless to stop the looters. Word finally reached Murphy.

"Pull those men out of there and keep them back until we can get help," he told other officers.

At 3:00 a.m., after touring Fourteenth Street with Mayor Walter Washington, Murphy went to the Pentagon to consult with the officers at the Army Operations Center. At this critical juncture, Murphy and his advisers, together with the military officers, decided that federal troops should stay in their barracks. They drew on the experience of previous disturbances, which showed that most rioting took place at night. Since the streets of Washington were beginning to calm down, Murphy assumed that he would have the following day to make his next move.

The mayor spoke to reporters waiting outside the police command center a short time later.

"The crisis is not over yet," Washington said. "It's still out there, but the police have it well in hand."

Police Chief Layton even predicted that the Cherry Blossom festivities would take place as scheduled. He dismissed the special riot control units and told them to report back late next afternoon.

The official plan to defend the capital from riots had a name: Operation Cabin Guard.

Military brass and metropolitan police had written and refined it in the summer of 1967, when other cities were on the brink. It was a precisely choreographed series of steps to put military troops between angry civilians and the key federal office buildings. The blueprint called for elite, specially trained troops to set up machine-gun emplacements in front of the White House and the U.S. Capitol. Operating out of police headquarters, other troops would fan out across the city to prearranged sectors. The troops were trained in riot control, and they were integrated. Under set procedures, the mayor and the police chief would have to certify the status of "serious domestic violence," but the president had to initial the order for military intervention.

On Friday morning President Johnson canceled a trip to Hawaii, where he was scheduled to consult with General William Westmoreland. U.S. forces were recovering from the Tet offensive, and the first American aircraft had just been shot down over North Vietnam, but the violence at home took precedence. The president called civil rights leaders, including Mayor Walter Washington, to the White Home to seek their views on how to calm the unrest that was breaking out across the nation. Should he address the nation? Call out the National Guard? Announce a national day of mourning?

Without arriving at any set course, Johnson proceeded to the National Cathedral for a special memorial service for Dr. King. Defense Secretary Clark Clifford and Mayor Walter Washington rode in the car with Johnson to and from the church. When they returned, Johnson read a proclamation to the nation that flags were to be flown at half-mast until King's burial on Tuesday. He declared Sunday an official day of mourning. He saw no reason at that point for Operation Cabin Guard.

Midmorning on Friday Stokely Carmichael arrived at Gaston Neal's New School for Afro-American Thought. The school, located just north of Fourteenth and U streets, was a gathering place for black radical intellectual, but on the day after King was killed, SNCC took it over, and Carmichael held a press conference.

"When white America killed Dr. King last night," he told the reporters, "she declared war on us. There will be no crying, and there will be no funeral…. The kind of man that killed Dr. King last night made it a whole lot easier for a whole lot of black people today. There no longer needs to be intellectual discussion. Black people know that they have to get guns. White America will live to cry since she killed Dr. King last night.

From the New School Carmichael went ten blocks east to Howard University for a rally called by campus militants. They raised the flag of Ujamma, the school's black separatist organization, and listened to speakers rail against "whity" and "honkies." At one point a young man grabbed the microphone to announce that parts of downtown Washington were ablaze, and a cheer rose from the crowd. Then Carmichael's voice rose from he back of the crowd of about six hundred students.

"Stay off the streets if you don't have a gun," he shouted more than once, "because there's going to be shooting." He pulled a gun from his jacket and waved it over his head for emphasis. Then he left and was sighted by reporters only one more time during the entire period of unrest. He and other activists tried in vain to control the streets, according to Ivanhoe Donaldson, who was close to Carmichael at the time.

"We didn't want to see black people burn down a black town," he says. "Everyone—poor and middle class—had an excuse to engage in the city's largest urban demonstration. It gave everyone a chance to go out and throw a fucking brick."

Carol Thompson, who would one day run the city government, walked to Roosevelt High School that morning in the Petworth neighborhood, two dozen blocks north of Howard University. It was hours before the downtown went up in flames, but the students were on edge. As soon as she arrived, Thompson felt the tension and wanted to go back home.

Home had changed over the years since her family moved into a large row house on Emerson Street a few blocks north of Sherman Circle. It had been an integrated, working-class neighborhood back then in the mid-1950s, but gradually the white families moved out. By 1968 there were three left. The Thompsons got along with everyone. Way back, her father's family had been oystermen on the Chesapeake Bay, and her grandfather, Leon Thompson, had been personal steward to Herbert Hoover. He went on to manage the Alibi and Metropolitan clubs, two of the most exclusive white clubs in the city. Following in Leon's footsteps, Carol's father worked in the White

House through the Kennedy years. The oldest of six children, Carol grew up in an extended family that revolved around her grandparents, Asbury United Methodist Church, and school.

"From early on our goal was to go to college," she says. "We were taught that the system may present obstacles, but you have a chance to lead a decent middle-class life."

The Thompsons were just like their neighbors in most ways except for their exceptionally light skin tone. Carol's round face was framed by straight, reddish hair. She had freckles. "My parents didn't make an issue of it," she says. "People are people, they taught us. I wasn't even aware of it."

There was much confusion in the halls of Roosevelt High that morning, beginning with the question of whether the schools should even be open. SNCC, other civil rights groups, and the teachers' union wanted to close the schools out of deference to Dr. King. But the last thing police wanted was teenagers roaming around with nothing to do. Carol Thompson recalls being in the stairwell and hearing people yelling. She realized that they were screaming at her, taunting her because of her light skin.

"I knew what it felt like to be ostracized," she says. "I couldn't wait to leave."

At noon the superintendent closed the public schools.

A few blocks away Carol Thompson's younger sister was on the bus home from Rabout Junior High. All of a sudden kids started screaming at her, people she knew were attacking her and calling her whitey, even though they knew she wasn't white. They finally forced her off the bus.

Carol Thompson and her sister were badly shaken when they reached home. Many students never went home.

It was still more dangerous for white people caught in the wrong place. Two were beaten to death.

As teenagers began to fill the streets, the police department was reporting that the situation was "not too bad."

Shortly after noon, the police communication system lit up with reports of looting and arson. There were so few police on the streets that they were out of touch. As the scattered cops on the beat began to react, the situation careened from calm to crazy in minutes.

Police Chief Layton placed a frantic call to Deputy Mayor Tom Fletcher at 12:30.

"It's starting up again," he reported. "I don't think that we can handle it alone."

Fletcher tried to locate Patrick Murphy, who was on his way to the Pentagon. He raised the public safety director as he was lunching just before 1:00 p.m. An hour later military brass and civilian leaders, including the secretary of the army, were meeting at the Pentagon and poring over Operation Cabin Guard.

From the top floors of their buildings along Pennsylvania Avenue, workers in the federal and city offices could look north and see smoke rising over Fourteenth Street and closer by on Seventh Street. Radio stations flashed bulletins about looting close to the downtown. Workers panicked, made frantic phone calls, or fled their offices. The federal government shut down in midafternoon, and fleeing bureaucrats caused the most massive traffic jam in the city's history. The phone system seized up with the overload.

The downtown jam made it even more difficult for police and firemen to reach the riot zones. In the vacuum, looters left Fourteenth Street to ransack stores up and down the Seventh Street and H Street corridors, which run northeast from the Capitol. At the height of the uprising, mobs had free rein along the city's three principal downtown shopping corridors.

The looters came in all ages and from diverse backgrounds. Most were male between the ages of fifteen and forty, according to arrest records. Three out of four were employed at low-paying, blue-collar jobs. The majority had been living in the District for years. But there were also a sprinkling of women, quite a few Howard University students, and plenty were high-school kids on a rampage. They created a surreal atmosphere that was part carnival, part consumer rebellion, part deliberate, destructive rage.

James Brown, the king of soul music, was in town for a concert, and city officials pleaded with him to help. He went on the air in midafternoon to say: "Don't terrorize, organize. Don 't burn—give the kids a chance to learn."

As soon as looters plundered a store, someone set it on fire, sometimes by lighting piles of paper but often by chucking Molotov cocktails. Looters barely had time to jump out before the structures burst into flame. Most of the twelve people who were killed during the rioting died in burning stores. Friday's first blazes were set just after noon along Fourteenth Street at Columbia Road. Firemen responded but had a difficult time getting through the crowds. One fireman interviewed by Senator Robert Byrd after the riots gave this account of those early fires:

"The company took a hose line, and I was assisting the pumping man to make the connection. They were calling for water, when a gang of Negro males came across the street and pushed and shoved the pumper man and told him not to hook up the hose."

One teenager shouted: "We didn't build the goddamned fire for any white people to put out. Don't worry, you will all be dead before the night is over."

Back at the White House, Johnson could smell the smoke and knew the situation was dire. He summoned Joe Califano and said, "Call Cy Vance and tell him to get the hell down here right away."

Cyrus Vance had served as undersecretary of defense and had done some special projects for Johnson, one of which was studying the riots in Detroit the previous year. He was working at a law firm in New York. He hopped a plane to Washington, arrived at National Airport, and fought the traffic to the White House.

Attorney General Ramsey Clark had flown to Memphis, so his deputy, Warren Christopher, went to the White House to deliver the official documents that Johnson would have to sign to call in the troops. Then Christopher headed on a reconnaissance mission with Murphy. It was about 3:00 p.m., and the riot was reaching its wildest period. The police were hopelessly outnumbered and outmaneuvered. Barred from using their service revolvers, they lobbed hundreds of tear gas canisters but still couldn't control the mobs. Rampaging teenagers had worked their way south and outflanked police at Mount Vernon Square. Looters laden with clothes darted between desperate commuters. The rioters sacked stores at Fourteenth and G streets, two blocks from the White House, before police drove them out of the central business district.

Throughout the afternoon there were thirty new fires set an hour, according to fire department records. Five hundred new fires were started on Friday; two hundred burned at once. Fire departments from the suburbs and as far away as Lebanon, Pennsylvania, sent trucks. Smoke billowed and hung over the central city. From a distance, it looked as though the entire capital was ablaze.

"I guess the significance of Martin Luther King was lost on us," Patrick Murphy now says.

Warren Christopher saw Fourteenth Street in flames, caught a glimpse of the chaos on Seventh Street, and took one look at H Street. That was more than enough. The general accompanying him grabbed a pay phone and called the Pentagon. At 3:30 the first troops began to move out. Christopher then called the White House and advised the president to sign the executive order.

With troops already converging on the city and the mayor virtually begging for help, at 4:02 President Johnson signed the documents ordering the military to restore peace to the streets.

Willard Wirtz was in Chicago on the day Martin Luther King was killed. Johnson ordered his labor secretary back to the capital. He flew into National Airport on the shores of the Potomac River across from Hains Point. As the jet banked in a lazy curve over the capital, Wirtz could see flames and smoke rising up along Fourteenth Street. He looked down ruefully. A decade of liberal programs up in flames, he thought. He wondered whether Marion Barry was playing the militant or the pacifier.

But Wirtz didn't have much time to think about who was burning Washington and why. Back at the White House President Johnson was trying to plan his response to King's death. Johnson had more to worry about than Fourteenth Street. A dozen other cities were burning; it seemed the nation was on the brink. Johnson asked Wirtz and a few others to compose a major civil rights speech, using King's assassination to rally the cause. As smoke and tear gas wafted over the White House, Wirtz worked late into the night Friday on a speech that Johnson never gave.

On Saturday, Marion Barry called.

"I know you must be wondering what the dudes are up to," Barry said. "All of my people are accounted for. We're setting up kitchens."

Barry had become one of the primary conciliators during the uprising. The city's leaders, both white and black, thought that Barry was one of the few people who could appeal to the looters. Mayor Washington, Walter Fauntroy, and John Hechinger invited Barry to help them plot their course. Compared to a crazed teenager with a Molotov cocktail, Barry was a moderate, and Pride, Inc., was one of the only community-based organizations that continued to operate.

Joseph Danzansky got through to the Pride offices early on Saturday. The chairman of Giant Foods, the largest supermarket chains in the city, had heard that his stores were going up in flames.

"I'm distraught," Danzansky told Carroll Harvey. "We'll lose everything."

"Hold on a minute, Joe," Harvey said. "Where are you getting your information? Your stores are fine."

Danzansky was among a group of liberal Jewish businessmen who went out of their way to work with the city's emerging black leadership. He had walked into Pride's offices unannounced back in the early days and said simply: "How can I help?"

From that offer, a working alliance had developed. Under the auspices of Giant Food, Danzansky and Pride had set up a landscaping service staffed by Pride's unemployed teenagers. They stored their equipment and the supplies at Giant Food locations. Carroll Harvey knew that Danzansky's stores were unharmed because Treadwell, Barry, and he had deployed Pride workers to guard Giant supermarkets.

Harvey told Danzansky to hold the line. He picked up another phone and called a Pride office across the street from the Giant supermarket on Fourteenth Street. The building was secure. He got back on the phone with Danzansky.

"Don't worry, " Harvey told him. "We have everything under control.

"I'm worried," Danzansky said.

On Sunday Harvey called Danzansky and asked if Giant Food would donate food to help feed people in the burned-out parts of the city. Danzansky agreed, and for the next week Pride ran caravans of cars and trucks full of free food into the ghettos. Along with other organizations, Barry's group set up and operated food distribution centers, and Barry was in the trucks and on the street delivering food.

When the last fire was extinguished, not one Giant store had been singed. Five Safeway stores, Giant's main rival, had been reduced to rubble.

The occupation of Washington had begun gradually on Friday evening.

Elements of the Third Infantry stationed at Fort Myer, just across the Potomac River, marched across the Memorial Bridge toward the Lincoln Monument. It was 4:40 p.m. One company set up gun emplacements at the White House; another surrounded the U.S. Capitol.

Mayor Washington invoked a 5:30 p.m. to 6:30 a.m. curfew. Though fires still raged and looters emptied stores on the side streets, the troops enforced the curfew and took the frenzy out of the ghetto. The riot, it seemed, had peaked. Vance and the mayor toured the city at midnight and held a press conference at 1:20 a.m. Saturday.

"The situation appeared to be quieting down," Vance said, "and, as of the moment, to be in hand."

Vance had arrived at the White House just before dark on Friday, absorbed a series of reports, and told President Johnson that above all, the soldiers shouldn't fire their weapons unless they were in mortal danger. If one looter died from a bullet fired from an M-16, the whole tenor of the civil rights movement could change, he said. Johnson agreed and told his military men to avoid shooting at all cost.

After the series of meetings at the White House, Vance got a firsthand look at the streets. John Hechinger picked him up at 7:00 p.m. in his black limousine driven by his chauffeur, Montrose. They headed across town and arrived at the foot of H Street. The car slalomed around fire hoses snaking across the avenue. Burned-out buildings steamed on both sides. Toward the far end of the street at Benning Road a fire still raged out of control.

"That looks like it's coming from my building," Hechinger told Vance.

The main warehouse that served Hechinger's hardware and lumber stores sat at the five-way crossroads where H Street meets Bladensburg Road. His office was on the top floor. As they drew closer Hechinger realized that a different building was ablaze, but they could see a lot of activity at the warehouse. Looters were hard at work.

"My God," Hechinger said, "they're using our forklifts!"

Hechinger radioed police headquarters, but he was told that every available officer was on Seventh Street. He asked Vance's advice.

"Let's drive in," Vance said.

At the sight of the big black car, the looters took off, and Hechinger's building was spared.

Overnight, five thousand more troops entered the capital, including paratroopers and military police flown in from Fort Bragg, North Carolina.

The troops were deployed along the main streets and intersections, but the alleys belonged to arsonists. On Saturday 120 more fires were lighted. The mood in the streets turned as ugly and hostile as it had been on Thursday night, but now all the stores had been ransacked. The community faced the cold reality of fourteen thousand men in uniform enforcing President Johnson's order. The troops lobbed hundreds of canisters of CS, a strong form of tear gas, but they never fired a shot, according to John son's wishes, and most of the rifles weren't loaded. Senator Bob Byrd called the White House to demand that looters be shot in the legs. After a tense weekend with one or two serious yet peaceful confrontations, the troops set up checkpoints in every neighborhood. There were tanks at the intersection of Georgia and New Hampshire avenues, where black teenagers taunted black soldiers for betraying their soul brothers; there were machine-gun emplacements along Wisconsin Avenue, where white teenage girls flirted with soldiers in camouflage. For the most part, the soldiers calmly patrolled the streets.

On Palm Sunday, the city was quiet. Washingtonians in their Sunday finest walked to church past burned-out buildings and tanks. Senator Robert Kennedy toured the steaming streets on foot with his wife. The uprising was over. On Tuesday Dr. Martin Luther King, Jr., was buried in Atlanta. On Wednesday night the Washington Senators lost their opening home game to the Minnesota Twins, 2-0. The curfew was lifted on Friday. The troops left on Saturday, a week and a day after they had arrived.

After the spring riots, the nation careened through one of its most traumatic years.

The Poor People's Campaign came to Washington and set up Resurrection City, a muddy hellhole on the Mall that broke up in mini-riots after forty-two days; in June, Robert Kennedy was assassinated in Los Angeles; Richard Daley's police bludgeoned protesters in Chicago at the Democratic convention in August; in November Richard Nixon was elected president on a law-andorder platform that used crime in the capital as an example of the nation's decline.

In countless ways, the city of Washington never recovered from the uprising. People will always define the city's history as "before the riots" and "after the riots." The greatest changes took place in the city's political arena. Power shifted to the black majority, and though Marion Barry was not a major player during the uprising, he would be the primary beneficiary of the changes that it wrought.

Statistics tell one part of the story. Approximately 20,000 people took part in the riots. According to police reports and arrest records, 98 percent were African-American, and 10 percent were women. About 6,300 persons were arrested; 1,660 were charged with felonies. Of those, 80 percent had jobs before the riot; many worked for the federal government. Twelve people died, mostly as a result of the fires. The value of property lost during the rioting was estimated at $15 million, according to a city council report. Half of the property along Fourteenth Street was destroyed, 15 percent on Seventh Street, and 10 percent on H Street.

Patterns of commerce that had developed over decades and sustained black neighborhoods were snuffed out in three days. Burned-out city blocks in some parts of the city were gradually cleared and re-developed; boarded-up storefronts in poor neighborhoods would remain for decades. The Senate Committee on Government Operations held hearings and reported that of the 668 businessmen burned out, half vowed not to return. Many would take their operations-and their jobs-to the suburbs. The riot affected 14,593 jobs, and nearly 5,000 were permanently lost. The violence and the sense that the city was out of control pushed more middle-class families—both black and white—to the suburbs.

Carol Thompson's family was part of the exodus, but the riots weren't the only reason or the most important reason. It was the declining quality of education in the public schools in the after math of Judge Skelly Wright's decision to abolish the track system. Before Wright's 1967 ruling, students were grouped according to test scores. Julius Hobson, Sr., believed that the track system kept poor black children down, and it was his lawsuit that prompted Wright's landmark decision that also ordered some busing of poor blacks to better schools, like Roosevelt High.

Carol Thompson recalls going to school the first day that Skelly Wright's decision took effect. She was in an English class when the teacher asked the students to practice writing a letter to a college they wanted to attend. Most of the students protested, and one said, "We're not going to college, so why write, a letter?" But Thompson and a few of her friends raised their hands and asked to complete the project. In a matter of weeks teachers had reinstituted the de facto track system.

"Abolishing the track system made sense," she says. "But it didn't work. Yes there was a caste system that locked people in, but at the same time you had good teachers who helped students who wanted to excel. Wiping all that away had a leveling effect, but it was the beginning of the end to a good school system."

Reluctantly, Thompson's father moved the family a few miles north to Silver Spring, Maryland. The move didn't affect Carol Thompson, but Martin Luther King's assassination changed her life.

"I wasn't angry, " she says, "but it was a defining moment in my life. Before Dr. King's death I had a feeling that things were going to work, integration would work, people would get along, racism was under control. I realized it wasn't going to work."

She had been a French major headed for the foreign service; instead she went to Smith College and majored in American government. Instead of taking her junior year abroad in Europe, she spent it in Mississippi registering voters.

Her younger sisters and brothers finished their schooling in the Montgomery County schools.

"My father hated to leave the District," she says, "but he wasn't about to sacrifice his children's education."

The riots shattered the myth that Washington was riotproof and replaced it with a pervading sense of fear. Whites felt suddenly vulnerable and started to avoid certain neighborhoods. On the campus of

Howard University, the bastion of high yellow elitism only a decade before, black nationalism was in vogue. "It was like a switch had been thrown," says Frederick Douglas Cooke, who grew up in Petworth and was a student at the time. "If they killed Martin, maybe there was a conspiracy to kill off the black leadership. Maybe Stokely and Huey Newton were right. The integrationists were discredited. It was dangerous to be white."

A few days after the weekend uprising, Polly Shackleton, a white liberal who'd been active in the biracial home-rule movement and in local Democratic politics for years, was asked to attend a community meeting about how to rebuild. It was at Fourteenth and Park Road in an area that had seen some rioting and produced many of the looter s. The smell of charred timbers hung over the neighborhood. Still, she had no qualms about going. There were twenty to thirty people in the room and only one or two other whites. The voices started as a murmur and picked up volume until she heard people ask, "What are these honkies doing here? What do they want here?" It was a bitterness and mistrust that she never had seen before.

Black separatists used the riots to demand that whites stay out of the slums and leave the rebuilding to the people who lived there. Build Black, Incorporated, ordered white storeowners to turn their property over to blacks.

"No more mom-and-pop stores, slumlords, and other exploiters of black people allowed in black communities," Build Black announced in flyers. "No more honky unions—without black members—and no more honky owners and contractors without black participation—allowed in black neighborhoods."

But Build Black and other radical groups never produced. They were poorly organized, and by cutting out whites they cut them selves off from the source of funds that would be necessary for rebuilding. There was no black capital. They lacked the sophistication, the leadership, and the persistence to accomplish anything substantial, and they disappeared shortly after their flyers turned to litter on Fourteenth Street.

The white backlash came swiftly from Capitol Hill and the merchants. Southern congressmen called Walter Washington and his chief aide, Tom Fletcher, in for closed-door sessions. Their constant question was, "Why didn't you shoot the looters?" Owners of the burned-out businesses, most of whom were Jewish, were on the phone to John Hechinger, who they believed should have protected their interests. "What the hell are you people doing?" they asked. "My mother and father built that business from scratch, and all you did was let those lousy mobs tear it down. Whose interests are you looking out for?"

The reaction from the white business establishment was much more measured, reasonable, and cooperative in spirit and in deed. The bankers and the lawyers, the builders and the retailers realized that an unruly, rebellious underclass could threaten their profits. The riot cost the city millions of dollars in lost revenues from the aborted Cherry Blossom Festival. Rather than bringing home pictures of pink blossoms against white monuments, tourists snapped shots of gun emplacements in front of the White House and cops chasing looters past burned out stores. The city's image couldn't survive another riot: The Board of Trade and other business groups were ready to deal, but on their terms.

"Both Negro and white racists have been trying to use the current ferment as a device to institute an apartheid system in our community," the Jewish Community Council wrote in a report to the mayor. "This must be opposed on moral grounds and because such a system would wreck the economic structure of the Nation's Capital."

The city council ventured out of the District Building to hold field hearings in the community. People came and vented their spleen. There was much talk from the usual suspects, but in the slums, the sense of alienation deepened. The presence of federal troops was just another humiliation. The rage was vented momentarily, but there was plenty left.

For a brief moment in the late summer of 1968, Stokely Carmichael tried to re-establish a base in Washington by taking over the SNCC office.

He'd resigned from SNCC in July and taken up with the Black Panthers. Arriving in town in mid-September, Carmichael and his lieutenants ordered the director of the local SN CC office, Lester McKinnie, to hand over control to the Panthers. McKinnie refused, at which point the Panthers attacked the office at 2203 Fourteenth Street with small arms and rifles, according to McKinnie and FBI records. The attackers returned on three occasions. McKinnie appealed to Marion Barry and Mary Treadwell for support, and they sent Pride workers to defend him.

"I felt that it was wrong," Barry told a press conference on September 8, "and that I should defend the right of any black organization to operate in this city."

"He was trying to Bogart his way into town at that point," recalls Mary Treadwell. "There was a siege mentality anyway. We all knew that a housing organizer had been shot in Chicago. People were carrying guns. We went through three days of madness."

In the end the SNCC office on Fourteenth Street was firebombed, but Carmichael was denied control. Armed men in fatigues attached to General Hassan's Black Liberation Army posted themselves on the building 's roof to make sure Carmichael and the Panthers stayed away. The "army" consisted of a dozen members whose stated purpose was to establish a black independent nation in Africa. They were allies of Marion Barry at the time.

Carmichael came back to town and acknowledged his role to Treadwell. "I thought Lester was by him self," he told her.

The black power leader then quit the Black Panther Party. He left the United States, adopted the name Kwame Toure, and moved to Guinea to await the revolution.

The power struggle that contributed to Stokely Carmichael's exit from Washington left Barry with the highest profile among black activists.

The white business establishment refused to deal with radical black nationalists or separatists, but Barry's brand of rhetoric was acceptable. He walked into a meeting of the Washington Urban Coalition, an organization of moderate blacks and whites, and listened to the members praising the police and firefighters. Dressed in green fatigues and sunglasses, Barry jumped up in the back of the room.

"We have a serious problem in our city with millions of dollars' worth of property damage," he said. "Why do we go on patting each other on the back like a mutual admiration society when this thing isn't over yet? It's not just the sixty-three hundred people who were arrested, but a whole lot of black people in this town are angry and just waiting 'til the troops leave."

His message to white business groups and to the city council was just short of a threat:

"When the city rebuilds the riot corridors," he kept saying, "if you don't let my black brothers control the process—and I mean all the way to owning the property—it might just get burned down again."

On the first anniversary of Martin Luther King's death, Barry addressed a rally at Meridian Hill Park, a lovely seventeen-acre square at the foot of Adams Morgan along Sixteenth Street. In the 1940s neighbors would spend hot summer nights sleeping by the fountains, but by the late 1960s it was a good place to buy drugs or get your throat slit. Barry told the crowd that he was "tired of mourning black people who die," according to an FBI transcript. He said that "Dr. King would appreciate" that blacks have to "join ourselves together and form a whole black unity thing of love and understanding for each other, " but there are different ways to "achieve the struggle.

"Those who want to do it through economic power, let's do that. Those who want to teach black history and black awareness, let's do that. "Those who want to get arms and guns and shoot the pigs, let them do that. But the point I'm making is we all got to fight."

Despite Barry's tough talk, or perhaps because of it, the operations director of Pride, Inc., was invited into the coalitions and committees that grew out of the efforts to heal the city's wounds. When Joe Danzansky and Carroll Harvey organized a new Economic Development Committee, Harvey carved out a seat on the board for Barry. The activist sat with the city's business elite and tried to find venture capital for black-owned businesses and guided federal funds coming to the city after the riots.

Less than three years after he arrived in town, two years after he called the city's businessmen "moneylord merchants," and a year after he was thrown in jail on a charge of destroying government property, Marion Barry started to take his place among the city's power brokers.

CHAPTER 5

BOMBTHROWERS TO BUREAUCRATS

I wanted to live in a black city, a place to call my home.
—Ivanhoe Donaldson on his decision to settle in the
capital

On a chilly afternoon in late January 1969, nine months after the riots and less than two weeks after he began his first term, President Richard M. Nixon took the ten-block ride from the White House to Seventh Street. Burned-out buildings and piles of rubble still lined the street. It looked as if the riots had taken place a week before.

Security was light, and the crowd pressed in on Nixon as he got out of his long black limousine. He turned and waved.

"Soul brother!" someone shouted from the crowd. Nixon waded right in and shook the man's hand.

"This is our capital city," he told Mayor Walter Washington during a press conference set against the backdrop of a collapsed storefront. "We want to make it a beautiful city in every way." An aide produced a poster-sized rendition of a shopping center, and Nixon pointed out where the trees would go. Mayor Washington nodded stepped to the microphone. "We will make Washington a model city," he said.

During the presidential campaign, Nixon and running mate Spiro Agnew had cast the city as a perfect example of urban lawlessness and degeneration. They peppered their stump speeches with statistics of muggings, murders, and rapes in the District of Columbia and held it up as "the crime capital." Once in office, Nixon showed an unexpected interest. The first Republican president in eight years came into the slums bearing $30 million in promised federal aid. Nixon had diagrams and maps to clear the rubble and build new housing, parks, and businesses. Like his immediate predecessors Kennedy and Johnson, he'd lived many years along the Potomac and dreamed of making Washington a showcase.

"Washington today is reaping a whirlwind sown long since by rural poverty in the South, by a failure in education, by racial prejudice, and by the sometimes explosive strains of rapid social adjustments," Nixon stated. "It is not enough merely to patch up what now exists. We must truly rebuild."

The moment of goodwill was illusory.

Community groups grappled for rights to control the funds. With few organized political networks in place, groups with official-sounding monikers sprouted and claimed a role. Their anthem was "grassroots control," but they couldn't take advantage of the funds and wound up squabbling over who was closer to the community. Little rebuilding took place. Millions in federal funds went unused. Thriving neighborhoods became desolate, crime-ridden zones. Suburban commuters rolled up their car windows and locked their doors during rush hour laps up and down Fourteenth Street. The blight was a blur in their windows.

But closer to the White House, the impending real estate boom of the 1980s took root. The fires struck fear into most developers and sent the price of downtown property through the floor. A fourth-generation homebuilder from the Maryland suburbs named Oliver Carr, Jr., saw opportunity in the city's misfortune. A mild-mannered and quite colorless entrepreneur, Carr started to snap up key corners in 1968, beginning with the Mill Building at the corner of Seventeenth Street and Connecticut Avenue, overlooking the White House. From that first bold move, Carr built an empire and pioneered the path for a slew of white developers—and eventually investors from London, Amsterdam, and Tokyo.

While nothing in the riot corridors seemed to change, the District's political structure was being created. Walter Washington started transforming what had been a federal agency into a municipal government, and kept order in the streets during a period when waves of antiwar protesters tried to shut down the federal government. "No one taught me in public policy classes how to handle riots and marches," Washington says, but when one million peace protesters descended on the capital in May 1971, Richard Nixon called him from Camp David to say, "You're in charge."

In one of the least reported and documented developments of Washington local politics, the timing of the District's movement toward independence coincided with the continued ingathering of former student civil rights leaders. Many of the men and women who had stood on the front lines of the movement—Ivanhoe Donaldson, John Wilson, Courtland Cox, Lawrence Guyot, Frank Smith, and others—saw the city's unique black majority community as fertile soil to carry on a civil rights movement as it changed into a struggle for economic power. Eventually, nearly the entire leadership of the student civil rights movement found its way to the capital and joined the battle to wrest power from Congress, the white power structure, and the native black elite.

"It was a natural here," says Ivanhoe Donaldson, who was emerging then as Barry's closest adviser.

In the months after the riots, Barry cultivated his disparate constituencies of ex-cons in Pride, Inc., and corporate leaders at the Board of Trade. He wore a tie and jacket to disarm the businessmen; he wore a dashiki and an amulet with a bullet around his meek and armed himself with a .38 for his work at Pride, Inc.

In July 1969 Barry walked into Pride's dilapidated field office in a townhouse on Maryland Avenue NE, in a neighborhood with a view of the Capitol but far enough away to be on the borderline between poor blacks and young white families. No one had paid the rent for a few months, and the landlady was threatening eviction. Barry started lecturing a group of Pride workers for not keeping the place neater. A young man in a yellow hat stepped out of the group.

"Man, Marion Barry, you just getting too big for your britches," he said. "I might have to shoot you. I might just have to kill you."

"That right?" Barry said, a bemused smile on his face. No one broke the silence.

"Yes, sir, Marion Barry, I might just have to kill you one day," the man repeated. The standoff lasted for another moment. Then the young man abruptly broke it off. Barry had passed another test. He didn't back down. He never backed down.

Guns and tough talk mixed with the daily social work in the Pride organization. The typical Pride worker was a black male, age sixteen to twenty-six, who had dropped out of junior high school and had a police rap sheet. More than a few were junkies. Some had never seen a family member hold down a job. Getting out of bed in the morning, putting on a uniform, and making it to the Pride office for a day of cleaning alleys was a relative measure of success. No organization—neither the Urban League nor the Black Panthers—had been able to reach these men and women at the bottom of the urban economic pile.

"What Hitler would have done in this situation with this population would have been to burn it up because they are no asset to society, because they are not putting anything into society, because it's a drag on society," Barry told the *Washington Star* late in 1970. "We're at the end of the failure syndrome."

By its second year of operation the goals of Pride, Inc. had become much more ambitious than alley cleaning. Barry and Mary Treadwell wanted to start a black capitalist revolution. They created a business arm, Pride Economic Enterprises, to become inner-city entrepreneurs and to take advantage of not only federal grants but private foundation monies. In theory, the idea was a perfect mix of Marcus Garvey's and Malcolm X's demand for black self-reliance, the federal government's liberal agenda, and the sixties brand of black power. Pride's business side operated a string of gas stations, went into the candy business, and became a landlord. Willard Wirtz was so impressed he sent Barry and Carroll Harvey around the country to advise similar projects.

Which is not to say that Marion Barry became the cool, corporate citizen.

On May 13, 1969, he and three friends rushed out of their offices to confront police writing tickets in the alley. "If you put a ticket on my car," Barry told the officer, according to the policeman's statement, "I'll kill you."

Officer Randy Lehman wrote the ticket; Barry ripped it apart, threw it in his face, and started to fight. Reinforcements came and arrested Barry and the three others for littering and assaulting an officer. At the station house Barry wound up with a blackjack welt on his head and spent the night in the hospital. The next morning Mary Treadwell dispatched Pride workers to the District Building where paid protesters demonstrated against Barry's arrest. Freed on bail, Barry walked out of the hospital wearing his bloody shirt and head bandage to address a crowd of three hundred.

"This shows me that the black people need to control the nation's capital police department," Barry said. "The police are like mad dogs."

A year later a jury acquitted the three Pride officials but couldn't reach a verdict on Barry's role. When the hung jury was announced on April 10, 1970, U.S. Attorney General John Mitchell sent a letter commending the prosecutor for convincing even one juror of Barry's guilt.

A month later Barry and Treadwell burst into the lobby of the Congressional Club, where First Lady Pat Nixon was having lunch with the wives of Republican senators. Outside the club, lines of cars were illegally double-parked and protected by police. Barry confronted Mrs. Winston Prouty, wife of the Vermont senator and president of the club.

"If we double-park we get tickets and are fined," Barry told her. "If you can do it, we want to do it, too."

Barry got headlines and a positive editorial out of the confrontation and went looking for more. At the time there were more heroin junkies in Washington, per capita, than in New York, but there was virtually no treatment available. Barry threw the issue at the city council. "Making some cat urinate in a bottle, then sending him off to jail isn't going to cure anything, "Barry testified at a hearing. He blamed poppy growers, called for stricter international enforcement, and later organized marches on the embassies of Turkey, Italy, and France to make his point.

"We maintain that the United States government is responsible for genocide by drugs," Pride, Inc. said in a statement.

In private, Barry had little patience with heroin addicts. "Goddamn junkies would steal from their mothers," he often told Carroll Harvey. "I don't know whether we should let them in the program."

At the start of the 1970 school year, with teachers threatening to boycott classes on opening day, Marion Barry lured the head of the teachers' union and the school superintendent into meeting by separately inviting them to Pride headquarters. Lying in wait were two-dozen community activists. The officials were trapped into an ad hoc collective bargaining session. Pride supplied food for the marathon talks that ended in a settlement near dawn the next morning. Barry mediated.

"I know all the people in town," Barry boasted. "There's not anybody in Washington I can't communicate with."

As Barry inexorably wove himself into Washington's power structure, federal law enforcement officials lavished special attention on his activities.

A Senate investigation into allegations of fraud at Pride, Inc. triggered a grand jury probe, and FBI agents used the opportunity to ask Pride officials whether they had had any dealings with the Mafia, Red China, H. Rap Brown, or drug dealers, according to Pride's attorney at the time. Eventually, officials with the U.S. Labor Department had to acknowledge that after more than three years of nearly constant scrutiny, the only hard evidence of wrongdoing that federal officials could muster was ten thousand dollars in phony payroll checks. In the same period, Pride's job-training and business entities had received about $8.5 million in federal grants. The amount of seepage was minuscule, especially considering the backgrounds of Pride's workers. But the government harassment set a tone and a backdrop that helped build the impression among many black Washingtonians that the white power structure was out to get Barry.

As early as 1967, the FBI's file on "Marion S. Barry, Jr., Negro Militant" had begun to swell. The agency infiltrated Pride, noted where Barry was living and with whom, filled out character sketches down to Barry's choice of clothes, and filed reports from informants together with a running narrative gleaned from newspaper coverage.

After the 1968 riots, a broad range of the city's black leaders came under more federal surveillance than just the FBI's. Army intelligence, operating out of the Continental Army Command at Fort Monroe, Virginia, monitored Barry and other civil rights activists, even the mild-mannered Mayor Washington and high school antiwar protesters. Barry, who also was monitored by D.C. police intelligence squads, got the most covert attention. According to formerly confidential FBI reports, informants tailed Barry to Atlanta in September 1970, where he attended a meeting of the Congress of African Peoples, a pan-African organization that protested attacks by Portuguese commandos on Guinea. At a meeting in Washington in March 1971, Barry advocated protests against the embassies of Rhodesia and South Africa as a means to bring down apartheid. Another source recorded Barry's attendance at an antiwar rally at Lafayette Park across from the White House on April 3. It resulted in an FBI file entry: "Among the speakers at this rally was Marion Barry who said that there were plenty of people around who would prefer to demonstrate in a war rally rather than a peace rally. He sug-

gested that everyone should learn how to put the finger on the trigger."

The FBI's surveillance continued into the early 1970s, when its reports noted in deadpan prose that the "negro militants" were becoming elected officials.

Walter Fauntroy was the first civil rights leader to become a major
force in local politics. But it was his fledgling group of white financial
supporters that would come to influence the capital's local elected
politics.

In 1971 voters were preparing to elect a nonvoting delegate to
Congress, the first true citywide election for an individual public official since 1874. The city's independent, elected political structure had
begun to take shape in 1969 with the election of an eleven-mem-
ber school board, but the delegate's race attracted much more attention. Richard Nixon and his chief domestic adviser, John Ehrlichman, briefly tried to install Mayor Walter Washington. "We created
the job out of whole cloth," Egil "Bud" Krogh, Jr., Nixon 's chief liaison with the city and also head of his Special Investigations Unit,
told Deputy Mayor Graham Watt, "and we have an obligation to see
that it's capably filled." As the campaign drew near, the Vietnam War
and the Watergate scandal occupied the White House, and the delegate's seat opened up to all comers.

Walter Fauntroy jumped into the race and became the underdog
against Channing Phillips, a liberal, progressive minister and Democratic national committeeman; Joseph Yeldell, the candidate favored
by Washington's black middle class and the business community; and
Julius Hobson, Sr., running under his Statehood party banner. Fauntroy was a graduate of Yale Divinity School and had become one of
Martin Luther King's disciples, traveling to marches and representing him in the capital. A tiny man with a high-pitched voice and
frenetic, bug-eyed energy, he used his pulpit at New Bethel Baptist
Church to become a housing activist and to land an appointment on
the first city council. Julius Hobson, Sr., belittled Fauntroy as Lit-

tle Lord Fauntleroy, because of his prissy, self-righteous nature, but Fauntroy 's campaign caught the fancy of Washington's well-heeled white liberals, who wanted to help a civil rights leader get elected.

John Hechinger, the young hardware baron, had served with Fauntroy on the appointed city council and became a cornerstone in the minister's organization. He brought along a number of wealthy white newcomers, most transplants to Washington, who together with the SNCC refugees would make a potent political team. Max Berry became Fauntroy's finance chairman. A native of Tulsa, Berry had grown up in a family of oilmen who were powerful players in Oklahoma's Democratic party. "I was one of two or three Jewish kids in a Baptist school district," he says. "The kids would feel my head to see if I had horns, call me Christ killer, beat me up. I had a lot of empathy with minorities. I was one myself. " He came to Washington in 1960 as a lawyer passing his army hitch in the Pentagon, fell in love with the city and later with a young woman named Heidi Lehrman, an heiress to the Giant Food fortune. On Fauntroy's behalf, Berry made his first fundraising pitch to a group of black businessmen.

"You have the right speech," said Ofield Dukes, a public relations executive, "but this is the wrong crowd. We don't have any money."

So Berry with Hechinger in tow went uptown to the corporate offices and the developers on K Street. They got a hearing and enough of a response to finance the campaign and establish an enduring pattern of white money behind black candidates. Much of it came from people like Bitsy Folger, who walked into Fauntroy headquarters from a world away in Washington 's wealthy white society.

A native of Cincinnati, Folger had arrived in the capital in the late 1950s when her father, Neil McElroy, gave up his post as CEO of Procter and Gamble to join the Eisenhower administration as secretary of defense. She traveled the world at his side, lunched with the shah of Iran and dined with Chiang Kai-shek. The young debutante danced the night away at embassy parties, swatted tennis balls at the elite Chevy Chase Club, and married Lee Folger, the son of Eisenhower's national finance chairman. But Bitsy Folger wanted more than the Junior League had to offer. Malcolm X's autobiography and Eldridge Cleaver's *Soul on Ice* changed her life. She invited Sterling Tucker and Marion Barry to speak at the Junior League. She sent her children to private schools but tried to raise them "colorblind." Pert, thin, and attractive, she found the energy of the movement irresistible. She tried to break the news to her father in Cincinnati.

"I really have to register Democratic to have a say in local politics," she explained.

"I understand," he said. "Local politics is different than national. But change right back after the election."

She never did. Instead, Bitsy Folger went on the Junior League circuit to raise money for black candidates. She and Polly Shackleton—also a Democratic activist with wealthy Republican roots—opened their Northwest Washington drawing rooms to informal sessions where Fauntroy, in tearful pleas, could describe the plight of the inner city and how he would fix it. Fauntroy's TV commercials, designed by David Abramson, showed the candidate in blue jeans leading an integrated gathering of happy people down a city street as they sang a jingle with the chorus: "He's going to get us all together."

In the January 12 Democratic primary Channing Phillips and Joe Yeldell split the electorate and allowed Fauntroy to win with 44 percent of the vote. Yeldell placed second with 31 percent, and Phillips, the local party's candidate, attracted only 22 percent.

"It was one of the most thrilling days of my life," says Bitsy Folger.

The outcome of the general election was a foregone conclusion. If the first law of Washington politics was white money behind black candidates, the second was that Washington was a one-party town. The Republican Party never organized in the capital and never attracted more than a tenth of the electorate, in part because it was run as a club for white conservatives. Liberal whites and black Democrats outnumbered Republicans nine to one. Fauntroy won the November election with ease; Republican candidate John Nevius finished dead last, far behind Statehood nominee Hobson and the Socialist Workers party candidate.

The lasting significance of Fauntroy's victory was not who voted for him but who backed him. The liberal, integrated organization that brought together John Hechinger, Max Berry, campaign cochairman John Wilson, Bitsy Folger, David Eaton, businessman Delano Lewis, Polly Shackleton, Dave Abramson, and civil rights veteran Jim Gibson would provide the foundation for other aspiring politicians, especially for Marion Barry.

At Walter Fauntroy's victory party, Marion Barry took the podium and called him "a minister in the Church of What's Happening Now. And what's happening now is we're going to send Walter Fauntroy to Congress." The crowd yelled "Right On," but Barry was beginning to think of how Fauntroy's new organization could send him into the emerging political network.

The chance came in late 1971. Barry was invited to the home of Marty Swaim on Capitol Hill. Swaim—a white, liberal member of the school board—was organizing a campaign against the sitting board president, Anita Allen. The board had spent its first two years squabbling over policy and position. Swaim blamed Allen and wanted her out.

Allen was a member of the city's high yellow elite. Her skin was lighter than cocoa, she wore her straight brown hair short and prim. Anita Allen could "pass." Born in Anacostia and graduated from the city's public schools and Howard University, she was a forty-five-year-old matron married to a well-connected Baptist minister. She worked for the federal Bureau of Higher Education, presided over the school board meetings, worked hard, and sent her children to college. Allen saw herself as the keeper of the black middle-class flame and an agent of the status quo. Swaim thought that the schools needed radical surgery, not conservative policies. But who could take her on-David Eaton or even Polly Shackleton?

Thornell Page, a tall, thoughtful activist working for the United Planning Organization, took the floor. He looked straight at Barry, wearing his leopard skin dashiki for the occasion, and said: "Why don't you run?"

"I can't," he demurred. "I'm not part of the Establishment. And it's not something that I want to do, anyway."

Actually, Barry had told some close friends that he was aching to run for office. The delegate contest came before he was ready. The school board was his only opportunity.

Thornell Page represented the city's new generation of ambitious, college-educated black transplants. Born in Dillon, South Carolina, the first member of his family to attend college, he came to the District after being discharged from the Army. Page was dark-skinned, which made him particularly sensitive to the privileged, high yellow caste of blacks like Allen who dominated city affairs. He believed the District needed to change, and · Barry was just what the city needed in a leader: tough, courageous, and admirable. "But it was more than just Barry," Page says, "it was a movement to change the city."

What followed was a key stage in Barry's metamorphosis from street activist to big-city politician. Just as Rufus "Catfish" Mayfield taught Barry the ways of the streets, Thornell Page groomed him for elective politics in a city where middle -class voters called the shots. "The first thing we had to do was make him acceptable—less offensive—to a larger community," Page says. He made Barry stop calling Pride workers "cats" and "dudes." Police couldn't be "pigs," and he had to drop his favorite adjective: "motherfucker."

"We're not electing an African king—we're looking to elect a strong school board member," Page told him. "You don't have to put the dashiki down forever—it's a matter of knowing when to wear it."

Reporters began to note the change. Was Barry more mellow? Was he betraying his image as a street-fighting activist who organized bus boycotts and challenged police on the street?

"Of course I've changed—the whole nation has changed," he told a *Washington Post* reporter, adding a rare personal insight: "I'm a situationist. I do what is necessary for the situation."

Barry knew that he needed an image-maker, and he arranged a meeting with David Abramson.

"I want you to work on my school board campaign, do the polling, write the ads," Barry said in Abramson's office.

"Do you know who I am?" Abramson asked.

"Yeah," Barry said. "You're the motherfucker who blew the whistle on me at McBride's."

Abramson flashed his trademark smile, bright and nervous at the same time. He talked in rapid bursts flavored by his Boston accent. Marvin Himelfarb, Abramson's partner, asked, "What happens if you don't win?"

"Can you outrun a bullet?" Barry said with a cold stare.

Abramson saw a winner in Barry. He was flattered, drawn to the power, and obviously aware that this rising political star would be great for his ad business. The firm agreed to handle the campaign and made Barry into a reformer, which the schools certainly needed.

Since the mid-1950s, Washington's schools had been in a steady tailspin. Though the system spent $1,208 per pupil, more than the neighboring suburban schools allocated, many buildings were dilapidated, the curriculum was outdated, and the bureaucracy was eating up precious funds. Test scores were low and the dropout rate was high. In 1971, 94.8 percent of the system's 140,000 students were black. If there was a place to affect the lives of poor blacks, it was here. Harry repeated the sad statistics at every stop. He promised to improve the schools or quit. A tireless campaigner, he rambled across the city in a rented Camaro plastered with "United to Save the Children" posters.

Anita Allen scoffed—at her opponent, at the money he talked about, and at his dawn-to-midnight crusades for votes. Her full schedule left little time to campaign. As Allen wrote in the *Washington Star,* to the epitome of the city's haughty black bourgeoisie, Marion Barry was a carpetbagger who "suddenly shed his dashiki and donned an Edwardian suit to become a member of the Establishment." The people who really wanted Barry were the white businessmen.

Allen asked why these backers, many of whom were white, have chosen to contribute so heavily to a person whose lifestyle is so different from their own. Allen felt the answer was apparent.

"For them, it is not a school board election at all. It is a campaign to build a political power base whereby a white minority in our city can continue to control the lives and destinies of the black majority as they have in the past…. This is what this campaign signifies to me, and if I am not re-elected, it may well be the wave of the future." Leaving a televised debate a week before the vote, she snapped: "I think if the people get you, they deserve you."

Barry swept Allen from office with 58 percent of the vote in a four-way race. Only 9.3 percent of city's registered voters cast ballots, but Barry proved he could attract middle-class black voters where Allen was expected to dominate. On election night, Barry bounded into the rousing victory party at the Pitts Motor Hotel at 10:55 p.m. "When January comes around," he said, "we're going to have a school board that's really hip—that's my street talk. "

During the campaign, Barry had supported a slate of four board members—including Marty Swaim and Hilda Howland Mason—all of whom won and in turn helped elect Barry president. From the president 's chair Barry tamed the fractious board and moved decisively to put the school system's finances in order. But he did little to improve the curriculum, buy new books, or repair broken-down classrooms, according to Dwight Cropp, Barry's executive assistant at the time.

"When he was president of the board, his interest was not education," says Cropp. "His interest was political growth, expansion."

At every community meeting, Barry instructed Cropp to bring two legal pads. "The most important thing to him at the town meetings was that he get his list of names," Cropp says. "He didn't care about anything else but getting names, addresses, and telephone numbers of everyone in the auditorium. That's how he built up his mailing list, which later became his political lists."

By the early 1970s, black politicians had begun to win office in America's cities and towns.

Richard Hatcher had been elected mayor of Gary, Indiana; Carl Stokes was running Cleveland; and Charles Evers was the mayor of Fayette, Mississippi. Black politicians formed a majority on Detroit's city council. A 1970 survey by the Metropolitan Applied Research Center reported that there were 1,469 black officials nationwide. Among these were 48 mayors, 168 state legislators, 362 school board members, 575 other elected officials, and 99 law enforcement officials.

Washington, D.C., was still the only city in the nation where black citizens were in the majority but couldn't elect a black mayor and legislative branch. It was not because of a lack of voting strength: There was no vote at all. Every president since Eisenhower had endorsed home rule, but a few aging segregationists in Congress stood in the way, especially John McMillan, who remained at the helm of the House District Committee. Harlem congressman Adam Clayton Powell decided to remedy the situation. He and journalist Chuck Stone, who was working for the *Washington Star* at the time, persuaded Charles Diggs to get on the District Committee and outlast the segs through the seniority system. Diggs, a black undertaker from the outskirts of Detroit, was an advocate for black causes and founded the Congressional Black Caucus in 1971. By 1972, McMillan was the last Dixiecrat between Diggs and the chairmanship.

Congress had established the Commission on the Organization of the Government of the District of Columbia. Chaired by Congressman Ancher Nelson, a moderate Republican from Minnesota, the twelve-member group was supposed to make sense of a municipal government that at the time had forty thousand employees, an annual budget of nearly $1.5 billion, and more than one hundred departments, boards, and agencies, yet was still controlled by the federal government.

The Nelson commission held three days of hearings in November 1971. It produced volumes of reports and issued 451 specific recommendations. Its mandate complete, the commission was about to dissolve when Nelson proposed another year of study. Home-rule activists saw more delay, appealed to the Nixon White House, and a few days later Ancher Nelson read in the newspaper that his commission was dead. A new home-rule bill was introduced and referred to the House District Committee, where John McMillan and Northern Virginia Republican Joel Broyhill were waiting.

"We don't have much interest in this issue," said Broyhill, the ranking minority member. McMillan nodded his approval.

The jowly segregationist normally won easily because black voters, who made up 40 percent of his electorate, never concentrated their vote against him, but in the crucial 1972 primary campaign, black leaders from Washington—including Walter Fauntroy and Sterling Tucker—organized the black vote, and McMillan lost the Democratic election to a young man named John Jenrette. Broyhill remained, but he was helpless without McMillan. The Watergate scandal was beginning to consume home-rule enemies in the Nixon White House like Attorney General John Mitchell, who'd once called the city government the "Amos and Andy cab company." The legislative path to home rule appeared to be wide open.

On May 27, 1973, in the midst of the home-rule campaign, Marion Barry married Mary Treadwell.

They had been living together since the spring of 1971 in an apartment at 643 A Street SE, a stately street of Capitol Hill row houses three blocks from the Supreme Court.

The formal union didn't make much sense. Everyone knew that Barry had a hard time with monogamy. Rumors of his affairs with a number of teachers and students were rampant. Treadwell certainly knew what she was getting into. She had discussed Barry's wanton ways with her friends.

"I'm just going to blow his dick off," she had told Carroll Harvey one day. "It will save us all a lot of trouble."

But she loved Barry and hoped marriage would change him. Their wedding at the Museum of African Art in the Frederick Douglass House on Capitol Hill was an elegant affair. *Washington Post* writer Sally Quinn, who usually authored sharp-edged profiles of the powerful, wrote admiringly in the *Post's* Style section about Treadwell's virginal, orange peasant dress.

"It was so funny to see Marion about to get married," John Hechinger's wife told Quinn. "They'd been going together so long, people just never imagined that they would."

Among the 150 guests were Sterling Tucker, Willard Wirtz and his wife, and Walter and Benetta Washington. David Eaton and Walter Fauntroy performed the ceremony. Fauntroy read from Kahlil Gibran. The service was nondenominational.

"I'm not a practicing anything," Treadwell told Quinn.

"We're humanists," said Barry.

Pronounced husband and wife, Barry bent and kissed the bride a few times until she pulled away.

"It ain't enough," he said.

"Be careful," she said. "You'll ruin my makeup."

Two months after the wedding, the police reportedly were called to the apartment of a young black woman active in local politics. Residents had heard screams coming from one of the apartments.

She told friends that she had run into Marion Barry at a reception earlier in the evening. The woman had recently met him and wanted to discuss a project she was developing. Their schedules were hectic during the day, so she invited Barry to her apartment to talk politics. Around midnight, as she opened the door for him to leave, Barry allegedly closed it, grabbed her, and dragged her to the bedroom. She screamed. In minutes police were at the door. She put on a robe, assured the police she was fine and refused to open the door. Unpersuaded, they roused the building manager. She let the manager inside but only in the living room. They talked long enough to satisfy the manager that she was not hurt and nothing appeared amiss. He left, and she said Barry—who had been hiding in the bedroom—spent the night as the squad car remained outside her building.

The woman told close friends that Barry called the next morning to apologize. He was in tears.

The story never became public, in part because the woman realized that if she exposed Barry it could hurt certain initiatives she was working on, including the home rule drive. She didn't want to give Congress another reason to keep the District from governing itself.

Charles Diggs took over the House District Committee chair and held thirty-eight days of hearings from February to July 1973. John Hechinger set the tone in his testimony on April 4. "How can the Congress continue this injustice—the absurdity that the capital of the leading nation of the free world is itself not free?"

Julius Hobson, Sr., was the only activist who didn't sing in the choir.

"I suspect that there are some members of this committee and of this Congress who don't want us to have it, because this is a black city," he testified. "I suspect that there are others who don't want us to have it because it would mean some economic difficulty for them. And now, I understand, we've got a man named Diggs, who is now chairman of the committee, and he looks like me and he is black, and

I am supposed to be happy because he is chairman of the committee, but he doesn't want (true) home rule either."

Following the appointed government established by LBJ, Diggs's bill called for the election of a mayor and a thirteen-member city council, all of whom would serve staggered four-year terms. The elected municipal government would have the power to police, to tax, to borrow capital from the U.S. Treasury, and to run the city largely independent of Congress. But as the legislation progressed through the committee, opponents started to chip away at full independence.

The Justice Department, at the urging of Deputy Attorney General Donald Santorelli, moved to keep prosecutorial power in the hands of the federal government. Language in the bill made the presidentially appointed U.S. attorney the city's prosecutor. Unlike every other major city, there would be no elected local district attorney. In that one stroke the District ceded its criminal justice system to the federal government. It would mean that presidents would appoint a succession of white male prosecutors and judges who would keep control over the city's majority black population.

Congressional delegations from surrounding suburban jurisdictions exacted a crippling price for their support by forbidding the District to impose any form of commuter tax, a lucrative source of revenue from the incomes of people who worked in the District but lived in the neighboring states' suburbs. In lieu of taxes on extensive federal properties in the city, the national government would pay the city an annual lump sum determined each year by Congress and the president. In that stroke, the city lost partial control of its finances.

Despite the compromises, Diggs was still dozens of votes short of victory in the full House. In the fall of 1973 he called a strategy meeting to deliver the bad news. Representative William Natcher, a crusty but well-respected conservative Democrat from Kentucky, was holding thirty crucial votes. Natcher was demanding that Congress not only keep authority over the city's budget but also maintain veto power over all city laws. A vocal minority wanted to demand full power, but Diggs said the Natcher deal was better than nothing and took it.

Still, at the eleventh hour the Republicans tried to kill the bill. Minority Leader Gerald Ford took to the House floor on October 30 to lead the fight. Joe Rauh and other home-rule supporters were in the House gallery listening to Ford rail against the District when an aide rushed up to Ford, whispered in his ear, and whisked him away. Congressmen started streaming onto the House floor. Rauh turned to Jason Newman, a wiry New York lawyer who'd worked on the bill. "Something's going on," Rauh said. "These people aren't here to discuss our bill." Minutes later they found out that Nixon had called Ford to the White House and appointed him vice-president to replace Spiro Agnew, who'd resigned because of his legal problems and mounting scandals.

With Ford out of the picture, the opposition fizzled and the home-rule bill passed the House. The banner headline in *The Washington Post* the next day announced that Agnew had resigned. The news that the House had passed the home-rule bill—the first in a century—was bumped below the fold. Nixon signed the historic legislation December 24, 1973. Four months later, on May 7, 1974, city voters gave overwhelming support to the new form of government. Even if their elected officials would still have to be supplicants before congressional committees, finally, after nearly one hundred years, the District would have a locally elected government again.

The elections would be held in the fall; neophyte politicians began lining up, and Ivanhoe Donaldson made his political debut with Marion Barry.

Donaldson was in the room one day in January 1974, when Barry called together his political advisers. Among those present were James Gibson, Thornell Page, and the Reverend David Eaton. With the home-rule referendum certain to pass, Barry's supporters wanted him to run for the first council. Four of the seats would be at-large in coming fall elections. In future contests, only two at-large seats would be on the ballot at any one time. But Ivanhoe Donaldson saw bigger things.

"Why not just run for the chairmanship?" Donaldson asked.

It was typical Donaldson—brash, insightful, and entirely plausible. Of the dozens of refugees from SNCC who gravitated to Washington, Ivanhoe Donaldson stood out as the sharpest political thinker, with the potential to influence black politics on a national scale. Harlem-born, the son of a cop, light-skinned with dark piercing eyes, Donaldson had a slight but athletic body that was in constant motion. His mannerisms were confrontational. His mind never rested. Donaldson's philosophy had helped set the tone for Stokely Carmichael's black power movement. When Carmichael went on the road, Donaldson served as his executive assistant, building crowds and prepping him on local community meetings. He helped get Julian Bond in 1965 to run for a seat in the Georgia House of Representatives, a move that brought Bond international attention when he objected to the Vietnam War and was expelled. Donaldson left Bond to organize voters in Ohio. He was a principal adviser to Andrew Young in his successful race for Congress in Georgia in 1972. He helped elect Richard Hatcher in Gary, and took all of his skills to the capital in 1967.

"I wanted to live in a black city, a place to call my home," he says, "and be an organizer in national politics and the local community at the same time."

Donaldson found a safe harbor at the Institute for Policy Studies, a left-wing think tank that provided an intellectual bridge between the preponderantly white New Left and antiwar movements on one hand and the black leadership of the civil rights movement on the other. Around the same time, Donaldson and two other SNCC veterans—Courtland Cox and Judy Richardson—founded the Drum and Spear, a bookstore on Fourteenth Street dedicated to black studies and literature. The bookstore immediately became a center for black activists. Wherever Donaldson moved, he established a place for other refugees from SNCC, and the Drum and Spear was their spot in Washington.

"Ivanhoe was brilliant, articulate, courageous," says Marcus Raskin, the founder of IPS, who gave Donaldson a refuge after SNCC. "He could have been a great figure in American politics, he's that brilliant."

Donaldson considered his paycheck to be communal property, according to Raskin, and he often sent H. Rap Brown by to pick it up and cash it. Rules and regulations weren't of great concern, either. He was for a time dispensing grants for the Cummings Foundation, which assisted community service projects. He would agree to five-thousand-dollar contributions over lunch without the usual bureaucratic niceties of grants or business plans.

Washington's increasing move toward local political power offered a new, hands-on venture for Donaldson and the other SNCC refugees to devote their considerable energies toward black empowerment. In the competition for political power in Washington, factions emerged in the black community that were not unlike the factions that cleaved the civil rights movement. Fauntroy, the SCLC leader, was too moderate. Julius Hobson, who came out of CORE, was too strident. Sterling Tucker from the Urban League was too conservative. Mayor Walter Washington was dismissed as a caretaker for the white power structure.

The SNCC group prepared to leapfrog the field.

Barry was ready to leave the school board. Education problems were intractable, the job nettlesome. Barry and Donaldson had failed to install Donaldson's uncle from New York as superintendent. Educator Barbara Sizemore got the job and turned the schools into a racial battleground by lambasting whites. For Barry, the question was simply whether his council run should be for an at-large seat or for chairman.

As he wavered in private, the issue was decided for him.

In June John Hechinger and a few other business leaders went to Barry's school board office and told him Sterling Tucker's campaign for chairman had their blessing. Barry, they said, should run at-large. They would help. If he ran against Tucker, it would be without their contributions. Mayor Washington, running for election to the appointed post he'd held since 1967, also was endorsing Tucker.

Barry bristled, postured, argued—then did as he was told. But he would never forget. On June 12, driving in his little red Volkswagen, Barry arrived at the District Building to announce his atlarge race and denounce unnamed "monied, machine politics." Barry was elected easily. Among a field of twenty candidates atlarge, he came in a close second to Douglas Moore, the veteran activist who in January had tried to publicly force Barry into promising to stay on the school board.

The first home-rule race for mayor was closer. Washington won the Democratic primary by only a few percentage points over Clifford Alexander, a black patrician who had served as secretary of the army. Alexander suffered from his image as a bureaucrat who had made his name on the city's national stage but had spent little time in local affairs. The familiar "Uncle Walter" at the helm of the new municipal government mollified Congress and reassured the city's white community. He was the perfect transition leader.

Sterling Tucker was elected city council chairman and promptly made his first mistake by appointing Barry to head the powerful finance and revenue panel, which controlled taxation. For the next four years, Barry used 'his committee as a club against Tucker and Mayor Washington on one hand, while with the other he began to woo white business interests.

The mayor kept sending down budgets that called for tax increases. Barry just as quickly rejected the budgets and vowed to cut taxes. "I think we're being taxed to death," he said; and blamed the rising budgets on the mayor's inefficient bureaucracy. Meanwhile, he and Ivanhoe Donaldson had assembled a racially diverse, crackerjack staff able to churn out alternative budgets that cut costs rather than raising taxes. Homeowners and businessmen who had been wary of Barry loved it. When Barry introduced an antispeculation real estate tax to stem the quick turnover of properties, some of the most active speculators got him to soften the bill and allow them to keep reaping huge profits.

It was during this period that Barry began to make the contacts that would finance his coming campaigns. One of the first was with R. Robert Linowes, a Jewish zoning attorney who represented the city's top developers. Linowes and Barry agreed to meet at Chez Camille, a restaurant across Pennsylvania Avenue from the District Building. Linowes thought he was dealing with a rough-edged activist. Barry smoothly ordered escargots and then artfully consumed them. More impressive was Barry's grasp of finances and his sensitivity to business interests. Linowes took the message back to the Board of Trade: Barry knew how to deal.

But he also kept faith with his activist edge. InDecember 1975, his staff issued a 102-page report that said the District was being stuck with social problems like public housing while suburban commuters earned high salaries in Washington and then took their paychecks—and payroll taxes—to the suburbs. "It is obvious that the District is being exploited by its suburbs," he concluded, and he started demanding a commuter tax. Congress wouldn't change the charter, but it was perfect rhetoric, and he applied it to the police, his tried and true punching bag.

"As it-now stands," Barry wrote, "a great majority of the present 1975 police department budget flows out of the pockets of D.C. taxpayers and into the hands of predominantly white male, suburban-residing police officers. This flow of money has some very nasty racial connotations—we're paying millions of dollars annually for an 'occupational army' of suburbanites to control our D.C. citizenry." In response, the council passed a residency rule for city employees, and Barry set himself up as the progressive force against the status quo of Mayor Washington and council chairman Tucker.

Barry ran for re-election in 1976 against a poorly financed Baptist minister. Barry campaigned as if he were the underdog, relentlessly visiting middle-class voters and housing projects across the Anacostia and middle- and upper-income black homeowners in Northwest enclaves. In a noticeable change, he also lavished public attention on white wards west of Rock Creek Park.

Was it mere re-election or laying the foundation for the mayoral campaign of 1978?

"I'll be mayor someday," he told a reporter in the summer of 1976. "The only question is when."

As Barry's political star was rising, his personal life was hitting the rocks.

Mary Treadwell couldn't corral him. Barry had told friends Treadwell was the only woman he truly loved, but that didn't keep him at home. She hated his continued philandering, threatened to move out, and left at least once. She had had two abortions, not because she didn't want Barry's children, but because their marriage was too unstable, and she didn't want to be a single mother. Early in 1976 Barry came home in the middle of the night, took off his clothes, and slipped into bed. As his head hit the pillow he felt the cold steel of a pistol pressed against his temple.

"Nigger," Treadwell said. "I'm tired of this shit. I'm gonna blow your fucking brains out."

Barry pleaded. He promised to mend his ways. He called his attorney and mentor Herbert O. Reid, who came to the apartment and talked Treadwell out of her rage. There were other violent confrontations. David Eaton says he was called to mediate at the Barry-Treadwell residence on a few occasions, once to disarm Barry.

Treadwell was still running Pride, but it bore little resemblance to the idealistic enterprise of 1967. Pride and its profit-making subsidiaries managed housing projects and owned subsidized housing. It did a lousy job, and poor residents suffered. Barry's ties to Pride were tenuous. He recognized the potential liability and publicly announced his resignation from the group. His marriage to Mary Treadwell was a casualty, too. They separated, and he moved out of their apartment.

With pretense of a home life no longer binding him, Barry was free to hit the bars. In the late 1970s that frequently brought him to the Gandy Dancer, a Capitol Hill fern bar near Union Station that was a melting pot for an integrated crowd of journalists, lobbyists, and politicians on the local and national scene. William Paley, Jr., son of the CBS chairman, was a part owner. Ed Bradley, a rising star in the CBS newsroom and assigned to the White House, lived up the street and visited regularly, as did Max Robinson and Jim Vance, two other black television reporters headed for stardom. But the Gandy Dancer was known for more than big drinks and good company. Some patrons in the fast crowd, like others across the nation, were beginning to play with cocaine, the hip drug of the late seventies and early eighties.

Barry lived on Maryland Avenue NE near the Gandy Dancer, often making it his last stop before going home. It was here, according to waitresses, bartenders, and friends, that Barry first came into contact with cocaine. To his political and professional colleagues, Barry appeared to be cleaning up his life. He'd stopped smoking cigarettes and he stopped drinking rum and ginger ale. In their presence, he sipped only white wine. The delicate deception completed Barry's transformation from a confrontational, tough-talking street activist to a polished pol. He had successfully split his life in two: During the day he was a hard-driving city councilman, stretching the limits of his power; at night he ran just as hard after women and occasionally drugs.

Neither intruded on his pursuit of higher office.

CHAPTER 6

A MAN FOR ALL PEOPLE

True, he would bring a certain sense of adventure to City
Hall-which means that there is a certain risk involved.
—The Washington Post *endorsing Marion Barry*

Sixteenth Street NW is a broad avenue that takes off at Lafayette
Square by the White House and shoots six miles north to the Maryland state line. It begins amid the elegance of the Hay Adams Hotel
and the power of the AFL-CIO union headquarters and the pomp
of the old Russian Embassy. On its path to Maryland, the street
cuts through the downtown business district, defines the eastern borders of Adams Morgan and Mount Pleasant—the city's only ethnic neighborhoods—and skirts Rock Creek Park before it bisects the
pastoral community of Shepherd Park. Here, along quiet streets with
flowered names like Jonquil, Holly, and Geranium, the black elite
dwells in large, center-hall Colonial and Tudor homes, side-by-side
with white families who first settled the neighborhood in the 1940s.
Martin Luther King's idea of a beloved community was Shepherd
Park in the 1970s.

In 1971 a large, extended family moved into a brick mansion at
7700 Sixteenth Street. The newcomers were Hanafi Muslims, a small
Islamic sect that numbered no more than one hundred in the Washington area, perhaps one thousand in the country. Los Angeles basketball star Kareem Abdul-Jabbar, a clan member, bought the house

for the Washington family. The Hanafis blended in the community that included other small religious groups.

On a January night in 1973, seven armed men burst into the Hanafis' home while group leader Hammas Abdul Khaalis and the other men were away. Wielding machetes and pistols, they slaughtered seven of the residents. Four children, including a nine-month-old infant, were drowned in a sink. Another child and two women were shot at close range. Seven Black Muslims were charged in the massacre; five were tried, convicted of murder, and sentenced to 140-year prison terms. But Khaalis, the gaunt and gray-bearded Hanafi elder, was unappeased. He turned his quiet mansion into an armed compound. Neighbors saw men with rifles guarding upstairs windows. The flowers died, and the backyard became a training ground. For four years and four months, the Hanafis seethed at Jewish judges for being too lenient on the murderers, at Black Muslims as part of a Zionist plot against Islam, and at the city government, which had somehow allowed the massacre. Then on March 9, 1977, they struck.

At 11:00 a.m. that Wednesday a U-Haul truck pulled up next to the national offices of B'nai B'rith, the Jewish service organization. Khaalis and six other Hanafis armed with rifles, handguns, machetes, and one crossbow burst into the downtown building and herded hostages into a back room. At the same time, three other armed Hanafis stormed the Islamic Center, a mosque beside the embassies on Massachusetts Avenue NW, and took their own hostages.

Khaalis's son in-law, Abdul Aziz, told reporters assembled in front of the house on Sixteenth Street that if demands were not met, "heads will be chopped off, a killing room will be set up at B'nai B'rith, and heads will be thrown out of windows."

Police cordoned off the two buildings and tightened White House security. Diplomats from Egypt, Iran, and Pakistan came to negotiate. At noon all of Washington was glued to television stations carrying the drama live.

When the Hanafis attacked, Marion Barry was speaking to a Kiwanis Club luncheon at the Roma Restaurant, a well-worn landmark on upper Connecticut Avenue known for walls hung with heads of wild animals, a sprawling grape arbor patio in the rear, and its owners, the Abo family. The bartenders in the attached watering hole look as if they've been there as long as the wild boar on the wall.

On his way to the District Building for a judiciary committee meeting, Barry heard initial radio reports about the hostage incidents. He was unaware that a smaller group of Hanafis at that moment was beginning to seize offices inside the District Building. He walked into the building, took the elevator to the fifth floor, and stepped off just as a Hanafi gunman fired a shotgun blast down the hall. Maurice Williams, a young WHUR-FM radio reporter, was mortally wounded. A security guard fell bleeding to the floor. Barry dived toward the council chambers. He felt a burning sensation in his chest. Someone dragged him into the council chambers.

"I'm hit," he said. "Get me a doctor."

Police officer Isaac Fulwood, Jr., was one of the first to arrive at the scene. "Help me. I'm dying," Barry told him.

With Hanafis holding hostages in parts of the hallway, firefighters eased Barry into a litter and lowered him down a ladder from the council chambers' window. Barry sat upright in the ambulance, afraid if he lay down he might die. At the Washington Hospital Center, doctors extracted a pellet from his chest two inches above his heart. Barry had suffered only a minor flesh wound.

"He's a very lucky man," said Dr. Howard Champion. "There was no injury to vital organs."

Mary Treadwell had thrown Batty out two months before, but she rushed from Pride headquarters to his side. Alert as he was wheeled to a recovery room, Barry asked her to sit on his bed. "This was a message from God," Barry said, according to Treadwell. "We're supposed to be together."

A nurse came into the room and took Treadwell aside. "Mrs. Barry," she said, "a woman is here to see Mr. Barry. She says she is his girlfriend."

"Is her name Cowell?" Treadwell asked.

"Yes," the nurse answered. "Show her in."

Barry objected, saying he didn't want to see her. Treadwell moved to meet her at the door.

The woman coming down the hall was a tall, statuesque beauty whose olive skin and high cheekbones gave her a regal Latin look. Effi Cowell, of Toledo, Ohio, was thirty-three, a former model who'd once posed in a swimsuit feature for *Jet* magazine. She had met Marion Barry six months earlier at a Bicentennial celebration. Cowell was a city restaurant inspector, but Barry didn't impress her at first. He called her night and day until she relented; weeks later she was replacing the other women in his life.

Treadwell took the younger woman down the hall, explaining that Barry was okay, but resting. Cowell felt slighted. She telephoned a friend to complain and demanded to see Barry. The two women were headed for a nasty confrontation when Ivanhoe Donaldson and the Reverend David Eaton arrived. Eaton called a truce and made sure Treadwell and Cowell visited at different times.

Barry, his bare chest wrapped in bandages, welcomed reporters to his bedside. "I heard two shots and dived to the right," he told them. "And then I felt a hot, burning sensation in my chest." The dramatic tale made great copy alongside photographs of the wounded hero. Cards, letters, and flowers arrived. Barry was so moved by the brush with death and outpouring of support that he summoned Thornell Page, the political adviser who had raised funds for Barry's previous campaigns.

Page was crossing a hospital parking lot to visit Barry when an acquaintance shouted to him.

"Hey, Thornell," the man said; "I hear Marion Barry's in the hospital."

"That's right."

"I bet somebody shot your boy because of a woman," the man said.

Page found Barry in a contemplative mood, focused on the upcoming mayoral race. The city's Democratic primary was eighteen months away, in September 1978. They discussed options until Barry gave the word: "Open the campaign account."

The city's second mayoral race of the home-rule era was up for grabs.

Walter Washington had been in office for a decade, counting his seven years as appointed chief executive. When he took over in 1967 the District Building was a powerless provincial bureaucracy run by whites who kept banker's hours. He'd replaced the lower-level officials with well-connected blacks, but he left whites in supervisory posts, and he never sank political roots into the community. He was a caretaker, a palatable transition figure.

"Everyone felt that Uncle Walter could keep things from happening," says Barry's early adviser Jim Gibson, "but he couldn't make things happen." Nevertheless, Uncle Walter wanted another term and announced his intention to run again with the backing of the black upper crust.

Sterling Tucker, chairman of the, city council, stepped up to challenge Washington. A slight and awkward politician, Tucker was a moderate who had joined the civil rights movement in the mid-1950s when he helped desegregate restaurants in his home town of Akron, Ohio. He arrived in Washington in 1956 to run the local office of the Urban League, perhaps the most moderate civil rights group. He'd served as appointed council chairman and forged establishment ties with Democrats and Republicans as an acceptable black alternative to the likes of Barry, Julius Hobson, and Douglas Moore. Tucker was approaching the mayoral campaign with a certitude that the job rightly belonged to him. He sent D.C. delegate Walter Fauntroy to inform Barry that he should run for the chairman's seat, but this time Barry refused to step aside and "wait his turn," as Fauntroy advised.

Instead, Barry took a poll that showed him positioned a close third behind Walter Washington and Tucker, but there were many undecided voters ready for change. According to the survey, Barry's core support lay among liberal whites and younger blacks. It was essentially the same coalition that had propelled the student civil rights movement in the early 1960s. Fifteen years after SNCC had peaked, here was the SNCC support system ready to be molded into a political constituency. The task of transforming that coalition into votes fell to Ivanhoe Donaldson.

Donaldson had been dabbling in small business, advising black politicians in other cities, but was politically and personally close to Barry, a man who had few friends. He took the poll numbers and forged them into a battle plan that cast Barry as a crusader against the status quo and the political bosses—Tucker and Washington—lumped together as has-beens. In a classic strategy crafted a year before the election, Donaldson figured that Tucker and Washington would split their base and allow Barry to slip into office by corralling white votes and picking off pockets of support from disaffected blacks and the emerging bloc of gay voters.

The city's unique, liberal white community would be a key factor. By 1978 there were no working-class whites in the capital. Most conservative and lower-income whites who might have felt threatened politically or economically by blacks had long since left the city for the Maryland or Virginia suburbs. The remaining upscale whites in Ward Three and urban activists in the center city were enamored of Barry's stirring rise from sharecropper to political leader, just as Willard Wirtz had been drawn to Barry and Pride in 1967.

It was the black middle and upper classes that still mistrusted Marion Barry. The established middle class was not anxious to put its young government in the hands of a forty-one-year-old former street activist. Black aristocrats loathed Barry's lifestyle and unacceptable pronunciation. He was still a cotton pickin' nigger to them.

"I'm an underdog in this whole situation in the sense that, among many people in the city, there is a feeling that Walter Washington or Sterling Tucker has a better shot than I do," Barry told *The Wash-*

ington Post's Milton Coleman. "It doesn't mean I can't win. It just means I have to fight a lot of battles."

The race was on for allies in a political network that was still young and fluid.

When Delano Lewis's secretary buzzed him with an "important" telephone call, the ranking black executive for the Chesapeake & Potomac Telephone Company reached quickly to pickit up.

"Mr. Lewis," said an officious voice on the line, "the chairman-would like to see you."

Lewis knew that "the chairman" was Sterling Tucker, who expected Lewis to support him for mayor. Lewis was worth thepursuit. A square-jawed, powerful man with broad shoulders and a quick smile, Lewis had become a bridge between the black and white business communities. Born in Kansas, Lewis was the son of a railroad porter and the first in his family to go to college. He came to Washington in 1963 after law school to work in the Justice Department under Bobby Kennedy. He spent a few years working for the Peace Corps in Africa and returned to work on Massachusetts senator Ed Brooke's staff. After an unsuccessful run in the crowded 1974 at-large council race, Lewis briefly worked for Fauntroy before becoming C&P's vice-president for corporate affairs and chief liaison to the fledgling city government. On paper he seemed to be the Tucker type.

"Tell the chairman that if he wants to talk to me, he can giveme a call," Lewis said and hung up. Days later, Marion Barrytelephoned.

"Del," Barry said, "I'd like to drop by and see you sometime. Can you fit me in?"

Like other businessmen, Lewis had found Barry friendly andaccessible, if not always agreeable in his role as chairman of the council finance and revenue committee. Lewis also was attracted by Barry's activism and energy. They had a natural bond, and after a congenial visit with the challenger, Lewis gambled his influence to align with Barry. His alliance was a metaphor for the 1978 mayoral campaign.

Tucker assumed the fealty of black professionals. Washington relied on the old guard. Barry hustled for supporters; some hungry for their own success.

Stuart Long, for example, was an Irish Catholic entrepreneur, born and raised in the city in an era when a thriving Irish community still worked at the Maine Avenue Navy Yard, manned the presses at the Government Printing Office on North Capital Street, and sent their boys for Jesuit schooling at nearby GonzagaHigh. Long joined the family restaurant and bar business after law school and ran it from an office over the Hawk & Dove, a neighborhood joint on the east side of Capitol Hill. When he inherited the bars, he felt hassled by city officials who nearly denied him required liquor permits. At the 1977 opening of W. H. Bone, a restaurant in Southwest that drew nearly all the city's political establishment, Barry sidled up to Long at a back table. "I'm going to run for mayor," he told Long. "Are you with me?"

"What are my choices?" Long said. "You know I want to get Walter out. Sterling's boring. You're fun. I'm with you."

"Well," Barry said, laughing, "it's you and me against the room."

That summer, Jeffrey Cohen was a guest at Long's beach house in Rehoboth, Delaware, Washington's summer resort town three hours from the capital. They drank vodka tonics and talked the business of politics.

Cohen was also a Washington native son. He'd grown up in "Hanukah Heights" in the heart of the city's well-to-do Jewish communities of Cleveland Park and Forest Hills. Cohen was the eldest son of a prominent businessman who had made a fortune in the oil business, but he was building his own development portfolio. As president of the local real estate association, he'd lobbied Barry to oppose rent control. Barry refused, saying rent control was not only politically popular but necessary to ease rising housing costs. Cohen didn't change Barry's mind, but like others he was impressed with Barry's grasp of city finances.

As they watched the waves and sipped their cocktails, Long and Cohen saw a grand future for themselves—if they backed the right candidate for mayor. "I have a sense that he'll be good for my business, and I'm ready to bring the rest of the saloonkeepers with me. It'll be worth big bucks for his campaign."

Cohen wasn't so sure. Barry was a long shot, but the race would be invigorating. And if their man won, the two young entrepreneurs dreamed of being on the inside of the city's power politics.

Ivanhoe Donaldson was famous for trying to anticipate and control every political angle, but his toughest chore was keeping a lid on Marion Barry's personal life, especially when there was a new woman in the mix, in this case Effi.

She seemed to have less chance than Barry's previous women. His tastes tended toward robust, voluptuous women who shared his passion for politics and activism. Cowell was tall and lean, cool and distant, and had had virtually no contact with the civil rights movement. Her mother, Polly Lee Harris, was an unmarried, sixteen-year-old African-American when Effi was born on July 4, 1944. Effi never met her Italian father, just as Barry did not remember his. When her marriage to jazz pianist Stanley Cowell, ended in divorce, she stayed in New York and worked a variety of jobs, including stints as a stewardess, a model, an entry analyst for Dun & Bradstreet, and a teacher at an all-black junior high school in Bedford-Stuyvesant. "It took them four months to accept me," she told an interviewer. "They thought that I was Puerto Rican."

In 1975 Effi headed to California but made it only as far as Washington. She found a job as a city health inspector, met Barry, and took aim at being his only woman. Near the time of Barry's mayoral announcement, she was moving some of her clothes into Barry's Capitol Hill apartment. The live-in relationship obviously worried Barry's advisers, who thought marriage would improve Barry's appeal. Ivanhoe Donaldson, according to a woman who was close to all three, gave Barry the word. "As a candidate for mayor, you cannot be living with someone. Either marry Effi or ask her to move out."

On February 17, 1978, just weeks after Barry formally announced his candidacy, he and Effi were married in a quiet ceremony at their apartment. Unlike the groom's second marriage to Mary Treadwell, there was no fanfare and no story in the *Post's* Style section. The new Mrs. Barry felt a wall of hostility from Barry's close male friends and advisers. Those inner-circle members still judged one another on whether they had paid their "Delta" dues. Effi hadn't contributed. "The civil rights movement kind of bypassed us," Effi Barry said in a magazine profile.

It got worse. When photographs of her began appearing, the campaign staff got telephone calls wanting to know why Barry had married a white woman. Her pale skin made her appear to be Caucasian, especially in the flat tones of newspaper ink. In a majority black city, the misconception could cost votes. Florence Tate, Barry's press secretary and a longtime veteran of civil rights activism, asked *Washington Post* city editor Herb Denton to clarify that Effi was indeed a black woman. The *Post* began characterizing Mrs. Barry as a "light-skinned black woman."

The *Post* delved into Barry's private life for other reasons during the 1978 campaign.

Despite his four-year marriage to Mary Treadwell and his new bride, Barry's reputation as a ladies' man was notorious. The gay community got the picture when Barry attended a fundraiser at Dupont Circle and left with the sister of one of his white, gay supporters. She was visiting from Dallas and started an affair that included her supplying him with cocaine, according to those familiar with the episode. His liaison with a striking African American hostess from the Gandy Dancer started during the campaign, too. But a politician's sex life was still off limits in 1978. It was ten years before Gary Hart dared reporters to catch him with a mistress and quit the presidential race after he was discovered dallying with Donna Rice on a boat named *Monkey Business.*

But in July 1978, city hall reporters fielded tips they couldn't ignore. One concerned the account by the young woman who told friends that Barry assaulted her in 1973. A reporter interviewed her and believed she was telling the truth. At the same time, *Post* reporter Leon Dash talked to a second woman who also said that Barry had sexually assaulted her. Dash visited the woman, heard her account, but decided that she wasn't credible.

Neither allegation was reported by the newspaper. In the case of the 1973 incident, the young woman refused to confirm it on the record, there was no police report of the incident, and Milton Coleman couldn't corroborate the story with secondary sources. (When approached for this book, she refused to talk about the incident.) Dash simply didn't believe the second woman. Their stories never became public.

If either of the stories had surfaced, Barry's campaign might have faltered. If he had dropped out of politics, the subsequent course of city government would have been entirely different.

Three months before the September primary, the mayor's race was too close to call.

A *Washington Post* poll showed Sterling Tucker leading with 24 percent of the vote, Walter Washington second with 20 percent, and Marion Barry last with 18 percent; 35 percent were still undecided. The three contenders chased endorsements in a city dazed by torpid summer air.

Most of the capital's black ministers, generally a conservative bunch, came out early for Tucker, the perceived front-runner. Big labor backed Washington, after building a ten-year relationship. Ron Richardson, the sharp-tongued executive secretary of the Hotel and Restaurant Employees Local 25, castigated Tucker for being "owned body and soul" by John Hechinger, the hardware mogul whose stores were staffed by nonunion employees. Richardson derided Barry as a turncoat who shamelessly abandoned the poor to appeal to business interests.

The Fraternal Order of Police, dominated by whites, endorsed the man who in his dashiki days had taunted the police for more than a decade as an "occupation army." The alliance was not as remarkable as it may have appeared. Now, instead of harassing cops, Barry was proposing legislation to give them annual raises. Crime was not the city's overriding problem. That Richard Nixon had ordered the city to hire fifteen hundred more officers, bringing the force to an all-time high of fifty-one hundred, helped keep the relative peace.

Dave Abramson's ad campaign portrayed Barry as a daring and dynamic progressive. Stark black-and-white posters said: "Take A Stand. Marion Barry. Mayor."

Barry's political genius shone on the campaign trail. He was born to hug babies, commiserate with men on the skids, stare into the eyes of old women who'd seen too much. He also threw well-aimed barbs at Walter Washington's "stumbling, bumbling" government and complained that no one answered the phones. He castigated the mayor for allowing the public housing complexes to rot; his promise to "take the boards off" became an anthem.

Jeff Cohen held intimate breakfasts with wealthy developers to show that Barry "isn't a devil with horns." Stu Long squeezed money from saloonkeepers on idyllic boat rides down the Potomac River. Campaign treasurer Max Berry conserved cash for a strong finish.

Though whites dominated the campaign's fundraising and advertising arms, Barry's black supporters controlled the heart of his field operation. Anita Bonds served as Donaldson's deputy. As the native Washingtonian in Barry's top campaign circle, she organized legions of volunteers who called themselves "Barry's Army." Bonds might have campaigned for Tucker or Washington. Her father worked for the National Park Service, and she spent an "idyllic" childhood in segregated Northeast Washington. Her politics turned radical at the University of California at Berkeley, where she befriended Mario Savio, the free speech savant who had marched with SNCC protesters in 1964. Returning to Washington, she helped Donaldson form a crucial link to the city's political activists.

Barry did not get support from Rufus "Catfish" Mayfield, the Pride leader Barry had booted out years ago. Mayfield, married and with two children, was campaigning for Washington when he encountered Barry.

"I'm going to be the next mayor," Barry said.

"Oh, no you're not," Mayfield responded.

"The mayor doesn't love ya," Barry said. "I still do."

"My people's blood is all over the streets of Washington.... Everybody flocks to Washington to try to make a name for them selves," Mayfield said. "Politics, well, it does some strange things to people. It did it to Marion in some way fierce."

The Washington Post, for all its national and international reputation after Watergate, remained still largely a white paper in a black town.

Its occasional coverage of black Washington centered largely on the failings of the city government, violent crime, and the downtown business scene. It reported on the deteriorating public schools and suburban growth. The vibrant black social, academic, business, and professional life rarely surfaced within the *Post's* local, feature, or business pages. Those lives were reflected in community news on local black radio and ethnic weeklies. The *Post* had few black reporters before the mid-1960s, and when more black reporters were hired, the city's black communities viewed them with suspicion.

Milton Coleman still felt the mistrust when he joined the newspaper in 1976. Coleman chose to live in a Southeast community of black professionals and city officials. He made it a point to dance at parties. "I had to dispel the notion that black reporters who worked for *The Washington Post* couldn't dance," he says.

But for white Washingtonians, the *Post* was the Bible on city politics. Ward Three had a tenuous understanding of the emerging black political system, and what it knew it learned through the *Post,* and to a smaller extent from the *Washington Star,* the venerable afternoon daily that was losing money and succumbing to the *Post's* power in 1978. Because of the *Post's* clout among whites—who voted in high percentages—the paper's endorsement was critical.

Each major candidate usually got two sessions at the beige brick building on Fifteenth Street NW—the first, an on-therecord lunch with the editors, reporters, and editorial writers; the second, a private affair with the editorial board alone.

Barry wore a jaunty, russet-and-white seersucker double-breasted suit for his luncheon session on August 23. He turned on the charisma and dazzled the journalists by talking about "a new creative direction" for the city. "People are embarrassed to say, 'I'm from the District of Columbia,' not because we don't have representation," Barry said, "but because they're not happy with the kind of leadership and the image this city has to them."

At his private editorial board session, Barry put on a dignified show for editorial page editor Phil Geyelin, an upper-crust liberal and Walter Lippmann protégé from Philadelphia's Main Line; Meg Greenfield, a brainy, independent journalist with a strong liberal streak who'd become close to owner Katharine Graham and would eventually replace Geyelin; Patricia Matthews, a young black professional who had close ties to Barry; Katharine Graham herself; and three other members of the editorial board. Graham had met Barry when he was working with Pride. She had found him "interesting." But now Barry was laying out his grand visions of harmonious integration, the importance of education, and plans to make the city a magnet for private business.

The editorial board heard from Tucker and Washington, but according to Geyelin—who made a point to cover some debates to see the candidates in action—Barry was the unanimous choice. "He was a hit of a roughneck," says Geyelin, "but there were a good bit more roughnecks in the city at large than there were in Ward Three. I thought Barry could take people who might run amok, who might he hostile to society and to the government, and lead them in a healthy direction."

Geyelin, like Willard Wirtz, believed that Barry could control "the street dudes."

Katharine Graham recalls that they agreed Barry was impressive, but that she left on a trip to New York and Martha's Vineyard believing the endorsement was still unsettled. Geyelin wrote the first endorsement on Tuesday, August 29, for publication the next day. He phoned Graham in Martha's Vineyard to alert her, but couldn't reach her. He went out to dinner and didn't try again.

The lead editorial said that Washington should he replaced, and in the choice between Tucker and Barry, "Our strong belief is that it should he Marion Barry." An unusually long paean took up half the editorial column and could have been written by Ivanhoe Donaldson. "We find it, in fact, very nearly grotesque that his work with disadvantaged street youths, at one particularly turbulent time in this city's history, and his service among the shock troops of a great national movement for human rights at a tumultuous moment in our national history, would somehow he counted against him in a campaign for mayor of the District of Columbia in 1978," the editorial admonished. "In our view, it is one of the basic arguments for him."

Katharine called Geyelin from the Vineyard and screamed in his ear. As he recalls it, the publisher was angry that she hadn't been warned. In his twelve years on the cditorial page, it was "her most violent reaction." Katharine Graham says that she spoke to her son Don when she returned to Washington. She wasn't pleased, he says, but she didn't consider it a "disaster" either

"Luckily," he said, "you won't have to live with your own endorsement."

The Grahams still figured he was a long shot even after the *Post* pleaded Barry's cause in five more editorials.

The endorsements crushed Sterling Tucker, but he had a few more cards to play.

Polls taken before the endorsement showed a close race with Tucker and Washington virtually tied for the lead and Barry trailing six points behind, but Tucker's tracking polls after the endorsement showed Barry closing the gap. He panicked and sent out an emergency mailing to five thousand voters in Ward Three. His campaign went forty thousand dollars into debt to buy television ads.

There was only one way to halt Barry's momentum. David Eaton, Barry's friend and spiritual adviser, and Polly Shackleton, the grand dame of Democratic politics who represented Ward Three on the city council, were scheduled to endorse Tucker five days before the primary—but they were wavering. Eaton still worried that Tucker and Barry would split the vote and put Walter Washington over the top; He convinced Barry to come to his home at midnight a week before the primary to meet with Tucker and perhaps join forces.

Max Berry smelled a plot. For weeks Tucker's two chief aides, Bob Washington and Harley Daniels, had been floating rumors that Barry would drop out of the race, throw his support to Tucker, and take a top job in the Tucker administration in return.

"You just want to pressure Marion into quitting," Berry told Eaton. "It's a setup."

"No," Eaton said. "It's not that way. I just want them to meet and discuss things."

"We have a deal," Berry said. "But don't screw around with me—just you and Sterling."

At 11:45 on the night of the meeting, Marion Barry parked his car around the corner from Eaton's home, positioned so he could watch the front door. He saw Tucker walk up the steps ahead of Bob Washington and Harley Daniels. Barry drove back to his headquarters. His legal adviser, Herbert O. Reid, called to tell Eaton the meeting was off. Then Max Berry leaked details of the botched rendezvous to the newspapers, casting what became known as the "midnight maneuver" as a blatant attempt by Tucker to muscle Barry out of the race.

"Even if I were not confident," Barry told reporters at a press conference the next day, "I would not drop out because we've established some principles in this campaign."

The next day's papers ran stories about the botched meeting and Tucker's strong-arm tactics. Eaton and Shackleton gave Tucker only a tepid endorsement. Shackleton told her constituents to vote their conscience.

Barry sailed into the final weekend riding a strong wind fed by the steady stream of *Post* endorsements, but the race was still a toss-up. Inside the *Post* newsroom, city editor Herb Denton and reporters Milton Coleman and Leon Dash all figured that Sterling Tucker would still come out on top. If not Tucker, then Walter Washington. Denton assigned Dash and Coleman to Tucker's headquarters election night.

The bad news came to Tucker shortly after noon on Primary Day, Tuesday, September 12. A city election official leaked a count of the morning ballot boxes to Harley Daniels, who slipped the paper in his sock and delivered it to the candidate. The returns showed Barry ahead of Tucker by a few points and Washington a close third. If the numbers held, as expected, Barry would win. When the morning returns were officially announced at 8:00 p.m., the party began at Barry's headquarters in the Harambee House next to the campus of Howard University. Delirious campaign workers and frantic reporters poured into the ballroom. It was a biracial, citywide party that lasted all night. At 10:00 Barry claimed victory.

"I'll never forget where I came from or how I got here," he told his screaming supporters.

The vote was excruciatingly close, so close that Tucker demanded a recount. The final tally was Barry, 31,265; Tucker 29,909, and Washington, 28,286. Barry had won by fewer than 1,400 votes.

The victory came just as Ivanhoe Donaldson had predicted: Solid majorities in the affluent white precincts and the city's gay community, a cohesive and politically growing minority, and a respectable share of black poor and middle-class voters punched Barry's ticket. Tucker and Washington split the majority of black votes; either one alone could have buried Barry. Fundraising, command of "Barry's

Army," and, of course, the *Post* editorial barrage had made Barry the winner.

The morning after, Barry called Board of Trade president R. Robert Linowes, who had backed Walter Washington.

"Okay," Barry said, "I've won now. Are we together?"

"You betcha," Linowes responded. This was vintage Barry: Make your enemies into allies. He embraced Eaton and Shackleton and stripped Tucker of supporters like Bob Washington. A few weeks later Linowes and the Board of Trade sponsored a $500-a-plate luncheon for Barry. In 1968 he had called these same people "moneylord merchants." At the lunch he collected sixty thousand dollars in contributions for his general election campaign. The backslapping lunch set the foundation for the fundamental quid pro quo of the coming Barry regime. In return for financing his campaigns, for withholding most criticism of his government, and for including Barry's friends in their deals, Barry would give the businessmen almost a free hand in developing Washington's downtown business district.

The November general election was a formality. The nine-to--one Democratic advantage overwhelmed black Republican nominee Arthur Fletcher, a novice in city politics who had been a federal assistant secretary of labor and former pro football player. The Republican tried to scare blacks into voting for him by accusing Barry of being the white man's candidate. The *Post* called his campaign "unforgivably shabby."

Barry won by a landslide on November 12.

The victory represented Barry's best, most untarnished moment.

His rise from Itta Bena to power in the capital city was Lincolnesque with a black face. His ascent was rougher, tougher, more improbable. Ten years before he became mayor, the city was still run by racists in Congress. Now the son of a sharecropper—not the progeny of a light-skinned black aristocrat—was in control of the city government. He'd achieved his goal of taking power in the capital city that he had only dreamed of in 1965, when he first told Dave Levy the town would be his.

It seemed as if the entire landscape had changed over the past decade.

Congress was transformed and no longer wished to run the capital. The racists were defeated or in retreat. Many of the current leaders, such as Senator Patrick Leahy of Vermont, who chaired the Senate appropriations subcommittee that oversaw the District's budget, were liberal Democrats rooting for the city's continued independent path. Black congressmen also were in position to promote the city's interests in the House. Jimmy Carter, a sympathetic Democrat, was in the White House.

The new mayor encountered Katharine Graham at a reception in New York that winter. They smiled broadly at each other.

"Here's the lady that made me," Barry said.

"Yes, Marion," she said, "and don't you forget it."

Black aristocrats, their hometown now in the hands of an uncouth outsider, were appalled, but they were in the minority. Much of the black middle class and the alienated poor were ready for change, and Barry seemed very much a man of the people.

The Board of Trade was willing to fall in line. Every power center was, for the moment, bowing to the new Barry era.

The resulting political constellation presented a unique opportunity in American urban politics: In 1978, in the capital city, there was a chance to create a truly integrated body politic. Barry was among the first big-city mayors to rise from the civil rights movement. And he didn't win political power by trying to be "white."

Barry had moderated his image, but at heart he was dark-skinned, unassimilated, and unashamed.

CHAPTER 7

BLACK POWER: THE MAKING OF A MACHINE

We're going to show everyone that black people can really
run something.
—*Ivanhoe Donaldson*

Inaugural Day, January 2, 1979, dawned under granite skies. A cold
drizzle rode gusts of wind down Pennsylvania Avenue. The ceremony
was moved inside the District Building, in part to accommodate U.S.
Supreme Court Justice Thurgood Marshall, who was to administer
the oath of office.

Bundled in an overcoat, Justice Marshall lumbered into the offices
of the mayor. A taciturn man in his seventies, he grumped a few
good mornings. Shaking off the cold, Marshall plopped his large
frame down onto a burgundy sofa and looked at mayoral aide Dwight
Cropp.

"Okay," Marshall said. "Where's the bourbon?"

"Uh, Mr. Justice Marshall," Cropp replied hesitantly, "maybewe
can meet that request after the ceremony."

"I want the bourbon."

Aides scurried to find a bottle of whiskey, and Marshall had a nip
to warm his insides before being escorted down the hall where he'd
help Marion Barry make history.

The festivities that morning began with a soggy parade, led by Marion and Effi Barry, from Malcolm X Park below Adams Morgan, across U Street NW, past Pride's former headquarters, down Sixteenth Street, and finally skirting the White House on the way to the District Building.

At 12:33 p.m., in a packed city council chamber, Thurgood Marshall asked Barry to raise his right hand. Marshall, the embodiment of the civil rights movement, had made it to the country's highest court. And there was Barry, with Effi standing by his side, the sharecropper's son who promised to carry the fruits of the civil rights movement to the capital city.

"I will," said Barry.

"You're in," said Marshall.

By Inaugural Day, Barry had been building his government for two months. The transition team had set up public offices downtown, but the Barry regime actually came into being around an oak conference table crammed into the small offices of the Potomac Institute, an obscure think tank that had helped bankroll the civil rights movement.

Each Sunday, a core group met at the institute's Dupont Circle office: Ivanhoe Donaldson, James Gibson, Herbert Reid, Courtland Cox, Carroll Harvey, and a few others. Here they sifted the boxes of studies and reports produced by transition manager Virginia Fleming, drawing organizational charts on blank sheets of paper to create the new administration. Their task was tantamount to designing a government from scratch to replace the bureaucracy that Walter Washington had barely changed from the pre-home-rule era.

"Well," the mayor-elect asked his inner circle at the first meeting, "what do you want to do?"

The question seemed naive, but it was a reflection of the communal spirit that existed at the top in the beginning.

"We were all part of the collective," Gibson says. "He wasn't the sole owner."

The Potomac Institute was a fitting venue. It was founded in the early 1960s by Steven Currier, scion of the Warburg fortune, and Audrey Mellon Currier, a Mellon heiress, to fund voter registration drives in the South and eventually SNCC. The Curriers hired a public relations firm to keep their names and their foundation out of the news. "It was," in Gibson's words, "a quiet mobilization of the well-motivated rich."

Gibson, one of the institute's three directors since the mid-1960s, was an agent of that mobilization. A short, energetic man with an analytical mind, he was a product of Atlanta's solid, middle-class black community. In 1959, after a stint in the U.S. Army, Gibson, with Julian Bond and Whitney Young, started a newsletter to communicate between the early civil rights groups. He understood early on that the black community's problems beyond elective politics were economic and structural. The Potomac Institute sent Gibson to Gary, Indiana, to advise newly elected mayor Richard Hatcher on how to use patronage, to wield political power as part of the establishment rather than as a protester. Gibson brought on Carroll Harvey to spread the good-government gospel. "We taught emerging black officials how to get into the game," Gibson says.

When Barry took office, Gibson became the city's director of planning. Harvey would take over the cumbersome General Services Administration, an agency that effectively serviced the entire government and controlled hundreds of millions of dollars in contracts. Ivanhoe Donaldson took the all-purpose role of "general assistant." Courtland Cox headed the minority business development agency. Tina Smith, who'd helped Barry run Washington's SNCC office in 1965, moved into the executive suite as a special assistant. It was achance for SNCC and the Potomac Institute to run the show, "not to picket the sheriff, but to be the sheriff," in Courtland Cox's words.

"Here we were," says Carroll Harvey. "We were in power."

Walter Washington's administration was disproportionately run by whites and suburbanites. The new leadership joked that in a city with eight political wards, the suburbs were "Ward Nine," and they moved swiftly to bring on more women and members of the gay and Latino communities—both to be fair and to pay political debts. Judith Rogers became city attorney; Florence Tate was the first press secretary. Betty King, a wealthy white activist who helped draw feminist support for Barry, took over the politically sensitive office, overseeing nominees to boards and commissions. Personnel director Jose Gutierrez knew the city's Latino community. Veteran gay activist Richard Maulsby was a special assistant to Barry.

But weeks before he took office, the new government lacked a city administrator, the one person who actually would run the day-to-day activities. It would take a professional to clean up what Barry had called the "stumbling, bumbling" bureaucracy. The search came down to Elijah Rogers, a short, wiry man with a shiny balding pate and a no-nonsense look in his eye. He was a natty dresser, with "Baby," his nickname, embroidered on his shirt cuffs. When Barry called, he was city manager of Berkeley, California, but he had attended Howard University, knew Washington, and had a reputation as one of the best black public administrators in the country. Rogers, a native of North Carolina, was about to take a job running Richmond, Virginia.

"Would you rather work in the capital of the Confederacy" he asked, "or the capital of the United States?" Rogers relented. For the next four years he played drill sergeant, while Donaldson played mother hen to Barry and dispensed political favors. Rogers goaded agency directors, bullied sluggish bureaucrats, and made the government function more efficiently than it ever had.

Still, there was friction between Donaldson and Rogers, and the question around the District Building was: Who was second to Barry? It was a longstanding joke that they settled the question by saying Barry was number three.

Ivanhoe Donaldson got in contact with Carol Thompson as soon as the phone was hooked up in his office.

"Well, kid," he said, "here's your chance. We're gonna do it. We're gonna show everyone that black people can really run something."

Carol Thompson idolized Donaldson. She'd met him in 1969 when she was an impressionable black student at Smith College, a New England school for bluebloods. Donaldson was teaching a course called African-American Political Science at the University of Massachusetts, and every black student in the area flocked to his three-hour lectures delivered without notes on everything from the civil rights movement to multinational corporations. "Ivanhoe was like a God in the five-college area," she says.

It was Donaldson who arranged Thompson's trip to Mississippi in the summer of 1970 to continue SNCC's work of registering voters in small towns. His lectures and that experience helped turn her into an activist bent on changing government from the inside. She was a twenty-nine-year-old rising star at the Department of Housing and Urban Development in early 1979 when Donaldson beckoned her to the District Building. Her coworkers at HUD said she'd be crazy to chuck her career in the federal government, but she couldn't wait to join Donaldson and the other SNCC leaders who were still her heroes.

"I was pumped up and excited," she says, "It was my hometown government. I believed I was part of a group that was making history. We had a real sense of mission."

She joined the government as a midlevel bureaucrat in the licensing division, but Donaldson said she could "go to the top" and brought her to the table with Marion Barry, Elijah Rogers, Jim Gibson, and Cox. "I was amazed at Barry's intellect, commitment, knowledge base at the start," she says. "People would talk black around the table; Barry would admonish them to be inclusive, that we had to bring together Ward Three and Ward Eight."

Donaldson even schooled her about corruption.

"People are going to offer you bribes," he said. "If you do it once, you won't be able to stop. So don't start."

In late February, a snowstorm shut down the city for a day. It wasn't overwhelming, but poor snow removal had people screaming, and Barry faced his first management crisis.

At the suggestion of press secretary Florence Tate, Barry invited *Post* reporter Milton Coleman along for Barry's tour of the city. The mayor's chauffeured car cruised major arteries that were passable. Barry was nonchalant. He told Coleman public works officials and Rogers, just on his second day on the job, would handle everything.

"What's to lead? It's not a crisis," Barry said.

Coleman asked about people digging out cars only to have plows block them again. How would they get to work?

"Take a bus," Barry responded.

Buses aren't running, Coleman said.

"Well, Milton, they can walk," the mayor snapped.

And that's the way Coleman wrote it. Barry's "let them walk" line set off another storm. Two months in office, he was cast as the cavalier ruler. Barry had learned a fundamental truth in media relations. Reporters did tend to love the underdog, but when they reported on top dogs, they changed into the adversary press. If Barry had assumed he could let down his guard around a reporter, he was wrong.

Once his government was in place and his goals were set, the new mayor and his enthusiastic entourage ran headlong into a huge budget deficit. Walter Washington's people had tracked the city's finances on three-by-five cards and scraps of paper, and the antiquated system disguised a $100 million shortfall plus a $300 million long-term debt. Barry and Donaldson found themselves in the basement of the District Building cutting expenses for rolls of toilet paper and contemplating the prospect of laying off city workers.

Image maker David Abramson and Barry's aides pumped out a forty-two-page "Report to the People" in April to announce that Barry had appointed dozens of panels and task forces to study myriad issues, as serious as infant mortality, as mundane as taxi cab safety.

"People may not always agree with what I do, nor how I do it," Barry said, "but they are going to know that at long last somebody is in charge and is doing his best."

The new mayor also crisscrossed the city as an ambassador of good will. He met with seventy-one citizen groups, attended forty ribbon cuttings or other ceremonies, met with reporters on eighteen occasions, "held literally hundreds of meetings with staff people to implement urgently needed policy," according to his report. Barry visited the president, the vice-president, the budget director, four cabinet secretaries, and various congressmen and senators.

Barry brushed off his activist credentials for an address to the annual meeting of D.C. bankers in Homestead, Virginia. He thanked them for their interest in the District, then announced that the city's human rights office would investigate their minority hiring and promotion practices. He expected law firms, accountants, and retailers to hire more blacks and women.

"You have to do better," Barry warned, and he left an implication that anyone hoping to do business with the city government had better hire blacks.

Barry's approach may have seemed heavy-handed, but he was only doing openly what Irish, Italian, and Jewish politicians had done behind closed doors. It was an honest attempt to bring blacks and women to the table in what had been a whites-only affair. He went further and ordered Courtland Cox to raise the percentage of the city's business with minority contractors from just over 10 percent to 35 percent. He demanded that developers who wanted to build on city property bring blacks into joint ventures.

"Suddenly law firms who never had minority partners had minority partners," says Elijah Rogers. "Same with banks and real estate developers. Some may not have liked it, but they knew the new rules of the game."

Courtland Cox still wanted to mix business with philosophy.

A tall and imperious native of the West Indies, Cox fervently believed that American blacks had to join hands with Africans to promote their mutual political and economic power. Pan-Africanism became a feature of SNCC's agenda during its final years, and now that Barry was in power, Cox said, it was time to make a symbolic trip to Africa, not as an American rejectionist like Stokely Carmichael, but as a bridge of power and influence. Barry and a small entourage embarked on a nineteen-day, fivenation trip on July 13.

Ivanhoe Donaldson didn't go. He was in the District Building days later when two U.S. deputy marshals placed him under civil arrest for failing to pay twenty-seven hundred dollars to a contractor for work on his condominium. The company had put in three skylights, a fireplace, and an office. After the marshals hauled Donaldson to court, Stu Long paid off the contractor. In the rush of news about Barry's grand trip, little was made of the episode.

In Africa, Marion Barry was received with the pomp usually reserved for heads of state. Local newspapers often mistakenly described him as the first black mayor of the American capital. In Monrovia, Liberia, Barry told the Organization of African Unity he would take a more active role in African affairs. First Lady Effi Barry was warmly received. Barry returned to the District on August 1 expecting to be greeted as a world player with the respect he had received in the foreign capitals. Instead, he found that in the eyes of many constituents, his campaign promises were overdue, and his first scandal was rushing his way.

The Washington Post's banner headline screamed "Pride Firm Tied to $600,000 Theft" on October 12, 1979. A yearlong investigation by *Post* reporters Ron Shafer and Lew Simons described in excruciating detail how Barry's former wife, Mary Treadwell, and other Pride officials had systematically skimmed funds, including rent payments from poor tenants at Clifton Terrace, a once-grand apartment building that had turned into a seedy subsidized housing complex under a Pride affiliate. The articles painted Treadwell as a woman who took from the poor while she lived in an apartment in the Watergate and drove a Jaguar. The *Post's* four-day series of articles triggered an investigation by the U.S. attorney. The articles repeatedly pointed out that Barry, who had divorced Treadwell in 1977, was not under investigation, but more than a few Washingtonians believed he must have known. Hadn't Treadwell given him a car? Didn't her lavish lifestyle seem odd to him? He testified before the grand jury and walked away unscathed, in a legal sense.

But in the midst of the Pride scandal, *Washington Star* reporters discovered that Barry's mortgage for his new $125,000 house in the Hillcrest section of Southeast Washington carried an interest rate of 8.75 percent, far below the market rate of 12 percent. The sweetheart deal came from William Fitzgerald, the president of Independence Federal Savings and Loan Association. Fitzgerald was a member of the city's black elite and one of its most successful bankers. He had supported Sterling Tucker for mayor and denounced the young challenger as an unwashed 'Bama who could not run the city. When Barry was elected, he cozied up to the mayor and opened a seat on his bank board for Effi, who had no banking experience. The ensuing uproar forced the Barrys to accept the prevailing rate, a move that added $247 to their monthly payment.

Lillian Wiggins, a columnist for the *Washington Afro-American,* smelled a plot.

A middle-aged, matronly native of the city, she'd lived through segregation, police brutality, and the racist plantation bosses in Congress. She was skeptical of the semi-independence under home rule. No one relinquishes power easily, she believed, and she had often written that the white power structure was aching to take back total control of the capital city. Reflecting the insecurity of a century of white rule, Wiggins raised the specter of the white apocalypse. She called it the "Master Plan," and the name stuck.

"Many residents believe that the Marion Barry era may be the last time Washington will have a black mayor," Wiggins wrote after Barry's first year. "If negative programming and characterization of black leadership are allowed to continue in the city of Washington and especially in the black community there is a strong possibility of the 'master plan,' which I have so often spoken about maturing in the 1980s."

Despite editorial support for Barry from the *Post* and backing for him from the city's white business community, Wiggins's warning took hold in parts of the black community and became enshrined as "the Plan." In ominous shorthand it embodied the city's racial tensions; it also played into Barry's hand. A year into office, he'd become the lightning rod that was hot-wired directly into that most vulnerable and insecure part of the collective black psyche.

"Many blacks feel that a part of their own future is wrapped up in Marion Barry's success as mayor," Milton Coleman wrote. "Heis a symbol—the most visible symbol—of those blacks who grew up in the '60s, began to achieve status, influence and power in the '70s, and don't want to lose it in the '80s....

"Barry has to demonstrate," Coleman said, "that a black man can run this government: that black people can answer the telephones right; that a black woman can be the budget director (black folks can count, too); that blacks not only can execute nickel-and-dime service contracts, but they can also construct skyscrapers downtown."

That kind of pressure led many black Washingtonians to circle their wagons around Barry to protect him—and the black citizenry—against white encroachment, even at that early moment in his regime. Unfortunately, the circle tended to exclude most whites, in fact or in sentiment. The racial divisiveness made it easier for some whites—who needed little from government except routine services—to disengage themselves from it all.

Psychologically, Ward Three west of the park began to break off from the city. Rock Creek, the stream that enters the District's northern line in Chevy Chase and empties into the Potomac River below Georgetown, became essentially a moat.

The federal government gave Barry's new government unprecedented independence. Jimmy Carter's White House ignored the city, and Congress was in no mood to meddle.

Early in Barry's first term, he and Ivanhoe Donaldson paid a courtesy call on Vermont senator Patrick J. Leahy, Jr., the man who controlled the city's finances by way of his chairmanship of the appropriations subcommittee on the District. Leahy was waiting when the two arrived a bit late for their appointment. They made for an incongruous ensemble. Leahy was a tall, balding, awkward Vermonter who could have passed for Ichabod Crane. Barry was nearly Leahy's height but already getting a gut. Donaldson was the short, fairskinned man in the middle. Barry shook the senator's hand, cracked a joke, and slapped himon the back, Senate style. Then he held forth for twenty minutes straight about balancing the city's budget and creating jobs and taking care of the poor.

"What can we do for you?" Leahy asked.

"Help us out with the budget," Barry said. "We want as much control as possible over our finances."

Leahy and other liberal senators wanted the District government to succeed for much the same reason that Willard Wirtz supported Pride. They wanted the District to be a showcase of their liberal programs: Head Start, food stamps, supplemental feeding under the Women Infants and Children program, housing subsidies. As long as they could limit their involvement to getting free tickets to Redskins games, other favors from the city government, and throwing money at the District's problems without getting involved, they were content.

A week or so after Barry's visit to the Hill, Leahy sent his aide, David Julyan, to the District Building to see Donaldson. Donaldson made Julyan wait for a half-hour and then ushered him into his office. A large black-and-white photo of Stokely Carmichael hung on one wall. It was the only reminder of his militant past.

"The senator has two proposals," Julyan said. "First, he's willing to pass your budget just the way you send it up. We will hold a hearing, but we will not review the budget line by line. In return, you have to take responsibility for the city's finances. You can't blame us anymore for meddling in the city's fiscal affairs.

"Second," he said, "the senator's willing to make the District a showcase. He wants to earmark block grants for education, jobs, housing, small business development. There's no reason why we can't use the District for all kinds of pilot projects."

Donaldson seemed distracted. He took Julyan down to see the mayor, thanked him for coming, and promised to get back to him.

A week later, Donaldson called.

"They're interesting ideas," he said, "but they aren't consistent with our plans for revitalizing the city. The budget autonomy is just too risky. We like it the way it is now."

Donaldson didn't believe the government was ready to take on the budget, or he thought the city still needed Congress to blame if things turned sour.

Midway through his first term, the strain of being mayor took some of the strut out of Marion Barry's walk and dusted his hair with flecks of gray.

Crime was up, waiting lines for services were still long, his 6 percent sales tax had been rejected. The early idealism had run aground on recession and double-digit inflation. He'd been forced to lay off hundreds of government employees and cut services, but the budget was still $125 million in the red. Public-housing residents protested outside his office about rats in their hallways. The man who had made his mark by shaking his fist at "the man" was forced to close off a public elevator so he could ride up to his offices and avoid protesters demonstrating in his reception area.

"You've got to find a way not to be overconsumed by the job because it destroys you," he told a reporter. "I really understand a lot of politicians winding up as alcoholics or pill-poppers, because the pressures are so enormous."

Barry's son, Marion Christopher, had been born in June 1980, but the mayor couldn't seem to make himself go home in the evening. Instead, he would work late, attend a few political functions, and hit the clubs. A favorite spot was Elan on K Street in the heart of the downtown business district. By day lawyers and lobbyists strolled by the doors; by night a fast crowd arrived. The bartenders supplied cocaine, and the patrons snorted it in the restrooms.

In early November of 1980, a young woman came to his table. She was twenty-eight, pretty but not striking, full-bodied with great legs, and self-assured—the kind of woman that Barry couldn't resist. She gave the mayor a card with her home phone number. They left separately, but a few hours later Barry's car, driven by a plainclothes police officer attached to his security detail, pulled up to her apartment house on Sixteenth Street. He called from the car to ask if he could come up. She told friends that they consummated their relationship in the wee hours of the morning. Her name was Karen Johnson.

Washington was a mecca for women like Karen Johnson. She was born in San Francisco and raised in a strict, churchgoing, Baptist family. In the mid-1970s she moved to Washington, got a college degree, married, and divorced, according to a friend who had met her in 1976. "She was not a virgin to the social whirl," said the friend, who was often in Johnson's apartment when Barry came for a quiet dinner party or a few drinks. The mayor was sometimes quiet and engaging, occasionally rough and raunchy, but always magnetic. "It seemed as if Barry and Karen were just friends," she says; He got her a job working as an energy specialist for the District government. But Karen Johnson kept a diary that eventually would fall into the hands of TV reporter Mark Feldstein and still later the FBI.

As reported in an entry from November 15, 1980, she described Barry as "down-to-earth, intelligent, imposing, commanding, masculine, very verbal in bed + + + ! (turns me on), good sense of humor, a good lay." She meticulously listed the pluses and minuses of her affair, but she was also worried about "being one in a long line of lovers," or the "possibility of a leak as a result."

"What's in it for him?" she pondered. "Sexual gratification…a temporary escape from politics."

Drugs helped open the escape hatch—first marijuana and then cocaine. Karen Johnson never laid out lines of white powder during her dinner parties, but Johnson's estranged boyfriend, Franklin Law, told police that he supplied Johnson, who shared it with Barry and eventually sold it to him on at least twenty to thirty occasions. Gradually the romance cooled. In mid-1982, Johnson revealed to Barry that she was pregnant, perhaps by him. The mayor abruptly cut off their liaison. Outside of a small group, few knew the two had ever met.

Ivanhoe Donaldson was supposed to he the only one who could slap Barry around and yank him hack from the excesses of women and drugs, but Donaldson had his own problems in the summer of 1981.

On a particularly sweltering August day, security guards peering out of 500 C Street NW saw a milling crowd of angry people suddenly surge through the glass doors. Seventy-five unemployed cafeteria workers spilled into the marble lobby of the District's unemployment offices, a dreary, post-World War II office building a block from Pennsylvania Avenue below the U.S. Capitol.

In his administrative offices on the third floor, employment services director Ivanhoe Donaldson was told about the commotion. Donaldson was weary. Barry had installed him as employment chief, but instead of curing unemployment, Donaldson the activist found himself swimming in a bureaucratic sea, drowning on paperwork and daily crises, such as cafeteria workers storming his building and demanding long-overdue summer unemployment checks. He dispatched this one quickly by telling agency controller James George to write checks immediately from the Special Administrative Fund.

Donaldson had gone to great lengths to keep control of the Special Administrative Fund when he took over the agency. Kept in a First American Bank account, the unaudited revolving account was replenished by penalties on employers late in paying unemployment insurance fees. The resulting fund was supposed to go for emergency payments to eligible unemployed District residents in desperate need of cash, such as the cafeteria workers. The checks bore no official insignia or telltale government green.

A day later, accountant Haridis Unni posted the agency checks in his ledger, but he couldn't account for two checks made out to a Judy Richardson for $1,800 and $4,400. He made a note to review the checks when they cleared the bank. Judy Richardson didn't even live in the District, but she was a soul mate of Donaldson's from the SNCC days. She didn't know about the checks, which Donaldson cashed to pay his own bills.

That same month, Ivanhoe Donaldson called Charles Cobb, another close friend from SNCC. He and Ivanhoe had organized small towns in Mississippi and had maintained an unquestioned bond. Donaldson met Cobb at the First American branch and presented him with a check in Cobb's name for $6,200. Cobb deposited it into his personal account. The next day, the two men returned. Cobb withdrew $5,600 and gave it in cash to Donaldson. He trusted Donaldson implicitly and asked no questions. In similar transactions with Richardson, Cobb, and other unwitting friends, Ivanhoe Donaldson had embezzled $27,145 in five months from the emergency fund that became his personal slush fund.

Donaldson's lifestyle did not seem extravagant, but it was. He dined at the city's expensive restaurants, places where the business crowd ate on expense accounts, including Jean-Pierre, Duke Ziebert's, Joe & Mo's, Mel Krupin's. His Mercedes cost $30,000. He wore expensive, tailored suits and clothes from a Georgetown tailor that cost thousands. And Donaldson was generous, too. He would lend money to friends and hold expensive Christmas parties every year for poor children and orphans. His wife, Winifred, also worked for the government, but their salaries couldn't cover their expenses. As early as 1977, Donaldson had trouble paying the $550-a-month mortgage on his condominium, and over the years he regularly received dunning letters from his banks. He was too proud to ask friends for help.

At the Department of Employment Services, the series of unusual checks continued with little notice, except for bookkeeping entries by Haridis Unni: For each check Unni would ask his boss, controller James George, how it should be noted in the agency's ledgers. After a while, the answer was shortened to just two words.

"Expense it." Unni did.

Washington's red-light district in the early 1980s consisted of a one-block stretch of strip joints along Fourteenth Street below Franklin Square. It was minuscule compared to Boston's Combat Zone or the Tenderloin in San Francisco, but it was seedy just the same. The pimps and prostitutes would hang out in the square; porno shops and bars like the Golden Butterfly and This Is It? lined the street to the south.

At the height of the 1981 Christmas season, a dark-blue Lincoln Continental pulled up to This Is It? and idled by the curb. It was the mayor's official vehicle, and it was beginning to show up in odd places, like the Howard University dorms and apartment houses in Dupont Circle. The mayor got out of the car and walked in the front door of the bar. Herb Cole, the owner, had invited him to the strip joint's annual Christmas party. Word on the street was that strippers serviced Barry below the table, and he snorted cocaine from the top.

Three months later, on March 29, 1982, three women who worked at This Is It? corroborated the report in statements to police. Police Inspector Fred Raines, a black official who headed the intelligence division, took the report straight to the FBI and the Justice Department. The federal officials kicked it back to the police department, where it died and then leaked to the mayor. Barry ordered Police Chief Maurice Turner to bounce Raines back to night supervisor. The message was clear to other officers: Don't cross Barry.

Barry was desperate to keep that message from getting to his political supporters, because he was beginning to turn his full attention to campaigning for another four-year term.

He went back to his original base and invited liberal icon Joe Rauh to lunch at the Blue Mirror, a well-worn luncheonette across Pennsylvania Avenue from the District Building. Rauh's endorsement had been important in 1978 and would be for the coming 1982 campaign.

"Joe, you were with me in '78," Barry said, "and I need you even more against Pat Harris. It'll be another tough battle."

"I have some problems," Rauh replied. "I don't like these stories about your carrying on with women and getting involved with drugs. Is any of it true?"

"C'mon, Joe," Barry said. "You know me. You can't believe what you hear on the street. I'm clean."

Rauh wanted to believe Barry, and did.

Patricia Roberts Harris, a light-skinned African-American with an aristocratic bearing and national connections, thought she could waltz into the mayor's office, but her credentials became a burden. Even at her confirmation hearing to be secretary of Jimmy Carter's Department of Housing and Urban Development, Senator William Proxmire of Wisconsin said that HUD "needs someone sympathetic to the problems of the poor," rather than an elitist.

"You do not understand who I am," she bristled. "I am a black woman who even eight years ago could not buy a house in parts of the District. I didn't start out as a member of a prestigious law firm but as a woman who needed a scholarship to go to school. If you think I have forgotten that, you are wrong."

It was easy to get the impression that Harris was of the upper crust. Born in Matoon, Illinois, in 1925, the daughter of a Pullman car waiter, she came to the capital in 1940 to attend Howard University, earned a law degree from George Washington University, and served as ambassador to Luxembourg and later deputy U.S. delegate to the United Nations in the Johnson administration. She was dean of Howard University's law school for a brief time and spent the early 1970s in the politically potent law firm of Fried, Frank, Harris, Shriver, and Kampelman. In 1976 President Carter appointed her secretary of housing and urban development.

But Harris's resume was weak in local Washington politics, and she hadn't paid any Delta dues. During the civil rights movement, she was getting a law degree and leading the pampered life of a diplomat. When Washington was burning in 1968, she was at the United Nations. Harris lived in the city but was not of the city. Like such prominent blacks as Vernon Jordan, former head of the National Urban League, she had made a legal and social career of working in the highest levels of white American politics rather than the scruffy beat of local politics.

The background made her the darling of white voters west of Rock Creek Park, who were disillusioned because Barry was not the reformer they had dreamed of. The hometown black bourgeoisie still resented the usurpation of their government by Barry's civil rights crowd. They wanted to take the city back. Two black aristocrats urged Harris to run and managed her campaign: Sharon Pratt Dixon, daughter of a judge and former wife of the city council chairman, and socially connected Charles Duncan, Walter Washington's corporation counsel.

By early 1982 Harris had lined up enough support to consider a run. Four city council members also were running, but the race quickly became a contest between Barry and Harris.

Dressed in black tie and tuxedo, the mayor bellied up to the bar in a ballroom of the Sheraton Hotel in February when a reporter asked if he was worried about the Pat Harris challenge. Barry said he was glad that she was running, that he would "beat her ass" and show the media who was boss.

The mayor was attending the Board of Trade's midwinter dinner, an extravagant annual gathering of the city's local power elite: the bankers, the big developers and retailers, the corporate lawyers, public relations executives, and the politicians. Fat cigars and stiff drinks were in vogue for the night. Barry had been drinking scotch on the rocks. The topic turned to fundraising, and Barry said the money's rolling in. Zoning lawyer Robert Linowes had told him that many would contribute only for business reasons, and they still didn't like him. Barry looked around the room and admitted the only reason he was in the room was that he was the mayor. But it didn't matter if the suits liked him or not—just so they paid up at campaign time.

The press, according to Barry, had been all wrong in reporting on the city. No one really cared about the city budget or the financial management system. People just wanted services. And few people cared that he might be cheating on his wife or doing drugs, unless he became a hypocrite and started to crack down on junkies at the same time that people saw him doing drugs. What about the women who felt that he was embarrassing Effi? Barry recounted that a white woman from Ward 3 had told him that he had a reputation for sleeping with every woman old enough to say yes; he told her it was a private matter. But will women, the reporter asked, who vote in great numbers, vote against him? Barry reeled off his top female appointees—Gladys Mack, Carolyn Smith, Judith Rogers—who would say that he'd done more for women than any other mayor.

People vote out of self-interest, the mayor explained, and he looked at Leonard "Bud" Doggett, a straitlaced, white-haired, parking lot magnate and powerhouse at the Board of Trade. The white businessmen make campaign contributions to whoever can help them make money. The people in public housing are going to vote for the politician who will fix their stoves and clean up their buildings. In his view those people really didn't care about the budget or about reporters investigating reports that he used drugs or writing that his ex-wife was cheating Pride while she was driving a Jaguar and living in the Watergate. They care about crime, he said, and if they felt that he'd put the heat on criminals, they would vote for him.

By big margins, he added, and walked off to schmooze his contributors.

The mayor based his prediction on the three legs of his young political machine: campaign money from the business community, power and votes from the churches, and the loyalty that derives from political patronage. He was the first politician to make players out of Washingtonians who were used to being bystanders to power.

He began by courting the city's powerful black ministers. The majority of black Washingtonians hailed from a southern tradition steeped in the rituals and social life of the church and guided by their powerful pastors. The city's leading ministers were household names—such as Bishop Smallwood Williams of Bibleway Church, Bishop Walter McCollough of the United House of Prayer for All People, and the Reverend Henry Gregory of Shiloh Baptist Church—and they would make perfect spiritual ward heelers. Barry wooed them with special clergy license plates, invited them to high-profile meetings at the District Building, and showcased them at an annual citywide prayer breakfast. Most important, Barry put millions of dollars at the disposal of the ministers to fund church-based day-care centers, senior-citizen meals programs, and job-training efforts. He freed city land and low-cost loans for them to build subsidized housing and food stores. The city funds served the community and also served to blunt criticism of Barry's personal lifestyle.

The mayor also rewarded friends and mollified enemies with appointments to the two thousand seats on city boards and commissions. Appointees screened by Betty King reflected the city's diversity and geographical sections. Barry dispensed carefully controlled constituent services, merging that office with his political apparatus under former campaign deputy Anita Bonds. She handled routine complaints on one hand, enforced political discipline with the other, and also bused adoring crowds to Barry's community meetings.

Barry lavished attention on the city's sizable senior-citizen population, a reliable source of votes. He sharply increased their budget and improved daily services. "He has them convinced they'll all starve if he's not mayor," fumed council member Betty Ann Kane, a white at-large member who wanted to be mayor. The city's vast fleet of recreation buses took them to community and religious gatherings, as well as to the polls.

The mayor took care of his major contributors, too. Stu Long, for example, was appointed to the Armory Board, a three-person governing body that runs the city's stadium and many of its big ticket sporting events, like the Washington Redskins games. For an up-and-coming restaurateur, it provided invaluable contacts.

The mayor deftly used the Minority Business Opportunity Commission to spread hundreds of millions of dollars in city contracts to firms controlled by blacks, Latinos, and women. Barry's aides also made sure that they reciprocated with community support and campaign contributions.

Routine city services, such as trash collection and street cleaning, began showing up regularly in black neighborhoods unaccustomed to it. Barry also opened new libraries and fire stations. City Administrator Elijah Rogers made the cumbersome bureaucracy work better than it ever had, though there remained plenty to complain about, like the water billing system. Barry dispatched Rogers to fix it, he did, and the incumbent was ready to run.

Harris kicked off her campaign on April 3, 1982, to the cheers of five hundred supporters at her headquarters on K Street in the heart of the downtown, and largely white, business district.

"Today," she said, "less than eight years after home rule, we look to our local government and ask what has gone wrong. Instead of answers we get alibis. And chief among those who give us alibis instead of answers is the mayor, who says he is not responsible for the failures of his government."

She started out on a high note, with approval ratings as high as 70 percent. She had the support of a few private-sector labor unions and Oliver Carr, only then beginning to establish himself as the city's most prominent real estate developer. But as soon as she hit the campaign trail, her weaknesses started to show. She was aloof in small groups, a mediocre speaker who tended to speak over her audiences, and didn't mix easily with crowds. To Washington's black middle class, she came off as a quintessential high yellow aristocrat. The campaign tried to blunt the elitist image with a poster showing Harris tenderly embracing a small black child.

"Pat Harris would no more touch that towhead than kiss Marion Barry," said school board member R. Calvin Lockridge, a maverick politician who supported Harris. "If they wanted to make Harris more black, it had the opposite effect."

Barry opened his campaign in the Ann Beers Elementary School in his predominantly black neighborhood in Southeast Washington, far from the downtown spot Harris chose to announce her campaign. With Effi, his twenty-one-month-old son Christopher, and his mother by his side, he was led into the auditorium by Ivanhoe Donaldson and preceded on the podium by John Hechinger.

"The road has not been easy," he said, striking a gospel tone. "We've made mistakes. We've learned from those mistakes."

He held himself out not as a good man, but as a flawed man trying to do good. The *Post* agreed and endorsed him.

"I have suffered a thousand wounds in trying to do right by the city," Barry told one candidate forum.

"It's true, Mr. Mayor, that you have suffered a thousand wounds," responded council member Charlene Drew Jarvis, who posed a minor challenge. "Unfortunately, they're all selfinflicted."

Beneath the rhetoric, the mayor bought votes the political way. He vowed never to lay off another city employee, a promise that ensured the ballots of thousands of bureaucrats and clerks, in addition to their extended families. And he promised to do more about crime in hopes of soothing the middle-class whites and blacks. "As long as I am mayor," he said, "we are not going to be locked in our homes in fear of criminals."

He even made a promise to Pat Harris at one candidate forum when he leaned over and said:

"I'm going to kick your ass."

Washingtonians went to the polls on September 14, 1982, and punched Barry's ticket in overwhelming numbers. He took nearly 60 percent of the vote, trouncing Harris 54,465 to 33,173. Harris won only Ward Three, receiving 54 percent to Barry's 34 percent. Every predominantly black precinct went for Barry by margins of more than two to one. He vanquished Harris even in her home area of upper- and middle-income communities of Ward Four. Two council members had dropped out and two others—Charlene Drew Jarvis and John Ray—together won less than 6 percent of the primary vote.

The results marked the total shift of Barry's electoral support from an integrated base in 1978 to one that relied on the black middle class and poor. In 1978 the white vote put him over the top; in 1982 it alone couldn't defeat him. With the biracial coalition went the civil rights movement's liberal dream of social change, of helping the less fortunate, of bringing the races together. In its place, Boss Barry began to emerge.

With the idealism went the team of civil rights veterans and top bureaucrats who gave Barry's first term its energy, its tone, and its efficiency.

City Administrator Elijah Rogers left early in the second term, leaving a void that never was filled. James Gibson soon returned to foundation work. Carroll Harvey abandoned the government in 1981.

Bitsy Folger, the wealthy white woman who raised so much money for Barry in 1978, left dispirited long before the second campaign.

Just after the first victory, she had given Barry one thousand dollars when he asked for money to take Effi on their delayed honeymoon to the islands. Two years later, *The Washington Post's* Bob Woodward was pursuing a tip that Barry was taking money to buy drugs, and he had heard of her thousand-dollar gift.

"Tell Woodward that I gave you the money and that's it," she told the mayor. "There was nothing illegal about it."

"Bitsy," Barry said, "if anything ever comes out I will totally deny that it ever happened."

Folger was shocked and felt betrayed. Woodward kept calling. She simply denied it. Finally, he gave up, and Folger left the Barry camp with her secret.

Likewise, Willard Wirtz left with a bad taste in his mouth. Barry had come to him early in the first term and asked him to take a post on the city's Public Employees Relations Board, an independent board that ruled on labor disputes. Wirtz turned him down twice but finally relented. He stayed on until the end of the first term.

"I discovered that he was getting to members of the board on certain cases through David Wilmot," Wirtz says. Wilmot was a lawyer, lobbyist, and nighttime friend of the mayor. "It was nothing illegal, just out of order. I talked to him and he promised to stop. It happened again, at which point I resigned."

What happened to the grand designs for a model urban government developed over years at the Potomac Institute?

"Early on we were solving problems right and left;" says Carroll Harvey. "But so many people started to court Marion, people who didn't share the same beliefs we all had of making life better for those who had the least. They were looking out for themselves. The government became directed by greed. I could say no to Marion, but nobody who came after me had that ability, that history going back to Pride."

Jim Gibson says the "party bunch" and general adulation got to Barry. "There was no vision, no energy, no plan," he says. "Everything was done in context of keeping Marion in power and maybe doing some good things along the way."

Harvey says that he contended constantly with Ivanhoe Donaldson, who wanted to help direct contracts. Their battles came to a head over millions of dollars' worth of contracts to build and operate the new convention center.

"The convention center," he says he once told Donaldson before leaving the government, "is a straight line to jail.

CHAPTER 8

GREED CITY

There are only two things for sale in Washington-the land
and the government.
—*Mark Plotkin, political analyst*

The dominant industry in Washington is the production, administration, and manipulation of laws and regulations. The government can support legions of lobbyists and more lawyers per capita than any other place in the country, but it doesn't foster the creation of great wealth. In Washington, the way to create a fortune is buying and selling property, and the time to trade it was in the 1980s, when Washington real estate turned to gold.

Jeffrey Cohen understood the game, and his timing was impeccable. He was consumed with making money even when he was a student at Sidwell Friends, the elite Quaker school that serves the city's diplomats, politicians, wealthy, and in 1993, First Daughter Chelsea Clinton. His buddies would go out drinking and driving on Saturday nights in the 1960s; Cohen would sit around with their fathers and talk stocks and bonds. He began buying and renovating brownstones around Dupont Circle while he was getting his law degree at Catholic University. He started putting together syndicates, and the deals got bigger and bigger. Before he was thirty, Cohen had borrowed money to buy stock in D.C. National Bank, sold it for a profit, and bought a controlling interest in the National Bank of Commerce. They called him the Boy Banker.

162 | DREAM CITY

In 1979 Cohen organized a group to buy the Parkside Hotel, a flophouse at Fourteenth and I streets NW, a hot corner in the city's red-light district below Franklin Square Park. Cohen paid nine hundred thousand dollars for the dilapidated building. He was speculating that the first wave of the impending development boom would jack up the hotel's value, so he could flip the property at double or triple his investment. Still, Cohen needed to make a few hundred thousand dollars a year to carry the property until it was ripe. He didn't want to run a flophouse.

Enter Marion Barry. The new mayor awarded Cohen a contract to shelter homeless families in the broken-down hotel for $507,000 a year, more than enough to cover the mortgage. Cohen agreed to provide the tenants with "a pleasant, emotionally inviting, and safe atmosphere." The building lacked a fire escape, but the city issued the required certificate of occupancy. Residents complained that plaster was falling from the ceilings, that there was no drinking water, that roaches and rats had the run of the place, and that whores still worked in and around the building.

"It's not the kind of neighborhood I'd want my kids playing in," Cohen told *The Washington Post* when the city sweetened Cohen's contract by $23,000 and made it $530,000 for another year.

Meanwhile, he and his partners bought up a few surrounding buildings, including three strip joints. In 1985 Cohen's group flipped the Parkside Hotel and the adjacent buildings to Texas megadeveloper Trammell Crow for $12 million. Trammell Crow bought some adjoining property, held on to it for less than two years, and sold out to Manulife Real Estate, a huge Canadian developer, for $39 million. The Canadians actually put up a gleaming, glass-walled office complex where the flophouse had once stood.

What happened at the corner of Fourteenth and I streets was part of a pattern of speculation and development—laced with-politics—that transformed Washington's central business district and electrified the capital's sleepy lifestyle.

In 1980 the city's bureaucrats, lobbyists, and lawyers worked out of boxy; nondescript buildings, drove American cars, ate at hotel restaurants for a good time, and went to bed with the late news. Five years later, Washington was the hottest real estate market in the world, and the trappings of new wealth had put a glitzy facade on the company town. Investors invaded in waves. First came the carpetbaggers from Texas and Boston. Then came the British, the Dutch, and finally the Japanese, who swept in and gobbled up a dozen pieces of property in two years.

The sudden makeover could have happened only in the American capital city. It was stimulated, in part, by the tax and lending laws of the day, and it was sustained by the demand for office space to house the lawyers and lobbyists who flocked to serve the Reagan administration. But what made Washington into a high-stakes Monopoly board was the foreign money. International investors loved buying ground in the capital. They liked the federal law that limited building heights in the city to 160 feet because it made for a low-profile city of eight- to twelve-story buildings, much like Europe's capitals. But the height limitation also made the land more precious and valuable. Since you couldn't build up, there was a finite amount of building space—especially in the hottest development zone, between the White House and the Capitol. All the foreigners, but especially the Japanese, felt much more secure buying property in the capital city than, say, Philadelphia or Boston or Chicago.

The boom's outer waves turned suburban towns and farmland into small cities, such as Bethesda in Maryland, and Tyson's Corner and Ballston in Virginia. The entire metropolitan area became a corporate mecca. Mobil Corporation moved from suburban New York to Virginia's Fairfax County, and other major companies followed suit. By 1986, the Washington region had solidified its standing as the wealthiest metropolitan area in the nation. The average annual household income rose to $47,250, compared to a national average of $33,250. But unlike cities such as Detroit that suffered at the expense of the outlying growth, downtown Washington came alive with new buildings, restaurants, shops, and clubs.

In the space of four years, the District's real estate boom created a new caste of homegrown millionaires. Second-generation Jews whose fathers had bought downtown land for a song in the 1950s suddenly were moguls atop $100 million real estate portfolios. Entrepreneurs feasted on the fast money. Jimmy Moshovitis, a Greek whose father owned the Bell Restaurant on Twelfth Street, parlayed the profits from the sale of the building into a multimillion-dollar portfolio in less than a decade. Jim and Ted Pedas started with the small Circle Theater in 1970 and built a $150 million movie and real estate empire. Dominic Antonelli came to town penniless and built a multimillion-dollar parking and development empire. Brokers who fled the Houston real estate bust for the gold in Washington were pulling down six-figure fees. Bankers were throwing money at developers, who took the cash and bought more property.

The new wealth started to pour into the city just as Marion Barry took office. Revenues from commercial property taxes doubled and then tripled. The question became bow the new black political structure could ensure that the city's African-American community shared in the economic boom. Achieving economic power was supposed to be the second phase of the civil rights movement. The white business structure had accumulated economic power for two hundred years; it would not relinquish it unless the blacks forced the issue.

"Blacks in politics should see to it that more economic power is distributed to the black community," Barry told *Black Enterprise* magazine. "I feel that my job is to see to it that this power is achieved."

Although the mayor took full credit for the massive redevelopment of downtown, he was actually the passive beneficiary of a planning process that was put into place by Richard Nixon, of the spiffy new Metro system that began operating just when Barry took office, and of global market forces that were beyond his control. But Barry does deserve some credit, including naming James Gibson as his first planning director.

Gibson had been an architect of Barry's rise to power, but he was also uniquely trained in the use of power on the municipal level. He knew the planning and zoning issues in Washington because he had served on the National Capital Planning Commission since President Johnson appointed him in 1968. He believed it could be a simple transfer of wealth.

"You accept the political transaction as legitimate," he says. "Let the developers build, and use the commercial tax revenues for social programs."

It was Gibson who saw the potential in moving the central business district to the east, into the one hundred city blocks immediately north of Pennsylvania Avenue between the White House and the Capitol. This was the city's historic business district that had evolved from the Central Market at Seventh and Pennsylvania Avenue in the nineteenth century. The federal government bulldozed the market to make room for the bureaucracy, but the commercial district lived just to the north. Before 1980 it was a neighborhood of townhouse storefronts: millineries; pawnshops and print shops; hometown restaurants, such as Reeves Coffee Shop, which served up the best strawberry shortcake in the city, and Whitlow's Diner, which did the same with meatloaf. It was the only remaining part of downtown that had character and a sense of tradition. Developers associated the area with the riots and a poorer black clientele. Gibson deemed it expendable.

Speculators and developers bought up at least ten entire city blocks after 1982. Wrecking balls leveled the old structures in a matter of weeks, and builders erected new office buildings at a record-breaking clip. In the late 1970s developers put up an average of 2 million square feet of office space a year. In 1985 they constructed 11 million square feet, and 12 million the following year. Ten new hotels went up at the same time. Only New York and Los Angeles, cities with populations ten times Washington's, outstripped Washington's pace, and not by much, in part because the federal government fueled the capital's growth.

Back in 1961, John F. Kennedy had remarked on the dowdiness of Pennsylvania Avenue east of Thirteenth Street during his inaugural parade, and he wanted to restore the avenue's grandeur. His aides, particularly Daniel Patrick Moynihan, pursued the idea. Richard Nixon in 1972 finally persuaded Congress to establish the Pennsylvania Avenue Development Corporation, which became the engine of development for Washington's East End. PADC was a quasi-public corporation that had the power to target development sites along the avenue and adjacent blocks to the north, buy the necessary land, and pick the developers. It started the work immediately, but it wasn't until 1978 and 1979—just as Barry became mayor—that the first buildings came under construction and helped trigger the development boom to the north.

Gibson's post as planning director put him on the PADC board, and he soon had an ally. Max Berry asked the mayor to recommend him for PADC chairman. Berry used his Democratic party connections to wire the appointment, and President Carter nominated him for the job in 1979. With Berry and Gibson at the levers, PADC hired developers to restore the historic Willard Hotel and the National Press Building astride Fourteenth Street, redeveloped buildings down toward the Capitol, and stockpiled property for future deals. The new downtown's southern boundary was coming into place.

"We changed the atmosphere from 'can't do' to 'can do',"Gibson says. "It was a matter of pulling away impediments to development."

Cutting the city's red tape certainly helped the white pillars of the Board of Trade and other captains of local commerce who owned much of the land in the new development zone. But if the city's true economic power was equity in real estate deals, how could blacks get a seat at the table when the redevelopment deals were struck?

The city owned some choice pieces of property, especially over the downtown stations of the new Metro system. Barry controlled the Redevelopment Land Agency (RLA), which controlled the property and chose the development teams. The mayor and Gibson, with prodding from Ivanhoe Donaldson, established strict guidelines requiring developers to take on minority partners, even if the minority partners put up little or no cash. The city then gave away the land.

In 1980 the city sold a parcel over Metro Center, the subway's central crossroads, to Bethesda developer Nathan Landow and his minority partner, Robert Washington. The price was $2.5 million, or $133 a square foot, when other downtown property was going for $500 a square foot. Washington was the city's Democratic party chairman at the time and had just returned from a trip to Africa with the mayor. Likewise, the city was asking $51.6 million for another site near Metro Center. Oliver Carr and his minority partner, Ted Hagans, bought it for $37 million. Hagans, who had contributed heavily to Barry's campaign, then convinced the city to reduce the price to $14.5 million in return for a speculative share in the profits.

The trademark deal of the era was Gallery Place, a choice parcel on Seventh Street across from the National Portrait Gallery. A consortium of black bankers and businessmen organized a joint venture with developer Melvin Lenkin. In exchange for a low price, they promised to build offices, a hotel, shops, and apartments for low-income residents. William R Fitzgerald, president of Independence Federal Savings and Loan, described the deal before the Redevelopment Land Agency on October 15, 1979.

"In our situation," he testified, "we decided that the time had come, the atmosphere was proper and just and right that we no longer just sit at the lunch counter, that we own some lunch counters. So we formed the joint venture." They struck a deal with Lenkin because "they would be a member of our team, there would be no master/

slave relationship but it would be a marriage and a partnership, but we would be in control."

Bill Fitzgerald was a slick, angular banker with a thin mustache and a nose for the right political connections. He had put First Lady Effi Barry on his board of directors and had given the Barrys the sweetheart deal on their home mortgage. He also joined a regular poker game with the mayor, whom he'd denigrated as a 'Bama a year earlier. His development team also included Delano Lewis, the up-and-coming phone company executive whose support helped put Barry in office. The RLA awarded the Gallery Place development rights to Fitzgerald's group. In July 1981, with downtown land prices skyrocketing, the city sold the tract to the partners at approximately half its value. The RLA's own valuation put the fair market value at $31 million; Fitzgerald paid $17 million.

At the outset, despite the political overtones, the Gallery Place venture was a good example of how to redistribute equity. The minority partners put up significant cash stakes. Fitzgerald and attorney James Cobb each invested twenty-five thousand dollars. All told, the thirteen minority partners controlled 55 percent of the deal. But a decade later not a spade of dirt had been turned, the grand notion of building apartments was history, and Gallery Place was dead in the water. Though Fitzgerald promised the RLA in 1979 that the minority partners would never "divest our selves of our interests and control," the original partnership sold out to Oliver Carr, the city's biggest developer.

What started as an attempt to broaden the economic base of the city soon proved to be a rich source of political favors. The city would sell land at fire-sale prices to development teams that boasted minority partners, who always seemed to be the same people with strong social and political connections to Marion Barry. The U.S. Department of Housing and Urban Development said that the city was giving away its assets. Still, a white zoning attorney who was involved with a number of these deals said that Washington was remarkably free of the raw forms of bribery, kickbacks, and payoffs that he said were the cost of doing business in cities such as Philadelphia and Baltimore. Out-of-town builders would ask, "Who do I have to pay and how much will it cost?" But that's not the way the game was played in the District.

"The bribe was on the table," said one developer. "To develop city property you had to give a big piece of the deal to minorities, and that didn't mean Hispanics—it meant blacks. But what's the big surprise? Every ethnic group takes care of its own first. Blacks were simply asking, 'Where's mine?' "

The problem with Barry's version of the spoils system was that he always spread them to the same people.

"I call them the chosen ones," said John Wilson, whose Ward Two council district encompassed downtown. "What started out to benefit the minority community at large has meant some politically influential blacks can move out to posh suburbs like McLean or Potomac."

The same disparity between principles and practice guided the Barry administration's minority contracting program.

When Walter Washington left office in January 1979, minority firms had only 7 percent of the city's contracts. In his first year in office, Barry promised to give 25 percent of the city's contracts to minorities, and he later upped the goal to 35 percent. In theory, it was the most ambitious minority-procurement program of any city in the nation.

In practice, it didn't work, especially at first.

Vincent Reed was superintendent of schools in 1979 when Barry took office. A conservative black educator who came to the District in 1955 from St. Louis, he had moved up slowly but steadily from teacher to principal to administrator and finally to superintendent in 1976. When Reed started to get huge bills for some school supplies, he asked for receipts and found that Ivanhoe Donaldson had changed suppliers for some basic items. Before Barry, the schools had been buying cornflakes for $8.00 a carton; Donaldson had signed a contract to pay $13.50. Reed called the District building and got Donaldson on the phone.

"We had a good deal," Reed told him. "Why did you change suppliers?"

"I wanted to buy from a black entrepreneur," Donaldson explained.

Likewise, the schools had been buying fuel oil from Steuart Petroleum at steady, low prices for years. Barry and Donaldson fired Steuart and gave the contract to Tri-Continental Industries, run by a Barry supporter named James Hillman. The cost of heating oil went up 25 percent. Then, during a particularly frigid spell in the winter of 1979, Tri-Con didn't deliver fuel for two days. Reed saw the Steuart trucks at other work as his schools start d to run out of oil. On the third day he stormed into City Administrator Elijah Rogers's office and said: "I'm going to close schools unless you get Steuart Petroleum to deliver oil tomorrow morning." Rogers requisitioned a check on the spot; Steuart delivered this oil, but Tri-Con kept the contract.

Similarly, Barry took the school system's trash contract from a white firm and gave it to an African-American concern that didn't own dumpsters. Reed's office was deluged with calls from principals complaining that bags of trash were piling up behind the schools and rats were moving in. But what really bothered Vince Reed was the inflated prices for food. He finally confronted Barry.

"I understand that you want to give contracts to black companies," Reed said, "but when you tell me to take food out of a black kid's stomach so some black dude can get rich, I have to ask what's your rationale?"

"Black entrepreneurs are at the top of my agenda," Barry responded. "We have to do it this way. It's the only way to get them into the mainstream."

Reed resigned before the end of 1980, in part because of the contracting policies.

Carroll Harvey was head of contracting for the entire city government at the time in his post as director of general services. He was fully behind the goal of minority contracting, but he also believed in the fundamental practices of competitive bidding. Donaldson would come to him with sole-source contract proposals that jacked up prices and Harvey rejected them. "I have to make sure that we're not paying a premium," he told Donaldson. According to Harvey, Donaldson wanted to enter leases and sign contracts only with politically connected people. It was his way of paying back political favors. Harvey fought him for two years.

"It went from helping a minority class to helping a few minority individuals," he says. "That's when I got off the boat."

Rewarding political allies with government contracts is standard operating procedure in municipal politics. One of the best-known examples was in Chicago, where Richard J. Daley and his Cook County machine controlled every appointment and every contract. But the difference between Barry's patronage and Daley's machine was that Daley's organization demanded that the cronies do the work, provide the service, complete the job. Barry rained contracts on his friends, asked little in return, and often looked the other way as they gouged millions of dollars in city funds without performing the services.

The most egregious examples were in housing and the treatment of the homeless, the most vulnerable and powerless people in the capital. Barry bestowed multimillion-dollar contracts on political friends, who overcharged the city for warehousing homeless families in broken-down motels and apartment buildings. The most notorious was the Pitts Motor Hotel, owned and operated by Cornelius Pitts.

Pitts was a beneficiary of the 1968 riots. When real estate prices plummeted after parts of the city burned, Pitts was able to buy a small hotel off Fifteenth Street. He leased some space to the city to house a few homeless families. When black politicians started to run for office in the early 1970s, Pitts made his hotel available for fundraisers, parties, and victory celebrations. Walter Fauntroy held his first victory party there, and Marion Barry celebrated his early elections compliments of Cornelius Pitts.

When the city put out bids in 1982 for hotels or apartments willing to house homeless families, Pitts won a $1 million contract to provide forty-eight rooms and board. The next year, the city didn't bother to put out a competitive bid and renewed the contract with an increase to $1.4 million for the same services, even though the number of homeless families had actually gone down. In 1984 voters passed Initiative 17, which gave the right to overnight shelter to every homeless person in the city, over Barry's strong opposition. The District became a magnet for homeless people in the region, and the number of families seeking shelter started to skyrocket. The Barry administration was totally unprepared, but Pitts was perfectly situated.

Cornelius Pitts put his entire fifty-two-room hotel into the homeless business in 1984, and increased the contract to $1.5 million for the rooms and 144 meals a day. A contract review committee analyzed the arrangement and realized that the city was paying more than three thousand dollars a month for each family just for the rooms, which were shabby at best and lacked cooking equipment. The meals cost another $12.48 per person, per day. The city had also agreed to lease office space from Pitts on the ground floor for an astounding rate of ninety-seven dollars a square foot. Prime office space on Pennsylvania Avenue with a view of the Capitol brought twenty-five dollars a square foot at the time. The city paid Pitts well, too. As part of the contract he and his wife received $327,000 over three years and hired a staff of thirty-one. Between 1985 and 1989, when the city added food contracts, Cornelius Pitts received approximately $16.4 million in contracts.

An analyst in the Department of Human Services called the Pitts budget "a travesty of the procurement negotiation process" in an internal memo written in June 1984. "By all indications," the analyst concluded, "the proposal is a set-up, based on 'this is what the mayor wants.'" The man who made sure Barry got what he wanted was David Rivers, the director of the human services department. Rivers was not an experienced administrator, but he was one of Barry's closest pals. The mayor called him "Deputy Dog" and partied into the

night at Rivers's Southwest townhouse, and Rivers protected the politically proper city contracts.

As the homeless problem got worse and the city started to spend
many more millions, more Barry cronies came to the trough. Roy
Littlejohn, a Barry supporter from the early days, had been on the
receiving end of millions of dollars in city contracting awards, but
his company had still gone bankrupt. He came back in 1987 to go
into the shelter business and opened two, Urban Shelters and the R
Street Shelter, with millions of dollars in contracts. He charged the
government twenty-eight hundred dollars per apartment per month
and furnished the small, dingy rooms with metal folding tables and
chairs, or nothing. A member of Barry's 1986 finance committee,
Ernest Green, got a $4.5 million food service contract to provide
meals to homeless shelters. He had no experience in the business and
got the contract without competition.

Barry lambasted President Ronald Reagan for the city's housing
and homeless problems, but more than twenty-three hundred public
housing units that could have housed the five hundred homeless families and others remained vacant. Barry never "took the boards off," as
promised. Instead, the federal government started withholding tens
of millions of dollars in housing rehabilitation funds because Barry's
government was too inept to spend it properly. The social service bureaucracy that overpaid Cornelius Pitts was in such disarray that it
also failed to file the necessary paperwork for federal reimbursement
due the city for its homeless programs. More millions were lost, and
the poor suffered.

Otis Troupe, the city auditor who documented the irregularities
and gouging in the homeless programs, explained the government's
lavishness to a congressional committee:

"The problem as I see it, in all too many agencies of our city's
government, is that the financial flexibility needed to carry out the
agency mission is too easily subverted to the agenda of greedy, corrupt, highly placed individuals...in a class of privileged political insiders. We create sole-source business opportunities for certain con-

tractors because that, quite frankly, is the way that the mayor and his cronies like it."

No matter how many millions of dollars in city contracts flowed to Barry's friends, it was chump change compared to the hundreds of millions of dollars that enriched the white community during the real estate boom.

"The mayor's friends got the crumbs," says a former city official.

The high-stakes development game was out of reach of virtually everyone in the black community, and was available only to a tiny percentage of the whites. All that they had to do was pay homage to Marion Barry by way of a simple transaction: campaign contributions. By the 1982 campaign, every real estate player had gotten the message and contributed mightily to Barry's war chest, which he used to destroy Patricia Roberts Harris. The last to fall in line was Oliver T. Carr.

On his way to becoming the city's premier developer, Carr putup office buildings in the less risky West End and made his first major mark downtown by renovating the Mills Building, which overlooks the Old Executive Office Building next to the White House. He was also the first to start snapping up land around Metro Center, and he was moving to control the rebounding East End when he ran into opposition from the Barry administration.

Carr didn't support Barry in 1978, but the mayor had helpedhim anyway. As a candidate for mayor, Barry had courted city preservationists by promising to save Rhodes Tavern, which had served as Washington's first city hall. As mayor, Barry switched and supported Carr's demolition of the squat corner building to make way for Carr's large Metropolitan Square project just across from the U.S. Treasury Building and with a commanding view of the White House. Then Carr slapped Barry in the face by becoming Patricia Roberts Harris's finance chairman in the 1982 campaign. After Harris lost, Carr tried to get back on the inside through an intermediary, zoning attorney and power broker Robert Linowes, who called Barry a few days after the decisive primary vote.

"I want you to call Ollie Carr," Linowes said. "I know you're mad at him, and you have a right to be, but I want you to patch it up."

"Fuck Ollie Carr," Barry said. "I don't need him."

But Carr needed Barry to help get the zoning for a building that would relocate the Hecht Company, a major downtown department store, to Metro Center. Linowes represented Hecht's owner, the May Company. Carr was suing the city because Barry had reneged on a zoning deal at the site.

"Just have lunch with him," Linowes said. "It won't kill you."

"Screw him," Barry said.

Jim Gibson was Carr's ally on the inside. He worked on Barry to meet with Carr. Ivanhoe Donaldson knew that Carr was the last best source of cash for whoever might be Barry's next opponent, and Donaldson also urged the mayor to make peace and neutralize him. So Barry reluctantly called Linowes to set up the lunch. They didn't like each other. Barry's style grated on Carr, who felt a kinship with the city's black aristocrats, and Barry knew Carr was holding his nose to deal with him. Nevertheless they agreed to the arrangement that made Barry's machine work: Carr wouldn't challenge Barry, he would contribute to his campaigns and also serve on city commissions. In return, Barry cleared the path for Carr's developments.

Carr had a voracious appetite for downtown land, and for a short time he and a few local developers consumed at a leisurely pace, until foreign competition got tougher. The British had begun buying buildings back in 1977, but after 1982 they poured cash into the capital. During the next two years, investors from England bought ten major properties for approximately $300 million. The run-up in real estate values they started in turn touched off a frenzy of speculation. Downtown property that had been selling for a few hundred dollars a square foot breached one thousand dollars in a matter of three years. The Dutch followed the British in the mid-1980s and bought some choice property on Pennsylvania Avenue. Before 1985 the Japanese had yet to buy one piece of property; by early 1987 they had inhaled a dozen properties at inflated prices for a total investment of more than $400 million. Canadian companies joined the feast, and downtown D.C. became the capital's equivalent of Wall Street when junk bonds were king.

For the most part, foreign investors just wanted to buy standing buildings, but the developers from Texas, Massachusetts, and Canada came to compete with Carr in the game of buying up blocks of property and replacing dozens of small storefronts with gargantuan, block-sized office complexes. Besides ratcheting up the competition and the price of property, the Texas crew brought a new standard of style and quality to its developments. Houston developer Gerald Hines, for instance, hired distinguished architects such as I. M. Pei and Philip Johnson to design his projects. The local developers had to keep pace, and the result was a slick, postmodern veneer superimposed on the once dowdy downtown.

The Washington business community reaped the benefits of all the activity. Carr was worth more than $100 million, and five other local developers were in his league. Another fifteen to twenty businessmen and real estate professionals had built personal fortunes in excess of $50 million from downtown development. The real estate boom made dozens of new millionaires. Developers built palaces for themselves in the suburbs and second homes in Aspen; they bought Ferrari Testarossas and fifty-foot yachts. Zoning lawyers like Linowes helped wire the deals for a piece of the action. Linowes was an exception to the rule: He also donated his time and energies to civic projects; most took the money and ran.

These newly wealthy white Washingtonians inhabited a privileged world, almost as segregated as in the days of Jim Crow.

In harsh contrast, Washington's black business districts along Georgia Avenue in Northwest, neighborhoods across the Anacostia River in Southeast, and the H Street corridor in Northeast remained stagnant. More than twenty years after the riots, parts of H Street still showed signs of the weekend of burning and looting. To his credit, Barry chose the corner of Fourteenth and U streets, where the riots began, to build a new municipal center, and he seeded development along H Street with city offices, too. But even here, Barry's efforts were hampered by cronyism, and white commercial developers declined to invest in the areas.

The only white developer who tried to bridge the gap between Washington's two worlds was Jeffrey Cohen, and he did it by attempting a major redevelopment in the Shaw neighborhood.

Like his deal at the Parkside Hotel, the Shaw project was a mix of politics and profit. It began with Cohen buying up dilapidated brownstones on the cheap in hopes that he could make a killing in a speculative market. But midway through the buying spree, Cohen said that his real purpose was to restore Shaw to its former place as the mecca for Washington's black culture. He portrayed himself as the white knight of the black ghetto.

Cohen first scored on the abandoned Children's Hospital building at Thirteenth and V streets NW. He and a few partners had bought it for $5 million in 1978 and promised to build a new rehabilitation hospital that would "rival the Mayo Clinic" and bring new jobs to Shaw. Cohen applied for the necessary certificate of need from the city, but the staff of the D.C. State Health Planning and Development Agency said that the city didn't need a new rehabilitation hospital. The deal was in jeopardy until Barry stepped in and recommended that the certificate be okayed. In the fall of 1981, the city gave Cohen the green light to build a 240-bed hospital.

At the time, Cohen and the mayor were cementing their personal ties. Barry gave Cohen the honor of being a godfather to his son, Christopher. The Barrys started vacationing with the Cohens in Jamaica, at their summer home in Rehoboth, Delaware, and their vacation house in Nantucket. Cohen also used his banking connections to curry favor with other city officials—for example, walking them into the bank president's office to negotiate a car loan. He took special care of Ivanhoe Donaldson by recommending him for loans and seeing that they were extended.

Cohen never built the rehabilitation hospital. Instead, he sold the coveted certificate of need to the Washington Hospital Center for $8.7 million. As part of the deal Cohen's group received $5.7 million in architectural and legal fees. In all, Cohen's group made $14.4 million for not building the hospital. Shaw got no jobs and no nearby health-care facility. Cohen then turned around and sold the Children's Hospital property to the city for $5.8 million, for an $800,000 profit on the land.

By late 1984 Cohen had bought up more than $10 million worth of property in Shaw. He was having trouble carrying all the debt, and the speculative wave that he had hoped for was still years away. Bankers were beginning to pressure him for $7 million in overdue loans. By way of a creative bailout, he designed a huge project that would combine low-cost apartments, office space, and retail shops. He dubbed it Samuel Jackson Plaza, named after a deceased local activist. Cohen put together a limited partnership of investors—many of whom were the usual politically connected suspects—and a non-profit community group. Then he got the city to take out the banks. In a complex transaction, the city paid $12.5 million for the partnership's land. Of that, nearly $7 million was used to pay off Cohen's debt and $4 million to pay his legal fees.

The deal was struck on February 1, 1985. At his monthly news conference three weeks later, Barry claimed that he had steered clear of the negotiations.

"I've demonstrated in my twenty years of public service in this town that we don't mix up friendships and business-ship," the mayor said, adding that he didn't even know his close friend owned other land in the Shaw area. "The only piece of property I knew he owned was Children's Hospital. I was shocked. I didn't know he had all that money, quite frankly."

A few months later Cohen invited Barry, his wife Effi, and his son Christopher to his $4 million beachfront home in Nantucket. It wasn't the mayor's first visit there. Cohen took Barry for a stroll down the main street one day to show him a small commercial building that he was in the process of buying with some partners. Barry asked if he could invest. Cohen said that it would look bad if the press found out.

"Fuck *The Washington Post*," Barry said.

"Easy for youto say from here," Cohen responded, "but you have to live with it."

Cohen says that he vacillated over the deal, but he eventually agreed to make Barry a 10 percent partner in the $1 million building for the sake of Barry's son Christopher. Cohen then created a dummy corporation to hide Barry's stake.

Four months later, on December 2, 1985, the mayor sent city council chairman David Clarke a bill that would float $9 million in tax-exempt bonds for Cohen to use in the renovation of the Manhattan Laundry, a sturdy structure that Cohen wanted to turn into offices for himself. The bond passed, and once again the city picked up Jeffrey Cohen's tab.

CHAPTER 9

WHITE POWER

You don't get into a fight with the prosecutor over who has the bigger dick.
—Courtland Cox, SNCC activist and Barry insider

Pennsylvania Avenue between the White House and the Capitol is America's power corridor. The executive and legislative branches of government are balanced at each end. Midway between the two, straddling the avenue on two square blocks be tween Ninth and Tenth streets, the long arm of the national law reaches from two squat buildings. The FBI Building sits on the north side of the street; the buff-colored Justice Department faces it to the south. Any challenge to the domestic national interest—whether real or perceived, criminal or political—usually comes up against the lawmen within FBI and Justice.

On February 23, 1985, Marion Barry slid into the backseat of his dark-blue Lincoln Town Car to ride the five blocks from the District Building at Fourteenth and Pennsylvania to the Justice Department, where he rendezvoused with Jeffrey Cohen. They were there to attend the swearing-in of Edwin Meese III as attorney general, an intimate affair followed by a small reception. It may have seemed peculiar that the Democratic mayor of the capital, who was even at that time under heavy scrutiny by the Justice Department, would attend a ceremony for the Reagan administration's conservative standard bearer, but Jeffrey Cohen's connections reached right to the White House.

Cohen's key to Republican power came through his association with E. Bob Wallach, a San Francisco lawyer who was an old friend of Meese' s. Wallach would eventually be indicted in the Wedtech military contracting scandal and smear Meese in the process, but in 1985 he was Cohen's conduit to raw power. In a complex web that developed during the early 1980s, Wallach invested in Cohen's Washington real estate deals; Cohen helped get bank loans for Meese; and Meese gave Cohen and Barry entree into the White House. Using those connections, the mayor visited Meese at least once when he was counselor to the president in 1984 to lobby him on home-rule issues.

Meese had his own reasons to have Marion Barry by his side. The new attorney general was trying to blunt his image as a rightwing ideologue who was insensitive to blacks. For his part, Barry thought that it enhanced his power to be seen with the nation's new chief law enforcement official. But Barry had an ulterior motive. He hoped that his mere presence that day in early 1985 might have some influence on the Justice Department investigation that was closing in on his closest political adviser and friend—Ivanhoe Donaldson.

By 1984, Donaldson had become an accomplished thief.

Since he had first started embezzling city funds in 1981, his need for cash had grown with his lavish lifestyle. His $63,700 government salary simply couldn't cover the cost of his expensive taste and his various business ventures.

Barry had appointed Donaldson deputy mayor for economic development, a crucial position .in a city crying out for jobs and new business. Donaldson used it to wring cash from the government. Shortly after taking the job he ordered the employment services agency to hire a friend as a consultant, even though she'd moved to California to take another job. When the city issued two checks amounting to $16,500, Donaldson forged her name on the backs and deposited the funds in his personal account.

Donaldson then tapped into a computer services contract held by another friend, Marion "Duke" Green, a prominent, self-made businessman. Donaldson asked Green to write a $20,000 check for Judy Richardson, whom he described as a contractor in need of a quick payment. Green would be reimbursed, Donaldson promised, by increasing the amount of a separate city contract Green's company held. Green objected, but wrote the check. Richardson deposited it in her account and then wrote three personal checks to Donaldson. When Duke Green pressed for the paperwork to justify the transaction, Donaldson erupted.

"I don't understand why you're raising all this hell about it," Donaldson said as they were having lunch one day. "You can't even write a check—white boys in your company running your goddamn company and they're going to have questions about your writing a check?"

Donaldson was a bully, but Duke Green was no patsy. He had arrived in Washington fifteen years before with five hundred dollars to his name and lived in his car until he found work. He had built a computer consulting and software company called IBS that was doing millions of dollars' worth of work for the federal and local governments.

"In my business," Green told Donaldson, "I run it the way I want to run it because it's my two testicles on the chopping block, and nobody's going to stand up and take care of me. I have to make sure that my company runs right-and I run it right."

Donaldson kept putting him off, but Green demanded the documents that spelled out Richardson's contract. Eventually, Donaldson produced doctored paperwork to satisfy him and reimbursed him with money from the Special Administrative Fund, his personal slush fund in the employment services department.

No one dared question Donaldson's use of the funds. He was abusive to bureaucrats, and they were fearful of his wrath and mindful of his kinship with the mayor. Dave Eaton called him "Little Mussolini." Thomas Doyle, a controller who oversaw the fund, once steeled his nerve and went over the heads of agency officials to question Donaldson about his casual use of the account. "This is my account," Donaldson said, "don't mess withit." Doyle was later moved to another job.

When stealing wouldn't cover his debts, Donaldson found willing lenders, especially at the National Bank of Commerce, which was owned in part by Jeffrey Cohen. Donaldson borrowed $8,500 early in 1983 and promptly missed his first quarterly payment. Against the objection of the bank's lending officers, Cohen approved an extension of Donaldson's overdue loan into a new $78,000 loan backed by a third mortgage on his apartment. Cohen then gave his "personal, verbal guarantee" to another bank that granted an additional $45,000 bridge loan to Donaldson, who again missed the first quarterly payment.

At the time, Cohen was in the midst of organizing the complex refinancing of his real estate investments in Shaw that would result in a $12.5 million city bailout. When investigators later asked Cohen about the Donaldson loans, he said that "the loan looked good on the bank's record for community investment, in view of Donaldson's high visibility in the community." At one point, Donaldson's pile of debts unnerved Cohen, and he warned Barry that Donaldson's finances could embarrass the administration. Barry reported to Donaldson, who turned around and cursed Cohen for daring to bring his financial problems before the mayor.

In late 1983 Donaldson was ready to leave the government. Black businessmen were pulling down hefty salaries in the private sector. Elijah Rogers, for example, quit the government earlier in the year to take a high-paying job with Grant Thornton, a national accounting firm that had done substantial city business. Barry later appointed Rogers to the newly created regional airport authority, which undertook a $700 million public works expansion—the largest since the construction of the Metro subway system. That fall, Donaldson became a vice-president in the local office of E. F. Hutton and Company. His salary jumped to $140,000, but he was still in too deep, and he was still powerful enough to embezzle government funds from the outside.

Mary Treadwell was suffering the consequences of her mismanagement of Pride, Inc. In early 1984, she stood before U.S. District Judge John Garrett Penn and pleaded for leniency.

"I have done nothing wrong," she told the judge. Then the once strong woman in Marion Barry's life broke down and wept. "I am totally innocent. Please let me do free community service."

Marion Barry's ex-wife had been indicted in 1982 on charges of stealing and misappropriating thousands of dollars from federally funded, low-income housing projects that she and others had managed through a Pride affiliate. Prosecutors charged that she allowed the Clifton Terrace Apartments to turn into rat-infested hellholes while she siphoned money to keep up her apartment in the luxurious Watergate complex and her Jaguar coupe. Barry had escaped blame because he was not running Pride when the alleged misdeeds took place. After a long trial in the summer of 1983, a jury acquitted Treadwell of most counts but convicted her of conspiracy. In January 1984 she faced Judge Penn, who sentenced her to a three-year prison term, fined her forty thousand dollars, and gave her five years' probation upon release.

Outside the courthouse a short, broad-shouldered man with dark, thinning hair, a thick mustache, and deep, intense eyes stepped up to the microphones and television cameras. "This crime was a serious one and needed to be punished," he said. "Even today, there was not one iota of remorse. She is still recalcitrant and unrepentant."

It was the debut of Joseph E. DiGenova, the pugnacious new U.S. attorney for the District of Columbia. At thirty-nine, he was one of the youngest men to take on the job as the capital's top law-enforcement officer. The job came with an extensive mandate: From his office a block from police headquarters, DiGenova's prosecutors handled all the national and international cases from the local FBI office in addition to the District's criminal cases.

Joe DiGenova was appointed by President Reagan, but he was by no means a Reaganite. He had graduated from Georgetown Law School in 1970, served as a prosecutor in the District from 1972 to 1975, and spent the next seven years on Capitol Hill working for moderate Republicans. For the last six of those years, he had worked on the staff of Senator Charles "Mac" Mathias of Maryland, one of the District's best friends in Congress. Being appointed prosecutor was DiGenova's ticket to stardom.

Before he took office, federal prosecutors in the District—mindful of the fundamental political weakness of their office—had kept low profiles. In a city that was predominantly black, the chief prosecuting attorney was appointed by the president, and every president had appointed a white male prosecutor. That created a criminal justice system ripe for accusations of racism, especially if the prosecutor coveted a high profile. Joe DiGenova loved the media, regularly invited reporters into his office, and relished dispensing graphic critiques of the city government.

DiGenova was not only aggressive by nature, he was also getting a sense that Mary Treadwell's conspiracy and mismanagement weren't isolated incidents. There was no direct link between Treadwell's crimes and Marion Barry—though many Washingtonians believed that the mayor must have known about his ex-wife' s indiscretions—but DiGenova had reason to suspect that Barry and his government were not beyond reproach in other areas. DiGenova had been the number-two man at the U.S. attorney's office in March 1982, when police investigator Fred Raines brought in the allegations that Barry had snorted cocaine the previous Christmas at This Is It?, the strip joint on Fourteenth Street. At the same time, a group of officers, including union leader Gary Hankins, had also told diGenova that Barry was corrupting the police department from the top down. Moreover, informants regularly reported rumors that Barry used cocaine.

DiGenova was waiting for the first solid piece of evidence.

It came in the summer of 1983. Franklin Law, a dental-supply salesman, approached the FBI and said that his girlfriend, Karen Johnson, was selling cocaine to Mayor Barry. Law was jealous of Johnson's relationship with the mayor and angry because he couldn't get a city contract for dental supplies. In June 1983 he let the FBI wire him with a listening device and recorded a twenty-six-minute conversation with Johnson during which she discussed her cocaine sales to the mayor and other city officials.

There was enough evidence for diGenova to present before a grand jury. He called Barry before the jury in 1984, and the mayor acknowledged that he had once had a "close personal relationship" with Karen Johnson. But when asked about drugs, the mayor testified: "I've never bought, used, sold, or indulged in cocaine with Karen Johnson or anyone else."

Reporters found out about the investigation and asked Barry about Johnson. He replied that he "vaguely" knew her.

On April 17 Karen Johnson was indicted on charges of selling cocaine on nine separate occasions between early 1981 and February 1983. The next day federal agents arrested her at the city's energy office, where Barry had gotten her a job. She pleaded not guilty to all charges. The mayor appeared to be unfazed and issued a statement that prosecutors had informed him that he was not a target of the investigation. But the investigation was just beginning.

Two months earlier, on a cold January day, Ivanhoe Donaldson settled into a prominent table at Mel Krupins, a power-lunch spot on lower Connecticut Avenue, a gilt-edged chophouse where men in pinstriped suits cut deals and occasionally chomped on cigars.

Donaldson's guest on this day seemed painfully out of place. Cornbread Givens wasn't that old, but his gaunt face was etched with the wear of years in the civil rights movement and the rough life of the streets. He had come to Washington in 1969 to set up cooperatives in public housing projects and eventually founded the Poor People's Development Fund, a foundation that sputtered along for years, understaffed and underfunded. Barry had appointed Givens to an advisory commission on economic development and had awarded his foundation forty thousand dollars to train public housing residents in food co-ops. Still, Givens always was one step ahead of eviction from his spare apartment, and bankruptcy regularly loomed for him and his organization. When Donaldson called, Givens came downtown to sit at a table covered in crisp, white linen in hopes of landing another city contract.

"I have a problem," Donaldson confided, hunching over the table, "but it could turn out to be an opportunity for you and the foundation." Givens's back stiffened. A year earlier, Donaldson had offered Givens and his Poor People's Development Fund a contract for $27,500. Givens had been elated until he got Donaldson's instructions. Givens was to collect the $27,500, deposit it in the foundation's account, and then write a series of checks to Donaldson. Givens's organization got to keep $6000, but he cursed Donaldson for involving him in "bullshit."

He listened as Donaldson laid out the latest plan.

Jesse Jackson was making his historic first run for president that year and Donaldson was advising him. Donaldson explained that he wanted to use city funds to pay some Jackson campaign workers off the books. As a cover, Donaldson said he wanted Givens to apply for a $65,000 contract to train parolees. Givens said he had no experience with ex-cons or campaigning, but Donaldson told him it was all set: He would get two or three people to actually do the work and Givens could keep 20 percent—$13,000—of the contract for his foundation.

Givens was reluctant, but Donaldson was waving nearly a year's income in his face. As he wavered, Donaldson said, "Marion wants it."

It was Donaldson's second lie of the lunch. The money wasn't for Jesse Jackson's campaign workers and Barry knew nothing of it. Givens was desperate and willing to be convinced.

Donaldson arranged the $65,000 contract through his successor, Deputy Mayor Curtis McClinton, a former football player who was in over his head at the District Building. McClinton called employment services director Matthew Shannon. "I've talked to the coach," McClinton told Shannon, referring to Donaldson. Shannon set up the deal. The contract was wired, but the bureaucracy still moved too slowly for Donaldson. After several weeks passed with no action, he called up Shannon.

"Goddamnit, man," he said, "you don't even know what the fuck is going on in your own department."

On April 11, Givens was called to the employment services office to get $32,500 and passed the money, minus his share, to Donaldson. Several weeks later he repeated the process for the second $32,500.

"I got a feeling that this must be how you get contracts from the D.C. government because we hadn't been getting them," Givens would say later. "I knew I was involved in a scam. That was the first time in my life actually saw the insides of a government scam where contracts were moving without any interference. Now, ain't never seen that before. I guess I was fascinated by it."

As Givens marveled at the ease of fraud, an unrelated act of anger snipped the threads of Donaldson's corrupt network.

District police were called to investigate what at first appeared to be a routine case of sexual abuse. An enraged woman was charging that her live-in boyfriend had sexually assaulted her underage daughter. The woman was Nina Turner, the sister of employment services director Matthew Shannon. The boyfriend, Clarence Wade, was a Maryland Eastern Shore carpenter whom Shannon had first hired in 1983 to do work on his beach house. Shannon offered Wade a city job running a building trades program, even though Wade had no administrative experience. Wade began working for the District and living in Washington with Shannon's sister, Nina.

By the time of Wade's arrival, employment services had become a candy store for more than Ivanhoe Donaldson. His manipulation of contracts and thefts had encouraged some lower-level officials to use city money for their own needs. In time, a general atmosphere of corruption had subverted any pretension of helping desperate city residents to find needed jobs. That corruption of the government's mission—at a time when the unemployment rate of young black males ran as high as 50 percent—was Donaldson's greatest crime against the city.

In the summer of 1983, Clarence Wade and two other employment officials realized they hadn't spent all of the agency's money assigned to them. Instead of turning it back to the city, they went on a shopping spree, buying up thousands of dollars' worth of consumer and household goods, paint, and contracting supplies—all of which went either into their personal homes or into the homes of other agency officials. Wade even bought a chandelier for the apartment he shared with Nina Turner. It was a bountiful time, until Nina Turner suspected Wade of sexually assaulting her daughter.

In her fury, Turner told authorities that Wade had been stealing thousands of dollars from the agency. The allegations reached the metropolitan police department and the District officers alerted the U.S. attorney's office,

Joseph DiGenova was occupied with the Karen Johnson investigation when the report about corruption in the Department of Employment Services came to his desk. He assigned the case to Assistant U.S. Attorney Daniel Bernstein, a veteran criminal prosecutor. Bernstein looked over the case and saw potential corruption far beyond the petty thefts that Nina Turner reported. He called Clarence Wade in for an interview. Facing both sexual abuse and major theft charges, Wade spilled his guts.

Meanwhile, DiGenova dissected the FBI's tape of Johnson talking about selling cocaine to Marion Barry. She said that she had sold him drugs on twenty to thirty occasions that she could recall, and she mentioned that she kept detailed records in her diary. DiGenova's strategy was to squeeze Johnson in hopes that she would turn on the mayor, but there was a hitch-she wouldn't talk. DiGenova had to indict her.

Barry's friends contacted Johnson and recommended that she hire attorney John Shorter. Among criminal defenseattorneys, Shorter was not held in high esteem. Eventhen, he was under investigation for tax evasion, and he would later serve time on the charges. But in Johnson's case, according to her subsequent testimony, he did his job, which included carrying cash to her from the mayor's associates, who also happened to be city contractors. Shorter delivered the cash in envelopes containing a few hundred dollars each but never more than one thousand dollars. Johnson testified that the money came principally from two of the mayor's friends: John Clyburn, a businessman who built a computer company on city contracts in excess of $3 million; and Roy Littlejohn, another city contractor, whose businesses ranged from consulting services to housing the homeless. He also testified that Clyburn himself delivered some of the cash at her apartment building on Sixteenth Street, his office on K Street, a nightclub called Chez Maurice, and the Shoreham Hotel, where he and a number of the mayor's friends played tennis.

Johnson wavered but eventually decided to plead guilty. On July 23 she was sentenced to a four-month prison term. As she walked out of the courtroom, prosecutors presented her with a subpoena ordering her to testify before the grand jury. DiGenova was still hoping that she would give up the mayor. His ultimatum: Testify or face a contempt charge and more prison time—away from her infant son.

There was no hard evidence linking Barry to the case until DiGenova filed legal documents referring only to "an individual" whom Johnson had sold cocaine to "on twenty to thirty occasions." Reporters dug into the story and, based on unidentified sources, wrote that the individual was Marion Barry. The clear implication was that Barry was diGenova's new target.

"I'm not involved in drug sales, distribution," Barry told reporters who cornered him at the District Building: "I'm opposed to that. I fight that."

Not according to tips that came to the police department on the order of once a week. Most of the reports were easily dismissed, but on June 14, 1984, a more serious accusation came up. Dr. Alyce Gullattee, director of Howard University hospital's institute of drug abuse and addiction, told police investigators that Barry had been treated for a drug overdose back on September 25, 1983. Barry had been rushed to the hospital at 3.00 a.m. from a Congressional Black Caucus party at the Washington Hilton after complaining of chest pains and shortness of breath. The official statement from the mayor's office said that Barry was suffering from a hiatal hernia attack, but Gullattee told two police lieutenants that the mayor's problem "was the result of an overdose of drugs (cocaine) that occurred while he was in the company of a female companion who also overdosed," according to the police report. "Marion Barry was overdosed a second time," the report said, "however, he was taken to the District of Columbia General Hospital for treatment." Gullattee also said, according to the report, that she was "fearful of Marion Barry and Ivanhoe Donaldson because they would retaliate physically against any opponent."

Police Chief Maurice Turner read the report and assigned it to the Internal Affairs Division, which is supposed to investigate public corruption. But Gullattee's secondhand information was barely followed up, and the file with her statement was locked in a vault in the office of Deputy Chief Jimmy Wilson, a handpicked Barry appointee who ran the Internal Affairs Division. Chief Turner conveniently forgot about it; The Gullattee file came to light only years later in a report by WUSA-TV investigative reporter Mark Feldstein. It was a crucial cover-up. The Gullattee report, together with the Johnson tapes, might have convinced a grand jury to indict Barry. With the report locked in a safe, he escaped.

Ivanhoe Donaldson's problems were mounting.

Prosecutor Dan Bernstein's interrogation of Clarence Wade led him to other city employees who kept talking about an unaudited account that people dipped into for their shopping sprees. It was called the Special Administrative Fund, and it held the footprints of Ivanhoe Donaldson's trail of embezzlement.

In July, Donaldson and Barry were at the Democratic National Convention in San Francisco to support Jesse Jackson, who was mounting his first run for the White House. Every black leader in America was on the scene, and the two Washingtonians participated in the back-room political strategy sessions. While they were playing at national politics, FBI agents showed up unannounced at the employment services agency with a grand jury subpoena directing director Matthew Shannon to produce all records of expenditures from the Special Administrative Fund.

D.C. Inspector General Joyce Blalock, reacting to the subpoena, launched her own, parallel investigation of the fund. She met with Donaldson on October 18. The severity of the situation sank in as Donaldson was read his Miranda rights. His attorney, Willie Leftwich, sat at his side. Blalock carefully raised questions about one check, then another-six checks in all. Donaldson had a ready answer for each one. But there was the matter of documentation. Nothing was in writing. Surely, Donaldson said, there must be agency documentation. It was all very simple. He knew the agency. He would get the information that existed or detail what happened in writing and pass it on to Blalock.

Donaldson shifted his cover-up into high gear. He asked Charles Cobb to lunch. Looking sheepish and embarrassed, Donaldson explained how three years earlier he had cashed a $4,500 check in Cobb's name. Cobb, one of Donaldson's closest friends, looked at his longtime buddy. Cobb felt sorry for him and didn't want him to go to jail. He agreed to sign an affidavit saying he had earned the money.

That same week, Donaldson called Judy Richardson in New York. Without mentioning the grand jury inquiry or the inspector general's investigation, Donaldson told his old friend that an internal audit had raised questions about the $6,500 check that she had cashed for him in 1981. It was just a small administrative thing, he said. He had already replaced the money. Could she just sign an affidavit swearing that she had received the money? It was no big deal, he said. Richardson listened sympathetically to the man she had admired so long. She agreed to help, not knowing that Donaldson had lied to her again.

Things were looking up. He delivered the batch of false affidavits to Leftwich, who passed them on to Blalock. The investigation that had seemed so threatening now seemed somewhat contained. Blalock turned her findings over to the U.S. attorney's office.

Mayor Barry was campaigning in Minnesota for Walter Mondale and Geraldine Ferraro at the end of August when *The New York Times* reported that the mayor was under investigation for perjury in connection with the Karen Johnson investigation. Quoting unnamed "federal law enforcement officials," the article said prosecutors were matching Barry's denials of drug use against Johnson's testimony. The mayor returned to Washington and counterattacked.

"It's interesting that the leak came right at this critical moment when I was with other black leaders in Minnesota to come to some terms with our presidential nominee, Walter Mondale, and Geraldine Ferraro," Barry said when he landed at National Airport. "It's just coincidental, isn't it?"

The "leaks and innuendo" came from DiGenova's office, he said, because the prosecutors didn't have the goods but still wanted to discredit a black leader.

"I am probably the most successful administration around the country in terms of those of us who are black," Barry told the reporters. "I have been outspoken. I nominated Jesse Jackson. I am a pretty good target."

A good target for sure, but one with a solid shield. No matter how hard prosecutors grilled Karen Johnson, no matter how ominous their threats, she refused to testify about anything to the grand jury. She was held in contempt of court and saddled with a four-month prison term. On August 9, at age thirty-two with an eleven-month-old son to worry about, Johnson took her secrets and her cash from Barry's friends to jail to begin serving her sentence.

Barry took his complaints to a "toast, roast and boast" rally in his honor at the Shiloh Baptist Church Family Life Center. "They used to lynch people by a rope a long time ago," Barry told reporters. "After that, they're trying to lynch black people another way, and I'm not going to be lynched."

The FBI came to Cornbread Givens's threadbare offices in January 1985.

The agents had a subpoena for all documents dealing with his foundation and said he'd be called before the grand jury. Frightened, Givens called Donaldson. They hurriedly agreed to create a series of phony documents to suggest that Donaldson's firm, Datafacts, had worked with Givens's foundation to earn the city funds that Givens had accepted. They exchanged the bogus letters just before Givens's testimony. But it all seemed too desperate for Givens. He talked with a lawyer, then sat down in the jury room and told the truth.

Charlie Cobb had changed his mind and refused to back up Donaldson's story about the $4,500 check that Donaldson had cashed in his name. Donaldson's last chance was Judy Richardson. They met on the morning before she was scheduled to testify before the grand jury. How could she explain how she had spent the $6,500?

"The main thing is, did you give it to me? And if you say 'no,' they're not going to ask any more about it. They're not after you," he said. "They're after me."

It didn't work. The prosecutor threatened her with contempt. Her attorney urged her to tell the truth, and Willie Leftwich, Donaldson's lawyer, even advised her she could not continue to lie. On January 10, 1985, Richardson appeared again before the grand jury, recanted her earlier testimony, and revealed Donaldson's scheme. Prosecutors asked why she had gotten entwined.

"I believed that he would not ask me to do anything that would endanger me in any way," she said, recalling her SNCC days, "and he had never done that before... because there was a level of trust, because of the bond that a lot of us had."

A year later Ivanhoe Donaldson stood in a federal courtroom and admitted his guilt before U.S. District Court Judge Gerhard Gesell.

Donaldson had waived indictment and pleaded guilty on December 10, 1985, to a criminal information that spelled out how he had stolen $190,000 in city funds, attempted to cover his trail, and then tried to evade taxes.

The mayor was attending a National League of Cities conference in Seattle that day, but he took time to limit the damage. "It doesn't even come close to me or anyone around me," he said."There's not the slightest hint of any connection. It's not going to hurt us. People know of my high integrity."

Donaldson faced a maximum of twenty-three years in prison and fines totaling $360,000. He said nothing at his first appearance but sent a letter to Judge Gesell. In it he said that he was raised to respect property rights and that he had spent his entire life "committed to the struggle for social justice." He never asked for leniency.

"I state the above as a way of expressing that I have no excuses for what I did," he wrote. "I knew better. I am not only shocked and disappointed with my behavior for having defrauded a community that has shared so much love with me, but I am devastated by the violent emotional scars that I have left on my family, my friends and myself.

"There really isn't any justification for what I did," he continued, "and the acts went against every grain of every value I hold dear in life."

Those values were hammered in by a "very strict father," according to Jim Gibson, who had been best man at Donaldson's wedding and got close enough to see that Donaldson couldn't do enough to please his father. "Ivanhoe just didn't believe he was as brilliant as people said he was," Gibson says. "He knew it on one level, but inside he was always doubting himself. He didn't have that inner security."

On the day of the sentencing, prosecutors painted a different picture. Calling Donaldson "a predator," they said his crimes were "spawned by arrogance and greed" and enhanced by his "treachery." In a perfunctory session, Judge Gesell sentenced Donaldson to serve up to seven years in jail and pay $127,500 in fines.

Joe DiGenova called a press conference after the hearing to say that he was "very pleased" with the outcome, but he didn't stop there.

"This is not an isolated case," he declared. "The systems of controls in local government are not adequate. There appears to be pervasive evidence that these controls seem to be an affront to managers who have too much else to do."

DiGenova's broadside and promise of future investigations begged a response. That afternoon Barry took credit for ferreting out Donaldson's crimes through Joyce Blalock's investigation, though the federal probe had forced Blalock into action.

"There are some who would still raise the question of whether I knew what Donaldson was doing," Barry said in a formal statement. "These were transactions that would not ordinarily come to my attention, and I want to say emphatically that I did not know of them."

More than a few Washingtonians believed that the mayor was protesting too much. Prosecutors had tallied nearly two hundred thousand dollars in thefts by the mayor's alter ego. Certainly some cash must have gone into a secret offshore bank account or to support Barry's habits. But the same prosecutors were able to document every expenditure of the stolen cash. Donaldson had used some of the money to replenish cash that he had previously stolen from the Special Administrative Fund. Thousands of dollars had gone to tailors, mechanics, jewelers, credit-card companies, limousine services, and poker debts. But the lion's share went to pay huge bank loans and lines of credit that he had started to open as early as 1981. He was already in way over his head by 1983, when Jeff Cohen helped him get his $78,000 bank loan and his second $45,000 note. His businesses never succeeded. For example, the Natural Quencher soda that he had hoped would make him a fortune never got off the ground, and he was personally liable for the bank loans.

"There are a lot of us who aren't rich, but who have friends who are," says Jim Gibson. "They have to accept us that way. When they run off to Jamaica we don't go, but Ivanhoe had to go. He had to live the way they did, even though he really couldn't."

Barry knew that his friend was in dire straits. Jeffrey Cohen had alerted the mayor to Donaldson's bad bank loans. And Donaldson was in so much financial trouble in 1983 that Barry personally approved nineteen thousand dollars in bonus payments from June of that year until Donaldson left the government in the fall. Those payments, which brought Donaldson's government salary to $82,700, were not at issue in the criminal investigation.

The mayor said that he was "shocked, surprised, and saddened" by Donaldson's guilt. He called the entire affair "a tragedy." He already had watched Karen Johnson go to prison in August 1984. A year later Mary Treadwell exhausted her last appeal and left for her three-year term. Donaldson reported to the minimum-security prison in Petersburg, Virginia, a few weeks after his sentencing.

He had said privately a number of times that the only two people he could count on were Effi and Ivanhoe.

Now the mayor was almost alone.

CHAPTER 10

BOSS BARRY

The most important color in the city is green.
—*Dave Clarke, city council chairman,*
on record campaign contributions in 1986

Ivanhoe Donaldson's fall from grace robbed Marion Barry of the last person who could rein him in.

In public, the mayor played the betrayed friend and called Donaldson his Judas. "Any system can be broken by a person with a devious mind," Barry said when Donaldson began serving his seven-year sentence on January 27. "There are people who think there is no way I couldn't have known what was going on," he said when polls showed a rising belief that his government was corrupt. "It's just not true." But aides would often find the mayor alone in his office, sitting at his desk with his head buried in his hands. When they asked what was wrong he'd say: "I miss him." Donaldson's demise wasn't a clear-cut turning point for Barry, because he already was headed the wrong way; but without Donaldson, there was no turning back.

His friends and political colleagues tried to help. Since 1984 Barry had been attending prayer meeting every Wednesday at 8.00 a.m. with the Reverend Dave Eaton, city council chairman Dave Clarke, D.C. Delegate Walter Fauntroy, school board member Dave Hall, and a few others. It was a time for free association and free-form counseling. Barry gradually clammed up early in 1986 and finally quit late in the year.

"The man was lost," says Jim Gibson.

Barry had many more reasons to be demoralized in the late winter of 1986. Deputy Mayor Alphonse Hill resigned after acknowledging that he was under investigation for taking three thousand dollars in kickbacks. Mitch Snyder, an advocate for the homeless, was in the midst of a hunger strike to force the local and federal governments to finance his shelter. The city's prisons were overflowing. After procrastinating for years, Barry tried to house some prisoners in a renovated police station near Capitol Hill, which provoked an old-fashioned sit-in by Ward Six residents and their councilwoman, Nadine Winter. At the same time, three thousand parents, teachers, and students staged a massive protest outside the District Building to force Barry into adding $16 million to the school budget.

"Procrastination has become the watchword of his administration," city council member John Wilson, the mayor's civil rights colleague, told *The Washington Post.*

The government's mounting crises could have chastened Barry; instead he celebrated his fiftieth birthday as if he were a gangster. At one of two parties a stripper dressed as a policewoman popped out of a cake, handcuffed the mayor, and performed for the guests. "Free at last," Barry said as "Officer Goodbody" removed the cuffs and photographers snapped pictures of the mayor's release.

The task of keeping Marion Barry sober and focused on the government fell to Carol Thompson, who was having her own problems with Ivanhoe Donaldson's demise.

"I felt totally let down," says Carol Thompson, who revered Donaldson. "Here was somebody who really instilled in me a sense of good government, caught up in something that to this day I still don't understand. A lot of things were happening that were against what we were all about. It left the whole government discombobulated."

Thompson got a firsthand view in April when Barry appointed her his chief of staff. Effi Barry wanted to know one thing about

Thompson. "Is she one of Marion's women?" the First Lady asked her sources in the government.

Thompson set about the task of organizing the mayor's office and the public parts of his life, beginning with his schedule. She knew that the business community hated the fact that he always showed up late for appointments, be they speaking engagements, luncheons, or private meetings. It was another childish display of power. He would sometimes arrive on time and sit in his car chatting on the car phone until he knew that people were waiting for him. Thompson realized within a few weeks that on many levels, starting with his schedule, Barry was uncontrollable.

"He's a child," she reported to her mother after several weeks on the job. The notion that the man whom she had admired for so many years was fundamentally immature shattered Thompson. As a native Washingtonian, she wanted Barry's black-led government to prove that African-Americans could indeed run a tight ship. Barry was becoming an embarrassment. How could he conduct himself this way? What made him tick?

"We work hard every day together," she said to him one day, "but we don't relate as two people. You don't know me, who I am, what I think. And I don't understand you."

"You're going to be okay," Barry responded. "You're one of the black people who's going to be successful. I was never meant to succeed. I'm from a poor background. I'll never make it in some people's eyes."

Barry was right. The Gold Coast crowd on upper Sixteenth Street would never accept him because he didn't speak the king's English and because he lacked proper breeding. But Carol Thompson, who had light skin and a Smith College degree, couldn't understand why Barry was so preoccupied with measuring up to anyone's standards, black or white.

"How can you not believe that you're worthy? You've made it," she said. "You are the mayor."

"I have to constantly overcome odds," he said. "You're acceptable. White people will never accept me."

So this was the private Marion Barry. The public man would never bow down to "Mr. Charlie," the all-purpose bogeyman, whether Mr. Charlie represented the black bourgeoisie or the white power structure. Yet in his heart he yearned for the approval of both, and believed that it would never come. The strut, the late entrances—even the women and the drugs—were an expression of that essential conflict between what Barry needed and what he knew he could never have. It contributed to a man who, in Mary Treadwell's words, "had no center." In the words of a friend who played poker with him and built a business on city contracts, Barry was "a sociopath."

Faced with the bare reality, Thompson did her best to control the situation and the man. She made sure that Barry was chaperoned as often as possible. She would send aides with him or plant allies at his public appearances. He would order cognac; they would bring ginger ale.

The champagne was flowing the night in April when Barry went to a fiftieth birthday party for Robert L. Johnson, his old friend and former campaign adviser. Johnson, the founder of the Black Entertainment Television cable channel, was president of the company that was awarded the District's cable franchise, with Barry's support. From across the room the mayor caught sight of a voluptuous black woman with long eyelashes, deep red lipstick, and high cheekbones. He made his way over and introduced himself. Her name was Hazel Diane "Rasheeda" Moore, and she needed a job.

Hazel Moore was a local girl whose family lived on Taylor Street, a cozy lane lined with row houses. The Moores were a family of government clerks. Her mother ran the household and played the organ at the historic Nineteenth Street Baptist Church. Hazel Moore and Carol Thompson were classmates at Roosevelt High School. Moore grew up beautiful and rebellious. She got her college degree at Fisk University in 1972, but she also got arrested for credit-card fraud. After making restitution, Moore went to modeling school, moved to New York in 1975, and adopted her sensuous middle name, "Rasheeda." She made the cover of *Essence* magazine in 1977, but a few years later she was blackballed for testifying on behalf of her boyfriend, and father of one of her children, when he was arrested in England for trying to smuggle in $18 million worth of heroin. She sought refuge at home with her family on Taylor Street. Moore expected to have no problem opening a modeling agency in her hometown, but the opportunities were slim. She was disappointed and close to broke when she ran into the mayor at Bob Johnson's party.

A month later the mayor and the former model met at the home of Gaylord Tissueboo, Barry's photographer. Out of their discussions came a city contract called "Project Me." The government paid Moore sixty thousand dollars to teach modeling and "image consciousness" to teenagers in the mayor's summer jobsprogram. They made a date to meet at the city's annual Riverfest celebration on the Anacostia River. Barry slipped off with Rasheeda to a flat at the Tiber Island apartments that he and other city officials had reserved for trysts. Barry walked over to a corner of the room, lifted up the rug, and pulled out a folded dollar bill that contained his stash of cocaine. It was the beginning of a relationship that mixed sex and drugs.

That summer Barry invited Moore to accompany him on a vacation to the Virgin Islands. He contacted an acquaintance and former District government employee, Charles Lewis, an island native. Together with friends, they cavorted on boats, consumed drugs, and partied into the night. But early in the relationship Moore had second thoughts. Now that she was closer to her mother, she felt guilty about having sex with a married man. She met Barry at the Channel Inn on Washington's waterfront to talk it over.

"I'm fighting with the idea of adultery," she told him. "There are a lot of things I'm trying to get together in my life. I feel uncomfortable about this."

"I think that it's divine providence that we're together," Barry told her.

It would have been a good time for Barry to bow out of politics.

He could have left a hero in the eyes of many people, but he was driven to run. He wanted to make up for his dismal second term; he wanted to prove that he could win an election without Ivanhoe Donaldson; and he had no higher office to pursue, no potential appointments to a federal post, no job waiting. So he prepared for re-election to his third four-year term.

At a second fiftieth birthday breakfast, the city's real estate moguls, flush with cash from the building boom, contributed one hundred thousand dollars to the mayor's upcoming campaign. His only Democratic challenger, former school board member Mattie Taylor, compared Barry to Marie Antoinette and said: "I am incensed that the mayor would have a thousand-dollara-plate breakfast when our public housing tenants can't get stoves and refrigerators purchased for them to prepare breakfast on."

Taylor's barb was well aimed but ineffective. She was no match for the incumbent mayor. An early poll showed Barry drawing 56 percent of the voters to her 7 percent. Why, despite the mayor's weaknesses, were there no serious challengers?

The answer is that the District's twelve-year-old political system was a democratic disaster. The city had virtually none of the checks and balances fundamental to a democracy. It had become a one-party, one-man rule that allowed Barry to become the boss in the crippled experiment of limited home rule. The Republican party was powerless, in part because white conservatives shut out blacks. The local Democratic organization was an inept, petty debating society because Barry purged critics in 1979 and packed it with sycophants. So great was Barry's hold over the political system that Mark Plotkin, a candidate for the Ward Three city council seat, was the only Democratic candidate in 1986 who was independent enough to say he wouldn't vote for him.

The city council could have provided a legislative balance, but the majority of its thirteen members were under Barry's spell and dependent on him for constituent services. Once elected, most council members tried to turn part-time jobs into lifetime appointments and voted themselves the highest salaries of any local legislature in the nation. Reporters and staff dubbed them "Marionettes."

"For all practical purposes, you have a one-man show," council finance committee chairman John Wilson said. "We try to be a check and it does not work most of the time."

In other cities, politics was a way for ethnic minorities to stake their claim to economic and political power, but Washington never developed a true local political class. Irish Catholics in Boston, Jews in Philadelphia, Poles in Chicago had climbed political networks up from neighborhood activism, to ward level, to city jobs, state offices, and federal power. In Washington, congressional domination, disenfranchisement, and racism stunted the growth of homegrown politics. By the time an elective political ladder became available in the 1970s, ambitious black men and women who might have been interested in city government could command prestigious, well-paying jobs in the legal community, in the federal government, or in business. Municipal politics was a backwater.

"We are an infant government, no traditions and no sure paths to power," said Julius Hobson, Jr., the activist's son who worked as Barry's congressional representative on Capitol Hill. "That makes it easier for someone who does hold what little power there is to block everybody else out."

Said Wilson: "We hire everybody who complains about the city. There are no independent advocacy groups in this city."

The media didn't serve as a reference point, either. Washington's major media thrive on the national and international scene, with little day-to-day coverage of local Washington—or even nearby suburbs of Virginia and Maryland—that might encourage a sense of place either in the newspapers or on television. Apart from scandal-driven news, it's hard enough for top locally elected officials to get news coverage, let alone the neighborhood activist who might, with modest normal coverage, mature into a citywide politician.

The electorate was kept in check by racial insecurities. A few whites could make it onto the council, but a white mayoral candidate stood little chance. White voters, who elected Barry in 1978 in a coalition with gays and poor blacks, could not turn him out by themselves, so Ward Three was neutralized. White developers from the suburbs financed his campaigns, but that was a cost of doing business, not a measure of political favor. Barry might have angered the black middle class, but blacks weren't about to join in white denunciation of him. "We prefer to handle this within the family," said one black activist. The only power center was Marion Barry, and he knew it.

On May 17, Barry kicked off his campaign before one thousand supporters bused in for the event by the city recreation department. In the highly choreographed show, Barry gave an hour-long speech and showed off his accomplishments by way of a color slide show. The mayor said that he had learned from his mistakes, then he touted "our nation's leading jobs program, our housing program... our plummeting crime rates, our balanced budgets, our downtown revitalization."

No one in the city would dispute him; if they did no one would listen.

Wall Street, however, was listening to some very important signals out of the Barry administration.

In the era of leveraged buyouts and fat fees from the bond business, New York brokerage houses were eager to be wired into a government that liked to issue municipal bonds to finance its operations. Congress had granted the District the right to float municipal bonds in 1984, and the fees for underwriting those multimillion-dollar instruments were handsome. A $200 million bond could generate a 2 percent fee of $4 million. Washington's developers had bankrolled Barry's 1982 campaign when he needed the cash against Pat Harris; in 1986, when he faced token opposition, Wall Street started to throw money at the mayor.

One afternoon in July Barry and a small entourage took the shuttle to New York and checked into the Pierre, a posh hotel on Fifth

Avenue. That evening a group of investment bankers held a dinner dance and raised nearly fifty thousand dollars from the bankers. All the big houses—Drexel Burnham Lambert, Salomon Brothers, Prudential Bache, Morgan Stanley, and Merrill Lynch—eventually combined to contribute more than one hundred thousand dollars in two-thousand-dollar installments.

Kidder Peabody hosted the main event that night, but the woman who made it possible was Bettye L. Smith. Like many women in Barry's life, Smith played a dual role. Her apartment on Capitol Hill was a frequent stop on the mayor's late-night circuit. The relationship paid well, too. Smith was a consultant to the New York-based investment firm of W.R. Lazard, the city's financial adviser, another high-paying role at the mayor's discretion.

As soon as Smith arrived in her room at the Pierre she called room service to take care of a crucial chore.

"Got to order a bottle of Courvoisier," she told a campaign aide. "I want it to be waiting in Marion's room when he arrives."

The 1986 campaign turned into a besotted, drug-laden lark. Places in Barry's inner circle were taken by a fresh set of friends. The new crowd tolerated or encouraged the mayor's recreational use of cocaine. Barry started spending time with Hassan Mohammadi, an Iranian who ran a restaurant in Georgetown and supplied Barry with cocaine and other drugs. The mayor could often find late-night amusement with R. Donahue Peebles, an aspiring young wheeler-dealer the mayor had appointed to the influential real estate tax review commission; Tony Jones, a consultant whose firm received a number of city contracts; Willie Davis, another friend and Birmingham-based consultant who profited from city bond deals; and Darryl Sabbs, who started out in Barry's youth leadership program and wound up on Barry's party circuit.

"People who were not real city people, with stakes in our community, people with no commitment, no history, no depth came in," says Jim Gibson, who was working in New York for the Rockefeller Foundation at the time. Longtime Barry street soldier Marshall Brown, who remained loyal to the end, put it more bluntly: "The sleaze crowd is showing up."

Barry scheduled few campaign appearances and rarely showed up at his campaign headquarters, even though his devoted political strategist Anita Bonds begged him to participate. Of the $1.5 million Barry raised, little went to television or marketing to inspire either the voters or campaign workers. Instead, Barry's campaign hired hundreds of low-level, "paid" volunteers to put on the semblance of a campaign. It was a private version of his summer jobs program. The crusade of his first campaign in 1978 and the battle royal against Patricia Roberts Harris in 1982 were faded memories in the overripe summer of 1986.

"Everything got out of hand," says a chief fundraiser who worked with Bonds. "It was a caricature of a campaign."

Barry was doing so much cocaine during the campaign that he started having trouble coping with his daily schedule. It was at this time that he started taking Valium to bring him down from the cocaine. When the Valium proved too weak, he switched to Xanax, a stronger tranquilizer.

The Washington Post, despite frequent critical stories in its local news pages about Barry's missteps, weighed in with a tepid editorial endorsement. At a cocktail party at Katharine Graham's home before the campaign, the mayor approached Graham and editorial page editor Meg Greenfield. "Meg here thinks I'm a druggie," and he smiled.

It didn't matter what she thought. Barry no longer needed the *Post.*

The voters went to the polls on September 9 for a Democratic primary in black and white.

Seventy percent of the voters cast ballots for the mayor; fewer than 20 percent voted for Mattie Taylor. Barry swept every community except for Ward Three, the white precincts west of Rock Creek Park. Barry's opponent in the November general election was Carol Schwartz, a Jewish Republican from Texas who'd made a solid showing on the school board and in her first term on the city council. Despite her conservative politics, Schwartz was a straight-talking, knowledgeable, and respected politician who could hold her own in political debates. She ran a serious, integrated campaign, but in a city that was 70 percent black and 80 percent Democratic, she had absolutely no chance of winning. And though she was a Republican with a clear bias toward business, she got no help from the national party, few contributions from the local business community, and none from the developers. To Barry's $1.5 million, Schwartz was able to raise $298,000.

The general election vote matched the primary count. Barry commanded 61 percent to Schwartz's 33 percent. Barry won everywhere but Ward Three. White voters, though most were Democratic, backed the Republican 76 percent to 15 percent. Barry was the imperial boss. Ken Cummins, who writes a tart "Loose lips" column in the weekly *City Paper*, began referring to him as "Mayor-for-Life Marion Barry."

The mayor spent the weeks leading up to his January 2 inaugural pledging to close associates and skeptics alike that he knew he had lost his way in the second term, but that the third would be a time of renewal.

"We must all think positively rather than negatively," he declared in one of his inaugural speeches. "We take exception to those who think we can't do anything, because we can. Stumble we may, fumble we do sometimes, heads bloodied but not bowed, bodies straight up and not bent. That's the Washington I know."

Instead of a simple, dignified inauguration that might have established his new tone, Barry and his aides rolled out a celebration that cost over five hundred thousand dollars. After the official swearing-in, Barry and his entourage headed to a reception at the Frank Reeves Center, the government office building that Barry had built at the intersection of Fourteenth and U streets NW, where Stokely Carmichael had paraded at the start of the 1968 riots. Barry shouted into the echoing din of the crowded lobby, reminding the audience of government workers that he had walked the nearby streets of Washington as an activist and of how his mother, "who still does a day's work as a domestic," had bought him a new pair of shoes for this inaugural.

"My mother said they were a long way from when I wore pasteboard in my shoes," he declared. "And my suit is a long way from the overalls I wore to pick cotton."

U.S. Attorney Joe DiGenova put a crimp in the new era on January 15 when he announced an eleven-count indictment against Alphonse G. Hill, the former deputy mayor of finance. The indictment charged Hill with extorting $44,000 from two persons to whom he had steered more than $244,500 in city financial contracts. Hill was also charged with income tax evasion in schemes dating back to 1981. With Ivanhoe Donaldson in jail, Hill became the second deputy mayor within two years to face substantial criminal charges, undercutting the mayor's argument that U.S. Attorney Joseph DiGenova's various probes amounted only to empty political witchhunts.

"Marion was always supposed to be arrested," says Carol Thompson, who moved from chief of staff to deputy mayor for economic development in 1987. "We had to deal with a constant bunker mentality. It made governing close to impossible."

As January came to an end two blizzards dumped twenty-six inches of snow on the Washington region. The suburbs immediately began digging out, but the capital's streets remained an unplowed morass of stranded cars. The mess made national headlines and network television news. Three thousand miles away, Marion Barry was spending the weekend at the Beverly Hills Hotel. He had flown to California on Wednesday night, just as the first snow clouds rolled into Washington, to visit friends in San Francisco and see the Super Bowl game in Los Angeles between the Denver Broncos and the New York Giants.

The day after the game Barry was in Oak View Park partying and playing poker with friends, including Jeffrey Mitchell, a longtime companion who frequently traveled with him. That evening, after a day of drinking several bottles of champagne and a quart of cognac, Barry and two women friends disappeared into a bedroom and closed the door. When the two women left the townhouse, Barry slumped to a sofa, head thrown back. His nose ran, and he made low grunting noises. The mayor clutched his chest and said he was having trouble breathing. Mitchell had done cocaine with Barry at other times, and he believed Barry was having a bad reaction to the drug. An ambulance arrived to find Barry sitting curbside with Mitchell. At first Barry wouldn't give his name. They insisted. Barry said, "Don't tell the news media." At Daniel Freedman Hospital Barry was given oxygen and immediately began to feel better. He told the hospital that blood tests and other exams weren't necessary, and he was released.

Back in Washington, press secretary Annette Samuels issued a statement saying Barry's hiatal hernia had flared up because he had little rest and too little to eat, but reporters weren't satisfied. In a series of phone interviews, Barry pointedly described how he was relaxing, getting manicures, and playing tennis at the Beverly Hills Hotel. His aides could take care of the snow and, besides, he really needed more time off from his busy job. Milton Coleman, by then an editor, told Barry his odd explanation and behavior were fueling rumors of drug use.

"I guarantee you," the mayor said, "if I was doing anything, Milton, DiGenova would have my ass."

The unplowed streets were a metaphor for the city government's wretched record for serving its citizens.

"We managed by confusion," says Thompson, who had become city administrator.

Barry had been on a hiring binge since 1982 when he bought labor peace—and votes—by packing and then mollifying the city work force with raises. One measure of the confusion was that the city didn't actually know how many people were on the payroll. The 1988 census and an independent commission on budget and financial priorities put the count at forty-eight thousand-one worker for every thirteen residents more government workers per capita than any other city or state government, including New York, Chicago, Houston, Philadelphia, and Detroit. Barry's work force soaked up half the city's budget, which had grown from $1.2 billion to $3.2 billion under Barry's regime. But the high cost and the large number of workers didn't translate to high-quality service.

Delivering a welfare check in the District consistently cost twice the national average, for example. The District's child support collection agency had the rare distinction of being the only one in the nation to repeatedly spend more than it collected. City officials kept such poor track of children in the foster-care system that judges held the District in contempt; city-run boarding homes for the mentally retarded were neglected to the point where an eighty-eight-year-old resident covered with maggots and lice collapsed and died in a hospital emergency room; the city's largest nursing home was responsible for locking out an eightyeight-year-old woman who froze to death in twenty-five-degree weather. Barry cronies landed costly social service contracts that enriched them but delivered few services.

Tales of bungled rescue missions by the city's ambulance service dominated the news. Jean Dean suffered an asthma attack on February 26, 1987, and called 911. The ambulance got lost, and she died. In April, Phyllis Hussakowski collapsed from a suspected heart attack at the downtown Hotel Harrington. Her coworkers called 911. After a half hour an ambulance arrived and took her to. George Washington University Hospital, where she died. Emergency dispatchers received six calls about a woman who was "not breathing." The ambulance went to the wrong address. Units from a firehouse thirteen blocks away took another eleven minutes to arrive. The victim, Lisa Wills, died of cardiac arrest on the way to the hospital. Barry was slow to acknowledge the ambulance problem and never completely solved it.

The mayor was equally inept at improving the city's infamous infant mortality rates, which were consistently among the worst in the nation. In 1978 the rate was 27.3 deaths per thousand; ten years later the mortality rate for infants under one year was 23 per thousand births—still more than twice the national average of 10 per thousand—and with the advent of crack addiction among pregnant women, the rates climbed back to record levels. Babies born in third-world nations had a better chance of survival.

If children made it safely into the world and tried to get an education in the District's public schools, they found themselves on the short end of Barry's budget. Though elementary schools were improving, most junior and senior high schools were in a free fall. Buildings were in disrepair, schoolbooks were second-rate, violence in the schools was on the rise, and the dropout rate was above 40 percent, ranking the schools among the worst in the nation. Barry always dodged responsibility for the school system, because it is controlled by an elected, independent school board, but he couldn't escape the fact that he reduced the share of the city's budget that went to education. In 1978 one-fourth of the budget went to the schools; in 1988 Barry allocated only 16 percent. The mayor, however, took care of his own. His son, Christopher, attended St. Albans School for Boys, a posh private school in Ward Three, eight miles from his home.

The Barry administration was least effective with the city's poorest citizens—those who helped him rise to power but remained trapped forty thousand strong in decrepit public housing.

At the start of his administration in 1979, Barry had promised to "take the boards off and renovate three thousand units of public housing. Over a period of years, he dislocated thousands of residents, promising to completely rehab their homes. Barry gave out contracts, mostly to his friends or to well-connected associates, but much of the work was never done. In 1987, six years after the "modernization" strategy booted people from their homes, 19 percent of the city's public housing remained boarded up and unused, except by squatters, vagrants, and drug addicts. Meanwhile, the waiting list for public housing mounted to eleven thousand families.

For those fortunate enough to land an apartment, life inside the projects was hellish. Pipes burst and were never fixed; toilet drains broke and spilled feces on lower floors; rats and roaches took over basements and stairwells; neither heat nor light was guaranteed. City auditor Otis Troupe, appointed by the city council, discovered that more than half the maintenance requests were simply ignored for months and even years. The system was in a state of "complete breakdown." The city blamed the tenants for trashing their apartments, but a federal judge in 1987 found that the city wasn't providing heat or hot water in some cases. He ruled that housing officials had "ignored and walked away from their responsibilities to public housing tenants."

Barry blamed the problem on the Reagan administration's cut back in funds, but as in other cases, the city had plenty of money. The city had allocated $100 million for maintenance in 1987; the money simply wasn't well spent. Federal funds earmarked for the housing department languished so long that deadlines passed and the funds had to be turned back. One reason for the confusion was that Barry never hired a decent housing director. From 1983 to 1985 four different administrators ran the housing authority. Their offices at 1133 North Capitol Street were in great shape; Troupe found that 15 percent of maintenance workers' time in 1984 and 1985 was spent working at headquarters. The mayor appointed a blue-ribbon commission on public housing to study the problem. It concluded that since Barry had taken over, the projects had gotten much worse. The mayor didn't trumpet the results.

To make matters worse, the city's budget analysts began warning that the sharp revenue growth of the 1980s was beginning to slow, even as his social welfare programs and the city's huge personnel costs were skyrocketing. The D.C. council began voting against tax rises and curbing rising property tax assessments. Still, the city's expenditures for its six hundred thousand citizens were about twice the national average, $5,163 as compared to $2,685 per resident, according to the *Statistical Abstract of the United States*.

"We have enough money," said John Wilson, who was chairman of the city council's finance and revenue committee. "I think [the government's] inefficient and incompetent."

This was certainly the sense among the white community. "They rejected Marion because of his lifestyle, his womanizing, the scent of corruption," says Polly Shackleton, the white councilwoman who represented Ward Three until 1986. "Marion took good care of Ward Three, but my constituents believed he was neglecting the poor. Their disapproval intensified by the month."

Much of Washington's black population also was disappointed by the mayor's failings, but black residents saw Mayor Barry through an entirely different lens, which goes a long way in answering the question posed by Mattie Taylor in the 1986 campaign: "Why do the people love him so?"

The African-American poor- and middle-class communities credited Barry with improving basic city services that most people take for granted: accurate water billing, street repair, garbage collection. These services didn't work totally efficiently, but they worked better than they had before. For the first time these city services were improved for residents east of the Anacostia River, where residents had felt especially estranged from the government before Barry took over, a fact that was lost on many white residents.

Barry also saw that Wards Four, Five, and Seven—the heart of the city's politically active black communities—received new fire and police stations, libraries, and community centers. Economic development projects, though flawed by blatant cronyism, brought new buildings, rehabilitation, and jobs to Anacostia, Marshall Heights, Georgia Avenue, and other black communities. It was the Barry administration that revitalized the city's New York Avenue industrial-wholesale core. Both Black Entertainment Television and Federal

Express built new offices on the eastern edge of the city. These developments, and others like them, didn't get much press.

From the African-American point of view, Barry had dramatically improved city services for the elderly and provided thousands of summer jobs for young people. The recreation department under Barry shifted millions of dollars to neighborhood festivals, community events; and entertainment programs for the elderly. There are about 106,000 senior citizens in D.C.—one-sixth of the population—and they voted in great numbers for Barry. A typical black family might have one or two extended family members working for the city government, an elderly person in a city-subsidized home, a child in a summer jobs program, or a relative working either for the government or for a company that held city contracts.

Were they going to give all that up because Barry was a womanizer? Or wasted some tax dollars? Who had paid attention to them before? And who would do so if Barry were no longer the mayor? Beneath the facade of services and patronage, Barry's political machine was fueled by the fear in the black community that whites would take it all away if they could.

When Joe DiGenova became the U.S. attorney in 1983, he was greeted by a column in *The Washington Post* by Ronald White, an African-American staff writer, who said that DiGenova was the only check to Barry's imperial power. By 1987, DiGenova believed it, and he also believed that Barry's government was corrupt.

Actually, there was little old-fashioned graft yet in the District. Perhaps the government was too young to develop the deep-seated system of payoffs that lubricated commerce through the permit process in cities like Boston, Chicago, Philadelphia, and New York. But DiGenova thought he saw what he called "rampant corruption" in the steering of contracts to Barry's cronies, in particular John Clyburn, whose computer firms had reaped millions in city business, and David E. Rivers, the Atlanta native who had held several top jobs in Barry's cabinet.

Clyburn was a close friend of former city administrator Elijah B. Rogers. Rivers, in addition to his formal title as director of human services, was close to Barry socially and frequently hosted the mayor's late-night stops at his secluded Southwest townhouse. They ran in a pack of friends who played tennis together at the Shoreham Hotel and formed something of a kitchen cabinet for the mayor. Among the group were Rogers, advertising executive Jeff Mitchell, attorney Bob Washington, and David Wilmot, the consummate inside player who was at once Barry's friend, a top lobbyist for Anheuser-Busch, the dean of admissions at Georgetown Law Center, and a real estate investor. Their tennis coach, John Mudd, was part of the pack until he was busted for distribution of cocaine. They took on "dog" nicknames when Mitchell showed up one day with a bag of trinkets, with different dog tags for each member of the pack. Rogers became "Baby Dog," Wilmot and Rivers were "Deputy Dogs." Barry's was "Supreme Dog," shortened to Supreme. When Barry was on the prowl after midnight, members of his security detail would radio one another that "the dog is running."

The social contacts contributed to Clyburn's early business success. Since 1984, Clyburn had attracted at least $3 million in city contracts for either his own firms or business associates in such diverse fields as long-term health care, computer consulting and services, snow removal, and management analysis audits for the city's drug and alcohol agency. Rivers had even hired former Clyburn employees to oversee contracts that went to Clyburn or his associates.

In 1986, a consulting firm calling itself B&C Management got a small contract through Rivers with Clyburn's help. B&C owners Warren Barge and Leonard Carey then hosted a fundraiser for Barry in Rivers's hometown of Atlanta. They paid for Rivers's expenses at the elegant Peachtree Plaza Hotel and gave him a pair of expensive Tony Lama boots. Later, Rivers announced he was leaving as director of human services to become secretary of the District-a job that would give him access to the entire government.

"I'm gonna get you in with Metro," Rivers told Carey, referring to the regional mass transit system. "They got so much stuff it's unbelievable."

"A whole new cast of players?" Carey asked.

"Whole new cast," replied Rivers, who said that he was happy to leave the human services agency. "I mean, I was ready. I ain't gotta worry about all those welfare fuckers no more, man."

Rivers discussed with Carey one more vital issue. Rivers suggested that 10 percent of the value of every contract be invested for Rivers's future use once he'd left government. Carey promised to invest Rivers's share secretly in Atlanta land deals.

"It's all in my name," Carey told him. "There's nothing that could ever be linked."

When FBI agents burst into their offices on May 22, Rivers and Clyburn found out that Leonard Carey was an undercover FBI agent named Roy Carroll, and they were the targets of a sting that had been in the making for seventeen months.

Sharon LaFraniere, a *Washington Post* investigative reporter who had written a string of stories about scandals in the District government, got tipped off about the sting the day before it was scheduled to take place.

A small, deadly serious white woman, LaFraniere huddled with senior editors in a glass-walled office on the daily's fifth floor to plan the coverage of what she expected to be a massive plan to raid dozens of homes, private businesses, and city government offices the next morning. In the pent-up atmosphere of the newsroom, the breaking story seemed to be the coup de grace for the Barry administration, evidence of the "rampant corruption" that Joe DiGenova had alleged when he indicted Ivanhoe Donaldson in 1985.

The raids got under way Friday morning, with subpoenas naming forty different people and thirteen different banks and businesses in addition to the District government itself. Mysteriously, the agents also went to the home of Karen Johnson, Barry's former girlfriend, and seized boxes of her private papers. Among the items seized at Rivers's townhouse were the Tony Lama boots—with FBI agent Roy Carroll's ID number stitched inside; anunregistered Smith & Wesson .32 pistol; and traces of marijuana. At the urging of other aides, Barry placed Rivers on paid leave, but Rivers appeared at a news conference first where he was asked about drug use, to which he answered: "I am not currently using drugs."

The raids and series of leaked stories fed a classic media frenzy of banner headlines and TV footage of men in FBI jackets haulingboxes out of government offices that titillated the city for more than a week. It certainly kept Barry's government off-balance,but was there a case?

"The surprise moves apparently succeeded in sowing suspicionand confusion among dozens of District officials and well-knowncontractors," the *Post's*Nancy Lewis and Sharon LaFraniere observed in the quiet aftermath. "Nine days later, however, it is still difficult for observers to distinguish the theatrics from the possible evidence." More than four months later, there were still no indictments, but the news media carried a constant stream of stories about the probe.

"DiGenova has nothing on me," Barry told reporters whocaught up to him one afternoon at the Maine Avenue waterfront. "They're on the wrong track. It's a loose federation of black friends, not corruption, just like white community businesspeople. The prosecutors are way out on a legal limb and aren't smart enough to understand what's going on. Where there are casual, informal relationships among people who work for the city and those who get city contracts, the prosecutors see conspiracy."

Whether Barry was confident or blowing smoke, prosecutors were bogged down. In a conversation with *Washington Post* managing editor Leonard Downie, a senior prosecutor conceded the contract probe was difficult and would "go on and on." On the crucial issue, the same prosecutor told Downie: "No indictment of Barry is imminent." He also told some reporters privately that the investigation would likely last beyond Joe DiGenova's term as U.S. attorney, which would be ending in the next year.

Were the news stories part of an active conspiracy—indeed, an unholy alliance—between a white government establishment and a white media establishment bent on bringing down the Barry regime? In the narrow sense of the term, the answer is clearly no; prosecutors didn't sit in a room with reporters and plot the mediablitz. But Barry and his government were the victims of a system that essentially puts the government in control of the news, especially in cases where legal authorities are charging public corruption. Federal investigators want to give the impression of guilt. It "shakes the tree," a popular law-enforcement phrase that means that the perception of wrongdoing often encourages other people to come forward and describe corrupt acts. The bountiful leaks around the Rivers-Clyburn investigation and the subsequent Karen Johnson grand jury were an extreme example of the unholy alliance.

"I find the whole investigation most distasteful," said the Reverend A. Knighton Stanley, the normally mild-mannered pastorof the People's Congregational Church. Stanley's congregation is largely uptown and aristocratic; he is former Atlanta mayor Andrew Young's son-in-law. "I believe it is politically motivated.... It is consciously and unconsciously racially motivated."

The FBI had raided Karen Johnson's house because prosecutors believed she was taking payoffs from Barry's friends as a reward for spending eight months in jail on contempt charges for not talking about the mayor's cocaine use with her in the early 1980s.

In the aftermath of the raids, WUSA-TV reporter Mark Feldstein obtained Johnson's private diary and disclosed the early 1980s sex and drugs spree that she had so carefully documented. It's unclear who leaked the diary, but an embarrassed Barry denied everything. "I am appalled and outraged," he said, complaining that the leaks were "designed to break my spirit—which will not be broken. This is an attempt to run me out of office."

DiGenova said he was astounded by Feldstein's report, added that prosecutors didn't have the diary, and quickly subpoenaed the television station to get it.

Karen Johnson seemed to be a different person. With guidance from her attorney, G. Allen Dale, she told law enforcement authorities that she had received as much as twenty-five thousand dollars from Barry's close associates Clyburn and Roy Littlejohn. The two businessmen at first denied and then acknowledged giving money to Johnson out of sympathy, not as "hush money."

"It's a shame there aren't more people like Mr. Clyburn and Mr. Littlejohn," said Dale. "Most don't give away money just for the heck of it."

The story attracted media heavies. WRC-TV dispatched general assignment reporter Katie Couric, now the co-host of the "Today Show," in an unsuccessful attempt to woo Johnson. She also turned away *Washington Post* star Bob Woodward. Elsa Walsh, Woodward's wife and a *Post* reporter, knew Dale and invited him and Johnson to dinner at their Georgetown home. No dice. Mike Wallace tried to interview Johnson for "60 Minutes," but she backed out twice.

Enough facts leaked from the Johnson affair to paint a convincing picture for most Washingtonians that Barry had used cocaine and tried to silence a potential witness. But for all the leaked details, graphic news accounts, and innuendo, DiGenova couldn't bring charges.

In June, Barry loyalists led a counterattack with a crowd of seven hundred government workers, city officials, and Barry supporters brought together for Marion Barry Appreciation Day. They waved placards proclaiming, "We Thought Lynching Was Outlawed" and "Stop the Leaks," and they heard accolades for the mayor.

"If he's guilty, indict him. If not, leave, him alone," declared Calvin Rolark, Jr., publisher of a black community newspaper and husband of city council member Wilhelmina Rolark.

Jack Olender, a negligence lawyer who had made millions of dollars thanks to the city's unlimited medical malpractice damages laws, chimed in.

"He has brought great credit to our city, nationally and internationally," Olender told the crowd. "He has helped bring us from a sleepy southern town to a vital modern city where equal opportunity is more than a slogan."

John Hechinger, the hardware mogul and early supporter, called Barry's treatment "trial by innuendo."

At that moment, Barry was on his way to the Bahamas, but he did file a lawsuit accusing DiGenova of deliberately leaking information. Over the next year, D.C. Superior Court Judge Aubrey Robinson, a black jurist first appointed by President Johnson, ruled against Barry's lawsuit.

The mayor also turned to the media that seemed most sympathetic, in this case WOL-AM radio, the home of owner and on-air personality Cathy Hughes. With the help of a $25,000 loan from the Barry administration, Hughes had established her station in the middle of the H Street shopping district, which was still struggling to overcome the scars of the 1968 riots. WOL's storefront studio featured a huge plate-glass window that allowed Hughes to see out onto the street and, just as important, allowed motorists and passersby to see Hughes as she hosted her daily, four-hour morning show of commentary that was sometimes spiced with blatant anti-white tracts amid the fare of prayer and calls for black self-help. Hughes reached a slice of Washington's lower- and middle-class black audience and gave voice to its need for an identity. Many of her loyal listeners were elderly and loved the connection they felt with Hughes's "WOL family."

Though the station had relatively low ratings, the white community took notice of Hughes in 1986 when she helped lead protests against *The Washington Post's* new Sunday magazine, whose first issue was remarkable for its negative, fearsome stereotypes of blacks. Brandishing signs that read "Take It Back," hundreds of protesters tossed thousands of copies back on the steps of the *Post's* headquarters. It was a public relations nightmare for the city's dominant newspaper, which was already uncomfortable on matters of race. It helped build the Cathy Hughes mystique.

Barry scheduled an appearance one summer morning, but stood Hughes up, tapping her ire. "You don't follow anyone blindly, my brothers and sisters," she said. "We love Marion Barry. He is the mayor. But if Marion Barry disrespects us, we will cry out. We will not blindly drink the Kool-Aid any longer." A week later he was back on Hughes' s station to smooth things over.

"There are forces out there who don't particularly like what I do, how I do it, or who I stand up to," Barry said.

What about the new *Washington Post* poll showing the damage of six months of bad press, she asked. Two out of three people believed corruption was a major problem in the Barry administration, and 47 percent said that Barry's own ethics were either "not good" or "poor"—a nine-point jump from just a year earlier. Three-fourths of white respondents were critical of Barry. Blacks were split fifty-fifty—a dramatic drop for Barry in less than a year.

"I'm elated," Barry responded. "I'm excited and encouraged when we have had nothing but a daily dose of negative information about the Barry administration."

Barry attacked the FBI for bugging his home despite prosecutors' denials. "It has been clearly demonstrated that they are capable of doing these kinds of things," he said, conjuring up the FBI harassment of civil rights workers. "They just don't trust that we can be honest, good, outstanding public officials.

"This is the nation's capital," he said. "For a long time the town had a majority white leadership. Then Walter Washington came in. I think he did a good job. I just have a different style and I suspect there are people in this town and this country who don't want us to maintain leadership in the nation's capital."

An unseen "they" just didn't like him. "They don't know how straight I am... I'm just little ol' David against Goliath."

In minutes, Barry had managed to cloak himself in the tradition of black religious beliefs, U.S. government racism, and the civil rights movement. Hughes commiserated that Barry's home life with Effi had been "invaded."

"It causes me concern," Barry said, "particularly—this is a very delicate subject—in my bedroom in terms of personal conversations that Effi and I may have, personal activities that I may have. It interferes with our lovemaking, but we get around it," he said. "We make love anywhere."

The consensus among people who knew the Barry family was that Effi and Marion probably didn't make love at all anymore.

As the mayor's extramarital affairs and nightly wanderings became public, Effi Barry kept her silence, at least in public. Dutifully showing up at social events as the city's First Lady, she rarely appeared in public with her husband. Everyone on the fifth floor of the District Building knew Barry and his wife effectively led separate lives.

"I am an independent entity," she would later tell the *Washingtonian* magazine in a moment of candor, "separate and apart from my husband."

"She's strong enough to stay, too weak to leave," said a close friend.

In September, Effi Barry burst from the sidelines of her husband's political melodrama and agreed to sit for an interview with WRC-TV reporter Barbara Harrison. Barry's aides were apoplectic. Barry said he had no control over his wife, but Effi demonstrated perfect control as she led Harrison to the edge of the dark corners of their life.

"What I blame him for is his indiscretion," she said quietly, smiling a thin smile and arching one eyebrow. "Indiscretion," she repeated.

"When the papers start naming names," Harrison began to ask, "and saying these people slept with the mayor and someone saw it..."

The First Lady narrowed her eyes and cleared her throat. "There is a caliber of female in this world that tends to gravitate toward power figures. This kind of invasion is a necessary nuisance that a wife of a power figure has to deal with." Effi Barry was just another female attracted to a power figure back in 1977, but now she was the power figure's wife talking about one of his former mistresses, Karen Johnson.

"I have pity for her," Mrs. Barry said. "I never met her. I feel embarrassed for her...I think she was foolish to stay in this town. If she served her time or whatever she had to do, she should have gotten out of town for the sake of her dignity, and for her son's sake, and started a new life elsewhere."

"My husband is an honest man," she said, Han arrogant person,and you expect him to be. He has a right to be. His arrogance goes along with his charisma. It's the street dude in him."

The only people willing to challenge Barry were· a handful who knew the Marion of 1978, the idealist who could have changed the world.

In mid-November, Max Berry, telephone executive Delano Lewis, and Doug Patton, a white attorney who had first worked with Barry sixteen years earlier, met with the mayor in his office. They exchanged pleasantries and got serious, Berry recalled.

"Look, Marion," Berry said, "It's bad enough that your government appears to be full of cronyism. But all of your extracurricular activities are killing your image. You make Effi look bad, your son looks bad. You're ruining yourself politically.

"I'm fed up," he told the mayor. "Go home at night. Start acting like a family man."

Del Lewis didn't say much. His presence expressed his concern, but he was in a difficult position. Lewis was the most prominent African-American businessman in the city, if not the entire capital region. The Greater Washington Board of Trade that had run the city to the exclusion of blacks for so many years had just elected Lewis its first African-American president. But he still needed the mayor. Barry gave Lewis all the city's phone contracts and blessed his company's piece of the cable TV deal Barry's influence was crucial when the phone company brought rate changes before the Public Service Commission. He had more to lose than Berry or Patton—plus, he was the only black critic there.

"You're a good friend, Max," Barry said, appearing shaken by the visit and the tirade. "I'm going to turn over a new leaf. I need to be a better father, a better husband. I'm going to start right away. I'm going to the Bahamas with Christopher. Effi has to give a speech and can't go. I'm looking forward to spending some quality time with my son."

On the way down the long corridor with huge likenesses of the mayor at each end, Max Berry was encouraged. "I think we made an impression," he said.

Barry and his son flew to the Bahamas on November 25, the day before Thanksgiving. Later the same day, a separate flight to the Bahamas took off with Bettye Smith, Barry's late-night friend and financial adviser from W. R. Lazard.

Barry's security aides and son checked into room 865 of the Cable Beach Hotel. Barry checked into room 864. A short time later, a bellhop showed Smith to room 866, adjacent to Barry's. The hotel accommodations were arranged by Jeff Mitchell, the friend who had been in L.A. the previous January when Barry overdosed on cocaine. Barry also had another female guest, Theresa Southerland, who was in another room. Barry called Southerland "Miss T." An administrative secretary in the government, Southerland had first met Barry a year earlier at Chapter III, a popular nightclub and disco in the warehouse district of Southwest Washington. Southerland was twenty-three years old at the time. She had beautiful hands and long fingernails that she would use to scoop up powdered cocaine to put under the mayor's nose. The Bahamas trip was midpoint in an intimate relationship that did not end until October 1989.

Post reporter Lee Hockstader—whom Barry didn't know—followed the entourage and filed a story about Barry's vacation, which raised questions about Barry's private life and the lucrative contract held by Bettye Smith's boss, W. R. Lazard. Smith was later forced to resign. Miss T escaped notice. Max Berry read the story and called the mayor.

"It's over, Marion," he said. "How many times do you think we can be fooled?"

Barry laughed. "I'll call you in two weeks," he said.

"Don't bother, Marion," Berry said. "That's it!

CHAPTER 11

CRACK ATTACK

Cocaine distribution (including crack cocaine) appears to
be the first illegal market in which youths have opportunities to be primary entrepreneurs rather than supporters of
adult distributors.

—*The Rand Corporation*
on drug dealing in Washington, D.C.

Rayful Edmond III, the capital's first cocaine king, had a close call early in his career.

It was a brisk spring night in 1984, and all along the Strip, a notorious drug market ten blocks due north of the Supreme Court, cocaine in small plastic bags was changing hands. Back then the Strip was a marvel of free-market economics. Supply and demand controlled prices, there were no monopolies, and rival dealers competed on equal terms. Unlike New York and Philadelphia, Washington had no organized crime bosses controlling the drug business and snuffing out competition. Anyone could get in the game.

"The capital was a free-trade zone for drug dealers," said John Wilder, the special agent in charge of the Drug Enforcement Administration's local branch in the late 1980s. Rayful Edmond was a budding eighteen-year-old entrepreneur in those days. As his mother put it: "He started off selling drugs hand to hand."

But that night in 1984 would be one of his last on the street. A lean, athletic young man with a narrow face and a precisely trimmed mustache and beard that circled his mouth, he was wearing a warm-up suit and basketball shoes; a few dime bags of cocaine were left in his pocket. Midway down Orleans Place, a beat-up Pontiac pulled up by the curb. The man riding shotgun rolled down his window. Expecting a sale, Edmond approached and asked how much the man wanted. The door burst open, and a police officer in plain clothes jumped out.

Edmond turned and ran with the cop on his tail. The two of them pounded down the street, but Edmond was too fast. He rounded a corner onto Florida Avenue, ducked into a Chinese carryout, and ditched the three bags of cocaine in a trash basket before the policeman showed. Edmond turned and flashed his sweet smile. He was hardly out of breath. Daily basketball games kept him in great shape. He looked at the cop, and turned his hands up.

"Keep your hands out of your pockets and get out here," the officer said. He stood Edmond up against the brick wall, spread his legs, and patted him down. No drugs, no guns, no knives. He booked him anyway on a minor charge, and two hours later Edmond was out on the street. But the close call taught him an important lesson: Let peons handle bags of coke on the retail level. At age eighteen, Rayful Edmond retired from street sales and set his sights on becoming a major supplier.

To build his organization, Edmond turned inward to his mother, sisters, half-brothers, and cousins. He grew up in a warm, extended family at his grandmother's home at 407 M Street NE, a neighborhood of brick row houses across Florida Avenue from the city's bustling wholesale food market. There were summer crab feasts on the stoops and big turkey dinners on Sunday afternoons. His father, Ray Jr., or "Big Ray," was a numbers runner and small-time gambler who spent a lot of time in Philadelphia and Atlantic City once the casinos opened. For a time he held down a job as a driver for the U.S Department of Health and Human Services. He quit in the early 1980s "in order to pursue more lucrative employment on the outside," according to his letter of resignation. The lucrative employment was dealing drugs.

Young Rayful, his only son by Constance "Bootsie" Perry, was a handsome, gregarious kid who rarely got into trouble and did well enough in school. His classmates at Dunbar High, once the premier black school in the days before desegregation, voted him "Mr. Dunbar." Edmond loved basketball more than books. He'd started playing in the boys' club leagues at twelve, and though he never made it past six feet, he could pop, the ball in from every corner of the court. Two of his best friends—Royal Brooks and John Turner, who became a basketball star at Georgetown University—urged Edmond to continue in school.

"You'll miss out on something if you don't go to college," one of Edmond's coaches told him.

"I'm thinking about it," Edmond responded.

His thoughts at this crucial juncture were guided by his father, Big Ray.

Some parents provide their children with an education and send them out into the world. Others guide them into a trade. Edmond's father taught him by example. Sometime in 1984 he called his eldest son to New York and gave him a kilogram of cocaine. Edmond returned to Washington, cut the white powder, and sold it on Orleans Place and Morton Place, a few blocks from his home. "It all started with his daddy," Constance Perry told a friend over lunch one day. With the profits from the first kilo, Edmond bought two more, and an empire was born.

He organized a crew of friends to work for him. Most were childhood buddies who didn't have jobs, needed cash, and liked to stay in the neighborhood. Edmond offered them a simple deal: He would provide them with a steady supply of cocaine for sale in various amounts; they would put no money up front, but he would take most of the profits. It was an easy way to get into the business, a crude form of franchising. There were plenty of job applicants. He even ordered

T-shirts as a marketing tool for his salesmen. They read: "Top of the Line."

Rayful Edmond was among the first of a new breed of drug dealers in Washington's disorganized market.

During the 1960s, when heroin was the drug of choice, a line of unrelated major dealers controlled a piece of the market. The first was Lawrence "Slippery" Jackson, whose heroin supply came by car and train from New York Mafia families. Three hundred calls a day were coming into Jackson's headquarters, a fact that the DEA learned when they took him down with one of their first wiretaps. In Jackson's place, James "Dumptruck" Smith, affectionately called Smitty, or Big Head, came to the fore. More than a few law-enforcement professionals look back on Dumptruck—and his drug—with a touch of nostalgia. In his own way, he was a gentleman, and he never used violence. His generation of criminals viewed illegal activities as a way to get ahead, raise a family, and send the kids to college. Crime was one way to boost your kids into the middle class. And heroin, though terribly addictive and destructive, had a calming effect on addicts. Junkies shot up and nodded off; they were rarely a threat when they were high.

Cocaine changed both sides of the equation. Coke dealers tended to be young, violent, fearless, and greedy; selling dope and making money were ends, not means. The drug itself made users jumpy and paranoid. When cocaine became king, the streets of the District turned much meaner. The city's first cocaine kingpin was Cornell Jones, a violence-prone young man who ran his operation out of Hanover Place, near the intersection of North Capitol Street and New York Avenue. From the corner store where Jones would buy cigarettes and occasionally make deals, he could look down North Capitol and see the white dome of the U.S. Capitol a dozen blocks away.

As a juvenile, Cornell Jones racked up an alarming arrest re cord for violent crimes. He was always the gunman. He was first busted on a drug charge in 1979, but despite his violent record, he was released, only to be arrested and released six more times over the next six years. In that time Jones organized a multilayered cocaine distribution system. He or his lieutenants bought cocaine by the kilogram in Florida and drove it up to the capital. Middlemen would break it down and sell it to buyers who would knock on the doors of certain apartments at Hanover Place. When the city's vice squad finally infiltrated Hanover Place in 1985 and took down Jones in a classic sting operation, they found that he had more than $2.5 million in cash, jewelry, cars, gold, and real estate. He was moving ten kilograms of cocaine a week.

Taking down Jones did nothing to contain the demand for cocaine. It just opened an opportunity for a new entrepreneur to take his place. It was as if Giant Food, the city's largest supermarket chain, had decided to pull out of town; another store would simply move in. In this case, Cornell Jones had a lieutenant who escaped prosecution. His name was Tony Lewis, and he was a good friend of Rayful Edmond, who lived a few blocks away across New York Avenue.

The Strip, where Edmond set up shop, is an ideal setting for the urban equivalent of a Middle Eastern souk.

Orleans Place and Morton Place are short, narrow, parallel one-way streets connected by a series of alleys. Florida Avenue, a major east-west thoroughfare, lies a short block to the north for easy access and fast getaways. When the Strip was running at full capacity, dozens of coke dealers sold little bags to customers who came on foot or slowly cruised through in cars with Virginia or Maryland license plates. If a police car ventured into the maze, lookouts would yell "olleray, olleray, olleray," Pig Latin for roller, and dealers would scatter. The narrow alleys were barricaded by old washing machines or piles of tires. If the cops gave chase on foot, there were trip wires in strategic, blind corners.

Around this supermarket, Edmond organized a highly structured dope-peddling system. Edmond and his top associate, Tony Lewis, bought cocaine in bulk. The kilo-sized bricks were transported to the suburban home of Edmond's sister and brother-in-law, where they were cut down to twenty-five-dollar and fifty-dollar bags for street sales. Kathy Sellers, Edmond's childhood friend, delivered the bags to the Strip. Middlemen distributed the carefully counted bags to the runners and dealers who actually sold the coke; they would lob foam footballs that had been hollowed out and stuffed with cocaine up and down the short block. A dealer could sell as many as five hundred bags a day and generate twenty-five thousand dollars. Managers would collect the day's receipts and often give them to Sellers, who took the money back to the Edmond family's home in Prince Georges County, Maryland. On one occasion Sellers saw Constance Perry, Edmond's mother, Jeeding one hundred thousand dollars in small bills into a counting machine.

Edmond was twenty-two when his organization started generating enormous amounts of cash, and he became a hometown hero, a mythical figure in a downtrodden corner of the city. He bought cars—Mercedes-Benzes, Range Rovers, BMWs—but the one that everyone loved was the white Jaguar with the gold hubcaps. On a summer evening he would cruise his turf in the white chariot, and young children would run in his path. He was generous in the manner of old-style gangsters: He'd make sure neighbors had turkeys on Thanksgiving; he bought meals for the homeless, cars for his top staff, and clothes for his friends. He sponsored a basketball team in the Police Athletic League called "Clean Sweep," the name of the police operation designed to get drug dealers off the streets. Basketball was the neighborhood's relief valve. Talented athletes who never made it to college, college stars who played at Georgetown University, and drug dealers got together for tournaments. "Doctors play a round of golf to relax," said an Athletic League supervisor. "Drug dealers play basketball." The stands were always packed with teenage boys and girls who had come out to see Rayful and his team.

"He's a wonderful young man," a neighbor said. "I've knownhim and his family for years. He would make any parents proud."

Edmond had everything but the perfect gangster moll. He ran into her one day in the summer of 1986 when he stopped by the Florida Avenue Grill for lunch. The restaurant at the corner of Eleventh and Florida on the southern edge of Shaw is Washington's most celebrated southern food diner. It was also the home of a fencing operation run by the owner's sons.

On the way out of the restaurant, Edmond saw a woman waiting for her Mercedes Benz to come out of the adjacent carwash. He had seen her in the restaurant selling jewelry out of a case. Her hair was bleached platinum blonde and shaved on the sides in a severe punk style. She wore a miniskirt slit up the side and stiletto heels.

"My name's Rayful," he said. "Some people call me Ray."

"My name's Rae, too," she responded. "Alta Rae Zanville."

He asked if he could buy some jewelry, and she fetched her case. They talked about cars for a while. Edmond picked out a ring, paid for it, and gave it back to her.

"Why did you do that?" she asked.

"Because I like you and I don't need the money," he said. He handed her a piece of paper. "Here's my phone number. Give me a call sometime."

When Alta Rae Zanville ran into Edmond for the first time, she was a forty-five-year-old woman who'd been working as a clerk for the Navy for twenty-six years. In that time she'd been married and divorced, worked as a cocktail waitress, and gone into the jewelry business to make some extra cash. Zanville's husband had lavished minks and jewels on her, and she wanted to maintain her lifestyle after they split in 1984. She liked the black social scene and hung out at popular clubs like the Foxtrappe on Sixteenth Street near Dupont Circle. It took her closer to the edge, where she was comfortable.

A few weeks later she was driving down Connecticut Avenue in her Mercedes with the top down when a red Porsche passed her with the horn blowing. The Porsche stopped when she pulled over to park. Rayful Edmond got out and came back to talk with her.

"Why didn't you call me?" he asked.

They chatted for a while, and she gave him her pager number. He called a few days later and asked her to come to 407 M Street. Alta Rae Zanville was just what Edmond needed at the time. They may have had an affair, but he wanted her for business purposes. His drug-dealing cash was piling up. He was not sophisticated enough to launder the cash through businesses or hide it in foreign bank accounts. Edmond just wanted to put his wads of greenbacks into cars, apartments, and houses for his mother and other family members. But he didn't want to put his name on the cars or the real estate, which might create a paper trail for the law. Registering everything in the name of a stylish white woman would raise fewer questions and lead investigators away from him. He asked her to rent an apartment for him just across the Potomac River in Crystal City, Virginia.

Zanville agreed to rent the apartment. Edmond paid her five hundred dollars. He had much bigger jobs in mind for her. The Navy clerk with a taste for the fast life would make the perfect front.

Len Bias was a local hero of another sort in the spring and summer of 1986.

The six-foot-eleven-inch basketball star had just finished his senior year at the University of Maryland, a few miles northeast of the District line in College Park. With great fanfare, the Boston Celtics signed him to a multimillion-dollar contract and turned him into a national attraction. At twenty-two, he promised to be a franchise player, a role model, and a man made wealthy from contracts and endorsements.

On the night of June 18, Bias met his friend Brian Tribble and began a night of celebration. They made a few stops, including one at Montana Terrace, one of the city's most downtrodden and drug-infested public housing projects. Along the way they bought a few grams of powdered cocaine and returned to Bias's dorm. The basketball star consumed massive amounts of white powder, possibly more than a gram, dissolved in a Coke. His system went into shock. A few hours later, Len Bias lay dead on the floor from an overdose.

That a hearty athlete in peak physical shape could be felled by cocaine sent shock waves across the country. White yuppies who'd used cocaine on weekends quit abruptly. The press used Bias's death to whip the country into a froth over drug abuse. The politicians responded to the press and the public opinion polls with an avalanche of legislation and a gale of speeches. The frenzy grew to such a pitch that the next few months became known as "Drug War Fall."

A week after Bias died, Congressman Charles Rangel introduced a package of legislation designed to get tough on drug dealers and fund education programs. The price tag: $1 billion. The proximity to Bias's death was coincidental. Rangel, a Harlem Democrat, was trying to outgun the White House in a struggle over the antidrug high ground that would rage for months.

"Even though the administration claims to have declared war on drugs," Rangel declared from his office, a mere mile from Rayful Edmond's headquarters, "the only evidence I find of this war are the casualties."

Back in May, it first dawned on official Washington that cocaine and drug abuse in general were becoming a problem. Republican pollster Richard Wirthlin detected the anxiety levels rising among the voters and suggested in a memo that President Reagan could seize the antidrug issue. It was a perfect opportunity for the president to rally the nation against a common evil. The president agreed, and the "war on drugs" was joined.

First Lady Nancy Reagan had carried on the small-scale skirmishes against drugs during the administration's first six years. In dewy-eyed chats and demure speeches she had implored audiences to "say no to drugs." But while she talked about her great concern, the Reagan administration was cutting drug treatment and prevention programs 40 percent, from $333 million in 1980 to $235 million in 1986.

The media discovered cocaine around the same time. *The New York Times* was first out of the box with a report on crack and crime in Manhattan. *Newsweek* followed in mid-June with a cover article entitled "An Inferno of Craving, Dealing and Despair." Bias's death triggered a torrent of stories in magazines from *Sports Illustrated* to *Good Housekeeping* to *Life,* which pictured a man puffing on a crack pipe on its cover with the headline " 'I am a coke addict'—What Happens When Nice Guys Get Hooked." Television followed with hour-long specials on crack, and the nation was fully aroused.

The Democrats branded Reagan a latecomer to the war and rushed to outflank him. Congressmen started minting legislation at such a rate that Speaker Tip O'Neill called a halt and asked twenty-two committees to develop an omnibus hill. On September 11 the House voted 392-16 to approve a hill that would authorize $6 billion over three years to do everything from making money laundering a more serious crime, to increasing sentences for first-time offenders, to giving the military sweeping powers to interdict drugs, to adding the death penalty for drug kingpins.

"I fear this is the legislative equivalent of crack," said Massachusetts Democrat Barney Frank. "It yields a short-term high but does long-term damage to the system, and it's expensive to boot."

The White House countered with a made-for-TV fireside chat by Reagan and the First Lady. Holding hands and looking moistly at the camera, the Reagans took turns beseeching the nation to go straight. Mrs. Reagan completed her soliloquy with her trademark: "Say yes to your life. And when it comes to drugs and alcohol, just say no."

"My generation will remember how Americans swung into action when we were attacked in World War II," Reagan said. "Now we're in another war for our freedom, and it's time for all of us to pull together again."

Congress passed the Anti-Drug Abuse Act of 1986 on October 17. The grandiose legislation called for $1.7 billion of spending on all manner of drug and alcohol abuse in the following fiscal year. Ten days later the president signed it and intoned: "Drug use is too costly for us not to do everything in our power, not just to fight it, but to subdue it and conquer it." Reagan's next budget gutted the bill, cut the funding by more than half, slashed its drug treatment and education provisions, cut research, and curtailed interdiction. Preparing for the political season a year away, President Reagan glibly took credit for "beginning to win the crusade for a drug-free America."

Despite the media hype and the political machinations, the demand for cocaine along the Strip was high—so high that Rayful Edmond couldn't keep up with it. His organization was able to move a kilogram of cocaine a day, broken down into half-gram bags that went for fifty dollars each. He could sell twice that much if he could tap directly into a Colombian connection.

In early April 1987, Edmond phoned Alta Rae Zanville.

"You want to go to the Sugar Ray Leonard fight?" he asked. "We're going to Las Vegas. I got an extra ticket. Why don't you come on?"

Zanville said sure and joined the party of ten, including his father, Big Ray; his mother, Bootsie; Columbus "Little Nut" Daniels, an enforcer; Edmond's partner, Tony Lewis; a cousin named Little Frank; and a few others. Lewis brought three children: his son and two nephews. They flew first class and drove around Vegas in a white stretch limousine. Edmond put everyone up in separate rooms at the Imperial Palace Hotel and picked up all the meals and bar tabs. He sported a gold chain around his neck with a gold medallion encrusted with diamonds. He took everyone shopping at the Gucci store. On fight night they watched Sugar Ray Leonard beat Marvelous Marvin Hagler from $400 seats close to ringside.

Edmond's entourage caught the eye of Melvin Butler, a roving cocaine salesman from the Crips street gang in Los Angeles. The Crips dealt directly with Colombian importers and acted as middlemen in the cocaine distribution system in Los Angeles. Toward the late 1980s Crips members were marketing coke—and its cheaper, more addictive, smokable form, crack—across the country and carving out new territory in Minneapolis, Kansas City, and Detroit. Butler checked out Edmond and recognized that he could be a conduit to the lucrative Washington market.

Butler introduced Edmond and Lewis to Brian "Waterhead Bo" Bennett, the Crips member who dealt directly with a Colombian supplier, Mario Ernesto Villabona-Alvarado. The relationship between Butler and Villabona was perhaps the first between a Colombian and a member of a black street gang. Edmond was to become one of their best customers. Bennett and Butler could supply Edmond with unlimited quantities of white powder from Villabona. All Edmond would have to do was bring the cash to and transport the bricks of coke back to D.C., and they would be in business.

Edmond tested the network immediately. He dispatched lieutenants to Los Angeles with suitcases full of cash; they returned with bricks of high-grade cocaine. Once he turned on the L.A. pipeline, Edmond ran a surplus at the Strip and started to supply kilograms to other major dealers across the city. At his peak in 1988, Rayful sat atop an organization of nearly two hundred employees that moved an estimated $10 million to $20 million worth of cocaine and crack a month from Columbia via the Crips. He controlled 20 percent of the city's cocaine market, and the market was still growing because of crack, the most destructive drug in the city's history.

"Rock" had already infected Los Angeles, Houston, Detroit, Miami, and New York before it made its D.C. debut late in 1986. Crack was cheap and addictive: A dose cost as little as five dollars, and smoking it produced a high that was powerful enough to make mothers abandon their babies for one more hit from the pipe. Adding crack to Washington's dispossessed neighborhoods had the same effect as throwing a match into a bucket of gasoline. Crack tore through other cities, but its impact on the capital was far more destructive. From 1984 to 1987 the number of patients admitted to emergency rooms with cocaine-related problems tri pled, according to criminal justice reports. The number of adults who were arrested and tested positive for cocaine increased by 43 percent between 1984 and 1988. "Not only has the drug epidemic been spreading like wildfire," a report by the Greater Washington Research Center said, "it has also been reaching farther down into the age distribution."

Why was Washington more vulnerable to crack than most cities?

The market was ripe in the desperate black underclass, but crack was able to dominate the capital because the metropolitan police department was ill equipped, ill prepared, and morally corrupted by its commander in chief, Mayor Barry.

Barry mistrusted the police from his childhood days in Memphis, when white cops used to call him "nigger." Police were the enemy during the civil rights movement, and he was arrested a half-dozen times. Though he had allied himself with the police union in 1978 for political purposes, as soon as he took office he had begun to gnaw away at the police department's power. In sheer numbers, the MPD had reached its zenith in 1972 when President Nixon ordered the hiring of enough officers to bring the total to fifty-one hundred. The department had been one of the best in the nation, judging by the dropping crime rates, ability to solve homicides, and lack of corruption. After 1978, the closure rates on all crimes began to plummet, police lost touch with the communities, and the crime rate started to climb. There were many reasons for the decline in quality police work, but the root cause was what federal prosecutors called the "Barryization" of the entire department.

Barry cut the number of police officers as soon as he could and kept reducing the force to a low of 3,612 in 1981. At the same time he kept slicing the police department's share of the city's budget. When he took office the police department got 8.6 percent of the budget; by 1985 it was down to 6.5 percent, according to the Congressional Budget Office.

The lack of funds weakened the police in fundamental ways. Investigators lacked cars to get to crime scenes. Homicide detectives had to work three or four to a desk. The entire unit had to share four typewriters, including two manual ones, to write their reports. Barry's studied neglect kept the city police in the technical dark ages. While other police departments were becoming computerized and beginning to share investigative information between units and precincts, the District's cops were working with equipment from the

1950s that essentially put them in blinders. Ace detectives had to type statements, with carbons, on manual typewriters. The city wasn't even linked to nationwide computerized crime networks, Training and recruitment suffered, too. "I've seen people diagnosed as borderline retarded graduate from the academy," former instructor Mike Hubbard told the publication *Policy Review.*

If Barry's first message was that he would squeeze the force's numbers and dollars, his second was that he would punish anyone who challenged his authority or dared to investigate him. That word came through loud and clear when he busted inspector Fred Raines back to night supervisor for reporting the mayor's cocaine use and whoring escapades at This Is It? in 1982.

The mayor kept the cops under his thumb by more direct means. Every appointment above the rank of captain required his stamp of approval—and it was not a rubberstamp. Barry made sure that his friends rose to the top. Isaac "Ike" Fulwood, Jr., the street officer who helped rescue Barry when the Hanafi Muslims attacked the District Building in 1976, was promoted to command the Sixth District in 1981. Then in late 1984, Barry personally intervened in the promotion process to install Fulwood as the number-two man in the entire department, in line to become the chief. Fulwood was seen as a good cop who was beholden to Barry; throughout the department, the FBI, and the prosecutor's office it was assumed that Fulwood would not cross any legal lines himself, but would limit any zeal to investigate his patron.

The police chief at the time was Barry's appointee, Maurice Turner, a big-boned native Washingtonian and a dedicated, gentle man. But he was no match for the mayor in the struggle for control of the department, and he wasn't dynamic enough to modernize police procedures. Following trends set by his predecessors, Turner kept officers in squad cars, off the streets, and out of touch with the people whom they were policing. In some drug-infested neighborhoods, the balance of power shifted to the dealers, whose wrath was more feared than the power of the law.

The combination of Barry's antipathy toward the police, his meddling in the promotion process, and the lax leadership set the department adrift. There were plenty of good cops on the force, but they were frustrated by a system that gave them little technical support and promoted by the crony method. As long as the level of criminal activity didn't increase, the police could muddle through and maintain public safety.

Then crack hit the capital.

Warnings were sounded as early as 1980. Lowell Duckett, a leader of the Afro-American Police Association, was asked by Barry for a status report and recommendations. Duckett reported that the police were beginning to lose control of certain parts of the District, and the lawlessness left the city wide open for exploitation by drug outlaws. Barry ditched the report. A few years later Detective Bill Larman started compiling statistics on drug arrests that showed an alarming rise in cocaine use. He recommended a citywide strategy to prepare for the coming cocaine wars. The top brass ignored his report. Police departments across the nation were sharing information and preparing to fight the new drugs. The FBI, DEA, and other federal crime-fighting agencies were training local police across the country. Somehow, the capital cops stood still.

The first wave of cocaine broke over the city in 1980 and 1981. The powdered form started to overtake marijuana, PCP, and heroin as the drug of choice in the inner city. The first blatant, outdoor drug markets opened in 1985, often staffed by drug dealers from New York who'd come down to take advantage of Washington's free-market liberal bail laws.

"In New York, the cops take our money, our dope, and beat your ass," a dealer told a D.C. vice cop who was working a strip two blocks north of Fourteenth and U streets in 1984. "Down here, you take me in tonight, and you'll see me back out here tomorrow."

The drug markets popped up in obvious places: public housing complexes, shabby parts of Shaw, tough street comers east of the Anacostia River. The police began to lose control of neighborhoods like Division Street, on the District's easternmost border with Maryland, where drug dealers were more feared than the cops. There were no brazen drug zones west of Rock Creek Park in the white community—which is not to say that whites didn't patronize the cocaine dealers or buy the powder through more discrete networks.

While the police were taken by surprise, Rayful Edmond was perfectly situated to take advantage of the coming age of crack. His organization was as slick and well run as McDonald's. Morton Place and Orleans Place became so crowded that on some days Edmond's lieutenants had to order customers to form lines that stretched one hundred buyers long.

The police tried to respond by arresting street dealers and occasionally one of the middle-management types, but it would take a much better organized approach to bring down the entire organization. Any kind of serious response was more difficult when it became apparent that Marion Barry, the commander in chief, was on his way to becoming a pipe head.

In early October 1987, among the scores of people going into and out of the District Building one day was an inconspicuous citizen of the U.S. Virgin Islands, Charles "Chuck" Lewis. A special assistant to islands governor Alexander A. Farrelly, Lewis had hand-delivered a two-page letter from Farrelly to Marion Barry.

Farrelly noted that twenty years earlier the District government had helped the territory redesign its jumbled personnel system. Farrelly wanted help again.

"I have assigned Mr. Charles Lewis of my office to manage the project," Farrelly wrote.

Lewis was no stranger to Washington and the District government. A short, skinny man with slightly hunched shoulders, he was the black sheep of a prominent Virgin Islands family. His family's connections opened doors into the business and political worlds, but Chuck Lewis's business ventures never succeeded. He began dabbling in the drug trade and developed a craving for cocaine. When he first came to work in the District in 1979, he already was using the white powder. He was addicted in the mid-1980s when he and Marion Barry discovered that they had a mutual interest in sex and drugs.

A month after Lewis delivered Governor Farrelly's letter to the District Building, Barry wrote back.

"I have talked with Mr. Charles Lewis of your office, and he has met with my Director of Personnel, Mr. Theodore E. Thornton," Barry began. "As I understand it, the government of the Virgin Islands will cover the costs of transportation and accommodations..."

Over the early winter months of 1988 a gaggle of forty District government officials and personnel aides spent more than two hundred thousand dollars shuttling to and from the sun-drenched islands. No matter that the D.C. government kept its personnel records in cardboard file boxes on the floor, and that no one knew how many people actually worked for the city, and the government had yet to write its own regulations to implement the Merit Personnel Act of 1979. The highest-paid officials headed south to offer their expertise.

Meanwhile, the mayor in January proposed a drug summit with Maryland and Virginia and promised to make a "crusade against drugs my number one priority" in 1988. "Drugs threaten our stability. Drugs threaten our safety," he told a cheering crowd, "and drugs threaten the soul of our city." He led a march through the Potomac Gardens public housing complex. *The Washington Post* commended him in an editorial for his strong stand against drugs. He was feeling quite good as he prepared for a four-day business trip to the Virgin Islands.

On March 2, 1988, Barry and an entourage of seventeen city employees and city contractors flew to the islands for a four-day conference. Barry was to meet with Governor Farrelly to discuss interim reports on the personnel project. By this time, city employees and private contractors retained by the District had grown accustomed to $300- and $500-a-night suites during the peak tourist season. Despite rules limiting per diem expenses to $180, Barry and top aides moved into the luxury Frenchmen's Reef Morning Star Beach Resort at top rates.

"They were spending money like drunken sailors," one island official told *The Washington Post*.

The mayor did meet with Governor Farrelly, but he spent most of his time back at the hotel where Chuck Lewis was providing him with women and drugs. Lewis told the women that meeting Barry would be an entree into jobs or business opportunities in Washington.

When Lewis walked Zenna Matthias into Barry's suite, the mayor was lying on a bed, watching an X-rated movie. Matthias, a schoolteacher with three children, realized that Barry had more on his mind than job opportunities. He brought out some powdered cocaine and showed her how to snort it through a straw.

"We call it Hoovering," he said, then helped her put the cocaine up her nose.

But when the mayor tried to grab her and suggested that she watch the movie with him, she laughed him off.

"I have children," she told him. "I'm used to the human anatomy. I don't need to look at things like that."

And she left.

Linda Creque Maynard found Barry wearing only a robe when Lewis escorted her to his room.

"Ah," Barry said, "this one's for me."

"No," she replied, "this one is not for you."

The mayor brought out the cocaine. Barry was drinking, too. He came up behind Maynard and began fondling her. She moved away and sat on a bed. Barry sat next to her and began touching her. She tried to fight him off. The struggle lasted about ten minutes until Barry pinned Maynard on the bed and forced her to have sex with him.

Back in Washington, Barry didn't have to fight Rasheeda Moore for sex, but he was becoming suspicious of the drugs that she was doing.

"Are you smoking crack?" he asked.

They were in her apartment on Sixteenth Street. She didn't want to introduce Barry to crack because she knew its addictive power. Barry said he already had tried it. He found her pipe and smoked some crack. After a few more occasions, the mayor was hooked. Throughout the spring and summer he often stopped by her apartment to take a hit of crack from the pipe. He came by before meetings, after meetings, after work. Sometimes he'd just use crack with Moore, and sometimes he'd take some with him when he left.

Barry started using Moore as a supplier as well as a lover. She brought forty dollars' worth of the drug to his office on the fifth floor of the District Building. On one occasion, Barry was at the podium during a budget hearing at the Reeves Center when Moore arrived to make a deal. He motioned for her to approach and handed her a magazine that held an envelope with money to buy drugs. Moore went to Florida Avenue near Howard University to score some cocaine, returned to the Reeves Center, waited for the hearings to conclude, and left with Barry to do the drugs.

One day Barry called Moore just before noon. It was midweek, and she was working at the city's juvenile services division at Third and N streets NW.

"Come on over to Tony's house with me," he said. "He's in New York."

Tony Jones was a city contractor and late-night pal whose house near Catholic University was a rendezvous spot for Moore and Barry; Moore didn't want to go this time.

"C'mon," the mayor urged. "We'll have some fun."

She relented, left the job at her lunch break, picked up one hundred dollars' worth of cocaine, and met Barry. The cocaine was in powder form, but Barry wanted to smoke it. He sprinkled the cocaine into a jar with a little bit of water, added some baking soda, and heated it over the stove until the powder had dissolved. When the concoction was hot, the mayor added some cold water, and the cocaine crystallized into the rocks known as crack. He fished them out and smoked them with Moore.

On another occasion when Barry had a yen for Moore and some cocaine, Moore said she couldn't; she was caring for her children—then four, five, and seven—and it was too late to get a babysitter. Barry called back at 2:00 a.m.

"Why don't you come?" he said. "Take a taxi, and bring the children."

Again, she agreed, and brought her children with her to the home of a mutual friend where Barry was waiting. She left the children downstairs in front of a television set while upstairs she and Barry freebased cocaine and made love. The friend arrived later and found the kids asleep, and the city's chief executive in bed with their mother. The friend stayed with the kids.

On Mother's Day, 1987, Rasheeda Moore was at her mother's house preparing for church when the mayor called, asking if she could score some cocaine.

"Don't you want to spend the day with your family?" she asked.

"Sure," he responded, "but I have time."

Time enough for Moore to score and meet the mayor for a hit from the pipe.

No direct connection was ever established between Rayful Edmond III and Mayor Marion Barry, Jr., though there was the odd case of Edmond's, beeper that turned up in Barry's possession, and there were suggestions that Zanville once sold cocaine to one of Barry's girlfriends. It is entirely possible, however, that cocaine imported by the Edmond organization wound up in Barry's hands via dealers like Lydia Pearson.

Pearson grew up across Taylor Street from Rasheeda Moore's childhood home. They went to Roosevelt High together. When Moore struck out for New York and her modeling career, Pearson remained at home and attended Howard University for a year. After her mother died in 1978, Pearson became depressed and started doing drugs. She tried to shake her addiction through three separate treatment programs, but when Moore returned to Washington, Lydia Pearson was selling cocaine, and her home was a low-key crack house. A few weeks after Barry met Pearson in February 1988, Barry returned to Taylor Street and went into Pearson's house. Rasheeda Moore arrived separately. Pearson sold her some crack, and Moore went up to a bedroom and smoked it with Barry. The mayor came down an hour later, alone. "I'm worried about Rasheeda," he told Pearson. "She's doing too much crack. I think maybe she should go into a treatment program."

If she had gone, it would have been to a treatment program outside the District. Barry's government had failed to open many drug treatment clinics, and those open were poorly run: Across the Anacostia River in Ward Eight, where drug addiction was at epidemic levels, there was no clinic. Barry's inattention and a dispute with Ward 8 Council member Wilhelmina Rolark over who might get the city contract had delayed the clinic for years.

Barry had good reason to worry about Moore's addiction to crack. In the summer, they were doing drugs at another Barry hangout, the suburban McLean, Virginia, home of Bishop H. Hartford Brookins, a friend and adviser to the mayor. On this occasion, Brookins wasn't home. Barry and Moore went into a bathroom to smoke crack. Barry smoked first and handed the pipe to Moore. She hadn't smoked in a few days and greedily filled her lungs with the crack smoke. She started to shake. She felt her eyes dilate and thought that her head was blowing up.

"Marion, Marion," she called and grabbed the sink to steady herself. Barry turned to walk out, snapping off the light. Moore could see only the whites of her eyes in the mirror. Her body was quaking. "Stay focused, stay focused," she said to herself.

The moment passed. Moore walked out to find Barry bent over in the closet, putting the pipe in a shoetree and the cocaine in another spot.

"Why did you turn the light off?" she asked. "I almost went out."

"I'm not doing this anymore," she said. "I could have died."

But neither could stop doing cocaine, though they did stop having sex that summer. One night in June they returned to Barry's suite at the Hyatt Regency after attending a Dionne Warwick concert to benefit an AIDS program. They smoked crack, and the drug killed Moore's appetite for sex. She refused Barry's advances. He was enraged and accused her of sleeping with Willie Davis, a former aide to Birmingham mayor Richard Arrington who now was trying to broker bond deals for the District government. Moore denied it. Barry slapped her once. She slapped him back. His second blow knocked her to the floor. He stood over her.

"I haven't hit a woman in twenty years," he said. "You bring out the worst in a man. Just get out!

CHAPTER 12

MURDER CAPITAL

*Washington is not Dodge City, and I hope the media
would not depict our great city as Dodge City.
—Marion Barry, February 1989*

Rayful Edmond ran into competition from a neighbor in the
summer of 1988.Just to the east of the Strip at Orleans Place
lies a compact neighborhood of narrow streets and brick row homes
called Trinidad, named for the ten-block street that runs though its
center. Trinidad is sandwiched between two Washington landmarks:
Gallaudet University, the nation's premier college for the hearing im-
paired, and the U.S. National Arboretum, a pastoral park of rolling
hills and manicured gardens known for its world-class display of azaleas and every imaginable plant, tree, and herb. Trinidad was known
for its cocaine.

The streets of Trinidad were controlled by Michael Salter, a drug
lord also known as Michael Frey. In contrast to Edmond's nice-guy
reputation, Frey was known to be ruthless. He was one of the first
Washington dealers to stockpile guns, according to police and prosecutors. He was also a few years older than Edmond and resented his
rapid rise. Early in 1988 the taunting and fistfights between the two
crews escalated into gunfire, but no one had been killed. Then on June
13 one of Frey's people drove to Orleans Place and gunned down
Leslie "June" Wheeler and Anthony "Mad Dog" Thomas. Their murders could not go unavenged.

After midnight on June 23, Edmond and a few of his gang members went to Chapter III, the nightclub where Marion Barry had met Theresa Southerland, his twenty-three-year-old paramour. The club is a squat warehouse on First Street SE, adjacent to railroad tracks in a low-rise industrial zone sprinkled with bunker-like blocks of two-story garden apartments. The Capitol dome is near enough to light up the northern sky on misty nights when Congress is in session. Inside, the club is a dark warren of rooms and a dance floor that thumps with a constant disco beat. Rayful Edmonds came with his lieutenant and enforcer, Columbus "Little Nut" Daniels, a short teenager with close-cropped hair and a smooth, baby face. His size pushed him to prove himself, and he did it with his gun. That night, as usual, he was carrying a nine-millimeter semiautomatic.

Edmond and Little Nut walked into the club and immediately crossed paths with Brandon Terrell. He and Daniels were childhood friends, and both went into the cocaine business, but Terrell bad joined Frey's gang in Trinidad. The shootings of Wheeler and Thomas were fresh in everyone's mind. Edmond warned Terrell to stay on his side of Florida Avenue. Michael Frey joined in the verbal skirmish. Taunts were traded, threats were made, but nothing happened inside the club. Terrell left just before 3:00 a.m.

Daniels followed Terrell into the parking lot and drew his gun. Terrell saw him and started to run, but he was too late. Daniels dropped his childhood friend with two bullets in the back. Terrell fell face down. Daniels stood over him and pumped in five more rounds. A stray bullet grazed Frey, who ran to his car and escaped. Terrell bled to death on the asphalt. Little Nut fled to Edmond's headquarters at 407 M Street, where everyone celebrated the hit.

If the dispute between Brandon Terrell and Rayful Edmond had taken place even one year before, they might have settled it with fists or just let it go. What was so striking about that killing and the hundreds like it was how suddenly the capital's streets became murderous.

"One day these kids were in shoving matches," says Detective Sandy Austin, the first female officer in the tough Seventh District, "the next day they were in shootouts."

Being tough in the ghetto used to mean that you had quick fists and a good right hook. Maybe you carried a knife or wielded a baseball bat. It wasn't until the mid-1980s that everyone in the drug business started packing a gun. The escalation in violence, firepower, and random bloodshed overtook the capital city toward the end of 1987 in a spasm that caught city leaders totally by surprise. Some city officials argued that Washington was no different from other big cities besieged by crack and guns, but statistics show the opposite: Murder rates fell in New York, Boston, Baltimore, and Miami in 1987, when the District's rose dramatically; homicides in Washington shot up 65 percent in 1988, almost twice the rate of the next-quickest increase, in Houston; Chicago was unaffected by crack and its violent turf wars. Once Washington became a mecca for crack cocaine dealers, the violence proceeded with its own deadly logic for reasons of geography and history that are unique to the capital.

It became clear in 1986 that Edmond and other homegrown dealers couldn't satisfy the demand, and word of the lucrative Washington market spread to Jamaican gangs out of New York and Miami. The Jamaicans were the first vertically integrated black drug-dealing operations to hit the United States. They were capable of importing cocaine, distributing it through wholesale networks, and selling it retail directly to customers through apartments that became known as crack houses. The Jamaicans helped to introduce crack to Washington, but their legacy was gunfire and violence. D.C. police busted Jamaican crack houses and found AR-15 assault rifles, Glock semiautomatic pistols, and Mini-Tee Nines-all sophisticated, high-powered weapons that could fire bursts of bullets. Their brand of ruthlessness and coldblooded warfare was typical of Kingston but mindboggling to Washingtonians. It was exactly the kind of threat to the public safety that had been predicted by police Lieutenant Lowell Duckett and Detective Bill Larman.

"We have confiscated guns with silencers and with clips which will hold 100 bullets," then assistant police chief Isaac Fulwood told *The Washington Post*. "They have heavier firearms than the police carry."

The Jamaicans first fought among themselves for control of some D.C. neighborhoods in spectacular murder sprees that shocked the city in late 1987 and early 1988. Police were called to a newly renovated apartment on Meridian Place in the city's Mount Pleasant section one Saturday night in late February 1988, where they discovered four toddlers crawling over the dead bodies of two women who'd been executed, gangland style. One of the women was four months pregnant. A few weeks later four men and a woman were slaughtered in an apartment just over the District line in suburban Maryland. Once the Jamaicans established turf lines among themselves, they turned their guns on the local dealers, like Edmond's gang. At first the locals fell back, and the Jamaicans conquered communities along Georgia Avenue and parts of Southeast. But by early 1988 the young native dealers were ready to fight back with equal firepower. Once they were armed, the serious bloodletting began.

Within a year, the Jamaican gangs were in retreat, caught in a pincer movement by federal and local police on one hand and the local dealers on the other. Having chased the Jamaicans and tasted blood, the capital's drug dealers started shooting one another—sometimes over a disputed corner, sometimes over a drug deal gone awry, sometimes for revenge, sometimes over a woman,perhaps for something as simple as a hostile meeting of the eyes. Every day the newspapers carried at least one execution by gunfire. The body count started to rise from a low of 148 in 1985, to 197 in 1986, to 228 in 1987, but in 1988 the carnage was awesome, beginning in January. Two hours into the new year, homicide detectives were called to a street corner near Fort McNair where they found Michael Saunders, Jr., sprawled on the sidewalk, a trail of blood seeping from the place where a bullet exited his skull. He had sixty packets of crack in one pocket and one thousand dollars in cash in his jeans jacket. He was nineteen. He was the first of thirty-seven people to be gunned down that January, equaling a record set in 1971 and setting a pace that would make the capital city notorious for its carnage.

Crack and competition bred violence, but why were there so many guns all of a sudden?

The District government passed one of the strictest gun control laws in the nation in the mid-1970s. Private citizens cannot own or carry a handgun legally. The city issues no permits. There are no exceptions. Moreover, the federal agency charged with regulating guns—the Bureau of Alcohol, Tobacco, and Firearms—is headquartered in the District. But the District's law was impossible to enforce, primarily because there's an arms bazaar at the city's back door. Right across the Potomac River in Virginia, gun control regulations were virtually nonexistent and easily skirted. Any teenager from Washington with folding cash could belly up to a gun store counter, buy an arsenal of high-powered weapons, and cross one of four bridges into the District loaded with guns and ammo. So many handguns came into the capital that the prices went through the floor. Anyone could rent a handgun for a day, buy one for fifty dollars, or trade one for cocaine. Life was cheap; every death of a gang member was avenged.

Edmond's top enforcers, Jerry Millington and James "Tonio" Jones, knew that Michael Frey would retaliate for Brandon Terrell's shooting. They dispatched Greg Royster to a gun shop in Virginia Beach, and he returned with a small cache of semiautomatic weapons and submachine guns. Millington and Jones arrayed them on a blanket in the alley behind Orleans Place and called roll. Edmond's trusted gang members filed by with military discipline and were assigned weapons. At first, Edmond wanted the guns to defend his turf, but the result was that the two gangs on either side of Florida Avenue were bristling with semiautomatic weapons that could squeeze off seventeen bullets in seconds. The police still carried six-shot revolvers.

Rayful Edmond wanted to reward Little Nut Daniels for killing Terrell. Little Nut wanted a car, so Edmond gave Alta Rae Zanville fifty-one thousand dollars in cash to buy him a Mercedes Benz 300 CE. Little Nut took his mother, Bernice Daniels, to the car dealership to pick it up. It was a dark-blue beauty, and he drove it through the Strip slowly a few times just to make sure everyone saw his trophy. A few days later Edmond and Daniels were sitting side by side in a neighborhood barbershop getting a shave. Two men walked in wearing ski masks, pulled handguns from their waistbands, and shot Daniels point-blank, gangland style, in the chest, spine, and abdomen. They didn't do their job. Little Nut was only paralyzed from the neck down. He would never drive the blue Mercedes again. Rayful Edmond was unscathed. A month later police walked into Little Nut's hospital room and charged him with killing Brandon Terrell.

Even the shooters realized that things were getting out of hand, and they tried to stem the violence. In the last week of August 1988, Rayful Edmond, Tony Lewis, and other members of his organization met in a schoolyard near Howard University with Michael Frey and his crew. They agreed that the warfare was senseless. Moreover, it was attracting too much attention from the police and could be bad for business. They called a truce and retrieved the weapons.

Less than two months later, Gregory Cain and Ronald Curry, two of Frey's men, were sitting in their car on the 800 block of K Street NE in Trinidad. Tonio Jones and Jerry Millington ran up from behind, flanked the car, and allegedly fired through the windows from both sides with automatic weapons. Cain and Curry died instantly, and the truce was over.

"The killing won't really stop until the gangs carve up their turf," said Police Chief Maurice Turner.

The number of murders shot up again in 1988 to set a record at 372. The rate of sixty killings per ten thousand residents put Washington ahead of Detroit as the murder capital of the nation. By comparison, New York's rate was twenty-five. And it would get worse. On Valentine's Day, 1989, thirteen people were shot in one twenty-four-hour period.

"Washington is not Dodge City," Marion Barry told reporters at a news conference. "There are some neighborhoods that are not safe, but most murders are targeted assassinations."

The mayor was quite correct—it was a murder rate in black and white.

Washington split into two cities: one white and safe, the other black and deadly, though there were many black neighborhoods that were still relatively safe back then, such as Shepherd Park, Michigan Park, and Brookland, all in the northern part of the city. Eighty-nine percent of the victims were black; 96 percent of the assailants were black. Not one murder occurred in the white neighborhoods west of Rock Creek Park. Communities like Cleveland Park, Chevy Chase, and Spring Valley were some of the most idyllic and safe places within the borders of any city in the country.

"While there has been a dramatic and much-publicized increase in drug-related murders and assaults, and in drug crimes generally," the Greater Washington Research Center reported, "there have simultaneously been large decreases in rapes, robberies; and burglaries."

But subtleties escaped the media, the capital's bloody streets made news across the globe, and the national press came knocking at Barry's door.

"I'm not going to take full responsibility for all these murders," Mayor Barry told *Newsweek* magazine. "The city government didn't import this drug into Washington."

In the privacy of his office, Barry was distraught. Young black mendied every day. Theprisons were overflowing. Homelessness was on the rise. Teenage mothers addicted to crack weregiving birth to addicted babies and abandoning them at hospitals. The problems seemed insurmountable, and all the while the newspapers carried leaked stories about his alleged drug abuse and his government's alleged corruption.

Former city administrator Tom Downs returned to Washington for a visit in the summer of 1988. Six months earlier Barry had unceremoniously sacked Downs. Until that point, he had been the highest-ranking white official in the District government. The day Downs was being replaced, Barry planted a story in the *Post* that Downs was responsible for his government's major problems.

Downs avoided Barry but stopped in to see Herbert O. Reid, the mayor's legal adviser. If Barry had a father figure in the government, it was Reid, a big-boned, slow-talking, deliberate lawyer who had a kinship with Supreme Court Justice Thurgood Marshall. Reid believed that Barry was the living symbol of the civil rights movement, and any attack on the mayor could erode black influence in general. But Reid was also a realist.

"How's Marion?" Downs asked.

"If it walks, he fucks it," Reid said. "If it doesn't, he ingests it."

Barry was barely functioning, and the signs of his addiction were beginning to show in public and to his staff.

The public read about two separate car accidents, one in the dead of night. His chauffeur-driven car ran a red light and collided with a car driven by a radio reporter en route to work at 2:00 a.m. "I'm just a night owl," Barry said to explain his early morning meanderings.

The mayor's public display at the 1988 Democratic National Convention in Atlanta also begged for some explaining. At the 1984 convention in San Francisco, Barry had played a visible role as Jesse Jackson completed his historic first run at the presidential nomination. Barry was asked to give his nominating speech before a prime-time television audience. Four years later, when Jackson had amassed power and seven million primary votes, Barry was just among the hangers-on. At a crucial moment in the negotiations between Jackson and eventual nominee Michael Dukakis, Barry darted from the sidelines at the start of a press conference and placed a Jackson baseball cap on Dukakis's head. He smiled and cameras clicked, but the prank affirmed Barry's image as a bit player. He cruised Atlanta in the company of four bodyguards, brought ahalf-dozen aides in his entourage, and lodged himself at a pricy hotel while the rest of the D.C. delegation stayed in budget rooms.

The mayor was chairman of Dukakis's Washington steering committee, but he spent the weekend before the November general election vacationing in the Bahamas as a guest of the Resorts International hotel and casino chain. As Dukakis flew around the country to plead for votes, Barry played tennis and predicted Dukakis would lose.

"I think it's because of his lack of organization among blacks," Barry told a *Washington Post* reporter at the resort.

The drug gangs were organizing children to run cocaine, act as lookouts, and make the deals hand to hand, which led to the other startling feature of Washington's bloodiest years: Child play was becoming gunplay.

One day in early January 1988, a twelve-year-old girl walked into Peerless Cleaners at 1202 Bladensburg Road NE, in a neighborhood bordering Trinidad. It was 3:00 p.m. and there were customers at the counter. She asked for the owner's daughter, who wasn't there, and left. A few minutes later she returned and demanded cash from the owner, a forty-three-year-old African American woman. "For what?" the owner asked. The girl pulled out a starter pistol and pointed it at her face. The woman screamed, and a customer burst in to chase away the girl. Her mother brought her to police headquarters that night and explained that her daughter wanted the money to buy cocaine because she was addicted.

That same night police arrested two fourteen-year-old boys in a hotel room near the Maryland line. They found guns, crack, PCP, and marijuana and the teenagers in the midst of a drug deal.

A month earlier teenagers killed a fifteen-year-old boy in an argument over his new ski jacket. A seventeen-year-old was shot and killed by younger boys who wanted his radio. Mark Settles, age twelve, was shot with his German shepherd in an argument over drugs.

At least half of the people killed were African-American males under the age of twenty-five, and the numbers of juveniles arrested on drug charges climbed from 1,111 in 1986 to 1,658 in 1987. In 1984 there were no children twelve or younger arrested for drugs; by 1987 there were thirty-five. Twenty-five juveniles were charged with murder in 1988; fifty-two would be up on murder raps in 1989.

The problem of kids and drugs and guns was more than any government could handle, but Marion Barry promised "bold new programs" on at least three occasions. "Our children are our future, and our future is in jeopardy," Barry said in April 1986. "I want to assure the citizens of this community that this administration is exerting leadership, is being forceful, and with their support, we will solve the dilemma with which we are faced."

He later launched Operating Services Assisting Youth. A year later it was a program called Invest In Our Future. None of the programs or promises were carried out. Barry's government neglected recreation centers, public basketball fields, and athletic programs at public high schools-all of which could have diverted children from the streets.

Barry's top aides realized that they had to cover for the mayor.

In a daze from his nightly indulgences, he was useless in the mornings. His security detail had to roust him from bed in the mid-morning. His staff stopped scheduling meetings for him before 10:00 a.m. When he missed those meetings and started arriving at noon, they scheduled meetings after lunch. At a meeting one afternoon about overcrowding at the city's prison in Lorton, an aide watched in horror as Barry's eyes rolled back in his head and he almost fell out of his chair. Barry's nose bled often.

"He was always running to the bathroom," said John C. White, Barry's press secretary at the time. "He could be sleepy and nodding off, and then he'd go to the bathroom and come back wide awake."

John White, city attorney Frederick Cooke, and Carol Thompson, who replaced Tom Downs as city administrator, were in charge of the government's public facade. Keeping it up was nearly impossible.

Barry's dissipation placed his young aides in a wrenching predicament. They were talented, honest, highly motivated African Americans. They felt indebted to Barry for his leadership in the civil rights movement. They believed that Barry and his comrades, such as Ivanhoe Donaldson, had changed the world and paved the way for their success. They also were totally committed to the notion that blacks could run the city government. It was their city. Carol Thompson and Fred Cooke were both native Washingtonians. Their hopes and dreams—their sense of identity—were entwined with Marion Barry.

"We had to face the massive disappointment," says Thompson, "the constant bunker mentality." And in Thompson's case, the mayor's sexual appetite.

One evening a year earlier, when Thompson was deputy mayor for business and economic development, Barry dropped in unexpectedly at her fourth-floor offices at the District Building. After small talk about business, Barry edged closer. She backed away. The mayor reached for her. She circled a conference table with Barry in pursuit. When she neared her door she was able to open it and step into a hallway where other staffers were also working late. The moment passed. Barry never tried again.

The unavoidable evidence, confirmed almost daily by Barry's behavior, was that the mayor was hooked on drugs and more interested in sex than in social problems. In response, his aides engineered a massive cover-up to protect the city government and the mayor—and to some degree themselves—from embarrassment. The cover-up took the benign form of arranging the government around Barry's schedule, running it in his absence, and covering for the mayor when he was too fuzzy to function.

"What was I going to do?" asks Thompson. "Call the press?"

Barry's staff became one more layer in the wall of silence that protected the mayor. But the wall had many more elements. Barry's friends kept their silence; his cocaine dealers never squealed; Effi Barry witnessed the damage and kept it to herself. The city watched Barry slur his speech, sweat profusely in cold rooms, stare from dilated eyes. Call them facilitators or enablers, to one degree or another, dozens of people were culpable. The whole town knew that the mayor was falling victim to drugs. "What's the surprise?" an African-American cabdriver said one day. "Everyone knows Marion's a street monkey who's addicted to cocaine."

The mayor's erratic behavior had become oddly routine. Friends said he was bored with his job. His cool arrogance, fueled by his superior knowledge of the city and his political skills, infuriated critics and confounded the news media. Though nearly all reporters believed Barry used drugs, no one could confirm it. From a distance it was also hard to tell whether Barry was addicted or using drugs only recreationally while he drank into the night. Barry's public grasp of issues—just when you thought he might be out of touch—always raised nagging doubts that Barry was indeed losing his grip.

And when Barry was on, he was still powerful and magnetic. He blamed Ronald Reagan and lax federal enforcement for the city's drug problems. He continued his crusade against drugs. He was a master of duplicity. He promised to hunt down killers "like mad dogs" and said in a television interview: "We ought to be outraged. We ought to act as if we've got a war and rise up against it."

But by the late summer of 1988, even Barry knew that he was in grave danger. Some friends who suspected Barry's addiction suggested he "pull a Betty Ford" and check himself into a clinic for alcoholism. Some suggested he needed to take a real vacation and stop his party lifestyle. Barry was too proud and too scared politically to go public and check into a hospital.

He decided to try to heal himself.

The Hudson River Valley north of New York City and west to the foothills of the Catskill Mountains is a bucolic setting. Undulating hillsides, scenic vistas, and farmlands cradle thousands of summer and weekend homes for harried New York City residents.

One small community is the oddly named Neversink, New York, founded around 1800. With a population 2,940, it's barely a wide spot in the road, two hours north of Manhattan. The Neversink River runs in east and west branches from Slide Mountain, the highest peak in the Catskills. Down one tree-lined drive off Route 55 lies a 155-acre farm that for years was known as the Neversink Inn, an upscale retreat famous for its fine food and city clients. By 1976, it had become a health spa. A series of small, wood-carved signs dot the driveway, cautioning and cajoling visitors to leave any alcohol, candy, or drugs behind.

Marion Barry's rental car cruised slowly along the dirt-andgravel driveway, pulling up to a cluster of small buildings and cottages and a sign welcoming guests. He had arrived at the New Age Health Farm Spa.

Over the next four days, Barry went on a strict fast of juices while he swam in the spa's pool, received massages, did aerobic exercises, took long walks, and practiced Zen meditation. Barry's body was wrapped in paraffin wax to draw impurities from his pores. He underwent an even less traditional treatment called colon hydrotherapy, a health regimen in which rubber hoses are inserted in the rectum to flush out the lower intestine. Nights were filled with lectures on behavior modification and nutrition.

Barry's plan was to spend the week quietly and return to Washington refreshed and released from drugs and alcohol. But his insistence, for the first time, that a trip remain a secret raised suspicions in the press. Supporters said Barry had a right to a private vacation, but the news media pointed to Barry's mysterious health problems on previous trips and said that the mayor had forfeited his right to privacy. Barry stationed two security guards in a New York City hotel for the week to distract reporters. Their bill, paid by taxpayers, exceeded twenty-five hundred dollars.

While insisting on his privacy, Barry couldn't resist the temptation of calling reporters in the capital. In a conversation with *Washington Post* columnist Dorothy Gilliam, Barry denied that he was away for drug treatment. "If I used drugs, I'd be in jail right now. I'm the most scrutinized public figure in the country... by the FBI, by the media... that's a nonissue.

"I'm so antidrugs."

Barry said that he had to start taking care of his health, lest he wind up like other big-city mayors. When he had last seen Chicago mayor Harold Washington, before he died of a heart attack, Barry said, "he looked like a big balloon." Barry had seen Detroit mayor Coleman Young in Atlanta at the Democratic convention. "And I told him, 'it looks like you forgot your birth control pills.'"

After returning to town in late October, Barry invited reporters into his office. Sitting on a side table were cornsilk tea and ground licorice root. The mayor said he was walking three miles a day and never felt better in his life. He said he was no longer the "night owl." He liked to meditate. He even looked healthy and hearty. He glided toward his red leather sofa. He perched on its edge, crossing his legs at the ankles. The mayor raised his elbows outward and pointed his fingers at each other from across his chest.

"You move your thoughts out of your head," Barry said, demonstrating the technique. "I'm not boring. I'm more controlled, more contemplative, more reflective, more caring."

The photograph in the *Post* the next day showed Barry sitting there with a sublime smile on his face, clean-shaven, looking like a yogi in a blue business suit.

CHAPTER 13

THE SMELL OF DEATH

*Some governments are corrupt but are known for their
competency in running the city, others are incompetent
but considered "clean." [Washington's] government is
scandalously corrupt and hopelessly incompetent.*
—*Missouri senator John Danforth*

It was late evening on December 16, 1989, in the shank of the
Christmas party season, and the mayor of the nation's capital was
in high spirits.

His dark-blue Lincoln Town Car turned onto Rhode Island Avenue NW and pulled up to the Ramada Inn Central, just around the
comer from Fourteenth Street. Alone in the backseat, he was looking forward to an evening of formal affairs. He'd just left a Christmas party at the Citadel, a recording studio in a converted skating
rink in Adams Morgan. A cold, bracing wind slapped his cheeks as
he opened the car door and pulled his large frame up from the backseat. He gathered his topcoat tightly over his tuxedo. This would be a
quick stop.

The corner of Fourteenth and Rhode Island, ten blocks from the
White House on the northern edge of the central business district,
was safe enough by day but dicey after dark. Crack dealers peddled
their wares hand-to-hand on Fourteenth Street, and the Ramada was
getting a reputation for drug busts and overdoses. Barry strode into
the hotel lobby and flipped his broad smile at the concierge. The

mayor was at home in hotels. He spent more time in hotels than he spent at home with his wife and son. He took the elevator to the ninth floor and went to room 902. As a short, wiry man in stocking feet opened the door and let the mayor into the room, Lewis said to Barry, "Just watching a little TV."

Charles Lewis had checked into the hotel at the end of November. The scion of a prominent Virgin Islands family, Lewis had fallen on hard times. He was broke, jobless, and hooked on cocaine. He had provided the mayor with women and drugs in the past—especially in the Virgin Islands government. Now he needed a payback and called the mayor as soon as he landed in town. The mayor was busy playing general in his latest crusade against drugs. He started showing up at crime scenes and taking well publicized walks through drug-infested neighborhoods, but he still had his own needs.

The mayor walked into Lewis's room, reached into the pocket of his tuxedo, and took out a matchbox from the Capitol Hilton Hotel. He pulled the little box open and dumped a few rocks of crack cocaine on the bureau.

"You took care of me in the Virgin Islands," he said. "I'll take care of you up here."

They improvised using a pipe stem and some foil. The mayor stayed for less than an hour and left some crack. The next night he returned to help Lewis polish it off.

The following Monday afternoon, the mayor gave an envelope to Fred Gaskins, a police officer assigned to his security detail, and had him take it to "a Mr. Lewis" at the Ramada. Inside the envelope were five crisp twenty-dollar bills. The mayor had asked Lewis to buy "a working fifty," crack talk for fifty dollars' worth of rocks. The mayor called at 11:15 p.m. from the nearby Grand Hyatt.

"How did you do?" Barry asked.

"I'm in good shape," Lewis responded. He'd invited his friend James McWilliams to watch the Monday night football game. McWilliams was a black attorney who sported a close-cropped white beard, worked for the city, and was a drinking pal of the mayor's. He brought along cognac for Barry but didn't try the drugs. The mayor arrived fifteen minutes later to watch the game and smoke crack. Lewis smoked from a thin glass pipe called a straight shooter. Barry rigged a pipe by stretching tin foil over a sherbet glass, poking pinholes in it, and laying ashes on the holes to cradle the crack. He sucked in the smoke from a larger hole in the foil at the edge of the glass. Lewis and Barry were smoking and laughing in the bathroom. McWilliams was watching the game.

"Good stuff," he heard Barry say.

Three days later, on Thursday the twenty-second, Lewis propositioned a maid in the hall outside his room.

Carmen Alarcon was a recent immigrant from El Salvador who spoke a bit of English, but she knew that when Lewis waved a small bag of white powder in front of her face, he was offering her cocaine. Alarcon reported the incident to hotel security, and the management alerted the police. Two District detectives, Pierre Mitchell and Robert Thompson, decided to try to buy cocaine from Lewis. Posing as maintenance men, the detectives started up to room 902 shortly before noon.

The hotel manager was having lunch in a dining room facing the foyer when Mayor Barry strolled by and waved. He didn't want the mayor mixed up with the drug bust, quickly radioed to the detectives, and aborted the undercover operation.

Barry continued to room 902, smoked crack, and left with a few rocks. He then went uptown to Rasheeda Moore's house on Taylor Street. He and Rasheeda smoked crack in the basement and walked upstairs to chat with her mother. Mary Moore was troubled. She wanted the mayor's advice about her son, who had a drug problem and was serving a jail term. Mrs. Moore fixed a pot of tea. Barry slipped off his shoes and got comfortable.

Treatment, he said, was the answer.

Sharon LaFraniere, the investigative reporter who'd been covering Barry for years, happened to be at her desk that Thursday afternoon when the phone rang. It was an employee from the Ramada who wanted to tip off the *Post* about Barry's close brush with the undercover drug operation.

LaFraniere bolted to the Ramada, knocked on the door of 902, and found herself face to face with Chuck Lewis. She asked him about offering cocaine to the hotel maid and about Barry's visit. Lewis said the mayor had visited because they were friends, and there were no drugs involved. By 6:00 p.m. a half-dozen *Post* reporters were assigned to the story. One went to police headquarters; another sat up all night with two officers in the Ramada lobby and talked with Chuck Lewis as he checked out; a third started checking Lewis's background.

The *Post,* still scrambling for details, carried a low-key story the next morning on the Metro page. The lead flatly stated that police had abruptly canceled a drug bust at the hotel. In the third paragraph it mentioned that Barry had been visiting the guest in that same room. Executive editor Ben Bradlee read the story Friday morning and walked from his glass-walled office past the foreign and national desks to the metro section where reporters and editors were busy pursuing the story. Bradlee rarely showed interest in local stories unless he sensed scandal.

"What do we got? What do we got?" he asked. After taking in a quick fill from the overnight reports, Bradlee told the reporters:

"This one has the smell of death to it."

Across town that Friday morning, Sergeant Albert Lee Arrington reported for work at the metropolitan police department's Internal Affairs Division and immediately started to review the Ramada incident.

Arrington had been a D.C. cop for seventeen years, the last five on the public corruption unit at IAD. Since there were allegations that Barry had called off the police bust, Chief Maurice Turner had turned the entire investigation over to the thirteen-member IAD staff. In years past the unit had been the graveyard for potentially damaging reports about the mayor's cocaine use, particularly the allegations of his overdoses in 1983, but Barry's friend Jimmy Wilson was no longer in charge. Some members of the squad started to trail Lewis, others went to the Ramada to seal room 902 and check for traces of cocaine. Arrington and Sergeant Gregory Wells interviewed Carmen Alarcon in her suburban Virginia home. They didn't take a formal statement, but Arrington returned to IAD's offices on the top floor of police headquarters with no doubts. "She's telling the truth," he reported. "Lewis offered her drugs." In the meantime, the sweep in room 902 turned up traces of cocaine.

That afternoon Barry summoned two *Post* reporters to his District Building office and sat at the head of his polished conference table, reporters to his right and Herbert O. Reid to his left.

"I want the police to investigate this matter fully. Let the chips fall where they may," he said. "You know, I don't ever want—if I'm around anybody who uses drugs, has drugs, I'm gonna call the police. I'm not crazy. You know I'm not going to sit around and let people—I suspect that at some point some people might try to set me up… I expect that to happen any time.

"I'm in a dangerous situation," he continued. "'I'm taking on these drug dealers and fighting this war. I'm subject to being killed, as well as being set up outside. I understand that. I'm worth a million dollars [dead]."

Charles Lewis had checked out of the Ramada and gone to stay with an old friend, John Olson, in suburban Virginia. Late Friday night, Barry called to tell Lewis to appear at police headquarters the following morning for an interview with IAD investigators. The whole mess would blow over, the mayor said.

"What if they give me a drug test?" Lewis asked.

Barry recommended that he drink a lot of lemon juice to wash the cocaine from his system. Lewis pumped tea with lemon all night and reported to IAD the next morning. The interview was amicable. Lewis believed that Barry controlled the cops and the investigation would be killed. Midway through the interview, the phone rang. The mayor was on the line asking to speak to the officer in charge. He was put on hold, and Captain Winfred Stanley was called out of the interview room.

"Tell him I can't speak with him," Stanley said. He knew that Barry had called the day before and spoken with Inspector David Faison, Stanley's superior. From that moment on, Faison was cut out of the investigation. Stanley refused to take the mayor's call. "He can talk to the chief," he said. Barry already had talked to Chief Turner, but both Turner and Assistant Chief Isaac Fulwood refused to speak with him about the budding investigation. The mayor ordered Turner to transfer Winfred Stanley, but he refused. Barry made the same request to Fulwood to remove Stanley. "Put it in writing," Fulwood said. This time the police wouldn't cover for the mayor.

In the interview room, the investigators were pressing Lewis to trace his whereabouts before and after December 22. Lewis pulled out a tattered address book, crammed with names and addresses and scribbled notations in the margins.

"Can we hang on to this for a day?" one of the officers asked. "No problem," said Lewis.

It was a crucial break. The address book provided an investigative road map for IAD. They made copies, analyzed the scribbles, decoded the script, and discovered a trail of friends, drug dealers, and customers from Miami to the Virgin Islands. In scouring the phone calls made from room 902, investigators found a few made to a house on Taylor Street. For the moment, they filed this item away.

A few days later Al Arrington and a few other police investigators were called to a brand-new building at 555 Fourth Street, a block up the street from the run-down metropolitan police headquarters, for an audience with the new U.S. attorney, Jay Stephens.

Joseph DiGenova, Barry's tough-talking nemesis since 1982, had left office in late 1987 for a job with a private law firm. He'd built an impressive record of national and international prosecutions, and he'd put two deputy mayors behind bars on guilty pleas and successfully prosecuted a dozen minor city officials. But DiGenova never got the mayor, and he left office with the main corruption investigation of city contractors up in the air.

Stephens was DiGenova's opposite in many ways. Where DiGenova was given to hyperbole and loved the press, Stephens was tight-lipped, methodical, and severe. At forty-one, the new prosecutor was a small, pink-faced lawyer with piercing blue eyes, a helmet of brown hair that never seemed to be out of shape, and a perfectly groomed, bushy mustache. He was appointed by Ronald Reagan and had strong ties to the White House, where he'd worked as deputy counsel since 1986. He was born and raised in Iowa. His feel for the city and African-Americans was academic at best. Immediately after taking office, he asked prosecutors to present their best cases for prosecuting Barry on either drug or contracting fraud charges. He wasn't impressed and said: "Drop them."

But the Ramada Inn investigation was a whole new ball game. Arrington and the other investigators from IAD found themselves in a room with Stephens, his chief lieutenants, and some FBI agents. A decision was made to split the investigation into two parallel but separate tracks. The FBI would pursue leads in the Virgin Islands having to do with Chuck Lewis and the city's bogus contracting work for the island government. The District police would work the drug case against the mayor, look into whether he obstructed the investigation, and try to make the case against Lewis in D.C.

"They thought that Marion Barry could never be gotten on a drug charge," says Arrington. "So they gave it to the MPD, thinking that the better case was in the islands."

One prosecutor told IAD investigator James Pawlik: "If you make this [drug] case I'll kiss your ass."

Reports about the investigation dominated the news for weeks.

"There is a kind of speechlessness—people are depressed," said the Reverend A. Knighton Stanley, the well-respected minister and occasional adviser to Barry who had previously complained that Barry seemed unfairly under attack. "People are concerned that it made national news."

The architect of Barry's defense in these crucial days was Herbert Reid, his seventy-three-year-old legal and personal adviser. He told Barry to stand up, proclaim his innocence, and blame the prosecutors for mounting a racially motivated investigation.

The mayor called a press conference for Thursday, December 29, one week after the Ramada episode. Barry entered the city council chamber in the middle of a wedge of police officers and high-ranking city officials. Effi was at his side and sat quietly behind him for the ten-minute appearance. Sweat poured from his puffy face; his skin was sallow and wan. Barry opened by evoking Thomas Jefferson and the fundamental rights of judicial process in a democracy. He compared himself to the disciple Paul, falsely accused by King Agrippa.

"What originally turned out to be an alleged incident has now called into question my character, my veracity, my integrity, my judgment, and my leadership," he said. He said he had spent his entire life building his leadership and sacrificing himself for the homeless, the drug-addicted, and the otherwise downtrodden. "We love this city," he said, mopping his brow with a kerchief. "We love the citizens in it and we're not going to let *The Washington Post* through innuendo, through rumors, do what they have done for the last ten years, try to turn it around…We're gonna win this war on drugs, we're gonna win the war on improving the quality of life, because Washington is the greatest city in the world. It deserves the best leadership, and I've given it all I've got."

The mayor turned and left the room, ignoring shouted questions about Chuck Lewis and the hotel.

That afternoon, Jay Stephens announced that he had ordered a full grand jury probe of the Ramada Inn incident.

The young telephone company clerk looked haggard the day she came for questioning at Internal Affairs.

"You look like you haven't slept in a week," Arrington said. "Maybe I haven't," she responded.

Arrington figured he was looking at a thirty-year-old African American woman who'd been attractive before crack put ten years on her life.

The police had discovered her by tracing names and numbers through Lewis's address book and the hotel's phone records. Arrington called and she came willingly. He and Jim Pawlik took her into the cramped, six-by-six interview room crammed with two desks and a file cabinet. There were no windows. On one wall Arrington had hung a poster of a menacing eagle holding a person in his claws. He had colored the eyes red. With three metal chairs in the room, the cops were sitting on top of their quarry.

For the next four hours they worked on the young woman. How did she meet Lewis? Who else was in the room? Did she see any cocaine? Had she ever met the mayor?

Arrington played the good cop and Pawlik was the bad cop. At first glance they made an odd pair, but they were perfect partners. Pawlik was a taciturn white cop, over six feet tall, with a head of thick salt-and-pepper hair, a generous mustache, and hangdog eyes that gave him a slightly sinister look. Arrington was a stout, broad-shouldered, cocoa-skinned African-American, who was dead serious and disarming at the same time. He often wore hats over his shiny head and grew a close-cropped beard that turned gray during the year.

Like Marion Barry, Arrington was the son of a sharecropper, but that's where their kinship ended. Arrington grew up on the farm and established deep ties to his family and to the Baptist church; He was born in 1950 into a family of tobacco farmers in Nash County, North Carolina. He was baptized in a pond in the cow pasture, the fifth oldest of sixteen children. He developed broad shoulders and thick arms by pulling tobacco and guiding a plow behind a mule. When Marion Barry and Ivanhoe Donaldson were leading SNCC in the southern civil rights movement, Al Arrington was attending high school and cultivating tobacco part-time. He married his high-school sweetheart after college at North Carolina Central. Then he made his move.

"I knew from the day I was born that I wasn't going to stay on the farm," he said. "I didn't want to owe my life to the man who owned the land."

He followed a handful of sisters and brothers to Washington, first in 1968 for summer jobs, and permanently in 1970. He worked at two jobs and joined the All Nations' Baptist Church at 502 Rhode Island Avenue NE. In July 1971, he became a rookie cop and rose quickly through the ranks as a uniformed officer, an undercover agent, and head of a vice squad unit. He busted drug dealers a dozen a day in the far eastern neighborhoods of Division Street, where the dealers controlled the streets, and River Terrace, a nice neighborhood that had become a drug bazaar for heroin, speed, Quaaludes, Valium, LSC, PCP, and cocaine.

In 1980 Arrington made sergeant and seemed to be headed for the highest ranks. One summer evening two years later he was driving home when a car crossed into his lane at a curve and rammed him head-on. The other car was aflame. Arrington was bleeding internally from the impact but managed to get out of his car and staggered across the road to help the other driver. As he did, a second car hit him and knocked him a hundred feet. "I'm dead, I'm dead," he told the first cop to arrive. He was rushed to the hospital and arrived showing no blood pressure. "We're losing him," he heard someone say. He had one operation, then a second. A pastor read the final rites. The next day twenty-five Arringtons came to pray for him, including his mother and others who came up from the farm. It took two hundred staples to close his internal wounds.

Eleven days later, Arrington walked out of the hospital. "It's a miracle," one of the doctors said.

Before the accident, Arrington wasn't very religious; now he prayed frequently. His faith gave him a benign view of the people he busted for doing drugs. "I have no bitterness, no animosity," he says. "They have an illness. It's an evil that possesses people." He felt somewhat the same toward Marion Barry. Long before the Ramada case, Arrington had no doubt that Barry was involved with drugs. He also believed that Barry was protected by "loyal crooks" in the government and the police department. But when he joined IAD after recovering from the accident, he had no idea that he would eventually try to take apart that wall of loyal crooks, beginning with bystanders in the drama like the telephone company clerk.

Arrington assured her she was not facing arrest. "We just want information," he told her, but she wouldn't admit to seeing drugs in Chuck Lewis's room, Arrington was about to let her go. As she got up to leave, Lieutenant Joseph Fairley decided he wanted to ask a few more questions. He bored in. She'd been in the room for nearly five hours.

"Okay," she said. "We did some cocaine at the hotel."

But there was more. She said that Lewis had phoned Barry one day and put her on the phone with the mayor. It was clear to her that Barry had been in room 902 before, understood that drugs were being used, and might rendezvous with her later.

Arrington immediately informed the prosecutors, who were already presenting evidence to the grand jury.

Jay Stephens asked the mayor to testify before the grand jury on January 5.

Barry convened a meeting at a friend's home to plot his response. On hand were Herb Reid; Marlene Johnson, his friend and legal adviser; celebrated local defense attorney R. Kenneth Mundy; and others. Still more joined the meeting by speakerphone. Two clear options emerged. Mundy, who came from outside the Barry circle, strongly advised the mayor to avoid testifying. If pressed, Barry was advised by Mundy to take the Fifth Amendment. If Barry denied using drugs at the Ramada, it could come back to haunt him as a perjury charge. Mundy didn't ask Barry if he had indeed done drugs with Lewis at the Ramada, but he knew that it was quite possible. Mundy's friends told him they had seen Barry snort cocaine.

Herb Reid argued the political side. By refusing to testify, Barry would be admitting some level of guilt for the first time in his entire career. It was a political Rubicon that Barry should not cross, Reid argued, and Barry agreed. There was no tangible evidence that he'd done drugs, and he thought neither Chuck Lewis nor James McWilliams, the city employee who had been in the room, would talk. If they didn't talk, there'd be no case.

Barry also retained Ken Mundy. It was a smart move. Mundy was a premier trial lawyer who brought a measure of respectability to Barry's cause. He quickly moved to minimize Barry's exposure. Without publicly invoking the Fifth Amendment, Mundy made a deal that would limit the prosecutors to questions about the Ramada Inn incident; they couldn't ask whether Barry had used drugs in the past, for example.

Barry testified on January 19 and again on the twenty-fourth. He told the grand jurors that he went to the Ramada Inn to help out an old friend.

"Did Mr. Lewis ever give you cocaine?" prosecutor Judith Retchin asked.

"No," he answered.

"Did you ever..."

"Let me say it this way," Barry said, cutting her off. "The answer is no. I mean, unless he put it in a drink or something and I didn't know what it was." And he laughed, along with the jurors.

Walking out of the grand jury room, the mayor confronted a gaggle of reporters with Mundy at his side.

"The public sometimes gets the impression that a grand jury means someone is guilty," he told them. "Because one goes before a grand jury doesn't mean anything."

Ben Bradlee was waiting when the mayor walked into the Retreat, a small restaurant in the posh Madison Hotel across from the *Post* building on Fifteenth Street.

It was 7:45 a.m.; the mayor was fifteen minutes late, but he looked sharp. He was wearing a blue shirt with a solid white collar—mimicking a combination that Bradlee had popularized at the *Post* and one that many junior editors also imitated. Barry complained of having a headache, and he asked the waiter for an Alka Seltzer. The mayor had asked for this meeting in hopes of blunting the *Post's* aggressive pursuit of the Ramada Inn story.

"Do you think that we're after you?" Bradlee asked. "Why do you say that?" Barry responded.

"Because you said yesterday that you were struggling against us."

"I'm not struggling," he said, toying with his scrambled eggs and sausage. "I'm all right."

Barry launched into his version of the Ramada story. Chuck Lewis, he said, was a hard-luck case who needed his help; the cops were not following standard police procedures when they came to the motel; the chambermaid was an unreliable, illegal alien who had disappeared. And he certainly didn't do any drugs. "You couldn't possibly be on drugs and be a leader," Barry said.

What about the stories that Barry had snorted cocaine at This Is It?, with Karen Johnson, and at the Super Bowl? The mayor admitted only that he had been drinking too much a year earlier.

"Nobody in leadership ought to support a mayor on drugs," he said. "Nobody in leadership ought to support a mayor with a serious alcohol problem."

Bradlee wanted to know why Barry appeared to sweat so much and to slur his words so often, symptoms that suggested to many that Barry was an addict. The mayor said he had a speech impediment. He acknowledged that he might be in serious trouble over the Ramada incident, and that's why he'd hired Mundy, who'd gotten off a number of clients who Barry said were "guilty as shit."

Barry dropped a few hints about preparing to run for office again. He looked at his watch, and Bradlee started to get up.

"Let me look you in the eye," Barry said, "and tell you that I don't do drugs."

"Do you swear to that?" Bradlee asked.

And he did.

Jesse Jackson was so concerned about his friend Marion that he had called from Africa to pray for ten minutes over the phone. When he returned to his home in Chicago, the reverend threw the mayor a brick in the form of overwhelming concern about Barry's "human frailties."

"I'm in no position to make a political evaluation of the current situation," he said when he called a *Washington Post* reporter at home on January 17. "My first consideration is his health and well-being. When people have been very powerful—and trouble comes their way—people have a tendency to abandon them. I have the opposite tendency."

The question became whether Jackson had political tendencies in local Washington. The day before the *Post* interview, a local TV station announced a poll showing that Jackson would clobber all comers in the 1990 mayoral election. It was an intriguing option. Jackson was under pressure to bolster his portfolio as a presidential candidate by holding a public office: a Senate seat from his native South Carolina or Illinois would do, but why not mayor of the capital? He'd be on the national stage and in the thick of urban policy debates.

"I have no plans to run for mayor," Jackson said repeatedly over the next few months, a comment that left the option open.

Though the mayoral primary was a year and nine months away, other political sharks tasted Marion Barry's blood in the water.

City council member Nadine Winter, a flaky pol who usually did Barry's bidding, invited him to her home on Capitol Hill in late January. The mayor was surprised to find three other council members: his civil rights comrade Johnny Wilson; at-large member John Ray, Barry's creation and water carrier; and Harry Thomas, whose Fifth Ward was bleeding from the ripple effect of Rayful Edmond's crack wars. They discussed Barry's future in general terms and one by one lowered the boom: The mayor shouldn't run in 1990. Barry clammed up and left. When a leaked story appeared in the newspapers a few days later, Barry called a *Post* reporter.

"Since they fucked me," he said, "I'm going to fuck them. I can deal with them individually."

The business community wasn't about to abandon the man who had helped to enrich them for the past decade.

"A little sleaze will never stand in the way of economic development," a lobbyist for the Greater Washington Board of Trade said.

The phone logs from room 902 led Al Arrington and Jim Pawlik to a white businessman named Blake Harper. Pawlik and Sergeant Greg Wells interviewed him for hours. Yes, he'd spoken with Lewis, but they hadn't discussed cocaine. No, the mayor wasn't involved. Harper stuck to his story so well that the cops gave up. He was halfway into his coat when Arrington squeezed into the tiny interview room.

"Sit down," the short cop said. "Let's talk a bit more. Forget the Ramada. Let's talk about past history."

Harper took one look at Arrington's eager eyes and lost his composure. He admitted that he'd started Chuck Lewis in the cocaine business and had used him to courier cocaine up from Miami. He described how Lewis started buying drugs himself. He even named the supplier.

"You have more to tell us," Arrington said. He had a hunch that Harper knew that Lewis had supplied drugs to Barry. "I can get on the phone right now and make a deal with the prosecutor. But if you 're not totally honest with us, you could face a perjury charge."

Harper refused. Arrington and Pawlik turned up more incriminating information to tie him in to a drug-dealing conspiracy. Confronted with the charges, Harper wound up both cooperating and pleading to a felony charge when he could have taken Arrington's deal and walked.

Pawlik and Arrington had worked up a smooth routine. Arrington would open with a monologue drawn from his experience as a church deacon. He would talk about religion, and black heritage, and how important it was to tell the truth. He would describe the investigation, how much he and Pawlik knew, and often more than they actually knew. He wouldn't read them their rights.

"We don't want you," he would say soothingly.

Then Arrington would sit back and Pawlik would start the hard questioning. Sometimes they heard more than they needed to know, like the account from the wife of a city contractor who said that the mayor liked to sprinkle cocaine on her labia and lick it off. Sex wasn't what they were interested in, but the mayor often mixed it with drugs. When the interviews were over Arrington would cite a line from the Bible, First Peter, second chapter, fifteenth verse: "For so is the will of God that with well-doing ye may put to silence the ignorance of foolish men." He would write it on a card and tell them to read it before they testified to the grand jury. "It will give you strength," he said.

When James McWilliams came in for questioning, they already knew that he was in the room when Barry was there. Arrington opened up with his heart-to-heart monologue, then he took out a sheet of paper and started drawing fish: one big fish at the top and four or five smaller fish below. He drew a bold arrow coming from the bottom toward the big fish.

"The big fish is Marion Barry, and the arrow is us coming to get him," he said. "At first the little fish swim in front of the arrow to protect the big fish, but we keep coming. Finally Marion starts throwing the last little fish in front of the arrow to protect himself. You're one of the last little fish.

"There was this loyal crowd around him," Arrington said, "but this time he's going to fall. Nothing on earth can save him. We have him. He's going to jail. There's nothing he can do for you. If you throw yourself in front of him, we'll squash you like a bug."

McWilliams still refused to testify before the grand jury.

"No problem," Arrington said. He dialed up the U.S. attorney's office and asked one of the prosecutors to send over a subpoena. Ten minutes later he slapped it on the desk in the interview room.

"This is big," he told McWilliams. "People are not playing games."

Chuck Lewis returned to the Virgin Islands after lying to the grand jury about the cocaine at the Ramada Inn.

A few weeks later the two FBI agents assigned to the case—Ron Stern and Pete Wubbenhorst—checked into the Frenchman's Reef Hotel, a luxury resort on St. Thomas that was one of Marion Barry's favorite haunts. They learned that Lewis was still buying and selling cocaine, using as a code word "avocados." The agents set him up to sell crack to a statuesque red-haired agent posing as a tourist at the hotel. Lewis took the bait, and on March 3, federal agents arrested him for attempting to sell twenty-five rocks of crack. They had video-taped Lewis boasting that he could sell coke by the kilo. Facing a maximum of twenty years in jail, he was held on two hundred thousand dollars' bond.

Back in the capital, Marion Barry had been telling friends that he had "dodged the bullet," until the banner headlines announced Lewis's bust.

"I know that this arrest will again raise the specter that something illegal happened when I visited Mr. Lewis when he was in Washington last December," Barry said in a statement. "I want to repeat that I never saw any drugs or drug paraphernalia during my visits with Mr. Lewis."

The mayor carried on his antidrug crusade and held a rally that week at Potomac Gardens, a notorious public housing project plagued with drugs and violence just twelve blocks from the Capitol. As Barry walked through the project parking lot, someone hung a banner from a top-floor window: "Mayor Barry, try some of our crack."

"It doesn't look good," commented Police Chief Turner.

It looked so bad that the mayor's top personal staff members tried to blow the whistle.

282 | DREAM CITY

City administrator Carol Thompson was most concerned about the effect that Barry's behavior was having on the government. He was coming to the District Building later in the day. He would sometimes arrive at 11:00 a.m. and sleep in his office until 2:00 p.m. He would closet himself with strange people and shun his staff. He refused to listen to his advisers. Thompson shared her worries with Frederick D. Cooke, the corporation counsel. They decided to take their concerns to Delano Lewis, now the president of the C&P Telephone Company and arguably the most powerful black power broker in town. Cooke asked Barry's press secretary, John C. White, to come along.

On the evening of March 22, they drove from the District Building on Pennsylvania Avenue toward the Capitol and pulled up in front of C&P headquarters on H Street. The building was officially closed, so Lewis himself had to come to the locked lobby and lead the city officials through a security door and into the elevator that took them to his executive suite.

"What is this," he joked, "a palace coup?"

Thompson, Cooke, and White weren't in a joking mood. For the next two hours, they poured out their frustrations. Despite the Ramada incident and the arrest of Chuck Lewis only weeks earlier, Barry's behavior was increasingly erratic.

"The government isn't functioning," Carol Thompson said, and she listed a litany of lost opportunities, disabled bureaucracies, bungled attempts at controlling drugs and crime, and a leaderless government.

John White scribbled a note to himself in the margins of his pad: "We're discussing the rise and fall of M.B."

Del Lewis was shocked. It was no surprise that Barry was in bad shape, but the negative effects on the government had never been detailed so starkly for him by such high officials. Barry's young aides got to the point. Maybe Lewis could talk to Barry and save him from his free fall.

"It's no use," he said, shifting dejectedly in his seat. Lewis revealed that he had gone to Barry in the past, and recently had urged him not to run for re-election, to get whatever treatment he needed, to at least leave office with some shred of dignity. Barry had rebuffed him.

Crestfallen, the trio left. "I guess we wanted some kind of magic to happen with Lewis," Cooke said of the meeting. "The magician had no magic." But at least the session was cathartic. "It was like a shrink session," White recalled. "It was awkward because we all had the feeling we were doing something behind Iris back. But we were desperate."

There was desperation in other quarters. Del Lewis said that many of Barry's closest political associates were discouraging him from running for a fourth term. Some of them—Herb Reid, zoning lawyer Robert Linowes, Max Berry, Jeffrey Cohen, Bob Johnson of Black Entertainment Television—had floated a plan to raise a $1 million fund for Barry's re-election, then donate the funds to the city's struggling college, the University of the District of Columbia. Barry would become an endowed professor with an $85,000-a-year salary.

When a reporter raised the idea, Barry said that he had no intention of being a teacher "at a remedial high school."

The FBI's sting of Charles Lewis made headlines, but it paled in comparison to the deep-rooted criminal network that Arrington and Pawlik were unraveling on their own.

Arrington was most intrigued by the phone calls from room 902 to the Moore household. IAD investigators had quickly learned that Hazel Diane "Rasheeda" Moore had some type of relationship with the mayor, but they weren't sure of its extent. They put together a dossier with her arrest record, her modeling credits, and her government contracts. Arrington thought she fit the profile of Barry's number-one lover. IAD officers tried to serve a grand jury subpoena on her several times, but she had moved back to New York. On a routine check of the house, Lieutenant Joe Fairley knocked on the door. Rasheeda answered, and he served her.

Moore called Barry and asked what to do. "Just go and do the best you can," he told her.

Moore arrived at the federal courthouse dressed in black skirt, black blazer, black stockings, black heels, and a black floppy hat that would become her trademark. Under oath, she testified that she had never gone to the Ramada Inn, which was true. But she also told the grand jurors that she knew the mayor only vaguely and never had seen him with cocaine.

The prosecutors reported immediately to Arrington. He knew that Moore was lying. He found her sitting with her attorney on a marble bench in the courthouse hallway. Prosecutor Judy Retchin made the introductions. He offered his hand.

"You just perjured yourself," he said quietly, "and you're going to be indicted. If you want to talk, here's my card." Barry called Moore that evening.

"How did it go?" he asked.

"Okay," she said.

"Were you careful?" he asked.

She said yes and he said, "That's good." Arrington called her lawyer the next day.

"Why don't you bring Ms. Moore to our offices," he said, "just to hear what we have to say. We won't ask her any questions."

It was a long shot, but she agreed, perhaps just to see how much the police knew. She arrived early one evening, once again wearing a sleek black ensemble with the floppy hat.

Arrington gave her the entire routine: the biblical references, the drawing of the fish, the warnings about perjury and the vulnerability of each witness. When he was through, she smiled politely to excuse herself. She never said a word, but she did write her name and address on a piece of paper.

"We'll get back in touch, I hope," Arrington said. A short time later, Rasheeda Moore moved to Los Angeles.

Arrington had a hunch that Rasheeda knew everything about the mayor and cocaine. He learned that her mother was an organist at the Nineteenth Street Baptist Church, Police Chief Turner's church. Arrington called and left a message. One night just before midnight, Rasheeda Moore's mother called Arrington's beeper. He called back and they spoke for a long while. Arrington mentioned that he was a deacon in his church and that she could talk with him. They commiserated about the frustrations of raising children. She said that Rasheeda had had trouble with men in her life: her first husband, the boyfriend who fathered her children—and then the mayor. Arrington didn't press her, but he now had proof that Rasheeda and the mayor had more than a passing friendship.

The next day he called again.

"Rasheeda is a grown woman," Mary Moore told him, suddenly cold. "There's nothing I can do. She's on her own."

In his fifth-floor office at 1400 Pennsylvania Avenue, the Democratic mayor twisted in the storm of drug charges; two blocks away at 1600 Pennsylvania Avenue, the Republican president licked his thin lips with the prospect of using the capital as a symbol of the country's drug epidemic. On March 13 George Bush moved to take advantage of Marion Barry's plight. In the White House, in the presence of his cabinet, Bush appointed William J. Bennett, a right-wing ideologue, the new federal drug czar.

"It's as bad as it can get here, it seems to me," the bearish former education secretary said after Bush swore him in. "And let's face it, this is the nation's capital."

Bennett became Bush's general in the nation's newest war on drugs, and the general chose the District to fight his first battles. "Why should we get in an airplane and fly three hundred miles when we are right here?" he asked. "This thing is right on top of us."

Bennett knew absolutely nothing about cocaine trafficking networks or drug treatment or drug addiction, except for his own addiction to nicotine. His qualifications consisted of being a high-powered conservative without portfolio; moreover, he took the drug czar job in a disgruntled mood because Bush refused to give him cabinet rank. He wanted to make a splash, so he jumped on the District and made it his "test case." He promised to assign more federal judges to process drug cases, build a new federal prison, create new "strike forces" to wipe out the city's ninetyopen-air drug markets, and direct federal drug-fighting funds to the city.

Over the next few weeks more grandiose plans emanated from Bennett's Office of National Drug Control Policy. He held high-powered meetings with FBI Director William Sessions and DEA Administrator John Lawn. The one person whom Bennett shunned was Marion Barry, the man who was running his own war against drugs. Their inevitable clash came to light in mid-April, when Bennett unveiled his plan to save the capital. "The plain fact is that for too long and in too many respects, the D.C. government has failed to serve its citizens," Bennett declared. "Here, where the problem is so glaring, so out of control, serious questions of local politics and governance can no longer he avoided or excused."

Bennett had a point, but his methods smacked of the kind of patronizing attempts at problem solving that federal officials always seemed to play out in the capital. He wanted to throw $70 million at the city and make it a model, but he hadn't invited any city officials to his press conferences and refused to consult them on how to use the money. Even federal drug agents thought Bennett's fulminations were flaky.

"It sounded good," says Al Arrington, "but it also sounded a lot like Joe diGenova talking about rampant corruption and how he was going to root it out. The question was could Bennett do more than talk?"

On April 13, three days after Bennett announced his big plans, Arrington and Pawlik's painstaking investigation bore fruit. A federal grand jury in the District of Columbia indicted Charles Lewis for possession of cocaine, based entirely on the IAD investigation. Prosecutors were able to charge him on ten counts, seven for perjury and three for possession. Less than a month later the government came back with a superseding sixteen-count indictment that added a conspiracy charge and five counts of cocaine distribution.

The indictment catalogued Lewis's drug deals beginning in 1985 when he was buying small quantities of cocaine in Florida and selling them in the District. It recounted a few transactions in 1986 and 1987 but focused on the deals that Lewis made while he was at the Ramada Inn during December 1988. It accused him of possession on December 22, the day that Barry was in his room. His lies before the grand jury had resulted in the seven perjury counts, and they landed him in a federal jail cell.

While Bennett and Barry were sniping at each other, federal agents and local police were preparing to take down Rayful Edmond III.

In the fall of 1988, Alta Rae Zanville retired from her job as a Navy clerk after twenty-nine years and decided to make some extra cash transporting kilograms of cocaine. On December 19, she drove her white Porsche into the parking lot of Hogates, a restaurant on the city's Maine Avenue wharf. She was wearing a squirrel coat and carrying 1.5 kilos of cocaine on the backseat. As she emerged from her Porsche, FBI and DEA agents swooped in. They hustled her into a car and drove off to the FBI's nondescript Washington field office on Buzzard's Point, overlooking the Anacostia River. After an hour of questioning, Zanville agreed to cooperate with the lawmen. The DEA placed taps on her phone immediately. The next day, Rayful Edmond called.

"I hear you been arrested," he said.

"Where'd you hear that, honey?" she asked. "Would I be here talkin' to you from my apartment if I was arrested?"

The agents fitted Zanville with a body wire and for the next four months she recorded incriminating conversations with everymember of the Edmond family. Zanville even wore a listening device to a lunch with Edmond's mother, Constance "Bootsie" Perry. The FBI tuned in as they chatted about their friends who'd been busted recently. Bootsie called Rae her "white sister." Edmond's closest associates were indeed getting busted, one by one, and DEA Agent John Cornille and lead prosecutor Betty Ann Soiefer prepared to take down his organization. They set April 17 at 3:00 a.m. for their coordinated blitz on twenty separate locations.

A week before the scheduled arrests, ABC news anchor Ted Koppel called Jay Stephens. The network star was planning to televise a town meeting about Washington that would be called "Divided City," and he knew every detail about the Edmond raid.He wanted his camera crews to tape the operation. Stephens turned him down, but Koppel said that he would send his cameras anyway. Then on Saturday morning before the scheduled Monday bust, an informant told Cornille that Tony Lewis had called Edmond with most of the raid details; Lewis even claimed that he'd seen the arrest warrants. It was too late to worry about the leak, subsequently found to be a courthouse clerk. The task force decided to strike that night; cops and agents were deployed to arrest as many as thirty suspects.

FBI agent Chuck Anderson wanted to arrest Edmund at his home, but he wasn't there, so Sergeant B. J. Parker, Lieutenant Shawn McGuire, and a few other detectives went to Edmond's girl-friend's apartment on Emerson Street. Parker knocked, Edmond opened the door, and officers aiming pistols piled into the apartment. The crack king had been upstairs watching a basketball game with his girlfriend. He was arrested in his boxer shorts.

"I heard that you were looking for me," Edmond told McGuire.

"Why didn't you call?"

Shawn McGuire cuffed him. The Irish cop and the homeboy dealer had become friendly during the long investigation. The tworode together to DEA headquarters and had a quiet moment there before Edmond was processed.

"What do I need to do to get out tonight?" Edmond asked."Can I call my lawyer?"

"Rayful," McGuire said, "I got something to tell you. I hopeyou fucked her because you're not getting another piece ofpussy."

On December 6, after a three-month trial held in a bullet-proof-courtroom, a federal jury convicted Rayful Edmond of running a continuing criminal enterprise, a count that called for life without parole, and he still faced a potential thirty murder counts. Ten other gang members, including his aunt and his sister, also got jail time. His mother was convicted in a separate trial. His father was convicted a year later on unrelated cocaine distribution charges.

Alta Rae Zanville testified during the trial and walked—into a life under the federal witness protection program.

On June 8, the mayor arose early, put on his finest white shirt and dark-blue suit, gathered his security detail, and made ready for an appearance on Capitol Hill. The Senate committee on governmental affairs had asked him to testify about crime and drug problems in the District.

At 9:30 a.m., he bounded into the hearing room on schedule, took his seat at the witness table, and started talking about "this scourge of drugs" that was destroying his city. The senators on the dais looked at Barry with unvarnished skepticism. Just three years earlier, some in Congress still had high hopes for Barry and the city. Now they saw him as a joke and the capital as a bloody mess. It was open season.

Warren Rudman, a Republican senator from New Hampshire, suggested that a federal police force take over from the city officers. "You can't have blood running in the streets like a third world capital run by a despot," he said.

"Some governments are corrupt but are known for their competency in running the city," Senator John Danforth of Missouri said, "others are incompetent but considered 'clean.' [Washington's] government is scandalously corrupt and hopelessly incompetent."

For the first fourteen years of home rule, the Hill essentially had allowed the District to run its affairs. But early supporters of home rule—such as Missouri's Tom Eagleton and Maryland's Charles "Mac" Mathias—were no longer in office. In their place Senator Jesse Helms of North Carolina called the District the "abortion capital of the world" and pushed through legislation to ban abortions; and Representative Stan Parris, a Republican from northern Virginia, took up where Joel Broyhill left off. After 1987, when Barry's peccadillos became public knowledge, Congress and the Reagan White House took it out on city residents by holding down the federal payment, the annual amount the city receives to compensate for untaxable federal land in the District.

"Home rule is at its lowest ebb in the nine years that I've been in the House," said Representative Thomas Bliley of Virginia, a member of the District committee. "We weren't elected by the people of the District to be the city's government, but we do have a federal responsibility."

D.C. Delegate Walter Fauntroy, whom District voters had reelected easily since 1971, was widely considered to be ineffectual and even at times damaging to the city's cause. He frequently made out-of-town trips and missed crucial sessions. When the House District committee approved a statehood bill in 1987, Fauntroy damaged hopes for passage by calling one moderate opponent "a racist." When quiet lobbying was in order, Fauntroy stalked the House floor with placards, as if he were running a street demonstration. He became a joke, too.

In effect, home rule, the city, and Marion Barry were inextricably tied, a sad irony in that Barry had had very little to do with passage of the home-rule charter in 1973. Now he was dangerously close to giving Congress an excuse to take it away. His performance before the Senate committee didn't help his cause, even though he stressed that Washington was no different from any other city and was indeed getting the situation under control.

"This cancer of drugs has the potential to destroy us all," he testified. "No one is immune, and we are all subject to its devastation."

CHAPTER 14

KNIFE IN THE HEART

*I got fucked-up up here with this goddamn bitch, setting
me up like this. Set me up, ain't that a bitch!*
—*Marion Barry*

Thirty miles south of the capital the flatlands of Virginia begin to undulate before rising into the mountains farther west. Here, in low hills near Quantico, Virginia, the Federal Bureau of Investigation maintains a well-guarded campus where it researches the criminal mind, trains agents, and interrogates its most valuable witnesses.

One morning in mid-August 1989, a dozen men gathered around a conference table three flights up in one of Quantico's most secure buildings. The large round table was in the center of the living room in a plush suite that had a full kitchen and bedrooms at either end and listening devices in the air vents. One large window overlooked a firing range and the wooded fields beyond. The mood in the room was relaxed but expectant. Much work had to be done. Over the next week the FBI, the prosecutors, and the metropolitan police would debrief Charles Lewis and build their case against Marion Barry.

The first session began with the signing of Lewis's plea-bargaining documents. The papers circulated around the table to Lewis's two attorneys, Mark Shaffer and Alan Soschin, to Assistant U.S. Attorney Richard Roberts, to Ron Stern and two other FBI agents, to Jim Pawlik, who was prepared to do the major share of the questioning, and to Al Arrington, who sat within touching distance of Lewis. Under the agreement, Lewis would cooperate fully and most likely get off without spending time behind bars. He had been ready to spill everything back in April, right after the first indictment.

"We knew he was ready to give it up right there," Arrington said. Lewis was facing a maximum sentence of two hundred years because of his conviction in the Virgin Islands and the sixteen counts awaiting him in the District. He wasn't a strong-willed man. "By then," Arrington said, "it was a matter of legalities." Federal officials worried that someone would try to kill Lewis in the District, so they moved him to a more secure jail in Alexandria, Virginia, right across the Potomac River, and later to Quantico for the serious questioning, beginning with Al Arrington's monologue.

He began with the Bible and eased gradually into his rendition of black history. He talked about how their people had been brought to this country as slaves and had risen from bondage under the leadership of models such as Frederick Douglass and Martin Luther King, Jr. He talked about the American Dream and how much it meant to African-Americans, but how it was being perverted by corrupt officials. He drew the pictures of the big fish and the little fish. He brought out a cardboard United States flag, opened it up on the table in front of Lewis and spoke about how many patriotic men—black and white—had sacrificed their lives for freedom.

"Let's have a moment of silent prayer," Arrington said, and Lewis, the lawyers, the agents, and the officers all bowed their heads for thirty seconds. Arrington drew closer to Lewis, picked up the Bible, and broke the silence.

"For so it is the will of God...lest ye confess in order tobe saved...purging yourself ofsin..." He laid the Bible onthe flag and watched the tears well up in Lewis's eyes. Everyone in the room was in the deacon's thrall, but he broke the spell togive Lewis a final analogy.

"Think ofus all in a football game," he said. "There are twominutes remaining. We're down 24-20. It's the Super Bowl. You're the quarterback. We're your wide receivers. The clock is ticking down. We can win this game together. Tell the whole truth and throw a touchdown. We're depending onyou.

"Please," he said, "don't let us down."

Lewis didn't disappoint. Over the course of the next eight days, they logged sixty hours in interviews. Pawlik, Arrington, and Lewis moved into apartments in the suite for the duration. The prosecutor and FBI agents participated, but the police officers controlled the sessions. Lewis described his first trips with Barry to the Virgin Islands back in 1986, when they first used cocaine together. He gave them fresh details of Barry's visit in 1988 as part ofthe government-to-government personnel project, and he described the parade of women that he brought to the mayor's room at Frenchman's Reef.

Ten days after the first briefing, some details of the Quantico briefings were leaked to WUSA-TV reporter Mark Feldstein, who aired them on August 30. In addition to describing where and when the interviews took place, Feldstein reported Lewis's account of Barry's cocaine use at the Ramada and the Virgin Islands.

The mayor was vacationing, but his office released a statement calling the leaks "blatant" attempts by federal officials to get headlines and assassinate his character. "They have attempted to do through the press what is not possible in a court of law," he said. "This is lawlessness by the government." Hounded by reporters at the District Building, Barry dismissed the latest Lewis stories. "Why, you 'll lie on your mamma to save your own hide," he said.

Arrington paid little attention to the leak or the mayor's reaction. Something that Chuck Lewis had said on the last Saturday of the debriefing riveted his attention. Lewis kept talking about the mayor's girlfriend who accompanied them to the Virgin Islands in 1986. She was a striking woman. They were lovebirds on boats in the islands, and they did cocaine together. The mayor talked about her all the time and got in touch with her from the Ramada Inn.

"What's her name?" Arrington asked.

"I just remember him calling her R.C.," Lewis said. "That's all I can recall."

Arrington asked Lewis to describe her. Lewis said that she was voluptuous, stunning, like a model. Arrington called IAD and asked a lieutenant to locate Rasheeda's picture and have it driven to Quantico. He showed it to Chuck Lewis.

"That's her," he said.

At 9:00 p.m. on September 5, nine months into his term, George Bush sat in the Oval Office to give his first national address as president. His war on drugs wasn't going very well, and he wanted to rally the troops and build his crime-fighting image.

"The rules of the game have changed," Bush said solemnly in a warning to South American drug cartels, declaring that he would spend billions more on drug enforcement, interdiction, and treatment.

The war was going especially badly in the surrounding city of Washington, D.C., where Bush's general, William Bennett, had chosen to engage the enemy. Bennett hired a staff, made promises, and pumped a few million dollars into a federal task force to bust more drug dealers. The agents were closing down crack houses and putting more people behind bars, but nothing seemed to cool the mayhem in the capital's streets. Drug abuse and drug related killings continued to rise and dominate the news. Four people were killed in four hours a month before Bush delivered his speech, and the murder rate was outstripping the record set in 1988. The arrest and trial of Rayful Edmond III were the only bright spots, but Bennett could take no credit for an investigation that began years before he became drug czar. And Bennett's two biggest promises—to build a jail and to set up state-of-the-art treatment centers—were unfulfilled.

Still, the president wanted to make an example of Washington. In mid-speech, he reached into a drawer with his left hand and held up a plastic bag of white powder for the camera.

"This is crack cocaine, seized a few days ago by drug enforcement agents in Lafayette Park, just across the street from the White House. It could have easily been heroin or PCP. It's as innocent looking as candy but it's turning our cities into battle zones and it's murdering our children. Let there be no mistake," Bush said as he shook the bag for emphasis, "this stuff is poison."

Even as the president spoke, secret service agent George Ogilvie stood just out of camera range, his eyes focused on the cocaine in the hand of the president of the United States. Ogilvie's job that night was not to let the cocaine—three ounces worth about twenty-four hundred dollars—out of his sight and to preserve it as evidence. When the speech ended, Ogilvie quickly retrieved the bag and delivered it to agent Sam Gaye of the federal Drug Enforcement Administration, waiting in a nearby room. Gaye took the cocaine to DEA headquarters, heat-sealed the bag in another container, and placed it in an evidence locker. The president's dramatic moment was over, and once again, the nation's capital had formed a convenient backdrop to a national problem. For shock value, the president evoked images of a drug crisis so great that even the White House itself was not safe. How brazen! And what a sham.

It turns out that the drug deal was pure theatrics, orchestrated by the White House for the sole purpose of hyping the president's speech.

White House aides concocted the cocaine gambit on August 31 and ordered the Drug Enforcement Agency to make a drug buy in Lafayette Park. U.S. Park Police had told the White House there was no history of drug sales in the well-lit and landscaped park patrolled by National Park Service officers on foot, car, and horseback. Homeless people and protesters of various kinds camp out there twenty-four hours a day. The only drug use was the annual marijuana smoke-in by yippies on July 4. DEA agents—and even the antidrug czar's own staff—tried to discourage the White House idea as "stupid propism." But the White House insisted and the DEA complied. The top brass ordered agent Sam Gaye to set up the deal. The agent enlisted a snitch who in turn set up a buy from a small-time dealer named Keith Jackson, a high-school senior who had no prior arrests. Jackson lived

296 | DREAM CITY

a world away from the White House in southeast Washington, so far away, in fact, that the agents had to direct him to Lafayette Park.

Jackson was so nervous at finding himself across from the White House with three ounces of cocaine at noon on September 1 that he made the snitch hold the drugs. For the Lafayette buy, Gaye strapped on a body wire to tape any conversations. But the recording device failed to work. The tape was useless. Another undercover agent—posing as a noontime tourist—moved in to videotape the scene with a camcorder. Suddenly a homeless woman who had been lying on the ground nearby jumped up, enraged. She cursed and screamed that she didn't want her picture taken. The startled officer retreated, his camcorder missing the actual drug transaction.

From the law-enforcement standpoint, the entire deal was botched. But Jackson was arrested September 26 and charged with four counts of cocaine distribution, three previous sales and the Lafayette Park incident, all of which had been initiated by federal drug agents. In a December and January trial, Jackson was convicted on three counts, but the jury refused to convict him on the Lafayette charge, and the president's drug bust collapsed in court.

When *Washington Post* reporter Mike Isikoff first disclosed the White House setup, reporters asked the president about the propriety of creating a crime for political reasons. Bush said, "I don't understand. I mean, has somebody got some advocates for this drug guy?"

When Chuck Lewis confirmed Al Arrington's hunch that Rasheeda Moore was Marion Barry's longtime lover and cocaine supplier, the former model was in Los Angeles, living with one foot in the gutter.

She had flown from New York earlier in the year to find her children—a nine-year-old son and two daughters, six and four. Their father had been jailed and the children were being shuffled around to family members of his girlfriend, who also was serving time. Moore had finally located them and taken custody. She had no means of support, three children on her hands, and a cocaine addiction. She applied for welfare.

The checks were for rent and food, but Moore had more powerful needs. She moved the family into a homeless shelter and used her welfare checks to buy drugs and liquor. As the Christmas season approached, the once-ravishing cover girl hit bottom. Unable to afford plane tickets to Washington, she was stuck on the coast with her kids and strung out on dope.

Back in the capital, Al Arrington was stymied. It was one thing to have Chuck Lewis ready to testify about Marion Barry's use of cocaine, but Lewis alone was not a credible witness. He was a convicted coke dealer who was willing to rat on the mayor to help himself. Arrington believed that Rasheeda Moore could testify to the mayor's abuse of drugs, and perhaps to his corrupt trading of city contracts for cocaine. He bet prosecutor Judy Retchin that he could bring her in. The FBI put out a warrant for her arrest as a material witness. The U.S. marshals also deputized Arrington and Pawlik so that they could arrest her anywhere in the country. Arrington persuaded a source to turn over one of Rasheeda's phone numbers on the coast, and FBI agents in Los Angeles began to track her down.

On New Year's Eve, police in L.A. County independently arrested Moore for driving under the influence of alcohol. They plugged her name into a nationwide computer crime network and came up with the FBI's warrant. The Los Angeles police called agent Ron Stern. Neither Pawlik nor Arrington, who was home sick with a serious sinus infection, could go. Stern and Pete Wubbenhorst made the trip and talked to Moore in the L.A. lockup. They gave her a choice: Cooperate with the investigation or face at minimum a perjury charge, which was enough to send her to prison on a felony count that would probably cost her the custody of her children.

Moore made no immediate decision, but armed with the warrant, the agents brought her and the children back to Washington where Moore encountered Al Arrington, again.

The *Los Angeles Times* had no inkling of the crucial break in the Barry case in the newspaper's own backyard when it published a detailed profile of Barry on January 9, 1990. Written by Bella Stumbo, a seasoned feature writer, the article captured Barry at the height of his arrogance and self-delusion: a big-city pol, taunting his enemies, touting his sexual prowess, and trumpeting his "invincibility" even as the moment of his disgrace raced toward him.

"Co-caaaaane? How folks use that stuff, anyhow?" the mayor asked in a playful mode as he and Stumbo sat at one of his favorite late-night bars. He drank wine, felt loose, and revealed himself to the out-of-town journalist, who happened to be a comely brunette. "You put it up your nooose? Ooooooooooeeeeeee!" Barry then excused himself for a sojourn in the bathroom. He emerged ten minutes later and smirked about how much the prosecutors or the news media would love to take a look at his urine specimen, leaving the clear impression that he had once again indulged and pulled something over on police, Stumbo, and the rest of the world.

Stumbo was doing research for the article in mid-November, a week after Charles Lewis testified in an open court hearing that he had provided crack to the mayor. The mayor agreed to the interview in part because Mary Treadwell's brother, a journalist in New York, had vouched for Stumbo. Treadwell had completed her prison term in 1987, and Barry had immediately appointed her to a staff job with the city's parole board. With Treadwell's blessing, Bella Stumbo talked to Barry's friends and enemies and spent a sixteen-hour day by the mayor's side, in his car, at his lunch table, and with him at staff meetings.

The day began at an elementary school in a tough neighborhood where the mayor spoke about his antidrug crusade. After giving his spiel, ending with a Jesse Jackson-style chant—"up with hope, down with dope"—the mayor took questions. A little boy asked, "Do people believe you when you say you don't do drugs?" Later in the day, Barry took Stumbo to the waiting room of the city's public assistance office. The mayor was at his best here, gabbing with city workers, commiserating with the troubled applicants, and bestowing a ten-dollar bill on a woman with sores on her face who said she couldn't

KNIFE IN THE HEART | 299

afford diapers for the baby in her arms. Stumbo described Barry as "high on public love," his other addiction.

At a bar after midnight the subject turned to local politics. The next election was less than a year away. Jesse Jackson was hovering. Many of Barry's supporters were abandoning him. "Isn't anybody in this town can beat me," Barry told Stumbo. "I'm invincible."

Not even Jackson? she asked.

"Hah," Barry replied, "Jesse don't wanna run nothin' but his mouth." Barry later would deny the comment and denounce the article as "racist."

The mayor's delusion was not lost on his allies or his best friends. After he flipped his middle finger toward hecklers at an Adams Morgan Day community festival that fall, it was clear that he was out of control. Stumbo contacted Ivanhoe Donaldson, who had been released from federal prison in January 1989 after serving three years of his seven-year term. He was keeping a low profile, but had been advising both Barry and Jesse Jackson on political issues. In the Stumbo interview, Donaldson defended Barry's record in office, but he said that the mayor should not run for re-election. "I think Marion's bored," Donaldson told Stumbo. "And image is image. You don't have to be a user to connect with the image. It's bad for the city, for the youngsters. That's reality."

The mayor continued to live his own reality.

On January 12, clunky blue city buses carried loads of senior citizens and other Barry supporters to pack the Convention Center for the mayor's annual State of the District speech. He spoke for an hour, cataloguing his accomplishments and dubbing the last decade "the boomin' Barry years" (referring to the real estate boom, not the sound of gunfire in what had become known as the Murder Capital). Barry and his diehard aides were painstakingly building toward another public event: the climactic January 21 announcement of his re-election campaign, just nine days away.

Arrington, Pawlik, and the FBI agents were building toward a spectacle of a different kind.

Rasheeda Moore was falling deeper and deeper into the arms of the law. In Washington and in FBI custody, she said that she was willing to cooperate because of a religious conversion and desire to straighten out her life. But the government's embrace was impossible to resist for a woman who had very little going for her. She spent long hours with Ron Stern and prosecutor Ricky Roberts. Arrington and Pawlik prepared her to testify before the grand jury, and this time she told the truth about her escapades with the mayor.

An investigator's ultimate tool is the undercover sting operation. It is by definition a setup—a trap—pure and simple. No one person came up with the idea of using Rasheeda Moore as the bait. It was an obvious option, if she would agree to play the role. In the second week of January, she did; The FBI would pay for the operation and provide the video recording equipment. Arrington and Pawlik would be equal partners in setting up the trap and busting Barry, if he would walk into it.

The officers discussed a date. Barry was out of town for the inaugural of Virginia governor L. Douglas Wilder, so it couldn't be done right away. The officers agreed on a date: January 15. Stinging the black mayor of the nation's capital was so potentially explosive that the details were reviewed at the highest echelons of the federal government. FBI Director William Sessions approved the plan, as did Attorney General Richard Thornburgh, but the Justice Department demanded a different day. January 15 was Martin Luther King's birthday.

Arrington didn't care. "I wanted to do it ourselves," he says, "make it a District police operation, forget about the FBI." He was overruled. The sting was postponed three days to Thursday, January 18.

The mayor invited two separate visitors to his offices that afternoon to discuss his re-election announcement the coming Sunday.

R. Robert Linowes arrived at 4:00 p.m. The influential zoning attorney could bring tens of thousands of dollars to Barry's campaign. But Linowes already had been quoted, along with John Hechinger and Max Berry, in a newspaper story suggesting that the mayor should not run for re-election. The three men composed an unofficial principal triumvirate of Barry's monied Jewish supporters. The day the critical story had come out, Barry phoned Hechinger and Linowes and filled the line with a stream of epithets. Now he wanted Linowes back.

"Do I have your support?" the mayor asked.

"I don't think that under the present circumstances I can give it to you," Linowes said.

"Why?" Barry asked.

They were sitting alone at the long conference table in Barry's office. "It's the drinking, the womanizing, the drugs," Linowes shrugged. "I just don't see how I can get behind you again."

"You don't believe that stuff, do you?" the mayor asked. "I'm a changed man. I jog every morning. Come on up and jog with me." He rose to his full six feet, three inches and thumped his stomach. "I've lost ten pounds. I'm down to fighting weight.

"I know I've made mistakes," Barry said. "It's affected my family, it's had a bad effect on Christopher. He came home from school the other day with a nasty crack in his lip. He got into a fight when some kids made fun of me. That hurt. I'm going to change. You'll see. In my next term I'm going to focus on education. We have to turn around the schools if we're going to have a decent city. Things are going to be different," he said.

Linowes said he had to leave. Barry put his arm around his shoulders as they walked toward the door.

"You'll see," Barry told him. "I'll make you proud of me."

"I hope so," Linowes said. "You're a tremendous guy, and you've contributed a lot to this city. I'm proud to be your friend. It would be a crime if you were remembered for this mess and not for your good deeds. You ought to zipper your fly and have it sewn up. "

The mayor laughed.

Barry needed Linowes, but there were developers who needed the mayor and took no persuading. Ted and Jim Pedas, two brothers who had made a fortune in the movie theater business, were trying to develop a huge building on Pennsylvania Avenue five blocks west of the White House. They needed new zoning and reams of city permits. They had agreed not only to help finance Barry's campaign but to host a fundraising party the night of his announcement. Another developer, Joey Kaempfer, had collected seventy-five-thousand dollars in checks for Barry's coffers. They were in Kaempfer's desk, uncashed, ready for delivery at the right moment.

Not long after Linowes left, David Wilmot arrived. Of all Barry's friends and political associates, Wilmot was the most successful. In his own right, he had done well as dean of admissions at Georgetown University Law Center, but he had parlayed his proximity to Barry and the city council into a lobbying business that brought him a small fortune. Developers had brought him into deals for political purposes, and he was one of the few minority partners to come out with huge profits. Wilmot knew that Barry was hooked on women and drugs, but he, still wanted him to stay in office and protect his own considerable financial interest. He came that Thursday afternoon to work on Barry's announcement speech. Wilmot, Barry, and chief of staff Maudine Cooper were discussing the draft when the phone rang.

"I can't make it tonight," Barry said into the receiver. "We're giving away houses in a lottery, and I have to be there. Maybe another time."

A half-hour later the phone rang again. The mayor picked it up and listened.

"Like I said, I have to go to the lottery," he said. "But I'll try and stop by afterwards."

The caller was Rasheeda Moore, phoning from room 727 at the Vista Hotel.

The mayor knocked at 7:35 p.m.

"It's good to see you again," Barry said. "You look like new money."

He didn't want to be there. He had called Moore twice from his car phone to arrange a rendezvous in the lobby or the hotel restaurant. "Too many Nosey Rosies around nowadays," he told her in the first call. He knew that a hotel room was a perfect place to set him up. He did float the idea of having sex, saying they could "make love." Moore laughed off the comment, and they agreed to meet after he attended a housing lottery at the Martin Luther King, Jr., Library a few blocks from the Vista.

The FBI had rented three adjoining rooms on the hotel's seventh floor. Moore was in 727; Al Arrington, Jim Pawlik, three FBI agents, and a prosecutor were in 726, separated only by the adjoining door; technical equipment filled 725. Wanda King, an attractive black FBI agent, was set to pose as Rasheeda's friend and dope supplier. Dressed in a tight leather miniskirt, she was supposed to sell crack cocaine directly to Barry and generally support Rasheeda Moore in the ruse. In the final minutes, Moore had a change of heart. She didn't need Wanda. "I can do it myself," she said.

While Barry gave away free houses, the police worried how they could lure the mayor upstairs to the room. IAD Lieutenant Bill Lynch suggested that Moore order room service so that she would be eating and unable to leave the room when he arrived. A half-hour later Barry called back from his car. She said he had to come up.

"I really don't wanna do that," he protested, at first. "All right," he finally relented, "but only for a few minutes." A moment later he was at the door.

They greeted each other in the manner of old lovers who were a bit ill at ease after not seeing each other for six months. Rasheeda Moore wore a gauzy blouse and a stylish scarf wrapped around her head and trailing down her back. "Wanda" was there, too, but left to go downstairs, saying she hoped to "get into trouble."

Barry got comfortable. He laid his walkie-talkie on the bureau and took off his blue suit coat to show his billowy white shirt and suspenders. They sat on the bed and watched TV. She poured him a four-finger shot of Hennessy cognac in a highball glass. They reminisced about old friends and old drug suppliers. Moore kept steering the conversation to drugs, but she was under orders not to specifically say anything about drugs unless Barry brought it up; Barry was focusing on her body and fondling her breast.

"Well, I love you still, you know," Barry said, "even if I don't treat you right. Once in love, always in love."

When Wanda left the room, Barry asked: "Does she mess around?" Given Barry's eagerness to paw Rasheeda Moore, it seems that Barry wanted to have sex with Wanda, but Moore interpreted "mess around" as a reference to drugs, and she seized the opportunity.

"She toots," Moore said.

"Mmm," Barry responded casually. A minute later he said that he didn't "have anything," and asked Moore, "How about you?" Rasheeda Moore took that offhand comment as a license to press the matter of buying drugs from Wanda. The mayor had polished off one glass of cognac. She poured him another.

"So what, you want to do something?" she asked. "I haven't done it. I've been doing it off and on in California."

"No, not tonight," Barry said. "Naw."

He phoned a friend, and then put in a call to his chief of staff Maudine Cooper to discuss press coverage for Sunday's announcement. Barry and Moore already had been in the room for forty-five minutes. He was ready to leave when Wanda knocked on the door. She had scored some crack, and Moore offered some for sale.

"I don't smoke no more, honey," he said.

That was bad news for the FBI. In what may have been a first-class blunder, the FBI had only crack cocaine on hand. The mayor was indicating he wanted powdered cocaine. There was some confused conversation between the two women about powdered cocaine and how long it would take to get some. Barry let them off the hook. He told Moore to buy some crack, and the women went into the bathroom to make the deal.

On the other side of the door to the adjoining hotel room, Al Arrington had his hand on the doorknob. He felt the button in the knob that would unlock the door to the worst nightmare in Marion Barry's life.

Arrington had been working toward this moment for a year; now he wasn't sure he wanted it to come. His headphones tuned in to room 727 were slick from the sweat on his head. His eyes were riveted on a monitor wired to video cameras that were secretly taping the mayor and the former model. Three FBI agents and Jim Pawlik were lined up beside him, watching the scene in the next room, preparing to pounce. Assistant U.S. Attorney Daniel Bernstein also was standing by. If and when Barry took the bait, Arrington was supposed to be the first one through the door.

Barry stood up and took a sip of cognac. His white shirt was rumpled from lying on the bed. He turned toward his former lover. She was still sitting on the bed.

"Where's your pipe?" he asked.

Moore got up and gave him a small pipe.

"I, I don't know how this work, how this work," Barry said. "I never done it before." Moore laughed. "That's what we used to do all the time," she said. "What are you talking about?"

"I'm new," he said. "We never done that before—give me a break."

"Put it in there," she said. "Let me give you a lighter."

"You do it," he said.

The cognac was affecting Barry's speech and his words came out in muddy phrases. It also weakened his resolve. Just as the lure of sex with Rasheeda Moore overcame his instinct to stay out of hotel rooms, the cognac lowered his resistance to crack. Still, he was suspicious.

"No," Moore said. "I'm not doing nothing." She said she had done something earlier, and it had made her too hyper.

"Nope," he said. "You do it."

As the mayor vacillated, Al Arrington's stomach twisted into a tight knot. He kept his hand on the door and his eyes on the monitor. To the federal agents, the man on the monitor was a trophy. Taking down the mayor of a big city on a drug rap was the catch of a lifetime.

But Arrington, the only black person in the room, saw another dimension. He believed Barry was hooked on drugs and had betrayed his own city. Still, there was a kinship of two sharecroppers' sons. A conversation that Arrington had that afternoon with another black officer flashed into his head. "I'm hoping he doesn't do it," that cop had said, and part of Arrington was hoping the same. From the scene in the next room, it looked as though he might not.

"I thought you bought this 'cause you wanted to take a hit," Moore told the mayor.

"Aw, naw, you do it."

In the back of his mind, Barry may have thought that he was being watched. But now he was breaking the crack into little pieces by the light of the table lamp. Moore coaxed him and coached him. They jousted and hustled each other for a full three minutes. Finally, he took the pipe and the lighter, put the pipe to his lips, lit the crack, took a long, slow pull, and drew the crack smoke into his lungs.

"How is it?" she asked, flitting around the room, moving quickly from the bed to the dresser to the door.

Arrington was supposed to get to Barry first. They watched the monitor as Barry put another piece of crack into the pipe and lit it again. As the crack hit Barry's bloodstream and made his heart race, Arrington's heart pounded, too. The law-enforcement team had worried about this part of the arrest. Anything could go wrong. The mayor might have a gun. They had to keep him in the room and arrest him on camera. Their greatest worry was that his security team might walk in at the moment of the arrest, see a bunch of armed men, and start shooting.

"Let's go downstairs," Barry said.

"You don't want to take another one?" she asked.

"No," he said. "You crazy." He took one last sip of cognac, put on his suit jacket, and looked into the mirror to straighten his tie. "Come on…"

It was close to 8:30, nearly an hour had passed. He reached for his walkie-talkie, turned it on, and put it to his mouth: "908, 907," he said as he walked toward the door.

"Nine-oh-seven back," came the response from Barry's security officer, who could be there in a moment.

Arrington hit the button on the door handle at 8:27. The four men behind him were starting to push against him and the door. Arrington wiggled the button and the door burst open, but Rasheeda had mistakenly placed her food cart against it. Arrington put his shoulder to the door, and the officers piled into the room.

"Police!" Arrington yelled. "You're under arrest!"

"FBI! FBI! You're under arrest."

The agent behind Arrington jumped on the bed and leaped at Barry, but Arrington got to the mayor first. The mayor stood six inches taller than Arrington. He looked down at him. Two glasses of cognac and two hits of crack fogged his brain. He tried to focus. He looked over Arrington's shoulder at the FBI agents and back at Arrington. In that horrible instant, Marion Barry's eyes locked on Arrington's. Face to face with the man he had pursued for a year, Arrington felt as if someone had plunged a knife in his heart.

"Why did he have to be black?" Arrington thought. "We don't need this."

"Mr. Charlie" had finally caught up with Marion Barry, and "Mr. Charlie" turned out to he black like him.

The FBI agents hustled Rasheeda Moore out of the room.

"Okay, Mr. Mayor," Ron Stern said. "We'd like you to put your hands on the wall."

"I don't have any," he said.

"Please put your hands on the wall."

"I understand."

He was still dazed. He kept saying he didn't do anything, didn't have anything. Then it began to sink in.

"That was a setup, goddamnit," he said. "It was a fucking setup."

"Listen to your rights now," Arrington said.

An agent told Barry of his right to remain silent and talk to a lawyer.

"Yeah," he said. "I know all that."

"Bitch set me up," he said, interrupting the recitation of his rights. He said it again and again like a mantra, as if understanding it could make it go away.

"I, I want to call my lawyer right now. I'll be goddamn. I got fucked-up up here with this goddamn bitch, setting me up like this. Set me up, ain't that a bitch!"

"Calm down," Arrington said.

Arrington and the agents were taking care of details. A team of emergency medical technicians came in to check the mayor's vital signs, which were normal. A technician asked how Barry felt.

"I feel fine," he said, "except that I'm pissed off."

Captain Stanley stood by the door to the next room and called Police Chief Ike Fulwood. He told him Barry was busted. Fulwood said he was joking. Busted for what? Where?

"Smoking dope," Stanley said. "Vista Hotel. No, I'm not lying.... We got a doctor checking him."

About that same time, another call was made. The first tip to the news media came into WRC-TV anchor Susan Kidd. After a few moments of disbelief, reporter Tom Sherwood was dispatched by editor Paul Irvin to the scene; he arrived in time to see the mayor's driver and a security aide being led away. But no one outside the hotel was talking.

In room 727, the medical technicians were taking the mayor's pulse.

"I'm not in that bad a shape, come on," the mayor said. "That shit she tricked me into doing, bitch. I'll be goddamn."

Through the shock and the crack, it was dawning on Barry that he was the highest-ranking black elected leader in the nation's history to he caught in a drug bust.

"Elaborate goddamn trap," he muttered to himself, "I tell you.... Man, I should have followed my first instincts."

Then, fifteen minutes after they had burst into the room, an FBI agent snapped on the cuffs.

"I mean, come on," Barry objected. Arrington, Pawlik, and two FBI agents were milling around the room. "I'm not going to go nowhere. Do we have to..." It was standard policy, everyone gets cuffed.

There were moments of awkward silence. The mayor, cuffed and cowed, sat on the bed, muttering, letting the full force of his predicament settle in.

Pawlik approached him.

"We're with Metropolitan," he said.

"I know that."

"Um," Pawlik searched for words. "I mean we didn't really want this to happen, really."

"I didn't want it to happen either. I should, if I had followed my fucking instincts tonight, I'd have been all right, I should have stayed downstairs. Bitch kept insisting coming up here. Goddamnit, I should have known better. I should have known better."

Seconds passed in silence, Arrington and Pawlik standing there, embarrassed by the sight of their cuffed quarry. Barry sighed and said, "Oh, boy." He paused. "What's your charge again?"

"Possession," an FBI agent said.

"Possession?" Barry scoffed. "What, what, intent to use?" He laughed. "That, little, that little bit, that, that speck?"

He complained that the cuffs were too tight, and they were loosened a bit. Pawlik stepped up again to fill the silence.

"So what do you think about all this?" he asked. Barry said he was pissed off.

"You knew eventually it was going to happen, I think, didn't you?" he asked. "Did you suspect someday it was going to happen?"

"I don't know," Barry responded. "I guess you all been checking on me for a long time, huh?"

"Obviously," Pawlik said. "Someday it's got to happen."

"Well," the mayor said, "I guess you all figured that I couldn't resist that lady. I should have stayed my ass downstairs like I wanted to, too."

Standing now at the edge of the bed, Barry could fit everyman's stereotype, a caricature to fit any prejudice. For the white racist, he was a typical black man, dumb enough to walk into a trap because he couldn't resist sex and drugs. For many African Americans, he was a black leader hounded and investigated, and finally humiliated by a racist white society. For those who could see beyond the caricature, he was the sad civil rights leader who had risen to political power, and by his own devices, squandered his opportunity.

Arrington cut the silence this time.

"It's a traumatic experience," he said, "but this too will come to pass."

"Sometimes it's better," Pawlik said. "Sometimes it's for the good, really, health-wise. You know…"

"You're assuming I got a problem," Barry interrupted him and laughed.

"Yeah," Pawlik said. "I am."

"You think I got a real problem?"

"Yes, sir. Respectfully, I say that."

Barry pressed Pawlik to find out how much he knew. Arrington cut off the conversation with details about the cars that would transport the mayor to the J. Edgar Hoover FBI building on Pennsylvania Avenue. Pawlik couldn't let the moment go.

"This is as traumatic for us as it is for you, I think," he said.

"Well… I know I wish it had not happened," Barry said. He shrugged his shoulders. "But I guess life goes on that way."

"Yeah. Well, we have to be strong enough to get over it," Pawlik said.

"Right," said Arrington.

A few minutes later, amid the crackling of police radios, they led Barry out the door, down a service elevator, out the hotel's basement door, and into a blue FBI Chevy Suburban with smoked windows for the thirteen-block ride. At the FBI offices, the mayor had his urine taken, his blood sampled, and his hair snipped to check for the levels of cocaine.

The operation was so quietly done that even many hotel employees did not realize what had happened. But within the next hour, WRC-TV broadcast news of the arrest. Cameras and reporters from the local, national, and international news media all arrived at the Vista to stun the city and country with the shattering news.

CHAPTER 15

CITY ON TRIAL

*This case is about the deals the government made with the
devil.*
—Ken Mundy, Barry's defense attorney

You have to know about Dan's place just to find it behind a dusty
blue door on Eighteenth Street in Adams Morgan. It's one of
the last honest neighborhood saloons in the city where blacks and
whites drink together. It has no pretensions, no ferns, no brass rail-
ings or skylights—just cold, longneck beers and bartenders who
know how to pour four-finger drinks from the rail. The regular
Thursday night crowd filled the long, scuffed wooden bar. There were
white guys in lumberjack shirts, jeans, and running shoes; the women
were dressed down, too. A few black men in T-shirts were playing a
desultory game of pool. Just after 10:00 p.m. news of the bust flashed
on Channel 4. Everyone elbowed up to the TV.

Jack Shafer, the editor of the alternative weekly *City Paper,*
couldn't control his glee. A dyspeptic white journalist, Shafer had
used his paper to ridicule Barry for years. Now he and a few friends
at the bar were clicking their longnecks and pumping their fists in the
air. It was their victory. The cops finally got the son-of-a-bitch. At
the other end of the bar, the black bartender took it personally, too.
Chin-in-hand, he talked quietly to the pool players, suddenly sullen,
shaking their heads in disbelief. At some level, it was their loss.

The reaction was repeated all over the capital as the news went nationwide and then global within two hours of the arrest. In Colombia, the South American country vilified for its cocaine production, newspapers called Barry the "narcomayor" of the drug-infested capital and suggested that Americans fight their drug war at home rather than blaming the suppliers. Suddenly people from Europe to Africa saw local Washington as a lawless city under siege. Many months after Barry's arrest, the superintendent of a suburban school district was traveling in the African bush with a guide who took him to a Masai village and introduced him to the local chief.

"Where do you come from?" the chief asked.

"America," he said.

"What city?"

"Washington," he answered.

"Uh," the chief said, and slapped his palm on his forehead. "Marion Barry."

The first flash of the camera taking the mayor's mug shot captured his haggard face, slumped in defeat. But he was ready for the next flash. He licked his lips, slapped on his wide-eyed smile, and grinned into the lens. Marion Barry still had enough presence of mind to wear his mask for the FBI.

It was about 9:30 p.m. The mayor had been at FBI headquarters for a half-hour. "When can I make a phone call?" Barry asked Al Arrington. "I want to call my wife."

Arrington led the mayor to a room where he could have some privacy. Barry phoned home and Effi answered. He gave her the news, and told her how he'd been lured into the hotel room.

"Who was it?" she asked.

"Y'know, that girl, Rasheeda," he said quietly.

His next call was to Herb Reid, who alerted R. Kenneth Mundy, the lawyer who had represented Barry before the grand jury. Mundy was playing his regular Thursday night tennis game at the Sixteenth and Kennedy streets courts in far Northwest when the call came. An hour later the lawyer was at the mayor's brick home in Southeast, comforting his wife and child. Barry was still at FBI headquarters.

Mundy, dressed in his tennis togs and cap, put in a call to Police Chief Isaac Fulwood.

"Ike, I'd like you to contact Jay Stephens," he said. "Ask him if he would accept a call from me."

Fulwood called back and said Stephens would talk. Mundy punched in the U.S. attorney's number and got Stephens on the line. The prosecutor outlined the charges, the evidence, and the implications.

"What would the mayor have to do for you to drop the charges?" Mundy asked.

Stephens, according to Mundy, said that Barry would have to resign and make a complete public confession of his drug abuse over the years. In the heat of the moment, the white Republican appointee had shown the Barry bust to be little more than what some people suspected: a naked political takedown. Stephens's revealing demand set the tone for Barry's imminent counterattack. Though the content of that first conversation was not disclosed publicly, Barry would portray the entire investigation as politically motivated, with some justification.

At 12:40 a.m. the sound of sirens broke the silence on Alabama Avenue, SE, near the mayor's home.

The dark blue FBI Suburban pulled into the alley behind Barry's house. Herb Reid got out from one side, and Barry, with agent Ron Stern at his side, emerged from the other. Joe Johns, a hefty black reporter for WRC-TV, had chased the vehicle on foot up the alley. He got between Barry and the gate to the backyard.

"Mister Mayor," he boomed into the cold night air. "Did you have cocaine in that hotel? Did you have cocaine in that hotel?" Barry disappeared behind a high wooden security gate. Uniformed D.C. police stood on the other side, wielding shotguns. There was no panic or anguish inside the Barrys' home. If anything, there was a sense of realization—mixed with relief—that the secret of the mayor's drug use was out in the open. Barry asked Mundy to talk with him, alone, in an upstairs sitting room. Effi walked in, but the mayor said that he wanted to speak to his lawyer. "If anyone should be here," she said, "it should be me." Barry insisted that she leave. "I've had a problem," he acknowledged, and he explained to Mundy the extent of his drug use.

Christopher, ten years old at the time, came into the room in his pajamas.

"Daddy," he said, "you've been drinking."

Indeed, Barry had been sipping from a glass of cognac, but it was empty. The bottle was at his feet. He pushed it behind the couch.

"I'm not anymore," Barry said. "Why don't you go to sleep."

"Give me the bottle," Christopher insisted.

"There is no bottle."

"I see it under the couch."

Barry gave it to him. Christopher refused to go to sleep. A short while later, the owner of the private school Christopher attended came to take him for the night. She put a coat over the young boy's head to protect him from the harsh light and the TV cameras staking out the alley. Effi Barry watched the scene as her son was led away. It was the only time during the entire affair that she wept.

The U.S. District Court Building occupies an entire block on the north side of Constitution Avenue where it intersects with Pennsylvania Avenue at Third Street. Constructed of buff-colored limestone, it's not an unappealing structure, and the small park on one side together with the expansive courtyard in front give it an open, unimposing feeling. The National Gallery's East Wing is directly across the street, and the Capitol is just four blocks up the hill. It is a venue for trying local drug dealers, such as Rayful Edmond Ill, and it is a court for judging spies, corrupt senators, and such federal officials as Nixon appointees John Mitchell, John Ehrlichman, and H. R.

Haldeman, convicted for their role in the Watergate scandal. It is a courthouse for the capital as a fishbowl.

At 12:45 the day after the arrest, the mayor's Lincoln pulled to the curb in front of the court. Barry and Effi stayed inside the vehicle for a few minutes while police struggled to form a path through the gauntlet of journalists, tourists, supporters, and de tractors who mobbed the steps and courtyard. The two emerged, protected by a wedge of blue uniforms, and waded into the sea of faces. They looked dignified, if subdued. The mayor wore a dark gray, double-breasted suit, blue shirt, and red tie. Effi wore big framed, tinted sunglasses, gaudy gold earrings, a brown shawl. She was icy, impassive. Barry wore a sullen mask.

"All the white folks smoke crack, too," boomed a bass voice from the crowd. "Don't feel bad. They're the ones who created it."

"You're all right, Marion Barry," another voice said. "Keep your head up!"

And then they were inside, up the elevator and into the courtroom packed with reporters. Barry made his trademark entrance, head up, eyes clear, chest out, arms swinging, and. shoulders rolling. He nodded to the reporters and headed straight for the defense table. With steady hands, he poured a glass of water to the brim but set it down so hard that it spilled. When the courtroom artist focused binoculars on him, he made circles with his fingers over his eyes and peered back.

Jay Stephens watched, stone-faced, from the front row.

The mayor stopped clowning when the magistrate walked in and began the proceedings. It took all of five minutes to outline the charges, the penalties, and the terms of his release. Throughout, the mayor held his head high, except when prosecutor Judy Retchin said that he still had to be booked. When the magistrate said that he could spend up to a year in jail, the mayor winced.

Jay Stephens emerged minutes later to address more than one hundred journalists and TV cameras arrayed like a firing squad in front of the courthouse.

"I think the events of last night are a personal tragedy for the defendant in this case," he said, "but narcotics abuse and the violence that has followed the narcotics abuse in this city is also a tragedy for many of the people of this city, for the kids of this community, for their families, for their communities. I have said many times that narcotics abuse is not a victimless crime. Our families are victims, our children are victims, and I think as last night's events demonstrated, even a city can be a victim."

That afternoon Marion Barry turned the government over to city administrator Carol Thompson and the top bureaucrats who had already been running the government for more than a year.

Sunday dawned overcast, damp, and funereal. The mayor's advisers told the press to gather at St. Timothy's Episcopal Church across the street from his house. A host of handpicked ministers joined him earlier at his home and accompanied him in a silent, thoughtful procession to the church, arm in arm with Effi. The man who called himself the "night owl," whose wife called him "a street dude," put on a pensive face. He was still a mastersituationist, and this was another situation. It required humility.

Inside the church jammed with journalists, Marion Barry rose and dramatically told the TV cameras that he had come "face to face with my deepest human frailties." But he acknowledged only having an unspecified "problem" and portrayed himself as a victim. "I spent so much time caring about and worrying about and doing for others," he said, "I've not worried about or, cared enough for myself."

Effi, in an all-white Sunday dress, followed her husband to the podium and praised him for having "the strength to admit to the whole world that as a mortal human being he has reached the hour of reckoning when he realizes that he is truly in God's hands." She also referred only to his unspecified "problem" and said: "Truly a burden has been lifted from our souls." The mayor took no questions and retraced his processional back to his house.

Later that day his office announced that he would check into the Hanley-Hazelden Center, a drug and alcohol rehabilitation clinic in West Palm Beach. He would later move to a clinic in South Carolina, but not before he made several highly publicized visits to a small black Baptist church that had spontaneously adopted him, or so it seemed. It played well in Washington, but Barry never revealed that the minister wasn't a detached observer but the brother of Cora Masters, one of Barry's most loyal and longtime confidantes.

The press played right along with Barry's pathos. Headlines in *The New York Times* declared, "A Tearful Mayor Vows to Seek Help," and, "Barry's Pledge Wins Support." The news changed from trysts and crack pipes to thoughtful stories about addiction, recovery, and forgiveness. Jay Stephens was looking for something else.

"I didn't hear any acknowledgement of drug use, of drug abuse," he said on Monday morning. "And really, that is the issue that goes to the heart of this case. It's greed, corruption, betrayal of trust, betrayal of public confidence.

"What should this city believe regarding his activity?"

The Washington Post polled residents and found that nearly half of the blacks in the sample believed that federal investigators had targeted Barry because he was black, but even more said that the mayor should resign. More than 70 percent of the whites polled said that Barry should step down, and the combined number favoring resignation was 57 percent.

The city, according to the poll, had had enough of Mayor Barry, but he hadn't had enough of the city.

On March 13, after six weeks of rehabilitation, the most resilient politician in America was back.

The mayor looked fabulous—clear-eyed, sharp-witted, lean, and brimming with energy—and the crowds responded, at carefully staged events. "Four more years, four more years," filled the atrium of the Reeves Municipal Center as Barry mounted the podium for his first major appearance. "I'm back and I feel good about my treatment program," he said at the beginning of a twenty-minute speech, tele-vised live across the city. Amid the chest thumping, Barry obliquely admitted that he had been dependent not only on alcohol but also on two powerful tranquilizers, Valium and Xanax. He made no mention of cocaine. Or that city administrator Carol Thompson had pleaded with him to make only a quiet return to the city.

At noon the next day, the mayor swept unannounced into the lobby of the Washington Post with his covey of security aides. The newspaper's own security guard stopped them cold, and asked, "Are you expected?" Calls were made to the fifth-floor newsroom. A pho-tographer came to snap pictures. *"Now* can I go up?" Barry said. Most reporters were at lunch, but chairman Katharine Graham was on hand. "Send him up," she said, and trailed him as he strode through the newsroom, pumping the hands of stunned journalists as if he were on a campaign stop.

After raiding the Post building, the mayor orchestrated a blitz on the TV stations. The evening newscasts led with images of the high-spirited leader. Paul Berry, a black anchor for WJLA-TV, asked how Barry could casually lie for years about his drug dependency. "That was the disease talking," he responded. "I didn't do that purposely to you. I was a victim." To Jim Vance, the anchor on WRC-TV and once Barry's good friend, the mayor offered the closest thing to an apology. "I'm sure I've embarrassed, some people," he said, "and to those people I offer my deepest and sincere apologies, my sincere re-grets, and my feeling of remorse about it."

There would be no apologies a few weeks later at a rally at the New York Avenue Presbyterian Church, a grand stone structure in the heart of downtown with a rich civil rights history. The rally was billed as "Barry's Baack & Best for '90." The church was half-filled with the mayor's hard-core devotees. In their eyes he was the black David; the government and the press were white Goliaths.

"The bust was an attempt to kill the mayor because he's a strong black man," Audie Johnson, a senior-citizens organizer, said from the podium. "Why else would the FBI stand by and watch him take two hits from a crack pipe?" After a series of testimonials, Rufus "Cat-fish" Mayfield took the microphone. Mayfield, Barry's enemy from the Pride days, now held a cushy government job supplied by Barry. "We better understand something," he said, waving his hands in a menacing harangue, "the white folks want their city back. That's why they took down our mayor."

Barry fanned himself in the warm church, soaking up the praise.

"I will not let this man go down the tubes!" Mayfield yelled, turning to embrace Barry and leading him to the microphone as the church rocked with applause.

"It's great to be back," Barry said, blowing kisses to the crowd, "and Barry is back. This is not a political rally—this is a love-in." Actually, it was part of Barry's legal strategy. From the moment he set foot in the capital, every move Barry made was geared toward his trial, then just three months away. The government had the goods on him. He'd already seen himself smoking crack on the videotape of room 727, and he knew that some of his cocaine-snorting cronies were cooperating with the prosecutors. On the facts, Barry looked very guilty, so the master politician decided to portray the FBI as the bad guys in a racist plot. The rally at the New York Avenue Presbyterian Church was another step in a concerted effort to radicalize the entire black community. Eventually, a jury would sit in judgment on him, and the majority would come from the city's black wards.

So for the months leading up to the trial, Barry ran: to news conferences, to three churches every Sunday morning, to community meetings, to prayer breakfasts, to the White House and Capitol Hill, to tennis games with journalists and jousting matches with network news anchors. In May he took to the streets for a "People to People" campaign in a converted recreation vehicle that he called his mobile city hall. He hadn't campaigned this hard since 1978. Barry was at his best when he was pressing the flesh, and for a month before his trial, he did little else, grooming an entire city of potential jurors.

"The prosecutors have been dipping and dabbling in the politics of Washington for a long time," the mayor told two *Washington Post* reporters on May 29, "and it's unconscionable. And then they try to kill me. It's unprecedented."

After admitting that he'd indeed smoked crack at the Vista, the man who had spent the last twenty-five years mining the psyche of the black community showed why his drug use was irrelevant.

"I think the prosecutors know that in this town all it takes is one juror saying, 'I'm not going to convict Marion Barry. I don't care what you say.'"

Jury selection in case 90-0068, the *United States of America* v. *Marion S. Barry, Jr.,* began on June 4, and the next three weeks turned out to be a frenetic prelude to the actual trial. A demonic convergence of extremists turned the courtyard on Constitution Avenue into a setting for street theater of the most surreal sort. A black woman in an iridescent blue spandex body suit paraded around with a two-liter RC Cola bottle on her head. The Reverend James Bevell, once a venerated leader of the civil rights movement and disciple of Martin Luther King, accused the government of genocide by encouraging birth control, of infecting blacks with the AIDS virus, and of lynching Marion Barry. "The attack on Marion Barry is just the beginning," he warned. "They're coming for you next." Bevell and his colleagues distributed a newspaper, conceived and produced by Anita Bonds, which compared Barry's prosecution to the Holocaust and urged the populace to rise up and protect the mayor.

"I'll tell you," Reverend Robert Hamilton declared on June 9, "it's going to be a long, hot summer." Hamilton, a tall dandy given to all-white summer suits, became a prominent cheerleader among Barry's new zealots. Barry appeared on radio and TV with WOL radio personality Cathy Hughes and former comedian Dick Gregory to portray the federal government as the evil empire out to undermine all African-Americans. Gregory ranted that the government sent up satellites as part of the conspiracy, and gave Barry nutrition advice from Bahamian Diet formulas he also hawked.

Curtis Sliwa, leader of the Guardian Angels community cops, held down the other extreme. Dressed in red beret and combat boots, Sliwa and a group of followers marched in a circle in front of the courthouse and for days chanted: "Marion Barry should resign, 'cause he's had too much crack and wine."

The drama on what became known as "Barry Beach"—named for all the camera crews whiling away hot summer afternoons waiting for the trial to end—was one more surreal scene in a capital city that seemed to be beset by strange news during the spring and summer of 1990. Earlier that spring American University president Richard Berendzen, a nationally known figure on the academic and social scene, was arrested for making obscene phone calls about little girls. Congressman Barney Frank of Massachusetts came under investigation for allegedly running a gay prostitution ring out of his basement. And every day without fail, at least one young black man died of a gunshot wound in and around the city's thriving cocaine markets.

The weirdness, violence, and instability in the American capital contrasted with the exhilarating events taking place around the world. The Soviet Union was loosening its grip on Eastern Europe. In the glow of a new era, Soviet president Mikhail Gorbachev came to Washington on June 1, signed historic agreements with President Bush, and took triumphal tours through Washington's streets. South Africa's system of apartheid was crumbling, too, and African National Congress leader Nelson Mandela was freed after twenty-eight years in prison. He too was headed for the U.S. capital in early June as Barry's trial split the city.

Amid the circus atmosphere of the trial's early days, Jesse Jackson was a voice of moderation. While Barry tolerated the race-baiting vitriol, in private he encouraged Jackson to broker a deal with the white prosecutors, The government had filed a new fourteen-count indictment: Eleven counts were misdemeanors alleging cocaine possession from the fall of 1984 to 1990, including four counts of possession at the Ramada Inn and one at the Vista. There were three felony counts alleging perjury before the grand jury in January 1989, immediately after the Ramada incident. Barry and Mundy repeatedly denied that they were trying to make a deal, but they negotiated constantly with prosecutors. Barry was willing to plead guilty to as many as three misdemeanor counts, but he refused to admit to a felony because he'd be forced from office and face jail time. Jay Stephens demanded that Barry accept at least one felony.

"All parties should try to arrive at a point of mutual agreement and spare Marion Barry and his family and the city and the country the pain of a long, drawn-out process," Jackson declared on June 4, the first day of the trial. "The losses and the damage need to be cut."

On June 13 Mayor-for-Life Marion Barry played another card by bowing out of the mayoral campaign.

"I could win," he said defiantly from a bare set at Howard University, staring straight and unblinking into the camera, "but what good does it do to win the battle if in the process I lose my soul. This is not about my legal situation, but to my recovery and my wife and son who have suffered painfully. Accept my word, that stepping aside now is best for the city."

It certainly was best for Barry's case before the jurors, just then being picked and still subject to the news. In the eyes of prospective jurors, there was one less reason to penalize the mayor because he now effectively was driven from office.

It took the first two weeks of June to pick a jury of twelve and six alternates.

The potential jurors represented a good cross-section of the city. There were attorneys and plumbers, secretaries and clerks, underemployed and unemployed. Of the 250-person pool, 146 actually went through the voir dire questioning by the judge and the attorneys. Most were excused because they had a bias for or against Barry's conviction. But those who stayed to answer questions showed sympathy for Barry and disgust over the government's tactics in the undercover operation that led to the Vista bust. No doubt Barry's three-month publicity campaign helped to frame their opinions.

Both the government and the defense team spent hours poring over profiles of the prospective jurors. Ken Mundy relied on the analysis, the dossiers, and the instincts of Barry's chief political aide, Anita Bonds, who sat at her own table behind the defense table. The prosecutors worked with Detective Al Arrington, who sat at the government's table. Bonds and Arrington were fitting adversaries; they both had a great feel for the people of Washington, and both passionately believed in the fundamental rightness of their cause. Bonds, however, couldn't understand Arrington.

"How could you help them bring down the mayor?" she asked early in the proceedings. "You must be brainwashed. He didn't do all the things the government accuses him of."

"We'll see," Arrington said.

By June 18 the two sides had settled on the twelve jurors and six alternates. Of the twelve who would sit in judgment on Barry, ten were black and two were white, reflecting roughly the city's racial makeup. Seven of the blacks were women; both of the men were white. Anita Bonds had done her work well. Barry needed just one juror; Bonds had succeeded in getting at least five dark-skinned, lower-to-middle-class blacks on the jury who fit the profile of a Barry supporter, regardless of the evidence: There was J. Hilson Snow, Jr., a forty-nine-year-old truck driver from the far Southeast across the Anacostia River; Johnnie Mae Hardeman, a sixty-one-year-old retail clerk from Northeast; Joyce Hines, an unemployed forty-eight-year-old from Anacostia; Harriedell Jones, a fifty-eight-year-old government clerk; and Valerie Jackson-Warren, an outspoken forty-year-old Democrat from center city.

The plea-bargaining negotiations continued to the eve of the trial, but neither side would budge. Barry wouldn't accept a felony plea. Stephens would accept nothing less.

The jury was sequestered. The trial had to go forward.

Just before the case was to be tried, Arrington and his partner Jim Pawlik were riding along M Street near the waterfront restaurants and boats that sold fresh fish and crabs. The day was moist and the air was pungent. Pawlik was at the wheel.

"You know," Arrington said, "if I were on that jury, and I didn't know what I know about the case, I would vote to acquit the mayor."

Pawlik stepped on the brake and almost screeched to a stop. He pulled to the curb.

"Are you nuts?" he asked.

"Unfortunately," Arrington said, "a lot of those jurors are going to base their decision purely on the issue of race. If I'm a juror, and think that the investigation was racially motivated, I vote to acquit."

Pawlik simply couldn't believe it; he certainly could never accept it. "You're dead wrong," he said. He looked away for a moment and said, "I hope you're dead wrong."

On the morning of June 18, 1990, Judge Thomas Penfield Jackson peered down from the bench in Courtroom Two and surveyed the opening-day scene.

To his left at the defense table sat Marion Barry, looking dapper in a dark suit stuck with a fiery red carnation. Effi Barry, knitting a baby blanket, sat in the second row of seats. The mayor and his wife had not exchanged a glance when Barry made his debut at 10:05 and gave a hug to Mundy and a slap on the back to Mundy's associate, Robert Mance. The prosecutors and Al Arrington occupied the table to the judge's right. Jay Stephens, dressed in red tie, white shirt, and blue suit, sat on a row of seats a few feet away. Fifty journalists filled most of the public seats. Only fifteen spectators were permitted each day.

"Ready, prosecution?" Jackson asked.

"Ready, Your Honor," said Ricky Roberts, the Yale-trained prosecutor, standing tall and rigid.

"Ready, defense?" he asked.

"Ready, Your Honor," Mundy responded.

Jackson swore in the jury in the gallery to his right, and the trial began. Roberts opened.

"This is a case about deceit and deception," he said to the jury. "The unfortunate but seamy truth is that Marion Barry was snorting cocaine all over the District of Columbia and elsewhere. He was saying 'down with dope,' and putting coke up his nose." Roberts had a passionless presentation, even when he gave a preview of the Vista videotape, leaning back and putting an imaginary pipe to his lips and drawing dramatically. He said the mayor had a special way of smoking cocaine by emptying out a cigarette, mixing the tobacco with the white powder, and putting the combination back for a coke-laced smoke. "His friends called it an M.B. special," Roberts said, running down the government's evidence that he said would prove that Barry used cocaine regularly since 1984.

Mundy assumed that the jurors knew all about Barry's use of drugs. He used his time to put the government on trial.

"This case is about the deals the government made with the devil," he said, asking the jurors to remove the headlines from their minds, and pretend they had just awakened from a long sleep. "Seven years ago the government made a determination that it would get Marion Barry, and it would go to any lengths, any extremes to get him." He was pacing before the jury, his cheeks were flushed, and he confided in them about how the government went to "the recesses of humanity" to dig up people who would testify against the mayor. All of the witnesses, he said, were people who traded immunity from prosecution for their testimony.

"When this trial is history," Mundy said, "when it is over, you can look back and be proud of your jury service."

You could look back on the city's history over the last quarter century and divine how some of the jurors viewed the characters and the drama that would unfold over the next six weeks. For twenty-five years the city had been the federal government's unruly stepchild-demanding, rioting, lawless in some neighborhoods. The federal government was the stern and harsh father figure.

Judge Thomas Penfield Jackson couldn't have been a more fitting symbol of imperious federal power if he'd been cast by Hollywood. He was a gruff, uncompromising jurist whose plump, round face frequently screwed up into the mug of a bulldog. A third-generation Washingtonian who went to St. Albans School for Boys, he'd attended Dartmouth College and Harvard Law School, served in the Navy, and practiced law for eighteen years in Washington before Ronald Reagan appointed him to the federal bench in 1982. His sentences were stiff, except in certain notable cases. On June 3, for instance, he had sentenced former Reagan insider Michael Deaver to fifteen hundred hours of community service after a jury convicted him of lying to Congress and a grand jury. Barry supporters recited that case repeatedly as a sign that Jackson could be lenient, if he wanted.

"I love this city. I always have," Jackson said in an interview with the *Washington Times* before the trial. "I just want to see the best for it." It wasn't hard for jurors to see that he believed Barry was bad for his city.

Jay Stephens was even more chilly and severe, and the prosecutors he chose to try the case were in the same mold. Judy Retchin was a capable white attorney, but she had zero rapport with the jury. Her presentation was dry, thin-lipped, and humorless. Ricky Roberts—her tall, stiff, light-skinned African American partner—squinted at the jury through his glasses and never convinced working-class blacks like Hilson Snow and Johnnie Mae Hardeman that he was one of them.

Ken Mundy, on the other hand, was a master at making jurors see the world through his eyes. He played the homeboy attorney, talking to the twelve men and women as if they were neighbors. Ironically, he was also a longtime associate of Judge Jackson's. Mundy was unique in Washington legal circles. He came up through the gritty terrain of the criminal defense bar, but he gained a tremendous measure of respect from the uptown law firms. When Thomas Penfield Jackson was in private practice, he and Mundy worked side by side on a number of medical malpractice cases. In 1981, they were both inducted into the American College of Trial Lawyers, an elite club of one hundred top litigators from across the nation. Its members include Supreme Court justices and six-hundred-dollars-per-hour legal stars. Mundy was the only African-American.

Mundy had no special love for Barry and vacillated before taking the case after the Vista bust. He had supported his cousin, former council chairman Sterling Tucker, against Barry in the 1978 mayoral campaign. He knew that defending Barry now would require a frontal assault on the system of justice, and he wondered what the members of the "club" would think of him. In his moment of indecision, NAACP executive director Benjamin Hooks personally urged him to take the case. Mundy was deeply bothered by Jay Stephens's initial demand that Barry resign. Removing Barry from office was a political issue that should be decided by the voters, he thought, not by a federal prosecutor.

Mundy brought a measure of respectability and plenty of style to Barry's side. He was a jaunty, flamboyant man given to wearing an array of felt toppers, straw skimmers, and riding caps on his shiny head. He relished high-profile cases and knew how to handle the press with a flip of the tongue. But most of all, he had an extraordinary ability to connect with black jurors and convince them that the government had a bad case, regardless of whether his client had committed a crime.

The mayor made his entrances into the courtroom every morning from a door on the left side and passed in front of fifty journalists hanging on his look, his attire, and his style. He clearly enjoyed the attention. He adopted the role of a Mafia don, wearing double-breasted suits with flared lapels, rolling in with his sinuous stroll, flashing a catlike smile.

"The canaries are singing," he said on the morning of the second day, and he bent his head to sniff the red carnation in his lapel. Minutes later Chuck Lewis took the stand.

Lewis already had served his jail time for the Virgin Islands drug rap. At fifty, he appeared frail and wizened in a blue suit. He testified for three days in a clear, subdued voice flavored with an island accent. The prosecutors led Lewis through his tale of drug buys and drug use in hotels from St. Thomas to Washington. He performed well and told his story in precise detail. Mundy spent two days trying to break him down and drew little blood.

On June 25, Nelson Mandela arrived in the capital for a three-day visit, and the city gave the African National Congress leader a hero's welcome. Crowds lined Pennsylvania Avenue to catch a glimpse of the square face, squinty eyes, and kind smile of the man who had spent over two decades in prison to help bring down apartheid.

The mayor wore a tricolored African kente cloth scarf under his flared lapels for the occasion. He spent the day in court listening to women from the Virgin Islands describe their sexual and narcotic exploits with him. Linda Creque Maynard, a gaunt looking mother of two, testified that Charles Lewis brought her to Barry's room in March 1988, under the pretext of a job interview. She testified that Barry made sexual advances, which became physical, but she fought him off. On cross-examination, defense attorney Robert Mance pressed her for details and asked why she didn't walk out. Prosecutor Judy Retchin quickly moved to pursue details that were off-limits, by mutual agreement, until Mance raised them.

"Did you and Mr. Barry have sexual relations in the hotel room?" Retchin asked.

"Yes," Maynard responded.

"Did you want that to happen?" Retchin asked.

"No," Maynard said, and she broke down in tears and sobbed.

In essence, she testified that the mayor had raped her. Everyone but Marion Barry appeared stunned. The mayor smiled. The judge called a ten-minute recess.

That afternoon Barry sped to WJLA-TV in his Lincoln for an on-air interview with Renee Poussant, a no-nonsense anchor with feminist leanings. Carol Thompson called his car phone and pleaded with him to call it off in light of the testimony. He refused and turned away similar pleas by Herb Reid. Thompson called Ivanhoe Donaldson, who reached Barry at the station, but no one could deter him.

On the set, Poussant asked him whether he had forced Linda Creque Maynard to have sex.

"God has blessed me to relax, to feel strong, and to bless the victims," he said, sweating profusely. "It's one of those incredible bits of testimony...I'm not worried at all about this testimony. The public should not take all these statements as an indication of anything." He never answered Poussant's question.

On the way out of the studio, Barry ran into reporter Del Walters and news director Bob Reichblum.

"Are you at all embarrassed?" Walters asked.

"About the woman testifying about forcing sex?" Barry asked. "I'm on trial for fourteen counts, or twelve, or whatever, and not one has to do with having sex with a woman."

The mayor had vowed to keep a proper distance between his tawdry trial and Nelson Mandela's triumphant celebration and put his intentions in a letter to Mandela's tour committee, headed by Roger Wilkins. The mayors of Boston and New York had welcomed Mandela in those cities, but when Mandela arrived in Washington, Effi Barry gave the city's official greetings.

Mandela was scheduled to address a crowd of ten thousand at the Washington Convention Center Tuesday night. City officials and other honored guests were to sit on the stage behind him. Before the address, Mandela's entourage had scheduled a private fundraiser with donors willing to contribute one thousand dollars for a chance to chat with Mandela and his wife, Winnie. As the private session was about to begin, Barry showed up with ten aides, bodyguards, and a photographer. Pushing and shoving, they forced their way into the room just so that Barry could have his photograph taken with Mandela. Barry's stunt preempted the fundraiser, and thousands of dollars were lost as the mayor kept the Mandelas occupied while one of his aides went looking for a key to the city. Later, during Mandela's speech, which was televised live, Barry sat behind him on the podium and spent most of the time horsing around and whispering, like a high-school student at an assembly.

"I was absolutely disgusted by what the mayor did," said Roger Wilkins, the black political scientist, "and so was Harry Belafonte. Barry totally reneged on what he had promised, and in my judgment was disgraceful and dishonorable."

The next morning Barry waltzed into court with two glossy photographs of himself with the Mandelas. He showed them to Effi and flashed them a few times at the press section to make sure that the reporters understood that he was still the mayor, and he could still command photo opportunities with famous men.

"The government calls Rasheeda Moore," Judy Retchin said a few minutes later.

The door to the witness room opened and in walked Hazel Diane "Rasheeda" Moore, dressed in a simple black outfit. She looked more like a slightly overweight matron than a ravishing cover girl. Moore took the jurors through a three-year binge of cocaine and sex, describing with precision the places where she and Barry cavorted and the people with whom they used cocaine. In more than three hours on the stand she said that they had smoked or snorted cocaine more than one hundred times. Over and over again Judy Retchin asked, "Were you intimate with Mr. Barry?" and each time Rasheeda Moore answered, "Yes."

Effi Barry, in contrast to Rasheeda's stark black attire, wore a cheery, flowered dress that was open at the neck. Sitting in the second row of spectators, she shifted in her seat to get a better look at the woman whom her husband had found to be so irresistible. As Moore spoke in clear, careful phrases, the First Lady sat in granite stillness, stirred only by an arched brow or a slight sneer, her fingers hooking a small rug. Once, when Moore said that she and Barry had smoked crack in a bathroom in the mayor's house, Mrs. Barry shook her head in disbelief, or perhaps dismissal.

The pain inflicted by her husband's infidelity was nothing new to Effi Barry. If anything, she was numb after twelve years of marriage to a philanderer in a glass cage. There was no way of knowing how much she suffered, but an interview with Barbara Harrison of WRC-TV back in February gave some insight. Harrison asked if rumors of the mayor's womanizing and drug abuse were hurtful.

"Of course I was hurt, of course I was embarrassed," she said. "I felt abused, neglected, a whole range of emotions."

But she said she didn't want to he a nag; she chose to build a separate life around her own needs and her son, letting her husband lead his life, with or without other women.

"My husband has been connected with other women for years," she told Harrison. "It's nothing new. What we must do is judge the character of the women."

The street jury judged Rasheeda Moore harshly, especially after Mundy carved her up for two days in cross-examination and forced her to discuss her own bouts with drugs and how she had lured Barry into the hotel room.

"I believe it's all lies," Mundy told reporters.

Street vendors did a brisk business in T-shirts that said: "Bitch set him up."

Mary Cox, a radical black attorney who sat near Barry every day of the trial, said the mayor's yen for women was typical. "African men have polygamous relationships," Cox said. "Effi realizes that. She's not devastated because he had relationships with other women. I'm sure she'd rather not have them splashed all over."

Effi Barry escorted her husband hack to the District Building after Rasheeda Moore's first day of testimony, took him into his office, and slammed the door. Aides then heard the First Lady scream: "I'm a person too. I have to sit and listen to all of this. How do you think I feel?"

That night the mayor took his wife for a surprise appearance at a rally for Nation of Islam leader Louis Farrakhan at the Convention Center, just one night after Nelson Mandela's speech to a much different audience.

The Barrys walked on stage at 8:25 p.m. before Farrakhan made his debut. The mayor wore his kente cloth scarf; Effi wore white; Bishop George Augustus Stallings, a breakaway Catholic priest, accompanied them in flowing robes. The crowd of ten thousand jumped to its feet and cheered. The mayor, hungry for public love, clasped his hands over his head. In the midst of the ovation, Farrakhan strode to center stage, waved Barry to his side, and kissed Effi. "I want to extend greetings to our brother the mayor and his beloved wife," Farrakhan said. They shook hands, the mayor looming large in his dark suit next to the minister, whose chiseled features were set off by his white tuxedo and trademark bowtie.

The mayor had had a rocky relationship with Farrakhan going back to the minister's 1985 rally in the capital, in the aftermath of the presidential campaign when Jewish leaders demanded that Jesse Jackson rebuke Farrakhan for his anti-Semitic statements. "Any foolish black leader who would come out to repudiate me based upon Jewish control and Jewish money," Farrakhan told that audience "should be thrown out by any black organization." *The Washington Post* criticized Farrakhan's "big time bigotry," and Jewish groups urged the mayor to issue a public rcbuke. Barry, who was elected twice with Jewish contributions and advice, vacillated for two weeks before coming out against Farrakhan.

In late 1988, Farrakhan's local Muslim mosque took up residence in Mayfair Mansions, a housing project in the Northeast section that was overrun by drug dealers. The police had done nothing, but the young Muslim "dope busters" threw out the drug dealers and became heroes. Farrakhan's assistant, Dr. Abdul Alim Muhammad, asked Barry to honor them at a rally with Farrakhan in the fall of 1989.

"I would love to attend," Barry told him, "but if I came to an event with Farrakhan the Jews would crucify me."

"I think I have the pulse of the people," Muhammad responded, "and the people hate you when they see you weak and afraid, bowing to the Jews." Barry "bowed down" then, but in the midst of his trial, he would welcome support from virtually anyone, no matter that he would blow bridges to such Jewish allies as Jeff Cohen, Max Berry, Boh Linowes, John Hechinger, and dozens of others.

Louis Farrakhan was drawn to Washington for the same reason that Barry and Ivanhoe Donaldson came in the 1960s: its black population. His sect was very much on the religious fringe, and he wanted to turn it into a political movement. He came to the capital that night to announce that he would make his first attempt in the Washington area. The Black Muslims would field two candidates: one for Congress in Maryland and one for the school board in the District. But before he primed the crowd with his new political agenda, Farrakhan talked about the mayor.

"Our brother the mayor is in pain, great pain, because our brother is under attack," he said. "He sinned—are there any in this audience who have not? That is the bottom line. Where are the holy ones? Is the prosecutor sinless? The attorney general? President Bush? Well then, what are we talking about here?"

But Farrakhan always preached monogamy and abstinence from drugs and alcohol.

"If a man chooses to drink and smoke drugs, he's sinning against himself, and it could lead to sins against others," Farrakhan said, "If a man has sex with someone other than his wife, he sins against himself, his wife, and his family. It's a sin that's punishable by God, severely."

Barry wasn't smiling any longer.

"I can't defend wrong," Farrakhan continued, "but what I want to point out is that those who stand to accuse the mayor are unworthy to stand in judgment. We applaud the mayor for standing up," he said. "If he were a white man, he would have blown his brains out by now. I don't say the mayor should stop, I want him to run, Barry, run. I want him to beat the U.S. government!"

The crowd erupted in wild cheers and applause. Farrakhan's wife came forward with Effi Barry in tow. "Black woman," she said to the First Lady, "stand behind your man, no matter what he does."

The next day at 10:00 a.m. Farrakhan, guarded by members of his Fruit of Islam security force, arrived at federal court and marched lockstep down the marble hall. Farrakhan's appearance was part of a plan by Barry to bring four ministers into court to anoint him in the eyes of the jury: Farrakhan, Jesse Jackson, Bishop Stallings, and Walter Fauntroy.

Inside the courtroom, Mundy asked Judge Jackson if Farrakhan could attend as Barry's special guest. The judge's face flushed. His eyes narrowed and his features hardened.

"No," he said. "I think that his presence would be disruptive and very likely intimidating. He is persona non grata for the trial of this case."

"Can I inform the minister?" Mundy asked.

"No," Jackson said. "Somebody else can inform him. We're ready to go on with the trial."

Outside the courthouse, before the cameras of Barry Beach, Farrakhan said that Jackson's order was "part of the double standard that black people have been under since we have been in this country," and the Barry trial "demonstrates the wickedness of the United States government and the lengths to which this government will go when it targets a black leader to be discredited." In the coming days Judge Jackson also barred Stallings, and the ACLU filed an appeal to get the ministers admitted. Ten days after the ACLU complaint, under pressure from an appeals court ruling, Jackson reversed himself, and said Farrakhan and Stallings could indeed attend the trial. Farrakhan never made it inside, but the judge's initial dictatorial application of power had been a fitting prelude to the showing of the Vista video-tape, which made its public debut the day that Judge Jackson barred Louis Farrakhan.

The buildup to the showing of the tape had all the hype and tension of a major Hollywood sneak preview.

The video was grainy, the voices were garbled, the characters seemed listless, the entire movie seemed like a fuzzy dream sequence in a B movie. The jurors leaned forward in their chairs to see the monitors and followed the dialogue on printed transcripts. For the full ninety-minute show, there was hardly a sound in the courtroom except for the voices of Marion Barry and Rasheeda Moore on the tape.

The instant that prosecutors entered the tape into evidence, a copy was rushed to a local TV studio, and the scenes inside room 727 were aired across the Washington region. Plenty of people watched it all the way through, including late-night repeats with much of the vulgar language, but most saw the quick clips played on the TV news. The distilled version showed two scenes: the mayor drawing deeply and professionally from the crack pipe, and the authorities crashing noisily into the room. The people who judged Barry's guilt or innocence based on the single frame that made newspapers all over the world—the picture of Barry hitting the crack pipe—got an even more one-dimensional view.

The jurors saw the whole affair, from the greeting at 7:35 to the bust an hour later. It showed a somewhat pathetic, middle-aged man chatting with an old lover for forty-five minutes before there was a mention of drugs. Above all, the mayor was horny.

"Can we make love before you leave, before you leave town?" he asks.

Effi Barry couldn't avoid watching. There was a large-screen monitor six feet from her face. She couldn't miss her husband reaching for Rasheeda Moore's breast; the packed courtroom couldn't miss the grimace breaking through the First Lady's stone face.

The issue of who first mentioned drugs was debatable, but once Barry had the crack pipe, it was quite clear that he knew exactly what to do with it. There was no doubt that he bought crack, that he possessed crack, that he smoked crack. The evidence seemed to ensure a conviction, but it was neutralized by the following scene showing the police and FBI agents piling into the room. It was a violent and disturbing scene, for Barry and Moore, but also for anyone viewing the tape. Seen in its entirety, the tape could be interpreted in dozens of ways. It was certainly not the convincing piece of evidence that was used in other undercover sting operations. The Abscam tapes, for example, showed congressmen eagerly making deals and pocketing cash bribes. The Vista tape, besides being an embarrassing peep show, left the impression that Barry was hoodwinked twice: once to come to the room and again to smoke crack. It didn't fit the legal definition of entrapment, but that was irrelevant. It looked like a trap, a con job.

Ken Mundy knew that, and he made certain that the jurors saw the tape over and over again. It turned out to be his best weapon.

The premiere of the tape was the dramatic high point of the six-week trial.

In July the government brought on more witnesses to Barry's drug use. It produced Barry's dealer, a sad and worn woman named Lydia Pearson, who grew up with Rasheeda Moore and provided for their mutual crack addictions. Restaurateur Hassan H. Mohammadi testified that Barry had a yen for opium as well as cocaine. Jeff Mitchell, the mayor's longtime friend who gave him the name Supreme Dog, recounted Barry's overdose at the Super Bowl in 1987. Theresa Southerland, the young and alluring Miss T., arrived in her own floppy black hat and demonstrated how she would scoop up cocaine on her long pinkie fingernail and place it under the mayor's nostril.

For its final witness, the government called Doris Crenshaw, the tenth person to testify about using drugs with Barry. The prosecutors wanted to end with a formidable witness. Crenshaw went way back with Marion Barry to the days of SNCC. She was a capable and politically active woman who had worked with Jesse Jackson and had served as deputy campaign manager in Walter Mondale's 1984 presidential campaign. In spare sentences she testified that she had used cocaine with the mayor more than a dozen times since 1984, including on a visit to the capital in the late fall of 1989, a few months before he was busted. Her allegations became the substance of count twelve for possession. At the time, it seemed no more and no less credible than most of the other possession charges.

The prosecution rested in the last week of July, and Ken Mundy put on a perfunctory defense that lasted only a few days. Barry did not take the stand.

Al Arrington was biased, but he thought the trial had gone extremely well. He and his friends at Internal Affairs got together toward the end and predicted how many convictions Barry would get out of the fourteen counts. Arrington, despite his earlier reservations, guessed Barry would go down on all fourteen.

Based purely on the facts, Barry's defense looked weak measured against the government's overwhelming evidence. Ricky Roberts and Judy Retchin methodically presented, documented, and displayed their proof that Marion Barry abused cocaine for years. It was clear that he went to great lengths to obtain, the drugs and conspired to buy it. It was also quite plain that he'd lied to the grand jury about his drug use at the Ramada Inn. Witness after witness had described using narcotics with the mayor, and the government introduced the mayor's own phone logs that proved that he made calls to many of the people who testified. If the jurors believed only half of the evidence, there was enough to convict Barry on most of the counts, including the felonies.

But there was much more than simple evidence at work in this case. The larger issues of race and politics and government power loomed over the courtroom and permeated every piece of evidence. When the testimony was complete, power shifted to the jurors.

Barry could take heart from two federal jury verdicts handed down in mid-July.

David Rivers, the former head of the city's social services agency, was acquitted of steering $2 million in contracts to his friend John Clyburn. On July 16, the same federal jury acquitted Clyburn of the same charges. Both men were part of Marion Barry's political and social brotherhood and had been the focus of the sweeping federal investigation that publicly surfaced in 1987.

"The U.S. attorney's office has waged a long and underhanded campaign to discredit the minority business community in Washington," Barry said in a statement.

The government did get whipped badly. Back in 1987, then U.S.-attorney Joseph DiGenova unveiled his seventeen-month undercover operation and promised to prove all manner of corruption, kickbacks, and bribery. The dramatic FBI sweeps of evidence together with the leaked allegations appeared to implicate the mayor in a web of graft. The resulting stampede of stories—all based on sources—had a vicious, destabilizing effect on the Barry government. Yet the appearance of corruption was all that prosecutors could prove.

Clyburn initially would say only that the government went too far and that there were "racial underpinnings to the case." His understated reaction changed after a sip of champagne during the celebration that evening at Joe and Mo's, a downtown eatery and unofficial clubhouse for top Barry officials.

"They didn't have a case," he told a *Post* reporter. "When they spent seventeen… months with a wiretap and they can't find anything, you know there wasn't a case."

When Clyburn arrived just after 6:00 p.m., former Barry government heavyweights Ivanhoe Donaldson and Elijah Rogers were there to wrap him in bear hugs. Rogers said the government was "out there" looking for any reason to bring down black officials. The mayor came down the steps by the bar at Joe and Mo's fifteen minutes after Clyburn arrived, and the two men warmly embraced. The mayor was buoyed by Clyburn's success, but their cases were very different. In Clyburn's suit, the jury could find no smoking guns; in Barry's case, there were smoking machine guns. The question was whether the jury would pay any attention to them.

The case of *U.S.* v. *Barry* went to the jury on August 2, 1990.

Al Arrington wasn't the only one who figured the guilty verdicts would come quickly. The journalists, white or black, expected convictions. Judge Thomas Penfield Jackson felt the same way.

How could the jury not convict on drug possession at the Vista?

They saw Barry smoke crack. It should have been a simple matter.

But from the first hours of deliberation, the twelve jurors were deadlocked—some as frozen in their divergent views as were the people of Washington, D.C. There were two separate realities: One accepted and trusted the American system of justice; the other believed in a conspiracy against blacks. Across that chasm, consensus would be hard to reach.

The jurors elected Edward Eagles foreman. A reclusive fiftyfour-year-old history teacher at St. Albans School, he was a liberal—"timid" in the eyes of one juror—who lived in the wealthy, far northwest enclave of Spring Valley. He had little experience with black Washington, and he wanted to avoid racial conflict in the jury room. Without a strong leader, the sessions became chaotic. In the chaos, there was little discussion and plenty of anger.

The lone black man, Hilson Snow, Jr., identified closely with Barry and voted consistently not guilty but for one count, according to a comprehensive article by *Post* reporters Elsa Walsh and Barton Gellman. He was joined by Harriedell Jones, a fiftyeight-year-old accounting assistant for the Department of Housing and Urban Development. Jones, according to the *Post* account, bristled at the suggestion by a young black juror that Marion Barry put himself in the position of hanging around "scumbags" such as Charles Lewis.

"If you knew what kind of man [Barry] was—he was always a street person," Jones reportedly said. "If you knew what kind of man he was, you wouldn't be saying that. And I'm sick of you bourgeois blacks."

Another juror, sixty-one-year-old Johnnie Mae Hardeman, was totally predisposed against the government. She told jurors that there was one set of laws for blacks and another for whites. As evidence, she offered the light treatment of President Reagan and Oliver North in the Irangate arms-for-hostages scandal. The leader of the proacquittal group, Valerie Jackson-Warren, felt that the government was "out to get Marion Barry."

Some of the older women had grown up in the segregated South, and they tended to believe that Barry was a victim; they didn't believe Charles Lewis or Rasheeda Moore. So great was the level of mistrust in the minds of some jurors that they looked at the plastic evidence bag containing crack cocaine from the Vista bust and said that it held sugar or perhaps baking soda, even though an FBI chemist testified that it was 93 percent pure cocaine. Hilson Snow said the Vista tape was so fuzzy that he couldn't trust its authenticity. Jackson-Warren said the FBI had stuffed things in Barry's pockets after the arrest according to the *Post* account.

"Come on, you guys," said Joe Deoudes, a twenty-three-yearold white entrepreneur attending American University and trying to start amessenger service. "They don't make up evidence."

The vote on the Vista sting was 6-6.

In the end, after eight days of frustrating debate, the jurors cut a deal. On eleven of the fourteen counts, including the three felony charges, they were hopelessly deadlocked by scores of 7-5 and 6-6. They didn't vote on the conspiracy count. But on two counts they decided to strike a balance. They agreed to acquit on the charge that Lydia Pearson sold crack to Barry once at the Reeves Center, because they believed that Barry had an alibi. They voted to convict on count twelve, the Doris Crenshaw possession charge, because she was a credible witness.

The outcome had more to do with horse-trading than with weighing of evidence. The antigovernment, pro-Barry bloc denied the prosecution its felonies and gained acquittal on one misdemeanor. The other jurors saved face and some integrity by hitting Barry with one misdemeanor. It was a political rather than a judicial verdict.

The jurors sent a note to Judge Jackson at 4:25 p.m., August 10, a Friday. Ken Mundy reached the mayor at the District Building and told him to make the ten-block drive down Pennsylvania Avenue to the courthouse.

An hour and a half later Marion Barry was standing at the defense table, facing the jury box as Ed Eagles read the two verdicts. The mayor fumbled with the buttons of his gray, double-breasted suit jacket, no corsage.

"On count three, not guilty," Eagles said.

Barry was impassive.

"On count twelve, guilty," the foreman said.

The mayor frowned and looked down, but when Eagles said that the jury couldn't reach a verdict on the other twelve counts, he turned around and shook Mundy's hand. The judge sent the jurors back to try again. At 6:10 Eagles sent another note that read: "It is our unanimous judgment that no further deliberation will result in a verdict." Eight minutes later Jackson called the jurors back and declared a mistrial on the remaining counts.

Marion Barry wept. The jury had hung on the felony charges and convicted him on one misdemeanor count. He thought there was little likelihood of a jail sentence. He had taken on the government and won. His supporters in the room cried and grabbed him. He hugged Mundy and left the courtroom amid a throng of wellwishers.

Word already had spread outside to Barry Beach. The mayor walked from the side door around to the front in a victory march that thrilled his waiting fans but apparently infuriated Judge Thomas Penfield Jackson. In front of the courthouse, the crowd erupted in a chant of "Ba-rry, Ba-rry, Ba-rry!" The mayor soaked it in for a few minutes and headed off into the late summer evening.

Mundy told reporters on the way out that he felt "lucky." When Jay Stephens tried to hold a press conference on the steps, the raucous crowd booed and shouted him down. Horns of passing motorists honked along Pennsylvania Avenue. Not since the Washington Redskins won the Super Bowl had the town seen such a spontaneous celebration.

Al Arrington was disappointed, but he took it in stride. As Barry was making his way out of the courtroom, he caught a glimpse of the detective. "Arrington," Barry said, pointing at him over the heads in the crowd. "See you next time."

Arrington pointed back and said: "You never know."

CHAPTER 16

RESURRECTION

I come out of prison better, not bitter.
—*Marion Barry*

I t was lunchtime on a late August day about two weeks after Barry's case ended. Donald Graham and Meg Greenfield sat together at a small table in the dining room of the Madison Hotel, across the street from the Washington Post building. The boyish, lanky publisher and his matronly editorial page editor had a crucial decision to make. When the riveting soap opera in federal court concluded, it dawned on everyone that voters would choose a mayor on September 11, the day of the Democratic primary. Graham and Greenfield had to decide which of five candidates to endorse.

"Who do you like?" Greenfield asked.

Don Graham didn't relish these decisions. Unlike his father, Phil Graham, who cut a dashing figure in the capital before he committed suicide in 1963, Don took an "aw shucks" attitude to running the most important news outlet in the capital. Phil palled around with U.S. senators; Don tried to be tight with his newspaper's blue-collar workers. Phil loved to play politics with the editorial page and pushed hard for the city's Southwest urban renewal project; Don trod lightly in most local affairs, especially city politics. He wanted to know what Greenfield thought first.

Meg Greenfield regretted her endorsement of Barry in 1986 and wanted to make it up to the city. Following a set procedure, she and her editorial board already had met with all five candidates and reviewed their position papers on various subjects. In her view, David Clarke, the white city council chairman, was too liberal and lacked leadership skills; council member Charlene Drew Jarvis was capable but tarnished by past scandals; D.C. delegate Walter Fauntroy was irrelevant and running a racist campaign that sullied his civil rights history. The only attractive choices were at-large city council member John Ray, who was leading the polls, and Sharon Pratt Dixon, a power company executive who was trailing.

Ray was the obvious, safe choice. A poor kid from the pine tar forests of Tom's Creek in southern Georgia, he'd skipped the civil rights movement for a career in the Air Force and a degree in the law. On the council since 1979—he took Barry's seat when Barry became mayor—Ray had gotten the reputation for bowing to special interests, and the fact that the business and real estate communities contributed $1.3 million to his campaign allowed the others to portray him as the developers' pawn. He was generally uninspiring and left Meg Greenfield cold.

Sharon Pratt Dixon, on the other hand, was Greenfield's kind of woman. Both were articulate and tough-minded feminists. A divorced mother raising two teenaged daughters, Dixon was a native Washingtonian, daughter of a judge and member in good standing of the African-American elite, by breeding and by her education at Howard University and its law school. She was the only candidate who had the temerity to call for Marion Barry's resignation after the Vista bust. The others were too scared to risk alienating the mayor's supporters. Dixon was also the only candidate who didn't hold public office, freeing her to run as the fresh-faced outsider. She could belittle Ray, Jarvis, and Clarke as the "three blind mice" from the council, and Fauntroy was easily skewered as the delegate who'd done little for the District in nineteen years in Congress. The time was ripe for reform, and Dixon punched up her soaring rhetoric with promises to "fix the government's bloat" by firing two thousand employees and to clean out the bureaucracy "with a shovel, not a broom."

It sounded just right to Meg Greenfield, but the voters were as yet unimpressed. Going into the final month, Dixon was shining at community forums, but her campaign was broke, she had trouble attracting volunteers, and polls showed her with a miserable 7 percent of the vote.

"I like Sharon," Greenfield told Graham. "I like what she says and how she says it. She has guts. But everyone says that she can't win. We might be wasting the endorsement."

It was up to Don Graham. After all the editorial board meetings and position papers, one man would decide. "I've been thinking the same thing," he told Greenfield. "Let's go with what we think is best regardless of the polls."

"Don and I were on the same wavelength," Greenfield said in recounting the conversation.

The first endorsement, "Clean House—Dixon for Mayor," came on August 30 and was followed with three more glowing editorials and a smattering of op-ed columns. It was a quixotic, hard-driving editorial campaign, strikingly reminiscent of the *Post's* unprecedented editorial support that swung the 1978 election for Marion Barry.

The shift in momentum was almost immediate. Volunteers and contributions swelled Dixon's campaign. By the eve of the election, white voters in particular were abandoning John Ray, and his tracking polls showed Dixon accelerating from last to first. Still, Dixon's people were less than optimistic. Her exhausted volunteers went home the night before the voting hoping at best that she would make a strong showing behind Ray.

At the polls on September 11, white voters in Ward Three followed the *Post* in lockstep and punched Sharon Pratt Dixon's ballot in overwhelming numbers. She won by slight margins in some black wards, but the *Post* and the whites boosted her past John Ray in the overall polling. She won with just 37 percent of the primary vote, nearly the same percentage as Barry had received in 1978. Dixon's victory was just as stunning, equally rapturous. Hope is hard to come by in any city, especially one whose mayor was a drug addict and whose image brought to mind crack dealers and bloody streets. Dixon's ascension rekindled the long-lost feeling that Washingtonians could live in harmony. She talked about bringing the city's black and white communities together. She promised reform, efficiency, pride. Indeed, for the first time since 1978, black and white voters cast ballots for the same candidate. She wasn't a political hack; she was a corporate executive beholden to no one. Her beautiful smile and flashing eyes lit up the entire ballroom of the Park Hyatt Hotel when she claimed her victory on primary night.

In elevating Dixon, the voters swept aside the established politicians and their backers. Eleanor Holmes Norton narrowly defeated Betty Ann Kane, a longtime city council member, to replace Fauntroy as the delegate to Congress. Norton was another promising addition to the city's leadership. A former SNCC lawyer, she'd built a record as a capable, fair-minded activist for minority and women's issues. The developers, big labor, and many minority business leaders lost with Ray; fundraiser Max Berry went down with Jarvis; David Abramson took it on the chin with David Clarke; John Hechinger lost with Fauntroy. Not one Barry-era power broker took a chance on Dixon, and not one gained from her victory.

"They tend not to recognize change when they see it," Dixon told the *Post* when her victory was assured. "They measure everything from the existing power structure.... I wanted it to happen this way. It's the only legitimate way."

A day later Dixon offered her deadpan assessment to *The New York Times:* "The status quo lost."

Dixon was not Marion Barry, but she was the standard bearer for a different status quo—the city's African-American elite.

She had the Upper Sixteenth Street upbringing, the father who was a judge, the Howard degrees, the haughty arrogance, and the sanctimonious belief that the capital belonged to native Washingtonians of a certain pedigree. She was a direct political heir to former mayor Walter Washington, and she had run Patricia Roberts Harris's losing campaign against Barry in 1982. She was the revenge of the aristocrats against Marion Barry's civil rights rabble.

The bums were out. Could the native elite do better?

Marion Barry still had one more race to run.

On the Monday morning following the August verdict, the mayor—who had missed the primary deadline—gave up his lifelong affiliation as a Democrat and filed as an Independent to run in November for an at-large city council seat. Right after the primary, he started campaigning against Hilda Mason, a frail but well-respected council veteran who had invited Barry into her home to recuperate in 1977. When he was shot; and Linda Cropp, a former school board president. The voters could cast ballots for two candidates to fill the two at-large seats. Early polls indicated that Barry could win one.

But there was still the matter of his sentencing by Judge Jackson on the one misdemeanor count. Few judges would put a first-time offender convicted of a possession count behind bars, but the mayor wasn't taking any chances. Ken Mundy prepared an exhaustive filing to argue against sending his client to jail, and Barry included an emotional letter admitting his addiction to cocaine.

"I had hoped to leave only a legacy of leadership in human and civil rights," Barry wrote. "Instead, because of my actions, I must also live with the personal pain and shame that cannot be erased. When I sat in your courtroom each day, hearing things about myself that I had not wanted to face, I may have appeared to be calm and unmoved, but on the inside, I was suffering nearly unbearable humiliation and deepest regret."

But Barry didn't grovel enough for Jay Stephens. "In short," Stephens's memorandum said, "the defendant is not genuinely remorseful about his criminality. He is sorry only that he got caught."

Effi Barry joined dozens of leaders, including NAACP chief Ben Hooks, in pleading with Judge Jackson for leniency.

"I beseech you to search your humanity," she wrote. "What further punishment does this man deserve? For certain, there can he no greater sentence than to have the whole world tune in to your day in court as you are publicly castrated."

In court on October 26, Mundy looked straight into the eyes of his friend and fellow club member Thomas Penfield Jackson as he argued eloquently in his client's defense. "If a lifetime of good deeds doesn't stand a man in good stead," he said, "then a lifetime of good deeds means nothing."

But nothing could dissuade Judge Jackson. Looking stern and dour, reading from a prepared text, he said that Barry had "given aid, comfort, and encouragement to the drug culture at large, and contributed to the anguish that illegal drugs have inflicted on this city." He gave Marion Barry the maximum—a six-month jail term—for running it into the ground.

"I understand there are different sets of standards for different people," Barry said. "That's the American 'injustice' system."

If there was any question that Judge Jackson was using his raw power to overrule the jury, he dispelled it in a speech four days later at a forum for students at Harvard Law School. Calling the evidence against Barry "overwhelming," Jackson said, "I am not happy with the way the jury addressed the case. Some people on the jury... had their own agendas. They would not convict under any circumstances."

Two weeks later, in the November 8 general election, it would be the voters' turn to pass judgment on Marion Barry.

Any campaign needs money, and Marion Barry went back to the well. He placed a call to Robert Pincus, a bank president who had brought in Jewish money in the past.

"I feel great," Barry said, just back from a two-week vacation. "I haven't had a drink."

Pincus was leading an effort to bring a major-league baseball team to Washington at the time, and Barry agreed to help by denying a stadium lease to a rival group. What could the banker do for him?

"Help me with the business community and the Jewish community, too," he said. "I realize the ties are badly broken, but I need campaign contributions."

"Damn right they're broken," Pincus said. "The Jews won't forgive you for embracing Farrakhan."

"I was a man adrift," Barry said. "It may have looked like everything was fine, but I was lower than low. I grabbed on to anything and anyone I could find."

"I'll see what I can do," Pincus said, but he did very little.

The mayor's final rallies attracted few people. His appeals had lost their power. On the night before the balloting, he went back to the New York Avenue Presbyterian Church for one last rally. He imported his mother, Mattie Cummings, looking frail and a bit dazed in her pink, floppy hat. Effi was absent. Fewer than seventy people came to hear the once-mighty leader. Bishop Stallings recited a list of Barry's betrayers, among them Jesse Jackson. After a few testimonials, the mayor stood up and tried to stir the crowd.

"It's time for us to take the hoards off," the mayor said. It had worked in 1978; maybe it would play again in 1990.

"I want to make the education system work," he said. "Our dropout rate is unacceptable in a civilized society."

The absurdity of Barry's attempt to run against his own government was apparent even to the diehard supporters who came out for his last political rally. There was little response, no emotion, and no familiar chanting.

On November 8, the voters rejected Marion Barry at the polls. Although he got over forty thousand votes, he came in a distant third. It was a bitter defeat—his first. The only part of the city that voted in great numbers for the mayor was Ward Eight, home of the poorest people, segregated and neglected across the Anacostia River. They didn't like what the government had done to him. And many loved Marion Barry, no matter what he said, no matter what he did, and no matter how little he had done to lift them out of poverty and hopelessness.

A few weeks later, Effi Barry announced her separation from Barry. She and their ten-year-old son, Christopher, took an apartment on Connecticut Avenue.

Vernon Jordan stepped up to the microphone at the Bricklayers' International union building on Fifteenth Street after mayor-elect Sharon Pratt Dixon introduced him as the chairman of her transition committee. It was a few weeks after Dixon predictably trounced former police chief Maurice Turner, who ran on the Republican ballot in the general election.

"It gives me great pleasure to be here today to help my friend Sharon bring new dignity to the capital city," Jordan said in his deep, resonant voice. Tall and imposing, the former civil rights leader turned corporate lawyer had deep contacts in the national Democratic party and held seats on more than a dozen corporate boards, but his roots in local politics looked weak under questioning.

"How can you say you're in touch with the community when your very first appointment is somebody whose commitment to the city is pretty questionable?" WAMU political commentator Mark Plotkin asked Dixon. "I checked the voting records for the last few local elections and found that Mr. Jordan voted in three of the last six. Mayor Dixon, he didn't even vote in the election in which you were nominated."

"I was out of town," Jordan said, clearly annoyed.

"But there are absentee ballots," Plotkin pressed.

Jordan's selection sent the right signal to federal Washington, but most local activists were unimpressed. It was a harbinger.

On her sixty-second day in office, Mayor Dixon took a nighttime tour of the hard side of the capital, beginning with a visit to Montana Terrace.

She arrived in her dark-blue chauffeur-driven Lincoln at the head of a small motorcade of police cars and walked up the steps into the cracked concrete courtyard. A tiny woman, she stood barely five feet tall and looked even smaller in her long, black overcoat, taking small steps amid a wedge of big cops. From a distance, you picked up her pale face, her trademark glasses with the oversized lenses, her round, doe eyes. Broken glass crunched under her lavender suede high heels. Every step sounded as if she were crushing cockroaches. A hundred and fifty families lived there in garden apartments squatting like bunkers around courtyards where young men killed one another for the right to sell crack to the young mothers who lived behind the battered, unmarked doors. The place seemed deserted. Out of the darkness the children emerged first. Little boys danced and swirled and wheeled their bikes around her small entourage. Then the mothers approached with their pleas for jobs and safe streets. Every one was quite civilized until a testy woman elbowed her way toward the mayor. Her face was sallow and her eyes were sad and runny. Her matted hair was covered with a blue kerchief.

"I've been waiting for an apartment for six years," she said in a high-pitched whine. Suddenly she was in Dixon's face. "Six years. Six years."

"Give me six months," the mayor said, and the cops whisked her away to appointments in other ruined parts of the city.

It was hard for her to make contact with the capital's desperate people stuck in hellholes like Montana Terrace. She'd been in a highbrow orbit for years, in the upper echelons of the Democratic party, in the white world of the Potomac Electric Power Company, where she was in charge of community relations. Now she had to make promises to people who had heard them all before.

Dixon had a tough job, no matter what level her political and leadership skills. Barry had left the city and the government in terrible shape. Records were nonexistent; phones had been ripped from the walls; all the top bureaucrats had resigned, at her request. The one Barry official whom Dixon wanted to keep was Carol Thompson, but she had had enough of government. RJR Nabisco, the tobacco and food conglomerate, hired her to be a lobbyist. If Dixon had been able to keep Carol Thompson—even for a while, just as a consultant—she might have gotten off to a better start. Without Thompson, a hard job was made even more difficult.

In 1978, Marion Barry came into office with a team of highly trained, highly motivated activists and public servants who stuck with the new government at least through the first term. Dixon was slow to assemble her staff, and she had a hard time keeping it. She ran as a "native Washingtonian" and promised to hire local talent to manage her government, but either she couldn't find any or they wouldn't work for her. She wound up going as far as Alaska for a housing director, brought her economic development chief in from Oakland, hired an administrative services director from Boston, and chose a press secretary from East St. Louis via Arizona. She fired her first chief of staff, local attorney Joe Caldwell, and publicly blamed his leaving on the poor health of his father. She hired Jack Bond, a well-respected city administrator and native Washingtonian, but then she proceeded to freeze him out of decisions and forced him out in less than a year.

When she finally installed her team on the fifth floor of the District Building, dark-skinned blacks couldn't help but notice that she surrounded herself with extremely light-skinned African Americans, in her own image.

"The people up there are so light they're almost white," Rufus "Catfish" Mayfield told a crowd protesting the mayor's budget cuts. Mayfield's job was one of those being eliminated.

"We don't need to get back to that syndrome," commented Calvin Rolark, Jr., president of the United Black Fund, publisher of a weekly newspaper and husband of a city council member. "It shouldn't be an issue, but people are watching her."

For the last quarter-century, Washington had been a simple city to describe in ethnic terms: It was black and white.

In contrast, immigrants were turning the surrounding counties in Maryland and Virginia into an international bazaar. Indians and Chinese, Latinos and Iranians, Afghans, Vietnamese, and Ethiopians moved into suburban cul-de-sacs and opened businesses in the malls. Within the city limits, Korean merchants took up where the Jews leftoff and ran many of the small stores, but it was still a two-tone city, until the mid-1980s.

The civil wars and poverty in Central America propelled wave after wave of villagers out of countries like El Salvador and Nicaragua. Many went as far as Texas and California, but thousands came to Washington. The 1990 census showed that the Hispanic population had increased by 85 percent since 1980, from 17,679 to 32, 710. Most settled in theAdams Morgan and Mount Pleasant neighborhoods. Many wereillegal aliens, but they were highly motivated and willing to do themost menial jobs. By the late 1980s most busboys, janitors, and laborers in the District were Latino.

Friction with the local African-Americans was bound to become a problem. For thefirst time, blacks found themselves fighting for scraps at the bottom of the economic ladder. The new immigrants didn't speak English, many jammed into apartments the to a room, and more than a few of the men diverted themselves by getting filthy drunk in the public parks. Thejob of keeping peace on *the* tense streets of Adams Morgan fell to the local police force, which was overwhelmingly black, and in 1991, filled with poorly trained rookies.

Sunday, May 5, was a hot day, and Daniel Enrique Gomez was spending the cool evening hours with some friends, drinking in a small triangle of green in Mount Pleasant. The thirty-year-old construction worker from El Salvador had been in the country for two years, but his command of English was poor. Two policemen walked into the park, informed Gomez and his friends that they were violating public drinking laws, and asked them to leave. What happened next is a matter of dispute, but at some point Gomez pulled a knife and came at Officer Angela Jewell, a young rookie. She pulled her gun, and when Gomez kept coming, she shot him in the stomach. Word of the shooting spread quickly, embellished by false reports that Jewell shot Gomez after he was handcuffed.

Latinos already felt that they were the victims of police harassment, and it was time for revenge. Within hours, angry crowds of Latino and black youths took to the streets and started burning buildings and looting stores. The next night people around the world were treated to televised scenes of burning buses and overturned police cars in the American capital. For three nights roving hands of teenagers staged running battles with police and threatened to spread the riots east across the city. Faced with a major crisis just four months into her term, Mayor Dixon slapped a curfew on the neighborhood and ordered the police not to shoot anything but tear gas. When the rioting was over, at least thirty-one businesses in the two communities had suffered some damage, but the entire city was affected.

"I think we need to worry," Stephen S. Fuller, a George Washington University professor who studies the economy, told *The Washington Post*. "Tourism is a part of the District's economy. It may give people cause to evaluate their summer plans."

The Mount Pleasant riots might have altered Jeff Cohen's plans to develop in the Shaw neighborhood, just a quarter-mile away, but Cohen's projects were already dead, a victim of Barry's demise, the depression in Washington real estate, and Cohen's miscalculations. Instead of the gleaming $200-million Samuel Jackson Plaza, the blocks that Cohen had gobbled up in the 1980s were either hoarded up, fenced in, or piled up with rubble and refuse.

Cohen, the former Boy Banker, had built his real estate empire with Marion Barry's help. The mayor had given his friend sweetheart government leases and an $11-million city loan to prop up the grandiose Shaw redevelopment project. Cohen had repaid Barry with a pipeline into Jewish campaign contributions and a secret piece of a real estate deal in Nantucket. When the deal became public late in Barry's term, the mayor was forced to admit his error and pay a fine for hiding it. Cohen's project in Shaw and another on Georgia Avenue near the Maryland line had run into heavy opposition from the neighbors. That and the real estate recession put him and his empire on the brink of bankruptcy as Barry was leaving office. To the very last day, Cohen believed that Barry would save the. Shaw deal by signing a government lease for his office space.

"He cut me off at the last moment," Cohen said in an interview from his office in the renovated Manhattan Laundry building before he was forced to leave.

Cohen wasn't the only local real estate mogul staring bankruptcy in the face. Washington was supposed to be recession-proof, but the commercial real estate market collapsed completely in 1990 and 1991. The speculative game of musical chairs abruptly stopped when bankers called in credit lines, and some of the developers who had gotten fabulously wealthy in the 1980s went broke overnight. Oliver Carr, the first developer downtown in 1968, stayed in business but was forced to give up a few major projects. Dominic Antonelli, the parking lot magnate who was thought to be so conservative, had gambled, loaned millions, and borrowed to the hilt; he was a billion dollars in the hole when he declared bankruptcy.

The demise of the local real estate moguls marked a watershed in the District's business life. Washington was always known as a political colony because Congress maintained ultimate control; by 1990 it was becoming an economic colony as well. Real estate development was one of the last purely local businesses, con trolled by native Washingtonians, financed by local banks, built by homegrown construction companies. The depression knocked out many of the local players and replaced them with Texans, Canadians, and foreigners. The shake-up in banking was even more striking. In 1980 there were a dozen major banks based in Washington; in 1990 there was one, Riggs National Bank, and it was owned by a pint-sized Texan named Joe Allbritton, Nationsbank and First Union, two regional giants based in Charlotte, controlled the lion's share of the banking business. Homegrown retailers like Garfinkel's and Raleigh's succumbed to pressure from national chains. Woodward & Lothrop, the last local department store, was taken over by Al Taubman, a Michigan financier. Giant Food and Hechingers were the last native business of note, and Hechingers was being elbowed out by Home Depot and others.

"The local businesses just couldn't compete," said William Regardie, whose award-winning magazine, *Regardie's,* chronicled the hurly-burly "greed decade" of the 1980s. His magazine folded in 1992, a casualty of general business collapse. "It will never be the same," he said. He restarted in 1994.

When Jeff Cohen and his wife, Francine, filed for personal bankruptcy on March 26, 1991, Cohen and his partnerships owed more than two hundred creditors approximately $54 million against personal assets of $119,149. Among Cohen's creditors were twenty financial institutions, the mayor's office, the District's-billing and collection department, and its finance and revenue agency. But being bankrupt and being broke were two different things in Cohen's case. After filing for bankruptcy, Cohen took his family on a long trip to Alaska in the summer of 1991, and then he returned to try to pick up the pieces. Two years later he was still lunching at the Palm, sending his children to tony Sidwell Friends, and dreaming of more development deals. He even managed to get in a round of golf with Bill Clinton in 1993.

The plaintive voices of the a capella gospel "Lord come by here" spilled out of the fenced-in backyard of Marion Barry's house on the overcast afternoon of October 26, 1991. In better days, Barry had invited friends and labor leaders here for annual crab feasts. On his worst night FBI agents escorted him through the yard after the Vista bust. On this moist day friends and reporters came to send him off to prison for six months. His hair was showing flecks of gray and getting sparse. He was wearing a gray suit, crisp white shirt, kente cloth scarf, and matching bowtie. His mother was by his side. Effi and Christopher were not."

Because I'm being sent to jail does not mean I've lost my spirit, or lost my way, or lost my understanding of myself..."

The crowd nodded and murmured approval.

"I hurt myself and my family and many of you…"

More nods and encouragement.

"I've asked you repeatedly for your understanding, your forgiveness, and your love…"

And the crowd of one hundred or so working-class supporters, many wearing baseball caps, some with public works insignias, smiled and waved and said, "Yes, Marion, yes." He trashed the government one last time for its "political prosecution" and he made ready to head down the road to the minimum-security prison for white-collar criminals in Petersburg, Virginia, where Ivanhoe Donaldson had done his time. But before leaving, he clasped hands with Union Baptist Temple minister Willie Wilson and swayed back and forth as he listened to Reverend H. Beecher Hicks deliver the benediction:

"Return him safe whole and healthy, complete to this community where he shall be sheltered in the love of his people."

And the mayor for life said, "Amen."

Al Arrington took some satisfaction when Barry left for his six-month stay behind bars, but it came with a dose of discouragement.

A few weeks before Barry began his jail term, Arrington and his partner Jim Pawlik were asked to attend the Metropolitan Police Department's annual award ceremony at Eastern High School. There, along with a few hundred officers honored for everything from saving babies to writing record numbers of traffic tickets, Arrington and Pawlik were given an award for their investigation of Marion Barry. When Chief Isaac Fulwood called them to the stage, he never even mentioned that they were being honored for running a one-year investigation that brought down the sitting mayor. For other cops he went into long descriptions of how they got bad guys. Fulwood just gave them a piece of paper and stood for a snapshot. "We should have skipped the whole thing," Pawlik said afterward.

Arrington knew that Fulwood and many officers were ambivalent about the Barry probe, and the message was driven home.as soon as the trial was over. Jay Stephens invited Arrington and Pawlik to attend the post-trial press conference. As they were about to join the prosecutors in the grand jury room, Fulwood ordered them to stay away. For Arrington it was a real slap in the face, but he was getting used to it. During the trial Barry supporters had heckled him as he went in and out of the courthouse. One day he was grabbing a sandwich at a carryout on the District side of the Prince Georges County line when a young woman walked 'up. "I've seen you on TV," she said and narrowed her eyes. "You're gonna get yours."

One of his relatives even registered his displeasure at what he thought was Arrington's betrayal of blacks.

"It was frustrating and stressful," he says. "They didn't get the message that this guy was doing bad things. He wasn't a hero. He was a bad guy. They saw it all in black and white. The white establishment was going after the black mayor, and I was the Uncle Tom that whites had brainwashed and used to bring him down.

"It's not that I didn't think about my role as a police officer and as a black man," he says. "I thought about it plenty and was quite comfortable with my role. I had no second thoughts."

Arrington didn't have to face hostile neighbors within the District of Columbia, because he'd moved to a sprawling rambler in Prince Georges County back in 1984. When he came to the capital back in 1968 he was following a well-worn path of black migration up from the Carolinas; in moving to the Maryland county on the city's eastern border, he was in the midst of another migration. During the 1980s thousands of black middle-class families abandoned the city, its crime, and its substandard schools for split level homes in safe developments in Prince Georges County. The first blacks who moved to the county in the 1970s were met with court-ordered busing, white antipathy, and police brutality. But by the 1980s they were taking political power and moving into posh subdivisions all over the county. The 1990 census showed that blacks outnumbered whites in Prince Georges, 51 percent to 43 percent.

The District was losing population throughout the 1980s, and the trend accelerated in the early 1990s, but unlike the outmigrations of the 1960s, this was black flight. Working couples, families with young children, and people simply trying to escape the city's high crime rate moved out in droves. From its high of 802,178 in 1950, the city's population dropped to 606,900 in the 1990 census and fell below 600,000 two years later. Nearly one-third of those remaining—180,000—were on the public assistance rolls.

Al Arrington placed himself in a position to benefit from the exodus to Prince Georges County. He got his real estate license, announced his intention to retire from the police department and started selling homes at a fast clip.

As Arrington was leaving, the quality of the police department was taking a dive. He was among hundreds of veteran police officers and detectives to retire almost en masse. They'd been hired twenty years before when Richard Nixon called Washington the crime capital and ordered the hiring of fifteen hundred officers; now they could retire with generous pensions. The police department went on a hiring binge to replace the retirees and at the same time comply with Congress's orders to hire even more cops. In a rush to fill the rolls, the department neglected background checks, lowered entrance standards, and skimped on training. The shoddy policies bore fruit when the recruits hit the streets and started wrecking police cars at the rate of one a day, conspiring with drug dealers, and selling cocaine. The classes of 1990 and 1991 put dozens of dirty cops on the streets, so dirty that the FBI formed a special unit to police the police.

In 1992, thirty-five Washington police officers were indicted on criminal charges ranging from murder, theft, assault with a deadly weapon, and sodomy to kidnapping while armed and making threats. At least seventy more were indicted in 1993. Police employees were caught selling handguns that had been confiscated and stored by the department. Even if the thugs in uniform were thrown in jail, they wouldn't necessarily lose their jobs. According to a report by Tucker Carlson in Policy Review, a 1990 District law requires that the department decide within forty-five days if a dismissed cop should be punished. If not, the cop cannot be permanently dismissed. In October 1992, a District employee relations board ordered the reinstatement of officers fired for drug dealing, vandalism, and concealing past psychiatric treatment, Carlson reported.

In October 1993, the trial of District police officer Fonda C. Moore drove home the unprecedented amount of police corruption and the cooperation between the cops and the drug dealers. Moore, a highly decorated officer, was accused of working for a deadly drug lord whose organization dealt up to fifty kilograms of cocaine a month from the Deli Den, a lunch spot on Martin Luther King Avenue in Anacostia that was a favorite of 7th District officers. She allegedly tipped off dealers about raids, transported guns, and set up the murder of Billy Ray Tolbert, a rival dealer who was brutally beaten and shot a dozen times as he pleaded for his life. Moore was the first D.C. cop to stand trial in a murder case, but she was one of 113 officers who were under indictment for assorted criminal acts ill 1993, including twelve indicted for taking bribes and providing security for a bogus drug operation.

Mayor Sharon Pratt Dixon got off to a slow start running the government, but she was a comet on Capitol Hill, where she seems to have spent most of her first year in office.

The congressmen and senators were totally disgusted by Marion Barry. In his last two years they treated him with disdain and penalized the entire city by freezing the annual federal payment in lieu of taxes to the District. Anyone but Barry would have made them happy, but Dixon absolutely charmed them. "A breath of fresh air," gushed Robert Byrd, chairman of the Senate Appropriations Committee and the man whose hearings in 1961 portrayed Washington as a city of welfare queens. Majority Leader Tom Foley invited her to escort him to the annual Gridiron dinner, an evening of elite journalist and politician schmoozing and one of the hottest tickets in town. Dixon was comfortable with the federal politicians and they with her. She knew many of the Democrats because she'd been on the Democratic National Committee for years and served as party treasurer in

1988. The Democrats needed a boost, and this articulate, attractive new mayor gave everyone a high. She made such an impression that Senate Republicans invited her to breakfast and asked her, in jest, to consider switching parties.

The mayor had good reason to he on Capitol Hill. The city was close to broke. Barry's profligate spending programs had put the budget in the red, and the real estate bust dried up tax revenues. Dixon lobbied for months against long odds to extract a $200-million increase in the federal payment from a budget-weary Congress. She got the money and emerged looking like a lion tamer.

But down in the den of the city, Dixon failed to connect. Either she hadn't hired anyone to run the government, or she wasn't letting her staff do its job. Though the mayor continued to make rousing speeches, no one on her staff was answering mail, returning phone calls, or meeting with constituents. She bristled at any criticism, telling everyone she had a different style and they'd just have to get used to it. But her style angered both foes and friends, and within a year she had somehow squandered all the goodwill that grew out of her improbable victory at the polls. She managed to insult the police department, the city council, business leaders, the medical community, the arts community, and a few key members of the religious community.

"Black folks have an expression—some people talk good and think bad," said Cathy Hughes, WOL radio station owner and talk show host. "Sharon is a classic example. This city is screaming out in misery. Marion Barry did a better job cracked up."

Hughes was still a Barry fan then, though that would change, and she spoke for only a small segment of the city, but her estimation of the mayor's first term was widespread. "A homeless woman just thrown out of a shelter and Oliver Carr, who's still trying to develop buildings, share one thing," said an aide for D.C. delegate Eleanor Holmes Norton. "They're both mad at city hall."

City politics is a sweaty contact sport. People have to believe that they can touch their leaders and make their government work for them. Dixon was on the road so much during her first year that constituents would have had to grab her in the airport. She was on the road to New York City a half-dozen times, stopped in Los Angeles for a speech and a fundraiser, vacationed in St. Thomas and Martha's Vineyard, held a cabinet retreat in West Virginia, went back to Los Angeles twice more, gave a speech in Cancun, attended a luncheon in Boston, and stopped back in New York to accept the *Glamour* magazine woman of the year award. She traveled a total of more than seven weeks in that first year.

Around the District Building they started to call her "Mayor of America" and "Air Dixon." How could a woman with so much potential and so much hope have become such a disappointment?

Every leader has shortcomings, and secure ones hire people to compensate for them. Dixon did the opposite. Not a warm person, she surrounded herself with icy aides. She had no experience in running a government, yet she got rid of Jack Bond, the only seasoned administrator on her staff. She had no political organization, yet she hired few aides with deep roots in the community. She built a worshipful staff that reeked elitism and exacerbated her weaknesses. When aides plucked up their courage and told her that voters were unhappy, she froze the aides out, responding, "If they don't like it, let them impeach me." And that attitude permeated her fifth-floor suite.

"It's part of a separatist attitude that's formed," said Ted Gay, the mayor's chief political consultant in the early days. "People are isolated on the fifth floor. They have a them-and-us approach, I'm trying to help them think of the city as we."

Dixon simply couldn't make the transition from the candidate—whose candor and passion thrilled people like Meg Greenfield—to the empathetic politician who could manage a government and build coalitions. Her way of getting support was by threat and intimidation, and it wasn't working.

In December 1991, the mayor married New York businessman James Kelly III at a private ceremony at the home of her sister, Benaree Wiley, in Brookline, Massachusetts. Kelly kept his legal residence in New York, but the couple moved into the mayor's home in North Portal Estates, an expensive Northwest subdivision so close to the Maryland line that you could chuck a rock into Montgomery County. Mayor Dixon became Mayor Kelly, but she didn't change her style. She started to get a reputation for lapses in moral judgment. In the midst of tough negotiations with Jack Kent Cooke, owner of the Redskins football team, over development of a new stadium, the mayor accepted free tickets to the Super Bowl. She traveled on the city's tab to conferences where she was paid to speak.

She allowed her staff to bluntly ask city contractors for contributions to her political campaign, a violation of city and federal laws that triggered local and federal investigations.

After three years in office, the mayor couldn't get her administration in gear, and she was hampered by personal tragedies: Her grandmother passed away and one of her best friends died of an asthma attack when a city ambulance was slow to respond to an emergency call. She certainly was not filling Barry's shoes as a dominant political force, or as a capable chief executive, as he was in his first term. She battled constantly with the news media, bitterly complaining in private that some reporters were trying to make her look like a crook.

In the parking lot of the Day's Inn off Route 56 in the rolling hills near Johnstown, Pennsylvania, a dozen young waiters and waitresses—all white kids wearing white shirts and black bowties—watched with slack-jawed wonder.

Hundreds of elderly black women and men holding green and white balloons and a few younger African-Americans stepped out of five buses that pulled into the lot at around noon. The crowd clapped and sang "Victory...victory is mine. Joy is mine, joy is mine." At 1:00 p.m. a tall black man with freshly dyed hair, wearing a gray suit, a kente cloth African scarf, and a matching hat walked out of the motel lounge and into the bright light. His seventy-five-year old mother held his hand. Marion Barry accepted the crowd's adulation; it was April 23, 1992, the day of his release from jail.

He waved a Bible, gave a catlike smile, and pointed at his friends.

"I come out of prison better not bitter," he told the happy gathering and the television cameras. "I come out of prison stronger internally than at any given time in my life."

And he came out of prison with another sexual indiscretion to explain. In prison lingo they call it "doing the wild thing," meaning to sneak a sexual encounter in jail, and Barry supposedly did it on a female visitor. Her name was Patricia Holbrooke, a thirty-nineyear-old court stenographer who was living in the Bronx but who had once lived in the District. She was wearing a short black dress above the knee. They were talking at a table in the visiting room. What transpired next is a matter of dispute, and as always, great theater with heavy racial overtones.

Floyd Robinson, a white inmate who was doing time for selling controlled substances, was visiting with his wife and children at a table about eight feet from Barry. There were twenty other people in the room at the time. Barry and Holbrooke started fondling each other, according to Robinson, and then she leaned over his lap and performed oral sex on him.

"There's no way I wouldn't have seen it," Robinson told reporters. "My wife's eyes were as big as saucers. She was shaking." He later scaled back his assertion about the sex act and told WRC-TV only that the woman "leaned her head over his lap, and then I saw her head go up and down."

The *New York Daily News* ran the story under the headline: "Sex? How emBarrysing!"

Barry said Robinson, his former bridge-club partner, was lying and that the whole episode was yet another attempt by the white establishment to "break his spirit." Prison authorities at Petersburg held a hearing, determined that Barry had engaged in a sexual act with a visitor, and moved him to the medium-security prison in Loretto, a small town in the mountains of central Pennsylvania. The entire affair was vintage Barry. There were reports of illicit sex with a mystery woman, his accusers were white, the federal government applied the punishment, he denied the whole thing. Upon his arrival at Loretto, he called WRC-TV Channel 4, said the new prison was fine and in fact it had "a better salad bar."

The one constant feature of Barry's incarceration was his continued addiction to the phone. With any free time, he was on the line to Washington, calling reporters, supporters, friends, and potential voters. He spent his last three months in the mountains of Pennsylvania, but he was concentrating on the hills of Washington east of the Anacostia River. There, in Ward Eight, he would make his comeback.

The "buscapade" that escorted him back to Washington from the Johnstown Days Inn was part of his political resurrection. The five buses pulled up to the Union Temple Baptist Church in Anacostia at 8:00 p.m. and hundreds of screaming, chanting supporters exploded in "Barry's back, Barry's back, Barry's back."

He got off the bus, surveyed the crowd, punched his fist in the air. Voices from the crowd said: "Free at last."

A few weeks later Marion Barry moved to a small apartment in Ward Eight to establish residency and start running for the council seat that would be filled by the voters on September 15—four months down the line. It was, in the eyes of many Washingtonians, a preposterous, foolhardy proposition. How could a man fresh out of the federal pen expect to get elected to public office? Who would vote for him? In Barry's eyes, still guided by tremendous political instincts, it was a natural fit: the outlaw candidate with the outcast ward.

Ward Eight was the only place in the city that Barry could have hoped to start his comeback. He's always tapped the anger in the black community, and there's plenty there—for good reason. East of the river is across the tracks, the city's dumping ground. Blue Plains, the region's sewage treatment plant, lies in the ward along the Potomac River. The city's only halfway house for prisoners from Lorton is here, too. In all of Ward Eight, there are no movie houses, no shopping centers; no malls. One small Safeway serves the population of 69,000. There are more liquor stores than doctors' or lawyers' offices, more check-cashing stores than banks, more carryouts than restaurants. Of the ward's 3,921 acres, only 900 are taxable. The rest is federal or city land. Some maps designed for tourists simply cut off most of the ward.

It is the city's poorest ward. The median income is $16,000. According to city statistics, 15,000 people live in public housing and another 10,000 live in subsidized apartments, so that 35 percent of the population qualifies for government help. Forty-one percent didn't graduate from college. In the midst of the homelessness crisis, there are 5,000 vacant housing units, and at least 1,700 are boarded up. In comparison, there are five boarded-up units in Ward Three, where the whites dwell.

There are some middle-class neighborhoods in Ward Eight, but they are isolated pockets of tidy row homes and new, predominantly subsidized apartment complexes. The result is a patchwork of public housing complexes, some deplorable and some renovated, across the street from spanking new apartment buildings behind twelve-foot-high wrought-iron fences. Or streets of row houses with well-tended lawns close by bombed-out brick buildings. Or shopping strips along Martin Luther King, Jr., Avenue that cram variety stores and bars next to a carwash and a liquor store.

In his career as a political boss, Barry's value and his inherent threat was that he could relate to and control the poorest, most explosive class in the city. In the 1960s they were called street dudes; in 1992 they were lumped into the underclass. Barry derived power because he gave the impression that he could contain the disenfranchised by giving them a voice, or unleash them by inciting their anger. Now he was down to the nub. If the lower class rejected his emotional, racially tinged appeal, Barry would be out of business.

"If he can get the people in the projects who have never voted to come out and vote for him, he could win big," said businessman James Bunn, who worked for Barry in Ward Eight when he was mayor. Now Bunn, the ward's former Democratic party chairman, was with the incumbent council member, Wilhelmina Rolark. "He's the only one who can motivate them."

But why chance it? Why go directly from jail to the campaign trail? Virtually every one of Barry's friends and former political supporters advised him to wait, or try something different, or reinvent himself. They said he risked humiliation, or worse, a return to drugs. But in his mind there was no waiting or reinvention required. Why should he change? The conditions that had brought him to power in 1978 hadn't changed. He could keep playing the same role.

"This isn't a campaign," he preached in his kickoff speech, "this is a crusade to bring power and dignity and services back to us here in Ward Eight."

Us? When Barry was mayor for twelve years and at-large city council member from 1974 to 1978, he gave only occasional alienation to the far Southeast neighborhoods of Ward Eight. He appointed few Ward Eight residents to city commissions, he never put in a drug treatment facility, he let services wither away and—the most egregious example of his neglect—he failed to use hundreds of millions of dollars in federal funds earmarked to renovate public housing. The feds took back the money. But even with his shortcomings, Barry still did more as mayor in the poor neighborhoods than any other politicians.

Barry had pragmatic reasons to run. He needed a job, and the council seat paid seventy-two thousand dollars a year, more than any similar elected office· in the nation. He needed four more years on the city payroll to qualify for a pension. He was addicted to power and politics as surely as he was hooked on drugs and alcohol. And he had a vendetta against the people who had abandoned him.

"I'll tell you why Marion's running," says Absalom Jordan, a Ward Eight activist who was also running for the council seat. "He wants to run for mayor again in two years. It's just that simple."

The political equation in Ward Eight was simple and sad. Few people cared to vote. There were 21,000 registered Democrats, but most usually stayed at home on Election Day, especially in council races. Wilhelmina Rolark, a seventy-four-year-old lawyer had represented Ward Eight since 1976. In the last election, in 1988, she had beaten Absalom Jordan 1,900 to 1,500. Barry ran for an at-large seat in 1990, after his conviction, and attracted 6,000 votes. The most she'd ever polled was 3,200.

The mere chance that Barry could get back into the city's political game had united the political establishment against him. In the manner of Middle Eastern warfare, where the enemy of my enemy is my friend, even Mayor Sharon Pratt Kelly and city council chairman John Wilson found themselves backing Rolark against Barry. Every city council member came out for her. Police Chief Isaac Fulwood, who had clashed with Rolark in her position as chairman of the judiciary committee, said "any intelligent person" would vote for her.

Kelly's support actually hurt Rolark. The mayor had come in third in Ward Eight in the 1990 primary and remained weak. The working-class people did not identify with her, and she did not identify with them. But why was Wilson, Barry's friend since the civil rights days, working against him?

"I don't think it's in the best interests of the city," Wilson said at the time. "Congress will punish us if Marion gets on the council. In the long run, the poor will suffer even more because with less money we will have to cut services."

So with no support from the established politicians and little money, Marion Barry went to the streets. He donned his dashiki and his kente cloth and played all his old refrains about black power and pride and African roots. He went to the public housing projects and the beat-up basketball courts—places that Rolark hadn't visited in years. He hugged the old folks, and the kids danced at his knees. He held gospel rallies in the churches and picnics in the parks. He registered almost three thousand new voters.

"His premise is that people have short memories," said Absalom Jordan, "and he can keep playing the race game again and again. He says 'look at what the white man did to me.' He wants people to forget that for years he *was* the white man, he *was* the law, he *was* in control of the city when Lorton filled up with black men.

"Who's attracted to Marion Barry?" Jordan asked. "The people who sell drugs love him. He legitimizes what they do. In him there's legitimacy, sanctuary, acceptance. They can say the former mayor has the same problem."

Barry's support wasn't confined to drug dealers, however. He had 100 percent name recognition. He promised jobs to people who hadn't seen a politician in years. He was endorsed by a local of the American Federation of Government Employees, the union that represents many city workers and remembered the raises for its members. The gay community considered Rolark public enemy number one because as chairman of the judiciary committee she refused to back repeal of the District's sodomy law. Gays provided money and volunteers for Barry, just as they had in 1978.

That anyone could support Marion Barry was incomprehensible to most whites, especially if they didn't live in the District. "Inside the Beltway he has a great deal of support," said John Wilson. "Outside the Beltway he's a major joke."

At the Democratic convention in New York delegates and political pros from all over the country asked Wilson whether Barry could win.

"He has a chance," Wilson told them. They laughed.

On September 15 a record number of Ward Eight voters elected Marion Barry over Rolark by a 3-1 margin. Victory was his, and it was sweet. He celebrated that night with his delirious supporters and received politicians, hat in hand, in his small apartment. Council chairman John Wilson, at-large member John Ray, and Frank Smith of Ward One stopped by. Barry was wearing full African attire.

"When are you gonna take that stuff off?" the normally quiet John Ray joked. Barry smiled. He'd just completed the first stage of what could be one of the most amazing political comebacks in history. Many people were mystified that he'd won, but the reasons were clear. Neighborhoods with terrific views of the sparkling lights on the Mall and the national monuments were breeding grounds for violence and drug addiction, Why Barry? Because no one else had helped them. They had no better choices. At least he would bring attention. He could bring hope.

And he did. He even brought Mayor Sharon Pratt Kelly across the river to celebrate his victory. She came to the Panorama Room to give Barry a hug, to dance the Electric Slide, and to tell him that she'd be happy to work with him on the city council. The reform mayor who had run against Barry even rehired some of his field troops in city government.

The election of a new president has an energizing, cleansing effect on the capital city. If nothing else it triggers a changing of the guard, but the election of William Jefferson Clinton on November 3 brought a special excitement. Clinton and his wife, Hillary, were young Democrats replacing old Republicans, and Washington was hip again in their aura. The new president jogged through the city streets and dined in neighborhood restaurants. He appointed a Washingtonian as his liaison with the capital region. When a deranged man shot a dozen people and killed three in Mount Pleasant and Columbia Heights, he dispatched Attorney General Janet Reno to speak at a neighborhood church.

But Clinton's greatest impact was in giving hope to Washingtonians who wanted the District of Columbia to become the state of New Columbia. Statehood is the Holy Grail of Washington politics. It's basic political dogma, a mantra for every elected official. Clinton was the first president who openly supported the District's becoming the fifty-first state; he'd even testified before Congress in its behalf early in 1992.

During Marion Barry's twelve years as mayor and especially in the last six, statehood was a dead issue. City voters in the early eighties had approved statehood and even a strongly liberal constitution, but sporadic efforts to get the attention of Congress died quickly.

But in 1990, the tide shifted, largely because Jesse Jackson was elected "statehood senator," an unpaid, symbolic post that made him the city's official statehood lobbyist in Congress. Though Jackson continued to fly around the country and the world in support of various causes, he did focus attention on statehood. It wasn't completely selfless. If the District became a state, Jackson would become a real senator, but personal agendas are the stuff of politics. During the presidential campaign, Jackson tried to extract a promise from Clinton that he would make statehood a priority, but Clinton wouldn't make the deal, agreeing only to support statehood if it passed the Congress.

Statehood proponents support a shortcut to statehood. To avoid constitutional issues, they want the "District" shrunk to the federal enclave encompassing the Congress, national Mall, and the White House. The rest of the city would become the state of "New Columbia" by the normal simple majority votes of the House and Senate and the president's signature. Some opponents of statehood insist that such a plan still requires a constitutional change, with two-thirds of the states approving. But neither seems likely in the near future. Each year the statehood bill is introduced in the House and Senate. Senator Edward Kennedy of Massachusetts introduced the latest bill in early 1993, as he had for years. Republicans, fearing two new and liberal Democratic senators, vow a fight to the death if statehood ever becomes a remote reality.

The moral high ground belongs to statehood advocates. It's hard to objectively argue with the fact that six hundred thousand tax-paying Americans who happen to live within the District line are not represented in the Senate and have only a delegate in the House. It is, on its face, taxation without representation. Jesse Jackson and others also see it as a civil rights issue, implying that some in Congress don't want to create the first majority black state. And though Con-

374 | DREAM CITY

gress has changed since the segregationist days of Bilbo and McMillan, there is still plenty of justification for the civil rights angle.

Unfortunately, Mayor Sharon Pratt Kelly and the rest of the local officials didn't do much to help the District's case. Kelly used statehood as a political weapon, blaming Congress for the city's problems and leading people to believe that all would be fine if Congress would grant statehood. It was pure demagoguery, because statehood wasn't about to happen, and even if it did, the state of New Columbia wouldn't be a slice of heaven between Maryland and Virginia. Kelly's campaign served only to make enemies in Congress. As Kelly dangled statehood in front of the city, the prospect that Congress would appoint a federal financial oversight commission was much more likely. The District's finances were extremely shaky. Outside experts and council chairman John Wilson said the city was on the brink of bankruptcy, and might miss making summer payrolls.

City residents wince when outsiders complain the government is too poorly run to grant statehood—and point fingers at troubled governments like that of nearly bankrupt California. Still, it's a political reality that the city's myriad troubles make statehood a long shot. In addition to finances, the crime rate is among the highest in the country, and the government remains exceptionally inefficient. The infant mortality rate remains among the highest in the nation. The wait for public housing is years and for drug treatment is months. In 1993, the eighty-thousand-student school system was ranked among the worst in the country, with more money per pupil than virtually any other jurisdiction. Kelly's promises to cut the city work force were at best half-filled.

As if that weren't enough, the city's elected leaders were constantly at war. Kelly and city council chairman Wilson were sworn enemies and potential rivals. Wilson's often brilliant but petulant style was grating on other council members. The mayor was at odds with delegate Eleanor Holmes Norton, who was coming off as the most sensible arid capable official of all—but there wasn't much competition.

On Inauguration Day, January 20, 1993, when the capital city was in the spotlight of the world for the swearing in of a new president, the mayor had her aides changing locks to doors to keep council members away from choice seats to view the parade from the city's District Building. The mayor already had moved her staff to a brand-new building for which the government overpaid by $30 million in a sweetheart deal with a local developer. The council decided to keep its offices in the old Beaux Arts building overlooking Pennsylvania Avenue. Kelly didn't want to work in the building, but it was a fine place for an inaugural party. And so it went, as the new president came to town.

On any given day, at any given hour, a television viewer channel surfing in the District in 1993 was likely to see Mayor Sharon Pratt Kelly on the city's cable channel. She televised faux talk shows on current affairs, town meetings, speeches, monologues—you name it. It seemed as if she were trying to govern from the tube, but it wasn't working. Kelly's high-tech, video approach to politics made her even more aloof from citizens who wanted to see her in person. Kelly, on the TV and in her new, antiseptic, highly secure building, appeared to be untouchable, and she was. On the building's top floor she installed a suite of plush offices and even an apartment, outfitting the rooms with $140,000 worth of oak and cherry wood cabinetry and a $50,000 fireplace of polished granite, all at the expense of a city that was going broke. She talked about economic development as businesses fled the city in droves to escape its high taxes and crime. Her effort to keep the Washington Redskins in the city failed in part because Kelly, with her abrasive personality, couldn't negotiate with owner Jack Kent Cooke, himself a crusty billionaire who called Kelly "Her Worship." A *Washington Post* poll early in 1994 gave her an astounding 67 percent disapproval rating.

All of which created an intense nostalgia—and a wide political opening—for Ward Eight council member Marion Barry, Jr., who got very high marks in the same poll.

The former mayor, dressed in his tailored dashiki and African cap, was everywhere in his first year back from prison. It was the Marion of old: magnetic, savvy, sincere. The city council job was a cakewalk for him. He'd already been a councilman for four years before he was mayor, and he knew the executive branch better than anyone in the city. He had virtually created it. In private working sessions and public committee meetings, Barry applied himself to the task of representing his ward. He was studious and conscientious, asked intelligent questions, and cooperated with the other twelve; council members.

"I find him thoughtful and a pleasure to work with," said Ward Four council member Charlene Drew Jarvis, who'd jousted with him when he was mayor.

There was, however, the matter of the stolen car. On the first day of the council's legislative session, a young gospel singer made off with Barry's burgundy Chrysler, which was parked behind the District building. As the story went, he stole the keys from Barry's jacket. A short time later he was arrested, and a search of the car came up with traces of cocaine and marijuana. Barry proclaimed his innocence and refused to accept return of the car. A grand jury indicted the thief—Barry was never implicated; yet once again, as with the allegations of illicit sex in prison, Marion Barry was doing a two-step with a scandal. Many conversations about him eventually touched on the question of whether he was free of drugs, and if so whether he would remain clean.

Barry often looked worn. His face was at times puffy and leathery. He was starting to resemble James Brown in his beat-up, later days. He was getting a paunch. But he still cut a larger-than-life figure, especially in comparison to the city's other pallid politicians. Through his public degradation and jail term, he held his head high and never "bowed down to Mr. Charlie." No one had risen to take his place. When Mayor Kelly gave her State of the District speech at the Convention Center in the spring of 1993, the city council members were seated on the stage when Barry made his entrance. Unlike other politicians that day, Barry spent several minutes schmoozing and pressing the flesh in the crowd before he joined them.

He even said hello to his former wife, Mary Treadwell, among those hired by Kelly.

In March 1993, Barry and Effi filed for divorce, and he became a single father when Christopher, then twelve, came to live with him. Christopher fit well into his new image as a hard-working, churchgoing family man. When the Urban League honored fathers and sons at its 1993 dinner, Barry and Christopher showed up to walk down the runway in full African attire. Then in January he married the latest strong woman in his life, Cora Masters, his friend of twenty years and an intimate of Effi's, too. His fourth marriage was an extravagant affair graced with African rituals, Barry had remade himself.

And everywhere he went, he found people who wanted him to run for mayor. It was more than just political posturing by Barry himself.

"It happens all the time, two or three people an hour come up to me and talk about my running," Barry said in a radio interview. "I tell them I'm just trying to do the best job representing the people of Ward Eight."

In fact, he could hardly get his mind off a total comeback. The next election would be in September 1994. He could run for mayor and not give up his council seat, so there would be no risk. He loved campaigning more than anything else and he could parlay the threat of running to gain favors from Kelly or other council members. Kelly appeared to be weak. If another candidate or two got into the race and split the vote, even Barry's most vitriolic detractors had to admit that he had a real chance to win the Democratic primary. Five candidates ran in 1990. The prospect was tantalizing, and some of the city's power brokers were just frustrated enough with Kelly to come to his side.

Emily Durso Vetter, for example, was president of the hotel association. She'd been working in various economic development jobs since she served in Barry's first-term government. Now she was running a group whose members provided the District with hundreds of millions of dollars in sales taxes. She approached the Kelly government with a project to train young people in the hotel business. If the city provided the applicants, the hotels would find them jobs. Vetter tried to get a response for months and wound up frustrated.

She ran into Barry at the Urban League dinner and related her travails.

"I've got some kids across the river who would love to work with you," he said. "We can make that happen."

And he did. It was shades of Pride, Inc. He knew all about teenagers and jobs. He was planning a series of citywide hearings to make sure that every youth had a summer job. It had worked in 1967, and in 1978, and nothing had changed in 1993, so why not try it again? And why not run for mayor?

His old friends from the SNCC days and from the glorious first term and the ones who had stuck with him all the way to the Vista bust remained business and social acquaintances around the city, and any conversation naturally included city politics and Marion Barry. Many felt another Barry campaign would be bad for him personally, bad for business, and bad for the city. It was time for other challenges. Barry should let go. They shared some of their feelings with him, but just as in his race for the Ward Eight council seat, Marion Barry had his own sense of timing, his own vision.

"You can't talk him out of it," said Courtland Cox.

EPILOGUE

At the end of the blood-soaked summer of 1993, President Bill Clinton paused during a speech before a college audience in North Carolina to talk about violence. He mourned for the twenty-two people killed in one nearby county and the ten foreign tourists slain in Florida.

"But in our nation's capital, in one week this summer," Clinton said, holding up an index finger and dropping his voice, "more than twice that many people were killed. They were not famous, but they were the president's neighbors.... It is heartbreaking. What can we do about it?"

The carnage in Mr. Clinton's neighborhood during his first year in office was gruesome and widespread. The murder rate, which had dipped slightly in 1992, began to climb again. The city careened toward a new rise of more than 467 dead, easily earning its infamous title as the murder capital of the nation, perhaps of the world. More people were murdered during one two-week stretch in Washington than were slain in 1990 in all of England.

We didn't intend to write a book that portrayed the capital city as a violent caricature of urban America, but twenty years after the advent of home rule, that reality is impossible to escape. Acts of random, brutal violence riveted the city during the summer and fall of 1993, but one shooting touched the entire town. On a Saturday afternoon in late September, twenty-two-year-old Anthony Dawkins went hunting for Kervin Brown, his childhood friend who'd joined a rival gang. Dawkins found Brown watching a pickup football game at an elementary school playground and killed him with a hail of bullets from his 9mm handgun. In the process he shot four-year-old Launice Smith in the head. She died four days later.

The day after Launice Smith died, one of her aunts came to the playground of Weatherless Elementary School where her niece was shot. It was a listless, gray day. Delores Smith, a sturdy, straight-talking woman, addressed a small gathering that had been organized by community leaders and Jesse Jackson, who stood to her left. Mayor Sharon Pratt Kelly was on her right.

"I would hate to think that Launice's death brought all of this on and got all of you together in vain," she said. "We need to do something—now."

Smith said that she had been a metropolitan police officer, but that she left in the 1970s because she realized the streets were getting too violent.

"I wish I was still there because the other two [killers of Launice] are still at large. And I will hunt them down myself."

"Yes, Lord," Jesse Jackson murmured.

Delores Smith said the new police officers were too young and inexperienced to deal with the new breed of "vicious animals" and thugs. "Because this was a vicious animal that shot Launice down like he did. No remorse," she said. "None whatsoever.

"So, my thing is this, Mrs. Kelly," she said, turning to face the mayor. "I have the opportunity to ask you: Heat up the electric chair. Bring it back. If you bring back capital punishment, it will cut down on some of this killing. It's not right to say a life for a life. I know, 'Thou shalt not kill.' But some of these animals? You need to replug that electric chair over there at the D.C. jail and start frying some of them and make it public."

She thrust her hand toward the camera as if to plug it in herself.

"And then," she said, "they'll stop."

The barrage of bad news and blood on the streets bewildered Mayor Kelly. Her continued demand for statehood as a panacea for the city's problems came off as ludicrous at best, and a cruel form of demagoguery at worst. President Clinton in his North Carolina speech called for more police on the streets to prevent crime. In the District, Kelly short-changed the police budget and then appealed to U.S. Attorney Janet Reno and others for National Guard troops or assistance from the FBI to maintain order. Neighborhoods pleaded for beat patrols, but they were slow in coming. Meanwhile Kelly beefed up her personal security force to nearly twenty-five sworn officers. She also installed bulletproof glass in the windows of her new office, despite the fact that it would take a helicopter attack to reach her eleventh floor suite.

The same day that President Clinton spoke about his "neighbors" in Washington, Kelly was al the Marine base in Quantico, Virginia, to announce a new program that would allow District police to be trained by U.S. Marines, because the city was doing such a lousy job. After reviewing the recruits, the city's chief executive gave them a pep talk.

"We're talking about a war out there in the District of Columbia," she said. "I've called it a war of values. Whatever kind of war you want to call it, it is a war.... We need you. We'll support you. And this is one way to support you—give you the preparation you need—to fight the battle and win the war."

Sharon Kelly wasn't much of a field marshal, but even if she'd been George Patton, she would have had little chance of winning the war. The police force she inherited was not prepared to fight, because her predecessor, Marion Barry, had wrecked it.

For all his achievements and failures, the dispirited and desperate state of the city's police department in a time of turmoil was perhaps Barry's most damning legacy. It sapped the city's sense of security, the fundamental fabric upon which housing, education, social life, and a quality business community depend. Every city in the nation was fighting crime and poverty and budget battles in the late 1980s and early 1990s. Could the District have avoided their fate? Could Marion Barry—or any leader—have maneuvered the capital into some kind of harmony and prosperity?

We're talking about imponderables, of course. But Washington, D.C. was unique. It had the most prosperous, well-educated black population of any American city. It had a stable employer in the federal government. It had a wealthy white population that was among the most liberal in the nation. It was the beneficiary of one of the most lucrative development booms experienced by any city over a ten-year period. Congress could still meddle, but it was ready to help.

Given the uniqueness of the setting, Barry had the opportunity to help create a modern urban center that worked. The fundamentals of integrating poor African-Americans—many of whom came from the migration of sharecroppers that also brought Barry north—could have been systematically and successfully attacked here. Expecting Marion Barry and the idealists from SNCC to make the city function at an ideal level may be unrealistic, but there's no reason it had to sink to the level of poverty, infirmity, and fear that it occupies today.

One person who might have been able to pull the city together was Council Chairman John Wilson. He was the rare leader who could make genuine friendships with people, regardless of race or class. His knowledge of the city's finances and his popularity among voters across the city were unmatched. After nearly twenty years of serving on the city council and playing an irascible but crucial role just off center stage from Barry and Kelly, Wilson was poised to run for mayor in 1994. Reporters always described him as brilliant but moody and mercurial; only a handful of close friends knew that he had fought clinical depression all his life. Even as he lay the groundwork for his campaign, Wilson's inner war against depression was becoming unbearable. He made several attempts at suicide that never became public but frightened his wife and friends. He changed doctors and medicines. He bought a second home on his native Eastern Shore of Maryland to escape the pressures of Washington. Nothing worked. On a quiet, rainy day in May of 1993, Wilson descended the stairs of his Southwest town house while his wife, Bonnie, was at work. He placed a rope around his neck and hanged himself from a basement water pipe.

And the city was further adrift.

As it approached the year 2000, the District of Columbia had become a mesmerizing mirror for black and white America's inability to integrate African-Americans—economically, politically or socially.

The fact that parts of the city were still calm and quite luxurious places to live only served to drive home the disparities. In the black middle class neighborhoods of Michigan Park, Crestwood, Blagden Terrace, and dozens like them, tens of thousands of Washingtonians struggled successfully to raise their families. They went to church, tended their yards, sent their children to college, and sought only what the great majority of Americans wanted: a decent way of life for themselves and their children. The city's poor African-Americans lived in another world. The city's infant mortality rate was still twice the national average, higher than any large city or state. Washington also has the highest cancer death rate, with 223 cancer deaths for every 100,000 people, according to the National Institute of Cancer, located nearby in Bethesda, Maryland.

The technology gap is another startling measure of distress. Middle-class Washingtonians were tapping into computer networks and taking advantage of vast data banks. In 1993 Bell Telephone, whose telephone network included the city's phone company, bought cable-TV giant Telecommunications, Inc., placing the country on the threshold of a new era in communications. But in the poor parts of the capital city, thousands of households didn't even have phones. Against a national trend that showed the number of households with phones climbing slowly to 94 percent in 1992, the number fell in the District from a high of nearly 95 percent in 1988 to 88 percent in 1992. In numbers, 14,000 households didn't have phones in 1988; four years later, 27,000 were without phone services. In essence, the poor parts of the city were becoming unhitched from the upper and middle-class sections of the capital—and from the rest of America.

The message inherent in these grim statistics is that a fundamental dream died in Washington over the last thirty years. The dream was that if integration could work anywhere, it could work in the District. It was a dream that wasn't taken lightly by people like Willard Wirtz, the labor secretary who launched Marion Barry into Pride, Inc. in 1967.

"We wanted to see the black government work in D.C.," Wirtz told us. "It came from as deep a sense of civil rights and integration we could feel, one of the most sincere of beliefs in civil rights that one can find."

But integration takes work. After using the rhetoric of racial harmony to get elected in 1978, Marion Barry rarely mentioned it again. By 1984 he was whipping up racial animosity by accusing federal officials of mounting a racist attack against him. Barry said he refused to be "lynched" in the mid-1980s, and in 1990, when he was grooming an entire city of prospective jurors, he cynically used racist rhetoric to set blacks against whites. Finally, he linked arms with Nation of Islam leader Louis Farrakhan a white-baiting separatist.

Ironically, the process of integration is still working itself through in parts of Ward Three, pockets of downtown and Capitol Hill. In the public elementary schools, white children are growing up in a school system run by African-Americans, most of the teachers are black, and the bonding that goes on in this natural environment is what Wirtz and others were hoping to promote; The same melting process is taking place in the suburbs, but it works only along class lines. Class, it turns out, may be stronger than race. As Mayor Kelly and other politicians jockeyed for position in the 1994 mayoral and council campaigns, wealthy whites and middle-class blacks were voting with their feet. The District's population in 1993 dipped below 600,000 for a 25 percent loss from the high of 800,000 in 1950; Nearly 50,000 black Washingtonians had left during the 1980s, and the exodus picked up momentum in the early 1990s.

"I've never seen so many 'For Sale' signs in our neighborhoods," said Kevin Chavous, a rising political star who won the Ward Seven council seat in 1990. "The middle class is leaving in droves."

No matter how bad things get in parts of the District of Columbia, Washington, D.C. is not going away. Unlike other cities that die when their industries wither or leave, the city will remain at the confluence of the Potomac and the Anacostia Rivers, unless the federal government moves to Kansas. No amount of "reinventing government" by Bill Clinton or any other president is going to make Washington disappear or even shrink. The legislators, the lobbyists, the bureaucrats are here by the tens of thousan.ds. The tourists come by the millions. The government that often plagues or ignores its city ensures the city's survival.

Thus the conundrum: Washington, D.C. won't die because it's the capital city; but if it weren't the capital, it might not be in such dire straits. If it hadn't been under the thumb of racists in Congress for a hundred years, it might have developed politics such as those in Atlanta, Baltimore, Chicago, and other cities. Blacks might be more politically adept. The city might have developed an identity and sense of itself, instead of having the split personality of a federal city and a small town.

Lacking clear divisions of power and identity, the city and its residents have become addicted to the blame game. No one is responsible for his or her actions—not the people, not the politicians, not the criminals. The well-heeled whites in Ward Three have little stake in the city, and most don't care about the politics or the government. What happens east of the Anacostia River doesn't concern them. African-Americans often pin their problems on racism and blame Ward Three. The Mayor, with her limited authority, can scream at Congress for her shortcomings. Or she can blame the independent school board for the city's shabby schools. Or she can harangue the suburbs for staying wealthy at the city's expense. The city council can point its finger at the mayor or the Congress beyond. The murderers blame their crimes on the poverty and desperation of their environment. And only about ·a quarter of those arrested for murder actually wind up behind bars, because the criminal justice system-from the cops to the courts to the jails-is close to breakdown.

So now what?

Following the same track of limited self-government under the 1973 home-rule charter will lead to further frustration, alienation, and outward migration by the middle class. The city will likely follow one of two courses:

One leads gradually toward true home rule, full independence, and possibly statehood. This would require the kind of incremental change envisioned by Delegate Eleanor Holmes Norton, as opposed to any quick fixes. A necessary step might be a joint task force of Congress and local citizens to review and propose changes to the twenty-year-old home rule chatter. It could consider the scope of powers for the mayor and the council. Should the city, for instance, hire a professional city manager to run its day-to-day affairs? It might be necessary to open more avenues for elective office, perhaps by doubling the size of the council but halving the $70,000 annual salaries and limiting the number of chairmanships.

On the road to full independence, Congress could grant the city complete control over its $4 billion budget, eliminating the wasteful and demeaning congressional review of how the city spends funds raised from its own taxpayers, whose hard-earned cash supports 85 percent of the budget. In addition, the District deserves control over its judicial and criminal systems. Nowhere else in America does the appointed U.S. Attorney prosecute local laws. President Clinton's appointment of Judge Eric Holder as the first African-American to hold that post is encouraging, but not enough. Allowing the city to elect judges, or the council and the mayor to appoint them, could do much to erase the sense of racial injustice that prevails, and it could engender support for stronger public-safety measures. To spur economic development, laws could he changed to make the city into a haven for corporate headquarters, similar to Delaware. Or it could become a tax-free zone that would promote jobs and development on hundreds of acres of prime vacant land, much, of it east of the Anacostia. There are creative options.

On the other hand, the federal government could tighten its control over the city. As we finish our work, there is growing unease about the financial stability, of the local government, even as the city's social problems draw the attention of both demagogic and well-meaning members of Congress.

In the statehood debate that took place on the House, floor in November 1993, California Republican Dana Rohrbacher asked a common question: "Why not just give the District back to Maryland, and then the people would have a state and congressional representation?" A Texas congressman said he'd prefer to revoke home rule rather than allow the District to become a state. After the debate the House voted against statehood, 277-153. Although the Senate planned to hold hearings on statehood in 1994, most people believe it would take years to mount another vote, In the interim, if the District continues to be seen as a national embarrassment—or becomes insolvent—Congress would be in the position of stepping in and assuming de facto control. As statehood was being debated, a House committee was considering how it would deal with a bankrupt capital city.

We've argued that Washington is unique, but we can argue the other side, as well. It is enough like other cities with financial and racial strains to be a barometer for how well the nation tends to urban America. The problem of race—so evident in the District—is the paramount domestic problem facing America.

If it can't be solved here, in Mr. Clinton's neighborhood, then where?

AFTERWORD

FROM 1994 - 2014:

RACE, MONEY, CORRUPTION AND THE REVIVAL OF WASHINGTON, D.C.

Courtland Cox had been right. "You can't talk him out of it."

As the 1994 race for mayor of the District of Columbia unfolded, the nation was aghast that the city was on the verge of electing Marion Barry once again.

"Most people who go through what I've gone through don't come back," Barry told the *Los Angeles Times* just weeks before the crucial September primary. "Either they just wallow in their own self-pity or they're in jail or dead or in the hospital."

The *Washington Post* frantically had endorsed Council member John Ray. Incumbent mayor Sharon Pratt Kelly was still flailing politically, whether over city books in financial chaos, the loss of the popular Washington Redskins to the suburbs, or her perceived haughty attitude.

The city remained segregated by race and class. Downtown, jammed with law firms and lobbying groups, prospered. Whites lived in wealthy, stable neighborhoods, from Chevy Chase to Georgetown, between Rock Creek Park and the Potomac River. But east of the park and across the Anacostia River, middle-class and poor African Americans scraped by. And suffered.

Ambulances didn't show up when called. School buildings still were falling apart, and classrooms were failing to educate their children. Young thugs with guns fighting over drug turf controlled the streets in Shaw, Trinidad, Congress Heights, and scores of other neighborhoods. If they had the choice, many residents left for the Maryland and Virginia suburbs.

In that tense and unsettled landscape, Marion Barry recognized the familiar political terrain. He was 58, fit, and had reassembled his political team.

Meanwhile, Mayor Kelly was more than vulnerable. After one term, she had worn out her welcome.

The fate of the Washington Redskins was only part of the story. The city's pro-football team was one of the few things that united rich and poor, black and white. Everyone rooted for the 'Skins, especially when they won Super Bowls in 1983, 1987, and 1991.

The team's original owner, George Preston Marshall, made a name for himself as a racist. He branded the Redskins the team of the Old South, courting fans from Virginia down to Georgia. Marshall resisted integrating his team and was the last owner to field a black player. But that ugly past was forgotten by the 1980s, when the team joined the modern sporting era, assembled winning teams, and won the love of Washingtonians. Doug Williams became the first black quarterback to win a Super Bowl when he led the Redskins to a 42-10 victory over the Denver Broncos in 1987.

For decades the Redskins played in RFK stadium, where East Capitol Street reaches the west bank of the Anacostia River. Built for baseball, the stadium was small and out of date. In the early 1990s, Redskins owner Jack Kent Cooke signaled his desire to build a new stadium either on the RFK site or somewhere else in the District. Cooke was a cantankerous fellow. A Canadian-born media entrepreneur, he used his fortune to buy several sports teams, including the Los Angeles Lakers, but he adored the Redskins. Cooke made his home in the Washington area and became a colorful figure in a bland government town. He was married five times, twice to Marlene Ramallo Chalmers, a fiery Bolivian 40 years his junior.

Cooke was salty and old-school, to say the least. Not surprisingly, he and the prim Mayor Kelly didn't mesh well. On the few occasions they met to discuss potential stadium sites and financing, each came away disgruntled.

"A billionaire bully," Kelly called Cooke, accusing him once of patting her on her behind. He thought even less of her, referring to her as "little lady."

Talks broke off. Council chairman John Wilson, for whom the city's government center is named, met privately with Cooke and came close to striking a deal, but Kelly shut them down. Cooke eventually built a stadium in Landover, Maryland, a suburb in Prince Georges County, and yanked the Redskins out of the city. They were still the Washington Redskins, but fans pinned the physical loss of their beloved team on Kelly.

There was more distress as city agencies faltered under Kelly. During one state-of-the-District speech, Kelly actually acknowledged that she "didn't have a clue" as to the depth of the problems with some social services. Soon buttons appeared that read: "She Doesn't Have A Clue."

At-large council member John Ray tried in 1994 to steer his campaign between Kelly's failures and fear of Barry's return.

"I hope you know a hustle when you see one," Ray told about 300 supporters at his announcement. "We're not going to fall for a hustle this time like we did the last time."

Ray was a buttoned-down lawyer born in Georgia. He had served on the council for years, beginning in 1979, when he was appointed to fill Barry's at-large seat. He had won four terms, but like Kelly, he had failed to build the kind of camaraderie with voters that would compel them to see him as a mayoral leader.

It didn't take polling or deep political insight for Barry to realize that he could rack up more votes than either Kelly or Ray: They would split the opposition, much as Walter Washington and Sterling Tucker had split the vote in 1978. Barry's core constituency of African American voters east of the Anacostia River believed he had been run out of office by federal prosecutors in 1990. On the campaign trail, he portrayed himself as a flawed individual who had overcome his problems and was ready to lead the city once again.

"You don't know what the light looks like till you been in the valley" was Barry's mantra before black audiences. He talked about his "God force." He sought help in his redemption; voters empathized and bought the revamped Marion Barry.

Cora Masters helped craft Barry's transformation. Masters was a strong woman who had helped Barry rise to power, and they had been friends for nearly two decades. Their friendship turned into marriage in January 1994, and Cora Masters Barry would become a force in her own right.

Redemption aside, the former three-term mayor's political machine was oiled and ready to run. Barry added Rock Newman, a boxing promoter and native Washingtonian, to his team. Newman helped organize and operate a sophisticated ground game and get-out-the-vote operation. Barry's campaign organization registered residents in poor precincts and phoned potential voters. On election day, campaign workers got supporters to the polls in buses, vans, and taxicabs. In the September primary, Barry trounced his competitors. He won with 66,777 votes, 47 percent of the total. John Ray came in second with 37 percent. Sharon Pratt Kelly got just 13 percent of the vote, a measly showing for an incumbent in any election nationwide.

The vote mystified most everyone beyond the city's boundaries. How could Washingtonians reelect a drug addict busted by the FBI, a man who had admitted to his weaknesses for women and booze on national TV?

Howard Croft, chairman of the urban-affairs department at the University of the District of Columbia, explained it this way:

"There is a resentment factor in sections of the black middle class who feel they're being lectured to and condescended to when it comes to Marion Barry," he told the *Washington Post*. "Also, there are sections of the black middle class who did well under Marion Barry."

In a jubilant press conference after his victory, Barry said: "There was a broad cross-section of our citizens who voted for me."

In truth, though, his victory split the city along sharp racial lines. In largely white Ward Three, only 586 of the 17,333 votes went to Barry. In Ward Eight, where Barry punched up registration, 10,497 of the 12,791 ballots cast were for him.

At the same press conference, a reporter asked Barry what he would tell the voters of Ward Three who were not part of his victorious cross-section.

"Get over whatever personal hang-ups you got," Barry responded, according to a report by *Post* reporter Yolanda Woodlee. He said he could best balance the budget and avoid financial collapse. "So to those white people who have whatever hang-ups they have, get over it." The Democratic nominee also said he would be the mayor of all the people, but the headline "Get Over It" stuck.

Barry's opponents had a chance to knock him out in the November general election. Carol Schwartz, the popular, lone Republican on the council, ran against Barry in the general election, as she had twice before.

"Wake up, Washington! Wake up!" Schwartz exclaimed. "Our city is dying under the dead weight of my opponent's legacy! A legacy of fear, filth, frustration, financial chaos, and flight. The race is not about the redemption of one man. It is about the survival of an entire city."

Schwartz got 76,902 votes, 42 percent of the total. It was her best showing, but in an electorate where Democrats outnumbered Republicans 10 to 1, Barry beat her with 56 percent of the vote.

White voters would have to get over Marion Barry's unprecedented—and unexpected—fourth term, but Congress was not under the same constraints.

A year before the election, legislation to grant statehood to the District of Columbia went before Congress for the first time. It would have given DC residents voting representation in Congress: two senators and a House member with full voting rights. To DC politicians, statehood was dogma, if not the Holy Grail. One had to advocate statehood to win local office in the District no matter how slim its chances of becoming reality. Delegate Eleanor Holmes Norton introduced the bill to create New Columbia; it went before the House in November 1993.

"The question before us today is one of fundamental fairness," argued House Majority Leader Richard A. Gephardt, a Missouri Democrat. "Should Americans who live in this 70-square-mile area enjoy the same benefits of citizenship as all other Americans? The answer is a resounding 'yes.'"

The House voted no, 277 to 153. Statehood advocates knew success was a long shot. Republicans figured the Democratic stronghold would elect two liberal senators and another Democrat to the House. Congressmen and senators from neighboring states feared a state of New Columbia could levy a payroll tax on their residents.

"The District, a liberal bastion of corruption and crime, doesn't even come close to meeting statehood requirements," said Texas Republican Tom DeLay. Congress, he declared, "ought to take back control of the city and clean it up."

DeLay's sentiment gained traction a year later, when Congress watched residents reelect Marion Barry. From the viewpoint of Capitol Hill, he was both dissolute and corrupt. In the early months of his term, congressmen read banner headlines projecting a $722-million deficit in the District's $3.2-billion budget, most of which he had inherited from Kelly. The Congressional Budget Office in February declared the District "technically insolvent."

Barry vowed to cut costs and fire workers, but Congress had lost faith. Representative Tom Davis—a moderate Republican from nearby Fairfax, Virginia, who had deep interest in and empathy for DC—crafted a bill to install a financial-control board to manage the city's government.

"Life in Washington is coming apart at the seams," Davis said on April 3, 1995, when the measure passed. "This legislation will halt the decay in city services." Franklin Raines, then Clinton's budget director, who had helped draft the measure, called it "tough love" for an elected government that was failing.

The bill established the Financial Responsibility and Management Assistance Authority. Under the law, a five-member board had the authority to regulate DC spending, disapprove labor contracts, and delve deeply into agencies to reform the government. It reduced Barry's influence and rendered the 13-member council essentially powerless.

A "rape of democracy," Barry called it.

The legislation created a chief financial officer to run the city's day-to-day operations. The CFO would report to the control board rather than to the mayor. Barry would have the power to appoint the CFO, but he could not fire the newly empowered official. So Barry wanted someone he might be able to control rather than a new boss or, worse yet, a potential competitor.

As he surveyed possible candidates, Barry sought the advice of friends, advisors, and businessmen.

Jeffrey Earl Thompson had a suggestion. Thompson, 31, was an up-and-coming city contractor who had formed an accounting firm named Thompson, Cobb, Bazilio. Born in Jamaica, Thompson had put himself through the University of the District of Columbia working as a bookkeeper. He had built an accounting firm with clients nationwide. And he had made it his business to build relationships with politicians, often through campaign contributions. He also developed a network of promising potential leaders.

Thompson saw that potential in Anthony Williams, then chief financial officer in the U.S. Department of Agriculture. Thompson introduced Williams to Barry and suggested that he would be the perfect CFO for the District. Barry agreed and nominated Williams.

At first glance, Tony Williams seemed to be the perfect choice for Barry's purposes. Williams came across as shy and mild-mannered to a fault. He had few local connections beyond Jeff Thompson. A California native, Williams had a gold-plated résumé: undergraduate degree from Yale, law degree from Harvard, master of public policy from the John F. Kennedy School of Government, and a stint in the Air Force. He had gone into public service as deputy comptroller of Connecticut and executive director of the Community Development Agency in St. Louis. His only flirtation with politics had been his election as an alderman in New Haven while he was at Yale. Tony Williams seemed meek, wore bow ties, often spoke in a mumble.

In no way did Barry see him as a threat.

By late 1995, the control board had taken over the city government.

President Clinton appointed Andrew Brimmer chairman. A Harvard-trained economist, Brimmer had been the first African American appointed to the Fed. Time Magazine dubbed him "the Federal Reserve Board's Jackie Robinson." Appalled at the shape of District governance and finance, Brimmer used his authority to take over most city agencies, including police, fire, and schools. His dictatorial and at times secretive style opened him up to criticism from residents and his own board members.

While the control board earned an immediate reputation as a no-nonsense authority—and enjoyed glowing stories in the *Post* and other media—behind the scenes its members were uncomfortable with their total power over District affairs.

"They did struggle with being part of a group that, yet again, meant that DC residents were disenfranchised," says John Hill, who was brought in from the federal Government Accountability Office as executive director of the control board.

The board initially got bogged down in too many procedural issues. It too often recommended action to the mayor and council when it could have simply decreed changes. After a very a public fight in 1996 over its firing of Vernon Hawkins, then the head of human services under Barry, congressmen summoned the board members to Capitol Hill.

In a tense meeting with House Speaker Newt Gingrich (R–Ga) and House Appropriations Committee chairman Robert Livingston (R–La.), the board effectively was read the riot act for not being more decisive.

The five board members sat at one end of a long conference table, Gingrich and Livingston at the other. A dozen or so Capitol Hill aides filled the side chairs in the room.

"This was not a get-to-know-you meeting," Hill recalls. "This was a come-to-Jesus meeting. They weren't [messing] around, and we were there for a reason." The Republican leaders told the board members to take more decisive action and to forget trying to bring along the mayor and council. Just do it, they said, and the board got the message.

Says Hill: "That was a scary meeting."

Andrew Brimmer stepped down after three years,

Clinton then tapped Alice Rivlin. A city resident with an abiding interest in its politics, communities, and finances, Rivlin had been head of the Congressional Research Service and Clinton's Office of Management and Budget, as well as a member of the Federal Reserve Board. She ran the control board from 1998 to 2001 with a firm but softer touch, and she backed Tony Williams at every turn.

Marion Barry complained when Tony Williams got the authority to hire and fire, but the mayor was powerless to intercede. Williams drastically reduced the city work force that Barry had padded in his three terms. He worked closely with Hill, the control board's executive director. The two represented the post-Civil Rights generation of African American leaders. Where Barry ruled with emotion and led by appealing to the sense of both pride and discrimination among African Americans, Williams and Hill were technocrats who used PowerPoint presentations and talked of efficiency instead of exploitation.

By 1997 Williams had turned the $770-million deficit into a surplus. The law that established the control board called for it to turn power back to the District after four consecutive balanced budgets. Williams was on his way.

Marion Barry was no longer having fun.

On May 22, 1998, the "Mayor for Life" summoned reporters and supporters to the DC council chamber to call it quits.

"I believe I've been a good mayor," Barry told the crowd. "I also believe I've been a compassionate, sensitive, accountable mayor; a responsible and a sacrificing mayor who served the people with joy."

He was flanked by his wife, Cora Masters Barry, his son, Christopher, 17, and his minister, Reverend Willie Wilson of Union Temple Baptist Church, who had held daily vigils outside the federal courthouse in 1990 when Barry was on trial for the cocaine charges. Barry launched into a self-tribute for his years of public service, then took some jabs at Congress for trying to "break the spirit of our people and recolonize our souls."

He congratulated himself for stimulating minority business through a law requiring that 35 percent of all city contracts go to minority firms. In 1979, he said, he had inherited a government run by whites. "Look at our government now," he boasted. "In every agency, African Americans and women and other qualified minorities are making major decisions."

Among a few personal notes, Barry said he wished he had been at home to help raise his son. "I've had some dark and difficult days in my life, as you know," he said near the end of his address. "I succumbed to the demons of alcohol and illegal drugs. But God has been good to me. . . . I stand here eight and a half years later clean and sober."

Barry never actually said he was not running for a fifth term. The closest he came was: "I am moving away from electoral politics."

A reporter asked if he would run again.

"Unlikely," he said.

Three council members had entered the 1998 race to succeed Barry: Kevin Chavous represented Ward Seven, east of the Anacostia River;

Harold Brazil was an at-large member from Ward Six's Capitol Hill; and Jack Evans had been elected to John Wilson's Ward Two seat when Wilson was elected chairman. Evans's ward covered Georgetown and ran through downtown to the Shaw neighborhood.

Voters were unimpressed by their mayoral choices. They saw the three as uninspiring members of the old guard or, fairly or not, part of the hapless council that had led the city to financial ruin.

And while the control board had balanced the District's books, life in the nation's capital was still grim for many residents. Homicides had fallen but were still among the highest in the nation's big cities. Unemployment was high. The board had hired retired Army Lieutenant General Julius Becton to reform the schools. He had repaired some facilities, but absenteeism was high and the quality of education remained abysmal.

When Barry stepped aside from a reelection bid in 1998, polls showed he could have trounced any and all of the three council members. But with Barry out of the picture, whom could voters turn to to lead the city?

Why not Anthony Williams?

A small group of civic activists in Ward Seven, led by Paul Savage, formed a committee to draft Williams. Savage was joined by Marie Drissell, a veteran activist who had worked for Williams in the CFO operation. Unlike many "draft" movements, this one was actually begun by citizens rather than political operatives. Savage was a longtime DC resident who lived in Hillcrest, a black community of fine homes east of the Anacostia. Drissell, herself a reformer, had roots in the city's wealthy white neighborhoods.

"Not interested," Williams, then 47, said at first. He argued that he had taken the CFO job with no political ambitions, that he had no political connections in DC, and that he would be running against three elected council members. He demurred again in two more meetings.

Undeterred, Savage and Drissell gathered more supporters in black precincts and broadened the "draft Tony" movement to white political activists and potential contributors west of Rock Creek Park. Their appeal struck home with Doug Patton and Max Berry, two veteran fundraisers from the early Barry years. Williams and Berry were close. Berry said he could help raise funds for Williams and even serve as campaign chair.

In a matter of weeks, Tony Williams succumbed to the pleadings of his supporters. The ultimate bean-counter gave up the CFO job and stepped gingerly into the mayor's race in late June. Money and supporters flowed his way. Even though Jack Evans had been building a campaign war chest for more than a year, Williams quickly whooshed past him, Brazil, and Chavous.

Tom Lindenfeld, a seasoned political strategist, managed the campaign, which Williams grounded on two themes: his proven competence and the city's need for change.

A poll conducted by the *Washington Post* in August, weeks before the September 15 primary, showed Williams with a "commanding lead" over his rivals: 38 percent of those surveyed planned to vote for Williams; Chavous came in second with 19 percent; Evans and Brazil didn't break double digits. Two out of three white voters preferred Williams, and he also topped Chavous among black voters.

The poll revealed a major shift in voter sentiment from the Marion Barry era.

"Most of those surveyed said they place a higher premium on management than on charisma," the *Post* said. "Asked to choose between a mayor who is a good manager and a mayor who is an inspiring leader, six in ten favored a good manager."

Those preferences played out in the election. Williams won 50 percent of the vote. Chavous came in second with 35 percent; Evans got 10 percent and Brazil 4. In the November general election, Williams easily outpolled Carol Schwartz, the Republican.

In conversations on the streets and in barber shops, African Americans still wondered if Williams was "black enough" to represent their interests. "Mr. Bow Tie," Cora Masters Barry dismissively dubbed him. But the majority of voters were interested in a mayor who could manage a city government that was ready to emerge from federal control, regardless of how he talked or what he wore around his neck.

"The city was shell-shocked," DC Delegate Eleanor Holmes Norton told *Washingtonian* magazine. "We wanted someone to run the government. He didn't promise he'd change his personality. He didn't promise he would conform to the traditional, big-city, African American pol.

"I prefer that to the politician who is an open book you would like to close immediately."

Mayor Tony Williams governed quietly and without fanfare. He was the anti-Barry, boring but competent. Barry liked to party after midnight; Williams preferred canoeing, biking, and opera at the Kennedy Center after dinner, which he liked to cook for his wife, Diane, and their daughter, Asantewa.

Continuing his role as chief accountant from his control-board days, he made sure the District balanced its books. He lured competent bureaucrats to run city agencies. When he was CFO, Williams had hired Natwar Gandhi to run the tax office, which had been a mess. A native of India, Gandhi had come to the U.S. for college and worked his way up to a top job in the General Accounting Office. Under the control board, Gandhi reformed a tax office that had lost returns and functioned with file cards strewn about its offices. Knowing Gandhi's success with the tax operation, Williams appointed him to be the new CFO.

When Williams became mayor, five of the city's social-services agencies were in receivership or under court-ordered management. One by one, he gradually brought them back under District control—but not before some tragedies shocked the city.

Brianna Blackmond was faring well in a foster home as she approached her second birthday. DC social workers had placed her in foster care because her mother, Charrisise Blackmond, had an IQ of 58 and a history of abusing her children. Through a series of missteps,

D.C. Superior Court Judge Evelyn E.C. Queen ordered Brianna removed from foster care and returned home to her mother. Around Christmas 1999, the toddler joined her mother and her mother's roommate. Within two weeks, Brianna was found dead. Someone had beaten her and slammed her against a wall. Prosecutors charged Blackmond's roommate with murder and the mother as an accessory.

"This is intolerable, and it will stop on my watch," Mayor Anthony Williams told an audience at Ballou High School, where he gave his first state-of-the-District address the following January. "No one is more outraged than me."

The auditorium went silent.

"I was a foster child myself, and my mother adopted me when they said I was retarded," Williams said. "I'll never forget the lesson she taught me: There are no disposable people."

In fact, Williams had come close to being disposed of when he was a child in foster care. He didn't speak as a toddler; his foster parents thought he was retarded, placed him in a crib, and failed to touch or teach him. He turned three without uttering a word. They were about to put him in a home for the mentally retarded when Virginia Williams adopted him. She and her husband were postal workers.

Slowly, with much care from his adoptive family in a working-class neighborhood of downtown Los Angeles, Tony Williams had begun to speak and grow into himself.

Now Mayor Tony Williams was outraged by the killing of Brianna, but he was also outraged by the miserable condition of the city's education system. He earmarked $80 million for public and charter schools. "Make no mistake," he said. "My budget for next year is an education budget."

It was also an anti-crime budget.

"Since the first day of classes," he said, "thirteen school-age children have been murdered in this city."

Six had been students at Ballou High.

If Williams had a weakness, it was his disdain for the rituals of politics. Where Barry had nurtured his network in the neighborhoods and sensed every shift in sentiment, Williams was removed and tone deaf.

Take his first budget. To reduce spending, Williams proposed moving the University of the District of Columbia from prime real estate on Connecticut Avenue, near embassies and expensive homes in Ward Three, to Anacostia. To the new mayor it seemed a great idea: Build a new college campus, along with a new technology high school, with the hope of spurring development in the city's poorest community.

"Have you sold us out like a cargo of slaves?" UDC student Lawanda Johnson asked Williams when he rolled out his budget during a press conference at the college.

Granted, UDC was troubled, dysfunctional, and wasted millions in city funds, but for many black Washingtonians and other students who had come through the District's schools without a proper education, it represented a way to come uptown and attend higher-level classes.

Barry seized the issue: "It shows he has no respect for UDC, an institution that is mostly African American. He is trying to destroy and dismantle UDC, and he is closing the door for higher education and opportunity for black students."

In the same budget, Williams proposed cutting the city work force and farming out government functions to private companies. City union leaders howled. Williams seemed surprised.

"People said the whole idea of me running for office was naive," the mayor said. "But people elected me because they wanted change. I didn't get elected to adjust the air-conditioning. I need to deliver on my commitment."

When he delivered his budget to the council, the legislators gutted many of his proposed changes, preserved city jobs, and killed the UDC move.

Chagrined but undeterred, Williams gamely dug deep to reform the District's lackluster bureaucracy. He established the "management supervisory service" system. It offered salary hikes and other benefits to 3,300 managers, but it made them "at-will" employees in a merit-based system. If they didn't measure up, they could be fired.

Williams and his top assistants assembled lower-level line employees in the convention center. They held seminars to teach them how to answer phones and perform routine public-service tasks. Williams did what Marion Barry had failed to do: He trained the work force. For the city government, it was nothing less than revolutionary.

The mayor then took on two of the city's most troubled services: public schools and health care.

He proposed dissolving the elected school board and taking over the schools, which were rated worst in the nation. The school board and council objected. Williams backed down. He settled for a hybrid board, with five elected members and four appointed by the mayor. Voters approved the new board in a referendum in 2000, but the school system continued to deteriorate.

Health care for DC's poorest residents was expensive, second-rate, and a drain on the city budget. To fix the system, Williams proposed closing DC General Hospital, the District's only public hospital. Located on the west bank of the Anacostia River, it was the only health-care facility that many poor residents easily could reach. The mayor would replace it with a system of health-care facilities in the neighborhoods.

Closing DC General made sense in economic terms, but it was another political debacle. Activists portrayed Williams as an unfeeling tool of monied interests. They picketed the District Building and harassed him for months. The DC council voted down the mayor's plan 13 to 0 in the spring of 2001, but the federal control board stepped in and sustained it. DC General shut its doors.

Early in Williams's second term, Louisiana Senator Mary Landrieu called him to Capitol Hill. The Democrat had taken an interest in DC's failing schools and offered to give Williams total control. "I'm willing to write it into law," she told Williams and his top staff. Fearing yet another political uproar, he declined.

Tony Williams kept balancing the budget, with the help of CFO Nat Gandhi. After four consecutive balanced budgets, in September 2001, the federal financial-control board suspended its activities and put the city's government and budget back in the hands of the mayor and council.

It was a triumphal moment for Tony Williams, and it burnished his credentials as a leader. Yet when he ran for reelection in 2002, his campaign failed to collect the requisite number of valid signatures to place him on the ballot. He needed only 2,000. TV reporters with NBC4 found that half of the signatures the Williams campaign turned in were fake. The Board of Elections ruled Williams ineligible for the ballot and fined his campaign $250,000.

Williams had to run as a write-in candidate. Still, he won. His success at reforming the government overcame his political ineptitude.

Jim Abdo was a different breed of developer for local Washington.

The monied men who had rebuilt the District's center city in the 1980s came largely from local families that had bought office buildings for a song after World War II. They were able to cash in or redevelop them when city property got hot during Marion Barry's first term. Oliver Carr, for example, had bought the Mills Building near the White House shortly after the 1968 riots, rebuilt it to start his real-estate empire, then renovated the Willard Hotel near the Treasury Building.

Abdo could not afford to play in the downtown-development arena. By the time he came to the District in 1996, investors from Dubai, Amsterdam, and London were looking to buy up downtown office buildings in the nation's capital.

Abdo was 36 and close to broke. Where could an aspiring developer get in the game? How about Rhode Island Avenue where it crosses 14th Street, Northwest?

When he bought his headquarters building in 1999, crack dealers were camped out in the basement. North of Massachusetts Avenue, 14th Street was the lair of hookers, liquor stores, and pawn shops. Bordering the burgeoning downtown, it still had not fully recovered from the 1968 riots.

Abdo evicted the drug dealers, set up his office on the top floor, and began looking for lovely-but-shabby Victorian buildings with potential. He found plenty. Renovating properties one by one, Abdo built a business model that pushed the District's redevelopment east past Dupont Circle, beyond Logan Circle, into the long-time African American neighborhood of Shaw, and north into Columbia Heights.

Other aspiring builders followed Abdo's trail. Meanwhile, the central business district emerged from the recession of the 1990s, and properties started to change hands. The District was hot again.

Business cycles have lives of their own, based on credit and demand, but there's no question that Anthony Williams and his administration encouraged the new wave of development. Investors took note of the balanced city budgets. They tracked news that Wall Street had upped the District's bond ratings from "junk" to "stable" to "positive." Mr. Bow Tie in the executive suite—with his Ivy League degrees and popularity on Capitol Hill—gave them the confidence to do business in the city again.

Mayor Williams saw the potential of Jim Abdo's venturing into communities such as Shaw and Columbia Heights. In his second term, he set a goal: The District would add 100,000 new residents in the coming decade.

At the time, it seemed like a pipe dream.

City contractors did well during the Williams years, especially those in the health-care sector. Jeffrey Thompson, the accountant who recommended Tony Williams to be Barry's CFO in 1995, got closer to Williams when he became mayor. Thompson had bought Chartered Health, a company that provided health care to the District's Medicaid recipients. Over time it would become the city's dominant Medicaid contractor, managing the health care of more than 100,000 low-income residents and collecting upwards of $300-million in government funds.

Baseball lovers in Washington had been chasing the dream of bringing a major-league team to the nation's capital ever since the Senators left town in 1971. Over the years, banker Robert Pincus, developer Oliver Carr, and Giant Food executive Joe Danzansky had taken part in efforts to attract a team. In 2002, Major League Baseball bought the failing franchise in Montreal and began looking for a new home for the Expos.

Why not the nation's capital?

The major-league team owners searched nationwide to place the orphaned team. By 2003 they had settled on the Washington metropolitan region, triggering a baseball war from Richmond to Baltimore. Politicians and ownership groups from Northern Virginia battled the District to convince Major League Baseball it would be the best home for the franchise. And it would build the best new stadium—with public funds.

Baltimore Orioles owner Peter Angelos objected to having a team just down the Baltimore-Washington Parkway and I-95, close enough to compete with his franchise. He tried to kill any franchise within 100 miles of Charm City.

Tony Williams's reputation helped woo MLB, but winning the team would take a team effort.

To show the league owners that local businessmen had the money and muscle to support a team, financier Fred Malek formed the Washington Baseball Club. He brought in former AOL executive Jim Kimsey, Clinton appointee Franklin Raines, and real-estate investor Joe Robert. Jeff Smulyan, the former owner of the Seattle Mariners, weighed in with a potential ownership group. To add some loca clout, his team included former Washington Redskins stars Art Monk and Charles Mann. But he also added Eric Holder, the first black U.S. Attorney for the District and a former deputy attorney general, together with Jeffrey Thompson, a rising star with his minority accounting firm and his growing health care empire. Williams wanted a team.

Williams wanted a team, but Jack Evans craved one. The Ward Two council member had been coveting a franchise since 1996, when he and his buddy William "Bill" Hall had roamed the city scoping out potential stadium sites. As chair of the council's finance and revenue committee, Evans played a crucial role in lobbying MLB owners and persuading the council to pay for a new stadium with public funds.

Williams appointed attorney Mark Tuohey to chair the Sports and Entertainment Commission. A tough and savvy litigator, Tuohey helped lobby Chicago White Sox owner Jerry Reinsdorf, the main MLB negotiator. Tuohey said the District would be the best home for the Expos. Negotiations intensified through 2004. Angelos banged tables and threatened other owners. Virginians flew league executives over potential stadium sites near Dulles International airport. Tuohey and Evans cajoled and coerced baseball owners, especially commissioner Bud Selig.

The phone rang in the mayor's office at 4:00 PM on September 29, 2004.

"Congratulations," Selig said. "It's been a long time coming."

It took three more contentious months to convince the DC council to agree to finance the new stadium along the Anacostia River's west bank between the Navy Yard and South Capitol Street. Critics argued that the estimated $500-million in bonds would be better devoted to more pressing needs.

"Why can't the team owners pay their fair share?" asked Adrian Fenty, the upstart young Ward Four council member. "No, voting against the stadium doesn't mean money will automatically go to schools and other needs. But it does mean that a government that does not get those things right should not be exploring putting hundreds of millions of dollars into the pockets of multi-millionaires."

The Lerner family—multi-millionaires who sat atop a real-estate empire stretching from DC through Tysons Corner to Dulles—were chosen by MLB to buy the Washington Nationals. Family patriarch Ted Lerner had loved baseball since rooting for the Senators at Griffith Stadium while growing up. His son, Mark, became the family's most active owner.

After three years at RFK Stadium, the Nationals moved into the new ballpark in 2008, and Washington became a fully loaded sports town.

Politically, landing the team was a win for Williams and Evans. But Adrian Fenty, the lawmaker who said "no" to public financing, got his first dose of notoriety. It would not be his last.

Marion Barry tried to make it in the private sector.

Business cards billed him as a consultant. He did some work for the Corrections Corporation of America and tried to make money as an advisor in municipal-bond deals. Nothing seemed to work.

This would have been a perfect time for the people he had helped to lend Barry a hand. He had given Robert Johnson his start in DC Cable, upon which he had built BET and become a billionaire. Why not find an office and a salary for Barry? Dave Wilmot, a Barry friend and advisor in his first three mayoral terms, had become wealthy on city contracts and other ventures. Why not help the man who helped make them rich? Oliver Carr and countless developers owed Barry for opening up the city to their deals. Surely they could make him an executive vice president of something.

But no jobs and few opportunities that satisfied Barry materialized.

In early 2002 Barry announced his bid for DC council. He aimed to challenge Phil Mendelson for his at-large seat. Mendelson was a white Democrat with a base at that time in Ward Three.

"I'm 66 years of age, healthy, wise, and strong," Barry said.

In March, U.S. Park Police were checking an isolated stretch known to be a drug market on Buzzard's Point, which jutted into the Anacostia River's west bank near the South Capitol Street Bridge. Officers came upon a car parked by the river and asked the driver to step out. Marion Barry obliged. The officers said they found traces of marijuana and cocaine in Barry's vehicle.

Barry vehemently denied using such drugs and said he had been set up—again—but he announced that he would drop out of the at-large race.

Mayor Williams invited Barry to his office, applauded his decision to step out of the race, and suggested that he might find a formal role in the city government. Instead, Barry took the path that had worked so well for him in the past: He decided to again run for the Ward Eight council seat in 2004.

When he returned from prison in 1990, Barry had bounced his longtime supporter Wilhelmina Rolark from the council; this time the seat was held by Sandy Allen, who also had befriended him. Barry easily dispatched her in the September Democratic primary. In January 2005 he was back in his familiar seat on the DC council.

Later that year he was back in federal court. Prosecutors charged him with failing to file federal and DC tax returns for the six years after he had left office. He pleaded guilty to a misdemeanor and received three years' probation. In 2006, prosecutors returned to court after Barry failed to file his 2005 return. They asked for jail time; U.S. District Magistrate Judge Deborah A. Robinson gave him probation.

Barry's tax problems had no effect on his council duties or his strength in Ward Eight, where voters would elect him again and again.

After six years in office, in the midst of his second term, Mayor Anthony Williams went to Ben's Chili Bowl on U Street, Northwest, for a bite to eat. His black Lincoln Navigator pulled up in front of the homegrown eatery famous for its chili dogs and Bill Cosby's affection for the joint and its owners, the Ali family. It had become a funky, intimate, 24-hour stomping ground for blacks and whites. There was hardly a more inviting or friendlier place in the city, especially at lunch.

The mayor powered down his Blackberry and laptop. He surveyed the scene. His police detail checked the street and opened the door for the mayor. Looking to his right and left on U Street, Williams could see cranes and construction sites where condominiums and office buildings were rising in what had been a drug zone a decade before.

Ben's was jammed. The mayor made his way between the long counter and the booths to the last seat facing the grill. Along the way, not one person appeared to recognize him or stopped him to chat. Not one slap on the back or shake of the hand. It was an immaculate reception.

Did it bother him?

"I'm surprised more people don't come up and complain," he joked to a *Washingtonian* magazine writer.

Really?

"It surprises me," he allowed. Later he said, "I have given up. I really don't give a damn anymore about charisma, lack of charisma, and all this in terms of glad-handing people. I don't think people expect that of me anymore. I spent a whole summer trying to deal with that shit.

"I want people to respect me, and I'm going to serve the people as their public servant. I love this job. I actually love the people. I think people who get to know me know that, but I don't worry about it."

The "people" didn't warm up to Anthony Williams. In Ward Eight, where Marion Barry was a demigod, Barry had served 16 years as mayor and council member, but there was little evidence that he had done much to develop the community, to make the streets safer or the residents healthier. Williams had brought DC agencies to Good Hope Road, tried to beef up policing, and shifted health care to community storefronts.

Yet he got no love.

Did Tony Williams drop crime rates, fix the schools, and end poverty? No. When he left office after serving out his second term, many rank-and-file police were furious with Chief Charles Ramsey. Homicides, gunplay, and violent crime were still high in many neighborhoods. Williams had wanted to fix the schools, but he lacked the focus, political muscle, or will to take on its entrenched bureaucracy. Like others, he left a city split along racial and economic fault lines.

But after eight years with Williams at the helm, the city was better off in measurable ways. He valued competence in the bureaucracies, trained workers, and expected accountability. Trash got picked up. The motor-vehicle department actually issued licenses without making residents reserve a day to wait in line. City workers were less surly and more willing to serve the public. In short, Williams reformed the city government. He organized its finances. And he balanced the budget every year.

The city was open again at last for business and development. Williams had built a successful, new convention center and laid the groundwork for the revitalization of downtown and the city's waterfronts.

By 2006, local Washington had the feel of a metropolitan center poised to hit its stride as an international capital.

And the 100,000 new residents started showing up.

When Mayor Williams announced in September 2005 that he would not seek a third term, DC Council chairman Linda Cropp seemed to be his natural council successor. An Atlanta native, Cropp had been in city politics since her days on the school board in the 1980s. She moved up to the council in 1990 and had served two terms as chairman. She ran the fractious council with calm collegiality. Everyone in the District Building trusted and respected her.

Everyone but Adrian Fenty. He was the Ward Four council member first elected in 2000, when he unseated another stalwart of old-line Washington, Charlene Drew Jarvis, 56 percent to 43 percent.

To Fenty, Cropp was another standard-bearer for the city's old guard, the people who had failed to govern his native city for decades, going back to Marion Barry. Cropp's husband, Dwight, had been a respected director of intergovernmental relations under Barry. Linda Cropp appeared positioned to succeed Williams, but Fenty stepped in to challenge her.

From the start, Fenty's campaign focused on contrasts—youth against experience, change versus the status quo.

Fenty had grown up in Mt. Pleasant, a hilly neighborhood of town homes off 16th Street north of Adams Morgan. His mother, Jan, is Italian-American, his father, Phil, an African-American born in Panama. Jan taught special education in city schools before the couple opened Fleet Feet in 1984. The running-gear shop in Adams Morgan is considered one of the city's best. Fenty and his two brothers grew up working the floor.

Fenty graduated from Mackin Catholic High School, Oberlin College, and Howard University Law School. He briefly practiced law, then went into politics, first on Capitol Hill as an intern for U.S. Senator Howard Metzenbaum (D-OH) and later for DC Delegate Eleanor Holmes Norton (D-DC) and Rep. Joseph P. Kennedy II (D-MA).

He then joined the staff of at-large council member John Ray as a legal counsel. That post allowed him to start building a local network and test his political ambition.

Fenty's 2000 council campaign against Jarvis had drawn citywide attention. With tactics he'd later use in the mayor's race against Cropp, Fenty walked Ward Four, home to the city's African American elite and established middle-class, knocking on nearly every door and casting Jarvis as a captive of downtown interests who had lost touch with her neighbors and constituents.

On the council for six years, Fenty made few friends among his colleagues. He devoted his time and his staff's to constituent services. No street light, trashy alley, or dispute with the city escaped their attention. With two Blackberries connecting him to staff and the streets, he patrolled his realm in upper Northwest DC along 16th Street and Georgia Avenue in a white Suburban. He was executive rather than collegial. His council colleagues neither knew nor respected him. Fenty didn't care. He was looking past them all.

In early 2005 Fenty took reporters on a tour of the city's rundown public schools and proposed a $1-billion fund to repair them. His colleagues mocked him at first. "He did not know what he was doing. He was just grandstanding," veteran council member Jack Evans said. "I don't think he's a serious person."

But when school advocates bombarded the council with support for Fenty's plan, Evans helped pass the school-modernization fund. Fenty was able to take credit.

Fenty started quoting Margaret Thatcher's line: "Consensus is the absence of leadership." And he learned a crucial political lesson: Education moves the DC electorate.

Fenty began running for mayor in June 2005 at age 35. He set a goal of walking every street and knocking on every door, and by the height of the campaign in the fall of 2006, he had come close. Tall, lean, and athletic, with a neatly shaved head, he came off as the buff alternative to Cropp's grandmotherly demeanor.

In one campaign commercial, Fenty stuck a shoe with a hole in the sole towards the camera to drive home the point that he had walked the city from corner to corner. For substance, Fenty promised to reform the city's shameful public schools and pointed to the $1-billion fund to repair public-school facilities and athletic fields as his first installment.

The establishment fought back. Eric Holder, then a prominent Washington lawyer with Covington & Burling, had considered supporting Fenty, even meeting with him to test his mettle. But Holder signed on as chairman of Cropp's campaign. Mayor Williams, himself a reform mayor, thought Cropp better understood city government. Plus, Cropp had been an independent but stalwart ally in the fight to build the new baseball stadium that Fenty had opposed.

Williams, after two terms as mayor, was still averse to the showboat aspects of campaigning, but he hit the streets with Cropp.

Nothing derailed the Fenty train.

In the Democratic primary that September, Fenty trounced Cropp in all eight wards, 57 percent to 31 percent, carrying every one of the city's 142 precincts. That had never been done before. Fenty had swept the field in a city long divided along racial and class lines.

"We said the next mayor of the District of Columbia has got to be seen as a mayor for everybody," Fenty told cheering supporters. "And that's exactly the way you want to start a new administration."

Before he took office, Fenty began his transition with a learning tour.

"I want to visit big-city mayors," he told reporters, "and pick up some guidance." Fenty met with Tom Menino in Boston, Richard Daley in Chicago, and New York's Michael Bloomberg, who turned out to be his most constant advisor.

Their message: "Hire good people."

The mayor-elect scanned the nation for talent. To run his planning office, he hired Harriet Tregoning, a leader in smart growth and urban planning. As police chief, he appointed Cathy Lanier, the first woman to run the high-profile force. Fenty knew Lanier from her days commanding cops in his ward. Peter Nickles, a tough litigator with close ties to the Fenty family, was appointed attorney general and essentially became Fenty's personal attorney within the government. Fenty installed Allen Lew to run the massive school-reconstruction operation. Lew had managed construction of the new convention center and the new baseball stadium.

To mimic Bloomberg, Fenty rebuilt the third floor of the John A. Wilson Building in the open, bullpen style favored by the New York mayor. He spent $132,000 tearing down walls and creating a web of 32 cubicles surrounding him. Fenty disdained—and rarely used—the sprawling executive suite on the sixth floor.

In his first days on the job, Fenty made his boldest move: He introduced a detailed plan to dissolve the school board and place the city's public schools under mayoral control. Bloomberg was running New York City schools. Fenty could do it here.

Taking over the schools was at the core of Fenty's reasons for becoming mayor. As a native Washingtonian, he was familiar with the public schools and had seen their sorry state. He believed the best way to improve the lives of all residents and begin solving endemic poverty was by fixing the public schools. He was the first mayor brave enough to take full responsibility for a system that had been dysfunctional for half a century.

The council passed the takeover legislation, 9 to 2, in April. Congress approved it in May. In June, Fenty took control.

Education reform would come to dominate Fenty's time in office and be his most lasting legacy, but he was more than an education mayor.

Fenty defined himself as an athlete. He ran, he biked, he swam. He was a serous triathlete. He craved competition. He loved to race and win.

As mayor, he ran the government as if everyone was on his team. Every agency head had to run fast and win. He set goals and expected staff to meet them. "No is not an option," he would tell staffers in the bullpen. "Don't tell me why it can't happen. Make it happen."

Natwar Gandhi, the city's chief financial officer, learned quickly that the new mayor didn't want to be bogged down in the details of the nearly $10-billion budget. Quarterly financial meetings that in the past had taken hours now took five minutes. "Are we up or down?" Fenty would ask curtly, according to staffers.

District agencies had been a comfortable backwater for employees under Marion Barry. Tony Williams launched the cultural change toward efficiency and accountability. Fenty added fear. City workers got the message: Fix it or get fired.

Fenty's headlong approach to governing racked up accomplishments, especially of the bricks-and-mortar variety.

Allen Lew's team renovated schools across the city. They patched leaky roofs, fixed busted toilets, replaced broken boilers and air-conditioning units. They built, rebuilt, or renovated 31 public schools. Lew's crews also refurbished athletic fields at 10 high schools and vowed they'd be maintained with regularity. Neighborhoods long used to shabby facilities cheered Fenty. The mayor built or refurbished eight libraries and started work on seven more. He renovated or rebuilt recreation centers across the city.

Fenty pushed Harriet Tregoning's planning office and Gabe Klein's transportation department to build bike lanes, increase bus routes, and begin planning for light-rail lines. Critics called it a "War on Cars," but the city was growing, and a regime full of avid bicyclists thought the city had to break out of the 1950s view that automobiles ruled the road.

To tackle the District's perennial problem of homelessness, Fenty partnered with Housing First, a group that advocated finding permanent housing for people without it. He was able to house 1,000 families, but homelessness remained an intractable problem.

Fenty's bureaucracy was younger, whiter, and smaller than before. He had taken Tony Williams's reforms and ratcheted them up to warp speed.

When it came to speed, Fenty found an equal in Michelle Rhee, his choice as the District's first school chancellor.

In a dramatic moment, Fenty had walked Rhee out onto the ceremonial steps of the John A. Wilson Building to introduce her. It was the first time some council members and city leaders had laid eyes on her.

In the late summer of 2007, before the school year began, Rhee and Fenty toured a school warehouse. DC's schools had been plagued perennially by a lack of books and supplies, desks, chairs, blackboards, and more. In the warehouse, the mayor and chancellor found huge stacks of supplies and unopened cartons of textbooks, boxes of pen-

cils, and dozens of chalkboards. The system had the supplies and
books—it simply hadn't gotten them to the schools and students.

"We knew we had a huge uphill climb in turning around our
school district," Fenty told reporters. "Every day we find something
worse than we had imagined."

Rhee, a graduate of Cornell, had had no intention of running
a school system. New York Mayor Michael Bloomberg had recommended her to Fenty, and Fenty persuaded her to join him. Before
she took the job, she warned Fenty that her reforms would cause pain
in the community and damage his political future.

"What would you risk for a chance to turn this system around?"
she asked.

"Everything," he responded.

In her first five months on the job, Rhee met with 144 principals
and fired two on the spot. She toured the halls of the central bureaucracy and pruned its ranks. Word got back to Fenty that she was
causing too many problems. He called his top staff together in a small
conference room off the bullpen.

"I want you to know Michelle Rhee has 100-percent support
at whatever she does," he told his cabinet and agency heads. "The
number-one priority of this administration is to improve the schools.
There's only one person who's allowed to say no to the chancellor, and
that's me. Anyone else who does will be looking for a new job."

Rhee, 38, brought in allies from the reform movement. Kaya
Henderson became her chief deputy. Working for Rhee's New
Teacher Project out of New York, Henderson had gotten deep into
city schools and its tough battles with the Washington teachers
union. Abigail "Abby" Smith joined the reform team along with a
phalanx of other Rhee acolytes.

In her three years as chancellor, Rhee closed dozens of public
schools, mostly in African American neighborhoods where schools
were under-enrolled. She evaluated and replaced principals. She battled the council on school budgets. She preached the value of data
and instituted rigid testing requirements. In bitter sessions, she rene-

gotiated the teachers union contract. The new agreement set up a teacher-evaluation system, rewarded successful teachers, established a process to fire those who failed to measure up, and weakened tenure.

The first round of student test scores showed marked improvements, and Fenty trumpeted the results with Rhee by his side. The results would later be questioned amid accusations of tampering, but Fenty never wavered in his unqualified support.

Beyond the nation's capital, Michelle Rhee became a new breed of celebrity: an "edu-celeb." Educators rarely show up on the covers of national news magazines. Michelle Rhee broke the mold. *Time* magazine featured a stern Rhee on its cover holding a broom, the better to clean up the schools. Perhaps Rhee's bitter medicine was a way to heal public education, not just in the District but in urban districts nationwide. Reform-minded foundations and wealthy donors sought her out and offered millions to her cause.

But within the District, Rhee was piling up enemies, especially among teachers and some parent groups. Every school she closed wounded a neighborhood and forced students to travel to class. Many teachers were middle-class African American women who served as the backbones of families and communities. Firing a teacher who didn't measure up could disrupt an entire neighborhood.

Rhee's popularity plunged. Unions called for her head. Teachers and students rallied at school system headquarters.

In the fall of 2009, Rhee put in motion a plan to fire 266 teachers. She was aware that Fenty might get slaughtered in the media with his reelection campaign just a year away. She briefed him at a senior staff meeting.

"I am okay if you want to rethink this," she told Fenty.

"Are we laying off the people who are adding the least to the classroom?" he asked. "If that's the case, it's the right thing to do."

What about political repercussions?

"We haven't made any decisions on politics so far," he said. "The minute we start doing that, it's a slippery slope. We can't go back."

Fenty's popularity sank, but the damage came more from self-inflicted wounds than from Rhee's reforms.

Politically, the chancellor's tactics and rhetoric cut both ways: Many African Americans disliked the changes and believed she discriminated against veteran teachers, but white voters and many black parents tended to admire Rhee and her relentless focus on improving the schools.

In other areas, Fenty started to make political decisions that angered huge swaths of voters.

Fenty never warmed to the bare-minimum political practice of cultivating friends, let alone disarming enemies. Idle chats with voters bored him. He didn't like attending civic functions. If he showed up at a Chamber of Commerce reception, he arrived late and left early. He treated other business groups the same way—with the back of his hand.

Previous mayors had used the District's boards and commissions to build relationships with important political groups and communities. Fenty used them to punish veterans of DC politics. He required every person coming up for reappointment to step down. He often replaced them with his running buddies—literally, people he ran and trained with.

For example, he appointed Charles Brodsky to chair the Alcohol and Beverage Control Board, which rules on liquor licenses and sets alcohol policy. Brodsky, a close Fenty friend, had little experience in the matters at hand, but he did run The Nation's Triathlon, a major annual event in DC. In time, Brodsky was forced to resign amid conflict-of-interest charges.

Fenty's relationship with the DC council was strained at best. During his six years on the council, he had shown disdain for his colleagues and the legislative process. As mayor, he treated the council as a problem rather than a partner in governing. He picked a needless fight over tickets to Washington Nationals baseball games. The franchise gave complimentary seats to both the council and the mayor, but delivered all of the tickets to the mayor. Fenty made the council beg for its share.

He came off as petulant rather than powerful.

"His politics are unnecessarily abrasive, confrontational, disrespectful, and superficial," veteran at-large council member Phil Mendelson told the Washington *City Paper.*

Fenty came under fire during a council investigation into a scheme that allegedly wired contracts to renovate recreation centers to friends, in particular to Fenty pal Sinclair Skinner. The investigation cleared Fenty, but the suggestion of cronyism stuck.

Then came the Dorothy Height snub. When civil-rights pioneer Height and the poet May Angelou tried to meet with Fenty over a dispute about an innovative recreation project in Southeast Washington, Fenty couldn't find the time.

"Look," one veteran observer of city politics told Fenty, "if Dorothy Height wants to meet with you at midnight at the Lincoln Memorial in your underwear, you meet Dorothy Height at midnight at the Lincoln Memorial in your underwear."

Fenty had been focused on the fact that the recreation center was a nonprofit run by Cora Masters Barry, under contract with the city. Fenty had intended to turn over the operation to other vendors. But Cora Masters Barry had won support from tennis stars Venus and Serena Williams. And Dorothy Height, aging and in a wheelchair, had even come to testify at an administrative hearing on the center.

Fenty's plan fizzled, but his insensitive snub of the two African-American icons branded him.

Fenty's image also suffered when it seemed that he was spending more time training for triathlons than running the city. WTOP radio reporter Mark Segraves caught him using police escorts to guide his cycling runs through Rock Creek Park and other heavily traveled parkways. Segraves' cell-phone video became a hit on the station's website. It also didn't help when Fenty scheduled a trip to Dubai without disclosing either his plans or who paid for the travel, as required by law.

In town, a reporter spotted Fenty on New York Avenue, North-west, in his city-owned Lincoln Navigator with his friend, Keith Lo-max, behind the wheel. Lomax ran a landscaping company that had landed $12-million in city contracts under Fenty. He and his wife had contributed to Fenty's campaign. The reporter asked if someone who is not a city employee was allowed to serve as his driver.

"He is if I let him," Fenty responded, according to the *Washington Post*. Fenty admitted his "bad decision" the next day, but the impression that Fenty was arrogant and surrounded by cronies began to stick, especially in African American wards.

A poll conducted by the *Washington Post* in January 2010 showed Fenty's approval ratings had plummeted, especially among black Washingtonians. African Americans switched from 68-percent approval after his first year in office to 65-percent disapproval, according to the poll. Citywide, 49 percent of residents disapproved of his performance as mayor.

Nevertheless, Fenty started raising money for a second term in the summer of 2009, amassing a war chest of more than $4 million. He left crumbs on the table for a challenger.

It looked as though he would run unopposed.

Vincent C. Gray was a native Washingtonian who came to elective politics late in life.

He grew up in a one-bedroom apartment in Northeast Washington. His parents never attended high school. Gray graduated from Dunbar Senior High—a once-storied school for academics—and went on to George Washington University, where he became the first African American to be admitted to a fraternity. After graduating from college, Gray went into social work, first for senior citizens, later for people with developmental disabilities.

Gray was instrumental in closing Forest Haven, a District-run mental institution infamous for its deplorable conditions. On an early visit there, Gray had been horrified when he witnessed 20 naked patients being herded into a shower room and washed down with a fire hose as if they were barnyard animals.

Mayor Sharon Pratt Kelly appointed Gray to run her human-services department in 1991. When she lost reelection in 1994, Gray became executive director of Covenant House, an organization that served homeless and at-risk children. He ran it for a decade.

In 2004, at the age of 62, Vince Gray won the Ward Seven seat on the council, defeating once-rising star Kevin Chavous. Just two years later in 2006, Gray ran citywide for council chairman and won. Like Linda Cropp before him, Gray was a natural at running the fractious council. He was deliberate, patient, collegial—all qualities that helped the 13-member legislative group function well. He watched the new Mayor Fenty treat the council with indifference, including the episodes of withholding baseball tickets.

"It's ridiculous," groaned Gray, a huge baseball fan who was offended personally and politically.

Fenty had made a point of not catering to the District's longtime political and business interests. He considered them part of the reason his hometown had suffered and declined for decades. Cut out of lucrative contracts and plum political appointments, they began looking for a challenger who would restore them to power. Vincent Gray became their hope.

Fenty raised money. Gray vacillated.

Members of the "old guard" lobbied Gray and promised to raise funds for his campaign. Among them were Jeffrey Thompson, who had become a multi-millionaire thanks to contracts with the city to manage Medicaid services. Polls showed Gray could challenge Fenty. In March the council chairman declared his candidacy for mayor; a month later Fenty officially entered the race.

"We pledged early on that we would not always make the politically popular decision," Fenty said at his official announcement. His parents, Jan and Phil Fenty, joined him on the small stage along with his wife, Michelle, and baby daughter, Aerin. His twin sons, Matthew and Andrew, were off playing baseball. Over and over again, the mayor said: "We did it because it was the right thing to do."

On quality of life and civic accomplishments, Mayor Fenty could run on a solid record.

The city was safer. Crime was down. Homicides had fallen to 140 in 2009, a 45-year low. District agencies were running more efficiently. Fenty had renovated recreation centers, rebuilt schools, turned athletic fields from hard-packed dirt to soft grass. Residents said in polls that the city was headed in the right direction.

But Fenty could not shake the widespread impression that he was arrogant and insensitive. He refused to accept polls that showed his popularity in free fall. He figured that by going door to door, as he had in 2006, he could lure voters back to his side.

This round, many residents declined to open their doors; if they did, they might give the major an earful.

Fenty again hired political consultant Tom Lindenfeld to help run his campaign. A New Jersey native, Lindenfeld had advised Tony Williams in his two mayoral campaigns and Fenty in his first run. Lindenfeld tried to show Fenty the results of surveys and focus groups.

"It's clear that if you want people to warm up to you again, you have to offer an apology," he told Fenty. "You have to say you moved too quickly at times and that you missed bringing your constituents along. You have to tell them you hope to earn their trust again, and you have to do it repeatedly, over time, in letters, debates, and TV spots."

Lindenfeld had drafted a letter offering such an apology. He passed it across the table. Fenty pushed it back.

"I have nothing to apologize for," he said.

In the summer of 2010, Fenty froze out Lindenfeld. He ran his campaign staff meetings as if he were taking the field in a football game. After each one, he asked aides to raise their hands and chant: "One, two, three—Fenty!"

The air was thick and moist the evening of August 4, 2010. City police directed traffic along 16th Street by the St. Georges Church, where mayoral candidates would face off in a forum. The stately church lay in the heart of Ward Four, where Adrian Fenty had begun his political rise, and the forum should have been a rousing affirmation of Fenty's first term.

As the forum reached a climax, Sulaimon Brown berated Fenty. A minor candidate with little chance of winning, Brown interrupted the mayor, taunted him, belittled him. Fenty tried to fend off the verbal blows. Sweat glistened on his brow. He took off his sports coat. He slumped at the table. Brown suggested that Fenty "and his cronies" ought to serve jail time. The crowd roared with approval.

During the spectacle, Gray eased back in his chair and smiled. Here in Fenty's home base, the challenger came off as relaxed, confident, and in control. He joked with the crowd. He winked at four friends sitting in the front row: Marion Barry, Cora Masters Barry, Rock Newman, and Sharon Pratt Kelly.

An undercurrent theme in the campaign to unseat Fenty was that Gray would resurrect Marion Barry's power base, bring back his machine, and redirect the flow of city contracts to Barry's friends. Fenty had tossed many old-guard Washingtonians from his government and from city contracts. Encouraged by Barry, they wanted back in. The foursome in the front row seemed to confirm that narrative.

Fenty left immediately after the forum. Sporting a Panama hat, Barry strolled through the parking lot and predicted Fenty's demise.

"You saw what happened in there tonight," he said. "Fenty is beat."

Fenty finally took Lindenfeld's advice in early September, just days before the primary. At a forum, he offered his apology. In the audience, Fenty's wife, Michelle, cried softly. It was too little, too late.

In the decisive Democratic primary on September 14, Vince Gray trounced Fenty with 54 percent of the vote to Fenty's 44 percent. The city cleaved along racial lines: In black precincts across the Anacostia in Ward Seven, Gray polled 82 percent of the vote. Fenty got 80 percent of the mostly white votes in Ward Three. But Fenty lost in Ward Four, his home base.

Gray ran on the theme of "One City," but as mayor he would have to knit it together from the racially divided vote that put him in office.

Mayor Vincent Gray was in office for fewer than two months when more than a few voters experienced an extreme case of buyer's remorse.

Gray had run as the clean candidate—"Character, Integrity, Leadership"—and promised high ethical standards and a more approachable city government than Fenty had run. Gray had barely moved into the executive suite when news broke that his appointees and staff in top jobs in his administration were busy installing dozens of family members and friends in other posts with high salaries.

Lorraine Green, one of Gray's closest friends, had chaired his campaign and his transition. Job seekers reported that Green was parceling out jobs to buddies, such as Gerri Mason Hall.

Hall moved from the campaign to become Gray's first chief of staff. Her first hire was her son, for a job in the Department of Parks and Recreation. When news of the insider hires broke, Gray acknowledged "missteps." Chief of staff Hall resigned in silence.

Sulaimon Brown, however, didn't go quietly.

The fringe mayoral candidate who harassed Fenty during the campaign had landed a $110,000-a-year job as a special assistant with Gray's health-care-finance administration. When his past legal problems surfaced in the news, Brown was fired and escorted from his office by police.

Within days, *Washington Post* reporter Nikita Stewart disclosed that Brown was accusing Gray's campaign of having paid him to harangue Fenty. He singled out Lorraine Green and campaign staffer Howard Brooks for slipping him envelopes of cash to beat up on

Fenty. He also accused Vince Gray of promising him a job for his role in the campaign.

The mayor and his campaign advisors scoffed. Gray hastily called a news conference and called for an investigation to clear his administration's name. But Brown produced documents, money order receipts, and phone records to help prove his account. The council called Brown to a hearing. Sporting dark sunglasses, Brown regaled the council with allegations of corruption. He also called council member David Catania "delusional" and told Ward Three's Mary Cheh, "You shouldn't be a law professor."

Which prompted Marion Barry to say, "I've never been in a hearing like this before."

But Brown never backed down on his charges. He promised to forward them to the FBI and the U.S. Attorney's Office, both of which took an interest.

Mayor Gray denied Brown's charges until he provided documents of the payments.

"If someone did that, then they ought to be subject to whatever justice is required," Gray said of the allegations. "I would never condone anything like that. Period. Point blank."

When Gray could rise above the fray, he governed well—and with many members of Fenty's team.

Gray inherited police chief Cathy Lanier, planning director Harriet Tregoning, and longtime public-works boss William Howland, who had been keeping the streets clean and free of snow since Tony Williams was mayor. Gray kept them and more, appointing Allen Lew, who had overseen school rebuilding and construction of the convention center, to be his city administrator.

Michelle Rhee, who had called Fenty's loss "a disaster," stepped down before Gray took office. Kaya Henderson, Rhee's number two, became acting chancellor. Gray made her appointment official. Henderson replaced Rhee's brash leadership style with a more collegial approach, but she never veered from hard-core school reform. She closed schools, held teachers to higher standards, and instituted a city-wide curriculum. Test scores continued to rise, especially in many of the District's top charter schools.

To his credit, Gray attacked the city's perennially high unemployment. He financed training programs and connected jobless workers to jobs. An improving national economy helped, and the unemployment rate started to fall.

Gray made early childhood education available across the city.

His economic-development aides helped jumpstart projects that had been in the planning stages during the Williams and Fenty administrations. Construction cranes once again defined the District's skyline. Gray cut ribbons for the long-stalled Skyland shopping center in Ward Seven; new shops, offices, and housing at the O Street Market site along 9th Street, Northwest; and a total redevelopment of the Southwest waterfront along Maine Avenue.

From the mayor's executive bunker, all seemed well.

Ronald C. Machen Jr. was nominated by President Obama in December 2009 to become U.S. Attorney for the District of Columbia. He was confirmed by the U.S. Senate and took office in February of 2010, just as Gray was about to challenge Fenty for mayor. A Detroit native, Machen had degrees from Stanford University and Harvard Law School. He had done a stint as federal prosecutor in the District in 1997 and then worked for WilmerHale, one of the city's top law firms. When Barack Obama nominated him to be the District's top prosecutor, he was 40.

Machen projected an image as a tough, serious but approachable lawman. He and his prosecutors—the largest U.S. Attorney's office in the country—put drug dealers, murderers, spies, and government contractors behind bars. He ran a tight office near the federal courthouse; he also spent days and nights in the local community. At high schools, he told students: "Do the right thing, or you will have to deal with me."

To strengthen his local knowledge, Machen made Vincent "Vinnie" Cohen his second in command. Cohen, a former basketball player and participant in Marion Barry's summer jobs programs, was the son of Vinnie Cohen Sr., who had used his own successful law career to mentor hundreds of minority lawyers. As chief deputy, Cohen helped Machen navigate the local political scene and supported one of his goals: to root out public corruption.

Machen's tough image and revulsion of public corruption didn't have much effect on three budding leaders in the DC political scene. All were rising powers on the council. Each was the son of a prominent player in city or national politics. Machen took them down, one by one.

Harry Thomas Jr. didn't come up like his daddy. Harry Sr. grew up poor in Richmond, dropped out of high school, joined the Army, and came to the District for a government job. He started as a janitor and worked his way up to the Interior Department's public-affairs office. He won the Ward Five council seat in 1986. Until he lost the seat in 1998, he earned a well-deserved reputation as an easy-going but alert ward boss who worked hard to take care of his people.

Harry Jr., who went by "Tommy," was elected Ward Five council member in 2006. The son had a swagger, but he also appeared to work hard in the community, especially on athletic programs for kids. He also liked fast cars, motorcycles, and swank golf resorts.

The District's attorney general began investigating Tommy Thomas for siphoning off $350,000 in public funds from programs aimed at helping at-risk youth. Thomas denied the accusation, calling it a misunderstanding over paperwork and nonprofits.

Machen didn't see it that way.

In January 2012, Thomas resigned and pleaded guilty to a pair of felonies. At his sentencing, he told the federal judge: "Somehow . . . I lost my moral compass. I went astray and lost my way." But prosecutors revealed that Thomas had begun stealing even before officially taking office. The judge sent him away to federal prison for three years and two months.

Kwame Brown's star could have risen all the way to the mayor's office. His father, Marshall, had been one of Marion Barry's lieutenants before Barry even was elected to public office. Marshall Brown was responsible for getting crowds to Barry's events. He went on to a successful career in political consulting. He also wanted his son, Kwame, to be mayor.

A likable, affable politician, Kwame Brown grew up in the District and graduated from Wilson High School. He got an undergraduate degree from Morgan State in Baltimore and went on to study at Dartmouth and Harvard. He briefly worked in the federal Commerce Department. In 2004 he won an at-large seat on the council. Running citywide, he built a strong network from Anacostia to Chevy Chase. In 2010, Brown won the council chairmanship.

Brown ran the council well administratively, but he also liked to run around town. He demanded a black, "fully loaded" Lincoln Navigator similar to the mayor's. He docked a powerboat, "Bullet Proof," along the Anacostia. He lived in a modest Colonial house in the Hillcrest neighborhood with his wife and children but wore expensive clothes.

And he was running up major debts.

City campaign officials investigated his campaigns and passed the results to Machen. The prosecutor brought only a misdemeanor charge over the campaign violations. But he also discovered that Brown had falsified records in loan applications for a home loan—a felony.

In a plea agreement that set aside other charges, Brown resigned and pled guilty to bank fraud. He served one day in jail and was sentenced essentially to home detention, but he was out of public office.

Then there was Michael Brown. His father, Ron, had been a powerhouse in the Democratic Party, rising to become head of the Democratic National Committee. President Clinton had made him the first African American Commerce Secretary. Ron Brown was killed on an official trip when his plane went down in Croatia in 1996.

Michael Brown grew up in DC and became a lobbyist. Trouble trailed him, particularly of the financial variety. Like Tommy Thomas and Kwame Brown, he had a weakness for fine suits and nice wheels, but records and news reports showed he had difficulty paying his bills and mortgages. He ran for mayor against Fenty and Cropp in 2006 but dropped out and supported Cropp. It would be revealed years later that Brown secretly was paid $200,000 to drop out by an enemy of Fenty's. In 2008 Michael Brown finally won an at-large seat on the council but lost his reelection bid in 2012 to independent David Grosso.

Brown was trying to make yet another comeback in 2013 when he was arrested in an FBI sting for taking bribes from two business-men seeking city business. The "businessmen" were undercover FBI agents. They taped Brown taking wads of cash in a Redskins mug. Brown was out of office in July 2013, when Machen charged him with bribery. Brown pleaded guilty.

Machen had taken down three promising politicians, all of whom pleaded guilty.

He was not done.

Sulaimon Brown's contentions seemed far-fetched—until Ronald Machen and his investigators corroborated them. They took down Vince Gray's very close friends and campaign aides, one after another.

Howard Brooks and Thomas Gore pleaded guilty for their in-volvement in the scheme to pay off Sulaimon Brown for harassing Fenty. Until then, both Brooks and Gore had been upstanding mem-bers of the Washington community. Both went way back with Gray. Each agreed to cooperate with federal investigators.

Their leads, and the unspooling Sulaimon Brown investigation, began to unravel and unmask far more than one dirty trick against Fenty. Prosecutors discovered a "shadow campaign" that funneled $668,500 in illegal contributions into Gray's 2010 election bid, with two other longtime friends of Gray as lead schemers and conduits.

Eugenia "Jeanne" Clarke Harris, 75, was also a longtime Washingtonian. She had been a Gray insider for decades and had consulted on youth program for then-Mayor Barry in the 1980s and '90s. Through her public-relations firm, she had funneled the off-the-books "shadow" money into the secret scheme to defeat Fenty. The funds went for campaign materials, consultants, supplies, and other expenses. None of it was reported despite clear campaign-finance laws. Harris pleaded guilty in July 2012 to federal crimes for violating campaign finance laws.

"In 2010, the mayoral campaign was compromised by back-room deals, secret payments, and a flood of unreported cash," Machen said after Harris's plea. He said that campaign had "deceived" the voters. "The people of this city deserve better. They deserve the truth."

The day after Harris's guilty plea, Gray was trying to stick to city business. A crowd of reporters showed up at a routine press conference touting a new, environmentally friendly alley-paving in Northeast Washington.

"I never expected to see so many people in an alley in Ward Seven," the mayor weakly joked.

Asked about Harris's guilty plea, Gray begged off, citing his attorney's instruction not to talk. But surely, one reporter asked, he had some thought on his old friend Harris?

"This is not the campaign we intended to run," the mayor replied. "I have said to many, many people that I got into this for the right reasons."

Veteran WJLA-TV reporter Sam Ford was not satisfied. He bluntly asked, "Is the mayor corrupt? That's the question."

"Well," Gray began again, "There's lots of people who probably will have that question. I know who I am. I get up in the morning every day and look in the mirror and I see somebody I respect."

The truth had started to emerge a couple of months earlier in March of 2012 when FBI agents raided the homes and offices of both Harris and businessman Jeffrey Earl Thompson. The records from Harris and Thompson, combined with information gleaned from Gray's campaign aides, detailed a wide-ranging scheme, with Thompson and his cash at the center.

From the days when Thompson introduced Anthony Williams to Marion Barry and helped install Williams as CFO, the self-made businessman had become one of the District's most successful contractors. His firm, DC Chartered Health Plan, provided Medicaid services to 100,000 low-income residents. By 2012, Thompson sat atop a health-care empire; his firm had collected more than $300 million in government funds. But the company had begun to run into problems with DC regulators, who questioned its practices and demanded millions in refunds.

Worried that Fenty would press the investigations and cancel his lucrative contracts, Thompson encouraged Gray to challenge Fenty in 2010. Thompson promised to help finance the campaign, but he told Gray's supporters, such as Vernon Hawkins, that his money would have to be hidden to shield him from retribution should Fenty prevail.

Prosecutors unveiled a complex scheme where Thompson would ask "straw donors" to contribute to political campaigns. He would then reimburse them with his company's funds, which came from government contracts. It was a closed loop of corruption, in which Thompson used profits from government contracts to secretly influence political campaigns, to protect the contracts.

In their early court filings prosecutors didn't name Thompson, but he knew he was the target of their investigation. He hired renowned defense attorney Brendan Sullivan, who tried to block prosecutors from examining Thompson's records.

Slowly but surely, Machen closed in on Thompson. Throughout the early days of the probe, prosecutors only said the illegal scheme was to help "Candidate A." But everyone knew that Gray was "Candidate A."

Mayor Gray kept silent, as the scandal picked up momentum and aides took pleas. The mayor, on the advice of his defense attorney, Robert Bennett, declined to speak with Machen's investigators. For public consumption, Gray said he knew nothing of the illegal campaign funds.

But with his friends and associates falling one by one, his comments did not ring true.

As Machen's investigators gathered evidence on Thompson, his checkbook, and Mayor Gray, the District of Columbia itself blossomed.

Center cities across the country, from San Francisco to Boston, were growing fast. Young professionals were choosing city life over the suburbs. Developers were renovating homes in downtrodden neighborhoods, and they were filling up with newcomers.

Mayor Williams had set the goal of attracting 100,000 new residents to Washington, and they had started to stream in. By 2010, 1,100 new residents a month were settling in the city. Young couples pushing baby strollers began showing up in traditionally African American neighborhoods like Petworth along Georgia Avenue. Newcomers moved into row houses in Bloomingdale and Eckington, east of North Capital Street.

They flocked to the District for jobs in politics and government, law and non-profits. Mayor Gray encouraged high-tech entrepreneurs with incubator programs, and the longtime government town sprouted new businesses.

Nowhere was the revival more evident than on 14th Street north of downtown. The eight blocks from Massachusetts Avenue to U Street became famous — and infamous — for redevelopment and gentrification. Developers knocked down warehouses and replaced them with condominiums. The Central Union Mission, which had housed homeless people for decades at 14th and R streets, sold its building and moved to another location. Developers turned it into housing for new Washingtonians, for the most part young, white, and wealthy enough to pay rents of as much as $3,000 a month for a two-bedroom apartment.

Redevelopment marched east along U Street toward North Capitol. The Howard Theater, which had its heyday when U Street was known as Black Broadway in the 1940s, had been idle for decades. Now it was refurbished and rechristened as a venue for drama and music.

Signs of the city's renewal showed up in hundreds of new restaurants and bars. Condominiums rose along the Anacostia River's west bank, creating a new neighborhood between the Navy Yard and Nationals Stadium on South Capitol Street. Artists and urban pioneers moved across the Anacostia into neighborhoods that were still the city's most troubled.

The city's revival failed to lift all boats: The District's poor residents still suffered from unemployment, poor health, and violent crime, especially if they lived east of the Anacostia.

Young parents demanded better public schools. Under Kaya Henderson, test scores continued to improve, but she and her reformers couldn't close the persistent achievement gap. Black, Hispanic, and other minority students lagged far behind white students.

Despite the city's troubled government, the population grew toward 650,000. For the most part, many new residents were oblivious to Ron Machen's pursuit of Jeff Thompson and Vince Gray. The economic forces trumped the burgeoning corruption scandal.

Still under suspicion, still under investigation, and still declaring his innocence—but still refusing to say what he knew about his 2010 campaign—Gray looked ahead in late 2013 to the 2014 reelection campaign fast approaching. The Democratic primary would be held on April 1.

Council member Muriel Bowser, who had represented Ward Four for seven years, jumped in first. At 41, Bowser was Adrian Fenty's handpicked successor in the ward. She inherited his political organization and his political baggage. But as a native Washingtonian and part of a family with deep roots in the city, she began with strong potential.

Two white council members entered the race. Tommy Wells, who represented Ward Six, ran on an urbanist ticket for a "livable, walkable city," but he added a dose of ethical purity: He declined to accept corporate contributions. Jack Evans, the veteran representative from Ward Two, ran on his 22 years of experience on the council.

Other candidates entered the race. Iraqi-born restaurateur Andy Shallal, founder of the popular Busboys & Poets eateries, ran as a progressive. But Bowser, Wells, and Gray presented the best chance of prevailing.

With Machen's investigation cooking along, would Mayor Gray dare to enter the race for a second term?

In December, with three months until the primary, Gray announced he would run. He apologized for the way his 2010 campaign had been conducted, but he steadfastly refused to say that he had any knowledge of the corruption that permeated his first election effort.

His silence raised the fundamental question: How could a chief executive known for micro-managing his affairs and for his love of details on nearly any subject not know that his closest aides and friends were running an off-the-books operation with $650,000 in dirty money in a room right next to his legitimate campaign?

After Jeanne Clarke Harris pleaded guilty, Machen's prosecutors meticulously brought more defendants in for guilty pleas.

Vernon Hawkins, perhaps Gray's closest friend involved in the 2010 race, admitted to managing the illegal campaign and pleaded guilty to federal charges.

Two former employees of Thompson's accounting firm admitted they had served as "straw donors" for political campaigns. Prosecutors also obtained the plea of a New York-based political consultant who described how Thompson had directed $600,000 in unreported campaign cash used to help Hillary Rodham Clinton's 2008 presidential campaign.

Two questions hung over the investigation: When would Machen indict Thompson, and would Thompson implicate Gray?

Thompson sold his home in Crestwood and other real estate. He divested his interest in his accounting firm and tried to sell his health-care business. In the fall of 2012, city regulators cited irregularities with Thompson's Chartered Health Plan and forced it into receivership. The receiver accused Thompson of diverting millions from city contracts and sued him for $17-million.

Perhaps because of the financial pressure, in early 2014 Jeffrey Thompson began negotiating a plea agreement with Machen.

The first polls in the mayor's race showed Gray with a lead, thanks to his base in black wards east of the Anacostia River and a field jammed with challengers. The three council members—Bowser, Evans, and Wells—were bunched at around 10 percent.

A January *Washington Post* poll also held signs of danger for the incumbent: Three out of four Democratic voters responded that Machen's investigation would play a role in their choice for mayor. Many questioned Gray's trustworthiness.

The *Post* endorsed Muriel Bowser—three times. Jo-Anne Armao, who wrote DC editorials, had excoriated Gray dozens of times for declining to describe his involvement in the corrupt practices during his 2010 campaign. *Post* columnists hammered Gray during the 2014 race.

Bowser, backed by the team that had brought Adrian Fenty to power, began to pull away from the pack of challengers. Polls in early March, a month before the primary, showed her even with Gray.

On March 10, three weeks before the election, Jeff Thompson pleaded guilty to violating campaign-finance laws. Among many admissions, he said he had paid former council-member Michael Brown to drop out of the 2006 mayor's race and endorse Linda Cropp against Adrian Fenty. He admitted to funneling more than $2-million in illegal contributions to local and federal campaigns over a six-year period. His plea detailed how he had raised and directed more than $650,000 for Gray's 2010 election.

The blockbuster: In open court, Thompson alleged that Vincent Gray knew of the illegal contributions. Vernon Hawkins and other Gray aides had asked Thompson for $400,000 to help Gray get out the vote.

Thompson said the candidate would have to come in person to ask for the dough. Gray showed up for dinner at Thompson's and gave his secret donor a one-page, $425,000 budget request, according to prosecutors. Thompson asked to be called "Uncle Earl," after his middle name. Gray complied.

"Jeff Thompson's guilty plea pulls back the curtain to expose widespread corruption," Machen said.

"Lies, lies lies," Mayor Gray said in a series of interviews.

Gray's supporters, along with veteran legal experts, questioned Machen's timing. He hadn't indicted Gray, yet he used Thompson's guilty plea to wound the mayor three weeks before the election.

Mayor Gray needed to rally his base in black wards. He never had much support among white voters, who pined for Fenty, believed Machen, and assumed Gray knew of the corrupt campaign. His best chance was to firm up his base and hope the other candidates split the white vote.

Whom was he going to call? Marion Barry.

Barry, now 78 and growing frail, had spent many weeks in the hospital battling a blood infection. Friends who visited the former mayor said he might not make it out of the hospital.

From the hospital bed, Barry tweeted that he was doing well. He recovered enough to go into a rehabilitation program. He emerged from the program in a wheelchair and headed home, physically weak but mentally alert.

On Wednesday, March 19, Barry showed up in the basement of Matthews Memorial Baptist Church in Anacostia to endorse Gray's reelection bid. He had to be helped onto the stage.

"That blood infection knocked me to my knees," he said. "I should be home resting, according to my doctors. But there's too much at stake for me to be at home."

Barry needed a cane and the help of his son, Christopher, to walk the 30 feet from the door to the dais, but after slowly climbing the few steps, he did his best to slip into rabble-rousing form. "Power to the people!" he chanted, punching (gingerly) his left fist in the air. A few seniors in the sparse crowd echoed the anachronistic chant, but they trailed off as Barry took his seat.

Reporters asked Barry and Gray whether the former mayor's support would help only in black wards. Gray said Barry had appeal across the city. Barry was more honest.

"This city, as most urban cities, is divided racially and class-wise," he said. "Washington has become a city of the haves and the have nots," he added. "It's up to whites to be more open-minded, and blacks are more open-minded than they are."

The weekend before the April 1 vote, Barry joined a caravan through African American wards. Riding shotgun, Barry used a megaphone to exhort voters to turn out for Gray.

Barry's health-care aides worried about his stamina and diet, but Cora Masters Barry waved them off.

"This is what his whole life has been about," she said, even as she privately worried about Barry's health. "He knows this is probably his last political go 'round. This is what makes him tick."

But just as Bowser's insiders had predicted privately for more than a month, Bowser won the April 1st primary decisively. She captured 44 percent of the vote to Gray's 32 percent. Council members Tommy Wells and Jack Evans led the rest of the field that trailed far behind.

Few voters showed up citywide to vote on April 1. The 83,000 votes cast represented the lowest turnout in nearly 30 years. Precious few showed up in the black precincts Gray needed to win. While half of the voters turned out in some white precincts, fewer than 10 percent bothered to vote in black precincts along the Prince Georges County line.

Gray had failed to assume the cloak of victimhood that Barry tried to pass to him. In his first campaign defeating Fenty, Gray had received more than 25,000 votes east of the Anacostia. In the new election, despite Barry, Gray got fewer than 9,000 votes.

Gray and his supporters blamed his loss on the Machen investigation, which they say unfairly made Gray seem guilty in the court of public opinion if not a court of law. Machen's office put out a statement that essentially said it was acting only on facts of the case, not politics.

At a Democratic Unity Breakfast a few days after the election, Gray had to be goaded into shaking Bowser's hand.

As the drama unfolded, another campaign loomed for Bowser.

Normally, winning the Democratic primary is tantamount to election in a city that is registered 75-percent Democrtic.

But at-large council member David Catania was preparing his run for mayor as an independent in the November general election, seven months away. Catania was first elected as an openly gay, white Republican in 1997 and had won four other citywide contests on the council. He had abandoned the GOP over its anti-gay policies.

On the council, Catania had fought hard for better health care in African American communities and to keep open the financially ailing United Medical Center, formerly known as Greater Southeast Hospital. Now, as chairman of the council's education committee, Catania had visited more than 130 schools, meeting with parents, students, and school staffers. Education would be his emphasis in the Mayor's race, and Bowser pledged that she would not be outflanked on such an important issue.

Catania, summing up the Democratic primary, said that contest "had been about Gray and who should not be mayor. The next election will be about who should be mayor."

Bowser, hoping to rally the Democratic base, suggested on WAMU 88.5 radio that the media was trying to fabricate a general-election contest between her and Catania. She said she wouldn't take votes for granted but left it unclear whether she would even engage Catania in campaign debates or seek to marginalize him.

Marion Barry showed up in a wheelchair at Gray's election-night party. He said it was time for city voters to rally against Catania.

Barry, the survivor, endorsed Bowser.

April 2014

NOTES

We've drawn most of the material for this book from our direct reporting of events, court records, official documents, newspapers, magazines and hooks, but we based our work primarily on interviews with more than two hundred people who were directly involved in the events that we describe. One person whom we did not interview specifically for the book was Marion Barry, Jr. Tom Sherwood interviewed Barry countless times since 1979 during the course of his coverage of city politics for *The Washington Post* and WRC-TV, and we relied often on transcripts and notes from many of his published and unpublished interviews of Barry and many others. I interviewed Barry a number of times in the 1980s. However, Barry declined to participate in any way in the research for this book, though we made repeated written and verbal requests. Effi Barry also declined written requests for interviews.

In order to achieve our goal of bringing the story alive for the reader, we present many scenes through quoted dialogue. In each instance, the quoted dialogue is reconstructed from the recollections of at least one person who participated in the conversation or who observed it and took notes. Most scenes and conversations are a product of more than one independent ac count, backed up by court testimony, affidavits, newspaper stories or other written accounts. Tom Sherwood's contemporaneous notes and transcripts were primary-source material for the chapters covering the 1980s. Other principal primary sources include the Student Non-violent Coordinating

Committee archives in the manuscript division of the Library of Congress; congressional hearing transcripts and committee reports; police records; confidential FBI memoranda and field reports; legal affidavits and court testimony; the Washingtonia Room of the Martin Luther King Public Library; the Washington Historical Society, and the Howard University Founders Library. The *Washington Star* and *The Washington Post* provided most secondary source material, and we are indebted to the many journalists who covered the city during the past thirty years.

In *Antecedents,* the first chapter, our description of the Barnes murder comes from police reports and court testimony, interviews with Barnes's roommate, Toof Brown, aides on Senator Richard Shelby's staff, and *Washington Post* coverage. For our brief history of the city we relied on documents from the House committee on the District of Columbia with the guidance of staff member Nelson Rimensnyder. Senator John Tyler Morgan's speech comes from the *Congressional Record.* Congress's treatment of the District under Senator Thomas Bilbo and Representative John McMillan came from committee reports, *Current Biography,* and Constance McLaughlin Green's *Washington: A History of the Capital 1800-1950.* Adam Clayton Powell Jr.'s comments were related to us by the Reverend David Eaton.

The account of Barry's arrest in *Roots of Anger* is based on interviews with the arresting officer, Thomas Tague; Mary Treadwell, who was at the scene; Landon "Jack" Dowdey, Jr., Barry's attorney; and court testimony. For Barry's early life we used, among other sources, a 1978 profile in the *Memphis Commercial Appeal* and interviews with Dr. Calvin Rolark and the Reverend Carlton Veazy, who knew him in Memphis. Barry's activities during the civil rights, years were drawn from SNCC archives in the Library of Congress (especially a memo from Barry to SNCC Educational Workshop—September 3, 1966, which describes in detail Barry's thoughts on creating a mass movement in the District); Clayborne Carson's *In Struggle,*

SNCC and the Black Awakening of the 1960s; and interviews with Representative John Lewis, Diane Nash, Connie Curry, Jane Stembridge, Mary King, John Wilson, Courtland Cox, Ivanhoe Donaldson, Charlie Cobb, Tom Rose, Lyn Wells, Joseph Rauh, Lonnie King, James Gibson, and Betty Garman. Sam Smith helped describe the 1966 bus boycott. Dave Levy, F. Elwood Davis, and David Abramson, together with Barry's SNCC memo, provided details of the Free D.C. movement. The account of Barry's trial stemming from the Tague arrest came from Landon Dowdey, court records, and newspaper accounts.

In chapter three, Willard Wirtz described his role in the creation of Pride, Inc. and the Johnson administration's concerns about potential racial violence in the District. The significance of Clarence Booker's shooting and Rufus ("Catfish") Mayfield's relationship With Barry came, among other sources, from our interviews with Landon Dowdey, Carroll Harvey, and Mary Treadwell. Roger Wilkins gave us insight into President Lyndon Johnson's appointment of Walter Washington as mayor, but we also relied on Joseph Califano's book, *The Triumph and Tragedy of Lyndon Johnson,* and Walter Washington's talks before the Washington Historical Society. John Hechinger described, among other events, his appointment as city council chairman.

For *Uprising,* we are indebted to Ben Gilbert's account of the 1968 riots in the book *Ten Blocks From the White House,* especially in tracking Stokely Carmichael's movements. Mary Treadwell and Carroll Harvey described Pride's role. Frederick Cooke, who was a student at Howard University at the time, Ivanhoe Donaldson, Frank Smith, and Carol Thompson Cole provided indispensable accounts. Patrick Murphy, former D.C. public safety director and now a consultant to the U.S. Conference of Mayors, gave us a sense of the politics and the White House response to the riots. For the riots' aftermath, we relied on the following primary sources: confidential FBI reports describing Barry's role; a U.S. Department of Labor report, ""Profile of Rioters"; the Senate committee on government relations hearing report; "The Response of the Washington D. C. Community and Its Criminal Justice System to the April 1968 Riot" in the George Washington University *Law Review;* and transcripts from field hearings held by the District of Columbia city council.

To describe the birth of elective politics in chapter five, *Bombthrowers to Bureaucrats,* and the 1978 mayoral race in chapter six, *Man For All People,* we relied on newspaper coverage, FBI files, the House District committee report "Governance of the Nation's Capital: A summary history of the forms and powers of local government for the Districit of Columbia, 1790-1973"; and interviews with members of the early political organizations, such as: Joe Rauh, Jason Newman, and Jacques Dupuy, who were active in the home rule drive; Max Berry, Bitsy Folger, Polly Shackleton, Dave Abramson and John Wilson, who helped elect Walter Fauntroy. Thornell Page provided an account of Barry's first school board race; Dwight Cropp gave us insight into Barry's role on the board; and Delano Lewis, Stuart Long and Jeff Cohen described their roles in Barry's 1978 campaign. Other key interviews came from Mary Treadwell, Cora Masters, Peggy Cooper Cafritz, Ivanhoe Donaldson, Florence Tate, R. Robert Linowes, and the Reverend David Eaton.

Our sources for the *Black Power* chapter included Betty King, Jim Gibson, Delano Lewis, Dwight Cropp, Carroll Harvey and Carol Thompson Cole. *Regardie's* magazine first published excerpts from Karen Johnson's diaries in a story .by Mark Feldstein, "The Mayor and His Mistress," December, 1988. We corroborated the incident at This is It? by police reports and interviews. In *Greed City,* Jeff Cohen's land deals were verified by landrecords and interviews with real estate brokers. William Fitzgerald's testimony comes from a hearing before the Redevelopment Land Agency on October 9, 1979. Dr. Vincent Reed described to us the school system's dealings with minority business contracts. Cronyism in the District's contracts to house the homeless is based on "Mismanagement in Programs for the Homeless in Washington, DC," a report by the House committee on government operations from the hearing on June 12, 1990. Barry's property deals with Jeff Cohen in Nantucket were first reported in *The Washington Post*. Ivanhoe Donaldson's embezzlement scheme and the dialogue reported in chapter nine, *White Power,* was drawn almost entirely from court documents in the case of *U.S.* v. *Ivanhoe Donaldson,* criminal No. 85-0433, especially the government's memorandum in aid of sentencing and government's oral proffer of evidence at plea of guilty proceedings, though we interviewed many of the other players. E. Bob Wallach's ties with Barry, Jeff Cohen, andEdwin Meese were described in *Legal Times,* 'A Web of Influence andFavors," April 17, 1989.

In chapter ten, *Boss Barry,* Barry's early relationship with Hazel Diane "Rasheeda" Moore, came from testimony in the 1990 trial *U.S.* v. *Marion S. Barry, Jr.,* criminal No. 90-0068. Wall Street bond firms' contributions to Barry's 1986 campaign were verified by internal campaign documents. The government's investigation of David Rivers and John Clyburn came from theindictment handed down on June 3, 1987, and interviews with Clyburn. Barry's cocaine overdose in 1987 was part of Jeff Mitchell's testimony-in the 1990 Barry trial. The November trip to the, Bahamas was part of the same court record.

Our account of the District's illegal narcotics business and the violence surrounding it in *Crack Attack* and *Murder City* came from legal documents, extensive interviews with law enforcement officials, and my coverage of the Rayful Edmond trial in the fall of 1989. James ("Dumptruck") Smith's network was described in *U.S.* v. *James Smith,* criminal No. 88-0073BDP, especially the sentencing memorandum. Cornell Jones's cocaine operation came from *U.S.* v. *Cornell Jones,* criminal No. 85-412. Most of the details and dialogue we used to describe Rayful Edmond's cocaine ring was drawn fromtrial coverage, affidavits and trial transcripts from *U.S.* v. *Edmond* et al., criminal No. 89-0162. We also relied on interviews with FBI Special agents Charles Anderson and Athena Varounis; Drug Enforcement Agency agent John Comille; and MPD Lieutenant Shawn Maguire. For statistical support we used "Drug Abuse Indicators Trend Reports" issued by the District's office ·of criminal justice plans and analysis.

The three chapters that encompass the investigation, arrest, and trial ofMarion Barry—*Smell of Death, Knife in the Heart,* and *City on Trial*—weredrawn from two primary sources: my trial coverage and extensive interviewswith Albert Arrington and other officers attached to the Metropolitan Police Department's internal affairs division. R. Kenneth Mundy described his strategy and events surrounding his legal defense of Barry. Benjamin Bradlee's meeting with Barry in January 1989 was based on a Bradlee memorandum. The substance of Delano Lewis's March 22 meeting with top-Barry officials came from interviews with all the participants. Press secretary JohnC. White took notes. R. Robert Linowes and David Wilmot described their meetings with Barry on the afternoon of January 18, 1990. All dialogue from the actual arrest that night came from verbatim transcripts. I covered the Barry trial and attended Louis Farrakhan's Nation of Islam rally on June 28. Our description of jury deliberations came from *The Washington Post* article by Elsa Walsh and Barton Gelman, August 23, 1990, and our interviews with alternate juror Anne Freeman.

In *Resurrection,* the final chapter, Meg Greenfield described her luncheondiscussion with *Washington Post* publisher Don Graham during a phone interview with me in November 1990 for a story published in the January 1991 issue of *Regardie's.* Barry's pleas for leniency were gleaned from court documents. Both Sherwood and I Covered Sharon Pratt Kelly's night tour inMarch 1991, and the critique of her administration was included in "Running On Empty," a story I wrote for the January 1992 issue of *Washingtonian.* Sherwood and I covered Barry's prison sentence, his release, and the subsequent Ward Eight council race and return to public life.

—Harry Jaffe

It would be impossible to list every person whose recollections and insights contributed to our understanding of the city and the events described. Thousands of people have touched us in the course of our reportage over the last decade and a half. We'd like to mention some of those we interviewed specifically for the hook who were not mentioned in the Source Notes above:

Roger Adelman, former federal prosecutor; Claude Bailey, assistant D.C. corporation counsel and former counsel spokesman; James Banks, a housing activist who hired Barry and others to work in the United Planning Organization in 1967; Jack Bond, 1991 city administrator for Sharon Pratt Kelly; Anita Bonds, Barry's longtime political aide; Donna Brazile, chief assistant to D.C. Delegate Eleanor Holmes Norton; Marshall Brown, a veteran local activist who worked in, the recreation department and created crowds for Barry's events; Joel Broyhill, former congressman from northern Virginia who opposed home rule; Peggy Cooper Cafritz, arts advocate; Joseph Caldwell, Washington attorney and first chief of staff for Mayor Sharon Pratt Kelly; David Clarke, veteran civil rights activist and city council chairman; Maudine Cooper, executive director of the Washington Urban League and former Barry chief of staff; Mary Cox, a radical African-American attorney whoadvised Barry during his trial; Ken ("Looselips") Cummins, *City Paper* columnist; G. Alan Dale, attorney who represented Karen Johnson; Harley J. Daniels, former political activist; Jane Danowitz, public relations executive and former director of the Women's Campaign Fund; Leon Dash, *Washington Post* reporter who covered Barry's 1978 campaign; Joseph DiGenova, former U.S. attorney; Tom Downs, president of AMTRAK transportation department and a former D.C. city administrator under Barry; Lt. Lowell Duckett, MPD; Virginia Fleming, former assistant city administrator and chief of staff of the Potomac Institute; Isaac Fulwood, veteran police officer who retired as chief in 1992; Jeff Gildenhorn, restaurateur; Donald Graham, *Washington Post* publisher; Katharine Graham, *Washington Post* publisher from the mid-1960s through the mid-1980s; Lawrence Guyot, SNCC activist and community organizer in D.C.; Gary Hankins, MPD labor leader during the Barry years; the Reverend Beecher Hicks, pas-

tor of the Metropolitan Baptist Church and anti-violence activist;
Julius Hobson, Jr., Barry's liaison to Capitol Hill; Charlene Drew
Jarvis, Ward Four councilwoman since 1979; Phyllis Jones, veteran
D C. political strategist and secretary of the District of Columbia
Council; Betty Ann Kane, former city councilwoman whose committee investigated the Virgin Islands scam; Max Krupo, assistant
chief in the MPD; Bill Larman, former MPD detective; Jane Freun-
del Levey, local historian and writer; Terry Lynch, housing activist;
Patricia Matthews, business consultant and former *Washington Post*
editorial page writer; the Reverend Douglas Moore, early civil rights
activist, former city councilman and businessman; Kojo Nnamdi,
WHMM-Channel 32 talk show host; Jerry Phillips, native Washingtonian and radio and TV personality; Mark Plotkin, political analyst for WAMU-FM; Brigid Quin, longtime aide to John Wilson; Marcus Raskin, Institute for Policy Studies director who hired
Ivanhoe Donaldson and other SNCC activists in the mid-1960s;
Bill Rice, freelance journalist; Ron Richardson, executive secretary
treasurer, Hotel and Restaurant Employees Union Local 25; Audrey
Rowe, former human services aide and personal friend of Barry; Annette J. Samuels, former Barry press secretary; Arthur Schultz, public relations executive; Sally Scott, press and public liaison for the
Greater Washington Board of Trade; Charles Siegel, former council aide to Marion Barry and Ivanhoe Donaldson; Kathryn Smith,
of the Washington Historical Society; Sam Smith, acerbic editor of
the *D.C. Gazette,* author and statehood advocate; the Reverend A.
Knighton Stanley, politically active pastor of the Peoples Congregational Church; Jay Stephens, former U.S. attorney; Harry Thomas,
Ward Five city-councilman; Joan Thornell, editor of the 1990 House
report on home rule; Leroy Thorpe, community activist; Sterling
Tucker, local Urban League director in the 1960s and city council
chairman who narrowly lost the 1978 mayoral race to Barry; Maurice
Turner, former police chief; Emily Durso Vetter, mayoral aide in the
first Barry term, and business leader; Superior Court Judge Reginald
Walton, former national deputy anti-drug czar under President Bush;

Jackie West, welfare activist; Ernest White, community activist and WDCU-FM talk show host; Joslyn Williams, president of the local AFL-CIO central labor council; and Joseph Yeldell, veteran city official and political advisor.

—Tom Sherwood and Harry Jaffe

Books

Arnebeck, Bob. *Through a Fiery Trial: Building Washington, 1790-1800.* Lanham: Madison Books, 1991.

Billingsley, Andrew. *Black Families in White America: Twentieth Anniversary Edition.* New York: Simon & Schuster, 1988.

Branch, Taylor. *Parting of the Waters: America in the King Years, 1954-63.* New York: Simon & Schuster, 1988.

Brinkley, David. *Washington Goes to War.* New York: Ballantine Books, 1988.

Califano, Joseph A. *The Triumph & Tragedy of Lyndon Johnson.* New York: Simon & Schuster, 1991.

Carson, Clayborne. *In Struggle: SNCC and the Black Awakening of the 1960s.* Cambridge: Harvard University Press, 1981.

Edwards, Audrey; Polite, Craig K. *Children of the Dream: The Psychology of Black Success.* New York: Doubleday, 1992.

Frazier, E. Franklin. *Black Bourgeoisie: The Rise of a New Middle Class.* New York: Macmillan, 1957.

Garrow, David J. *Bearing the Cross: Martin Luther King, Jr. and the Southern Christian Leadership Conference.* New York: William Morrow, 1986.

Gatewood, Willard B. *Aristocrats of Color: The Black Elite, 1880-1920.* Indianapolis: Indiana University Press, 1990.

Gilbert, Benjamin. *Ten Blocks From the White House.* New York: F.A. Praeger, 1968.

Gitlin, Todd. *The Sixties: Years of Hope, Days of Rage.* New York: Bantam Books, 1987.

Green, Constance McLaughlin. *Washington: A History of the Capital, 1800-1950.* Princeton: Princeton University Press, 1976.

Halberstam, David. *The Powers That Be.* New York: Alfred A. Knopf, 1979.

Hamilton, Charles V. *Adam Clayton Powell, Jr.: The Political Biography of an America Dilemma.* New York: Atheneum, 1991.

453

Johnson, Haynes. *Dusk at the Mountain: The Negro, the Nation and theCapital.* Garden City, New York: Doubleday & Co., 1963.

Katz, Michael B. *The Undeserving Poor: From the War on Poverty to the War on Welfare.* NewYork: Pantheon, 1989.

King, Mary. *Freedom Song.* New York: William Morrow, 1987.

Lemann, Nicholas. *The Promised Land: The Great Black Migration and How It Changed America.* New York: Alfred A. Knopf, 1991.

Lincoln, C. Eric. *The Black Church Since Frazier.* New York: Schocken Books, 1974.

Malcolm X. *The Autobiography of Malcolm X.* New York: Ballantine Books, 1964.

Melder, Keith, ed. *City of Magnificent Intentions: A History of the District of Columbia.* Washington, D.C.: Intac, Inc., 1983.

Moore, Reverend Douglas E. *The Buying and Selling of the D.C. City Council.* Washington, D.C.: Douglas E. Moore, 1978.

Newfield, Jack; Barrett, Wayne. *City For Sale: Ed Koch and the Betrayal of New York.* New York: Harper & Row, 1988.

Raines, Howell. *My Soul Is Rested.* New York: Bantam, 1978.

Rieff, David. *Los Angeles: Capital of the Third World.* New York: Simon & Schuster, 1991.

Roberts, Chalmers M. *In the Shadow of Power: The Story of The Washington Post.* Cabin John, Md.: Seven Locks Press, 1989.

Royko, Mike. *Boss: Richard J. Daley of Chicago.* New York: New American Library, 1971.

Sleeper, Jim. *The Closest of Strangers: Liberalism and the Politics of Racein New York.* NewYork: W.W. Norton, 1991.

Smith, Edward D. *Climbing Jacob's Ladder: The Rise of Black Churches in Eastern American Cities: 1740-1877.* Washington, D.C.: Smithsonian Institution Press. 1988.

Smith, Sam. *Captive Capital: Colonial Life in Modern Washington.*Bloomington: Indiana University Press, 1974.

Steele, Shelby. *The Content of Our Character: A New Vision of Race inAmerica.* New York: St.Martin's Press, 1990.

Stevenson, Lisbeth Gant. *African-American History: Heroes in Hardship.*Cambridge: Cambridgeport Press, 1992.

Taylor, Jared. *Paved with Good Intentions: The Failure of Race Relations in Contemporary America.* New York: Carroll & Graf, 1992.

Wofford, Harris. *Of Kennedys and Kings: Making Sense of the Sixties.* NewYork: Farrar, Straus, Giroux, 1980

Periodicals and Reports

Barry, Marion. *Letter on Addictions and Confessions. Sister 2 Sister,* Vol. 3, No. 5: March 1991.

Brisbane, Arthur. "Marion Barry Just Wants To Be Loved." *Washington Post Magazine,* April 26, 1987.

Carlson, Tucker. "D.C. Blues: The Rap Sheet on the Washington Police." *Policy Review.* The Heritage Foundation, winter 1993.

Dent, David. "The New Black Suburbs." *New York Times Magazine,* June 14, 1992.

DeParle, Jason. "The Worst City Government in America." *Washington Monthly,* January 1989.

Financing the Nation's Capital: The Report of the Commission on Budget and Financial Priorities of the District of Columbia, November 1990.

Girard, Keith. "Murdertown, U.S.A.: How Mayor Barry Destroyed DC's Homicide Squad." *Regardie's,* March 1989.

Grier, Eunice S. "The Changing Population of the District of Columbia." Washington, D.C.: Greater Washington Research Center, 1990.

Indices: A Statistical Index to District of Columbia Services, District of Columbia, Office of Policy and Program Evaluation, 1982-1990.

Mismanagement in Programs for the Homeless in Washington, D.C. Commit tee on Government Operations, House of Representatives, June 12, 1990.

Oversight of the District of Columbia Drug Problem. Committee on Governmental Affairs, U.S. Senate, June 8, 1989.

Pack, Robert; Sansing, John; Green, Debra. "The Charmed Life of Marion Barry." *The Washingtonian,* December 1984.

Reuter, Peter et al. of the Rand Corporation. "Money From Crime: The Economics of Drug Dealing   in Washington, D.C." Greater Washington Research Center, 1990.

"Segregation in Washington." Report by National Committee on Segregation in the Nation's Capital. Chicago: December 1948.

"The Other Washington." *Wilson Quarterly,* New Year's, 1989.

Archival Material

The Student Non-Violent Coordinating Committee Papers, 1959-1972. Manuscript room, Library of Congress.

INDEX

Abdul-Jabbar, Kareem, 115

PRAISE

"In *Dream City*, Harry Jaffe and Tom Sherwood tell a tragic and riveting story: how the bright promise of Washington, D.C., the capital that reflects America to the world, has turned into a nightmare for the city and the nation. Their careful and persuasive examination of all the conflicting strains that course through the nation's capital holds a lesson for all Americans who confront similar problems in their cities and communities. Both compelling and disturbing, this is a book that deserves the widest possible audience."
— Haynes Johnson, Pulitzer Prize-winning author and columnist

"A riveting, well researched account of D.C.'s stormy introduction to home rule, under the wary eye of a doubting Congress ... few heroes emerge on either side."
— Patrick Leahy, United States Senator

"A stunning achievement with breadth of vision and wealth of detail. Jaffe and Sherwood tell the definitive story of Washington in our time. Corruption, colonialism, crack cocaine — it's all here, and the principal characters fairly leap off the page. This book is required reading for all Washingtonians — natives, newcomers, and expatriates — who would dare to understand the past in order to rescue the future."
— Jamin B. Raskin, professor of law, American University

"A vivid account of how the complex legacies of white racism and white guilt commingled with the deep hurt and mistrust at the center of black politics to let one man, Marion Berry, preempt the development of an integrated civic culture in our nation's capital."

– Jim Sleeper, author of *The Closest of Strangers: Liberalism and the Politics of Race in New York*

"This is a terrific read. The authors, in a highly readable, page-turning style, take us through the recent history of America's least-understood major city. By all means – read it!"

– Larry King

"Two veteran Washington journalists offer a vigorous and resonant portrait of the 30-year decline and polarization of our capital...a memorable and disturbing reminder of much unfinished urban business."

– *Kirkus Reviews*

ABOUT THE AUTHORS

Harry Jaffe has been a national editor at *The Washingtonian* magazine since 1990. He has received a number of awards for investigative journalism and feature writing from the Society of Professional Journalists. He has taught journalism at Georgetown University and American University. His work has appeared in *Esquire, Regardie's, Outside, Philadelphia Magazine, National Geographic Traveler, The Washington Post, The Los Angeles Times, The Chicago Tribune,* and other newspapers. Jaffe was born and raised in Philadelphia and began his journalism career with the *Rutland* (Vermont) *Herald.* He is the co-author of *Dream City: Race, Power and the Decline of Washington, D.C.* He lives in Clarke County, Virginia, and Washington, D.C., with his wife and daughters.

Tom Sherwood is a reporter for NBC4 in Washington, specializing in politics and the District of Columbia government. Tom also is a commentator for WAMU 88.5 public radio and a columnist for the Current Newspapers. Tom has twice been honored as one of the Top 50 Journalists in Washington by *Washingtonian* magazine. He began his journalism career at *The Atlanta Constitution* and covered local and national politics for *The Washington Post* from 1979 to 1989. He is the co-author of *Dream City: Race, Power and the Decline of Washington, D.C.* A native of Atlanta, he currently resides in Washington, D.C. and has one son, Peyton.

Made in the USA
San Bernardino, CA
23 June 2014